Rethinking Identity in Modern Japan

Rethinking Identity in Modern Japan traces the changing shape of national hegemony in post-World War II Japan.

Examining the creative and academic works of a number of influential Japanese thinkers, including Maruyama Masao, Takeuchi Yoshimi, Yoshimoto Takaaki, Mishima Yukio, Etō Jun, Ishihara Shintarō, Katō Norihiro and others, the author explores Japanese intellectuals' articulations of the cultural crisis accompanying modernization and the deepening contradictions between native Japanese culture and the culture of the modern West.

Iida argues that the popularity of *nihonjinron* ('theories of Japaneseness') in the 1980s and the resurgence of historical revisionism in the 1990s cannot be satisfactorily understood within the conventional explanatory framework of nationalism. Instead, by situating Japanese knowledge production at the intersection of the historical, socio-economic and political-cultural contexts, the author conceptualizes the emergence and maturation of particular forms of knowledge as vital constituents of the shaping and reshaping of national hegemony. Exploring the overlap and tensions between the political-economic and the aesthetic-symbolic realms, this book will be essential reading for those interested in contemporary Japanese politics and culture and the intellectual history of twentieth century Japan.

Born, raised and educated in Japan, **Yumiko Iida** holds degrees from Yokohama National University, University of Toronto and York University, Canada. The author's cross-cultural experience and interdisciplinary training have provided a unique foundation for her scholarship. Her doctoral dissertation, on which this book is based, received York University's Faculty of Graduate Studies Dissertation Prize for 1999.

Routledge/Asian Studies Association of Australia (ASAA) East Asia Series
Edited by Tessa Morris-Suzuki and Morris Low

Editorial Board: Professor Geremie Barmé (Australian National University), Professor Colin Mackerras (Griffith University), Professor Vera Mackie (Curtin University) and Associate Professor Sonia Ryang (Johns Hopkins University).

This series represents a showcase for the latest cutting-edge research in the field of East Asian Studies, from both established scholars and rising academics. It will include studies from every part of the East Asian region (including China, Japan, North and South Korea and Taiwan) as well as comparative studies dealing with more than one country. Topics covered may be contemporary or historical, and relate to any of the humanities or social sciences. The series is an invaluable source of information and challenging perspectives for advanced students and researchers alike.

Routledge is pleased to invite proposals for new books in the series. In the first instance, any interested authors should contact:

Professor Tessa Morris-Suzuki
Division of Pacific and Asian History
Research School of Pacific and
    Asian Studies
Australian National University
Canberra, ACT 0200 Australia

Dr Morris Low
Department of Asian Languages
    and Studies
University of Queensland
Brisbane, Queensland 4072
Australia

Routledge/Asian Studies Association of Australia (ASAA) East Asia Series

1 **Gender in Japan**
  Power and public policy
  Vera Mackie

2 **The Chaebol and Labour in Korea**
  The development of management strategy in Hyundai
  Seung Ho Kwon and Michael O'Donnell

3 **Rethinking Identity in Modern Japan**
  Nationalism as aesthetics
  Yumiko Iida

4 **The Manchurian Crisis and Japanese Society, 1931–33**
  Sandra Wilson

Rethinking Identity in Modern Japan

Nationalism as aesthetics

Yumiko Iida

LONDON AND NEW YORK

First published 2002
by Routledge
2 Park Square, Milton Park, Abingdon, Oxon OX14 4RN

Simultaneously published in the USA and Canada
by Routledge
711 Third Avenue, New York, NY 10017

Routledge is an imprint of the Taylor & Francis Group

Transferred to Digital Printing 2005

First issued in paperback 2013

© 2002 Yumiko Iida

Typeset in Baskerville by
Florence Production Ltd, Stoodleigh, Devon

All rights reserved. No part of this book may be reprinted or
reproduced or utilized in any form or by any electronic,
mechanical, or other means, now known or hereafter invented,
including photocopying and recording, or in any information
storage or retrieval system, without permission in writing from
the publishers.

British Library Cataloguing in Publication Data
A catalogue record for this book is available from the British Library

Library of Congress Cataloging in Publication Data
Iida, Yumiko, 1959–
    Rethinking identity in modern Japan: nationalism as
aesthetics/Yumiko Iida.
        p. cm.
    Includes bibliographical references and index.
    1. Japan – Intellectual life – 20th century.   2. Nationalism –
Japan.   I. Title.
    DS822.25 .I339 2001
    320.54′0952—dc21   2001034983

ISBN 978-0-415-86282-0

Contents

	Acknowledgements	vii
1	Approaching the questions of Japanese identity and nationalism	1
2	'Overcoming modernity': towards an aesthetic politics of identity	25
3	Uneasy with the modern: the postwar revival of the modern and the return of dissent	67
4	The age of rapid economic growth and romantic resurgence: mass society and the erosion of popular politics and the social imaginary	114
5	Back to identity: 'postmodernity,' *nihonjinron* and the desire of the other	164
6	Japan in the 1990s and beyond: identity crises in late modern conditions	209
7	Japanese nationalism in the late modern world: in place of a conclusion	259
	Notes	277
	Bibliography	306
	Index	322

Acknowledgements

I would like to acknowledge my debt to the following institutions for having made the completion of this book, and the doctoral dissertation upon which it is based, possible with their generous financial support. The Social Science and Humanities Research Council of Canada offered me a two-year Doctoral Dissertation Award and a Post-Doctoral Fellowship, and York University provided a hard-to-get final year scholarship, 'President's Dissertation Scholarship,' thanks to which I could devote all my time and effort towards my research. At York, I was hosted by the Joint Centre for Asia and Pacific Studies, and the York Centre for International and Security Studies offered me travel funds for my research trip to Japan in 1998 as well as an environment conducive to intellectual labour.

In Toronto, I received a great deal of intellectual input from the following individuals, without whom this work would not have taken the shape it has. Robert Cox continuously encouraged me to expand my conceptual horizons and informed me with an open-ended sense of structured history, thanks to which I was able to pursue my research in an unconventional and interdisciplinary manner. Sandra Whitworth opened my eyes to new streams of literature experimenting with different ways of looking at global issues across various perspectives and theoretical camps. During the process of revising my dissertation into this book, I became increasingly influenced by Robert Albritton's Uno-Sekine approach to capitalism, and that became one of the principal theoretical threads running through the book. The sudden death of Ioan Davies in February 2000, whose fertile and creative mind was capable of effortlessly bridging the social sciences and the humanities, was a deep loss for me; my interdisciplinary orientation would not have developed without his influence and guidance, especially in his last years. Ted Goossen, the sole member of my dissertation committee with a literary background and an extensive knowledge of Japan, was without a doubt my greatest leveller, and helped me to strike a just balance. Michael Donnelly offered wonderful constructive criticisms of my thesis, and I hope I have made just use of his comments and suggestions. And, it should be mentioned, this book has benefited enormously from discussions with three distinct scholars in the field of Japanese studies: Gavan McCormack, Tessa Morris-Suzuki and Victor Koschmann.

During my residence at Cornell University as a post-doctoral fellow in 1999–2000, I had the great opportunity of meeting a number of outstanding scholars specializing in Japan, especially Victor Koschmann, Naoki Sakai, and Brett de Bary, as well as their excellent graduate students, all of whom substantially influenced me when I was reformulating my theoretical framework. In addition, I would like to acknowledge my professional and personal debts to Kyoko Selden and Mark Selden.

Comments at various conferences and elsewhere provided me with a great deal of intellectual stimulation and emotional support. Among the many who contributed in these ways were the following teachers, friends and colleagues: Setooka Hiroshi, Joe Moore, Yi Sookyung, Naoko Iida, Naoko Idesawa, Nishikawa Nagao, Arif Dirlik, Laura Hein, Adolf Ehrentraut, William Carrol, Hayashi Shigeru, Leslie Jeffrey, Feng Xu, Mary Young, Marshall Blair, Samantha Arnold, Davina Bhandar, Liz Philipoze, Marlea Clark, Katrin Oertli, Marta Marin, Carol Bigwood, Rosa Sarabia, Lynne Kutsukane, Diane Davies, Tam Goossen, Robert Plitt, Keiko Kikuchi, Maggie Holland, Himani Banajee, Ikeuchi Yasuko, Matsuko Katada, Micki Honkanen as well as Mark Crimmins who offered substantial editorial help.

Finally, I am dedicating this book to my family spanning the Pacific. Colman Hogan, my partner, has constantly encouraged, supported, helped and sometimes goaded me throughout the production of this book and its preceding works; he has, in addition, been the principal editor of the manuscript. While turning the pages of my Japanese sources and formulating my ideas, I have thought much about my own past and the imagined life of my parents, Tomio and Ryoko Iida, who lived through the turbulent Japanese history, before, during and after World War II, that I can only attempt to describe. Across the ocean in Victoria where I am currently settled, my parents-in-law, Keith and Barbara Saddlemyer have always provided me with warm support.

Chapter 6, 'Japan in the 1990s and beyond: identity crises in late modern conditions' is a revised and extended version of a paper first published in *East Asia Cultures Critique – Positions* 8: 2 (Autumn 2000).

Terry Eagleton, *The Ideology of the Aesthetic*, Oxford, Blackwell 1990, p. 3. Reprinted here with permission.

Note on Japanese names and translations:

Japanese names appear last name first, first name second, except where the author is principally known through writings in English; in this case they appear in the standard English order.

All unattributed translations are my own. In a few instances I have modified my translations by borrowing from others' translations, and these borrowings are marked in the endnotes.

1 Approaching the questions of Japanese identity and nationalism

> Yet the peculiarity of aesthetic discourse, as opposed to the languages of art themselves, is that, while preserving a root in this realm of everyday experience, it also raises and elaborates such supposedly natural, spontaneous expression to the status of an intricate intellectual discipline. With the birth of the aesthetic, then, the sphere of art itself begins to suffer something of the abstraction and formalization characteristic of modern theory in general; yet the aesthetic is nevertheless thought to retain a charge of irreducible particularity, providing us with a kind of paradigm of what a non-alienated mode of cognition might look like. Aesthetics is thus always a contradictory, self-undoing sort of project, which in promoting the theoretical value of its object risks emptying it of exactly that specificity or ineffability which was thought to rank among its most precious features.
>
> Terry Eagleton, *The Ideology of the Aesthetic*, Oxford, Blackwell 1990, p. 3 – reprinted here with permission

Decoding nationalism/reading the violence of modernity

Back in 1970, a dramatic series of pictures was posted at the end of the hallway of my elementary school, displaying a man's head and his decapitated body in army uniform. Next to these photographs were large Chinese characters for 'seppuku' and 'suicide.' Although the meaning and significance of the event was unclear at the time, the scandalous death of a famous novelist was sensational enough for a 10-year-old to ponder the how and the why beyond the headlines. Today, the death of Mishima is an even greater enigma; as one seeks for and fails to identify the 'true cause' and his intent, this indeterminacy conjures up, as he himself might have foreseen, various interpretations of the event and a search for some profound symbolic meaning about nation, cultural identity, and spirituality. In Mishima's own rationalization, the sensational suicide pact was an act of protest, an expression of rage at the spiritual degradation of postwar Japan, and a demand for the cultural revitalization of the Japanese. In *Geki* (*Outrage*), written just before the suicide, Mishima claimed:

> We have seen that the postwar Japanese have opportunistically welcomed economic prosperity, forgetting the principles of the nation, losing their native spirit, pursuing the trivial without correcting the essential, indulging in momentary convenience and hypocrisy, and leading themselves into spiritual emptiness. Politics has been solely devoted to the covering up of contradictions, the protecting of the self, the desire for power and hypocritical ideals, while we have stood by like helpless bystanders, biting our teeth hard, passively witnessing the sell-off of our national politics over the last 100 years, deceiving ourselves about the humiliation of defeat in the war rather than confronting it – the Japanese themselves have assaulted their own history and tradition.[1]

The misery and spiritual decay Mishima saw all about him he attributed to the modernization project initiated by the Japanese state, its revival in postwar Japan under the American occupation, and Japan's defeat in the war. It seems strange that the achievements of postwar Japan, including a democratic polity and rapid economic growth, should be painted in the single colour of the loss of 'native spirit' and that the 'origins' of shame lay in Japan's self-betrayal of its own history and tradition. This sweeping, bold and unfair generalization was a product of Mishima's frustrated vision and, perhaps, speaks to Mishima's nihilism and his increasingly troubled personal–artistic development, his inability to make peace with the outside world. Contemporary Japan and his fellow Japanese were, for Mishima, little more than a fountain of angst and disgust, the source of his own moral imperative to transcend decay.

The passage cited reiterates a number of key cultural nationalist notions – 'Japanese cultural tradition,' 'native spirit' and 'Japan's [own] history' – notions both loaded with excessive and ambiguous meaning and employed as self-evident, unquestionable categories. While one can easily problematize such terms and their singular meanings, one ought not to dismiss them too easily, for their overdetermination is surely the result of trying to articulate (and in such a way as to challenge the rational mode of thought shaped and nurtured by the modern world) all those things that were thrown outside the reach of modern language itself. In this sense, such over determination solicits exploration into the twisted tangle of nationalist discourse as the unwelcome by-product of particular aspects of modern knowledge and practice. Although risky, this endeavour is a necessary step nonetheless to opening up a theoretical ground where the 'problems of nationalism'[2] can be reconceived in terms of the inherent contradictions in the modern, rational and universal configuration of the world. With this end in mind, I view the key notions of nationalist discourse, however elusive of definition and successful in attracting emotional and moral sympathy, as instantiations of what Terry Eagleton calls the category of 'the aesthetic.' This category is characterized by 'a certain indeterminacy of definition which allows it to figure in a varied span of preoccupations' and to function as a flexible signifier absorbing and representing 'things excessive' and 'unrepresentable,' such as reactionary feelings and projected hopes, which cannot be easily articulated in the existing rationalist lexicon nor be contained in the synchronically codified system of modern language and the mode of being it projects.[3] Negatively correlated with the rise of enlightenment reason and modern rationalism, the aesthetic is the domain where the unspeakable stories of the excluded are given voice as a protest against the transformative forces in the modern configuration of thought and social order and against their violent inscriptions in the realm of 'the body.'

One purpose in this book is to disclose the structural factors underlying such 'excessive' nationalist voices. Rather obviously, these voices are not merely expressions of an immediate concern with the Japanese nation or of a love for it, but are, more significantly, articulations of the pain of disfiguration which the increasingly oppressive structuring forces of modernization impose upon the individual and society. Beyond their highly problematic literal expressions, the Japanese experiences of this pain and, indeed, Japanese criticisms of modern thought and institutions have tended over the course of the twentieth century to articulate themselves in 'nationalistic' terms; and it is the intimate relation between the problematic of modernity, a troubled subjectivity, and the rise of nationalistic voices that is the principle theme of this book. It was revealing in this context that the spectre of the aesthetic, or calls for 'Japanese identity,' revisited the Japan of the 1990s, a couple of decades after Mishima's suicide. Not only did the aesthetic return, it had a far greater influence in intellectual and popular discourses than it had had in Mishima's time, largely because the emotional landscape of the late 1960s came to be shared by a great number of Japanese intellectuals and the populace at large, and because nihilism had become an integral part of the cultural climate of the times. Building upon the *nihonjinron* (the discourse of Japanese uniqueness) of the previous decades, contemporary Japanese discourse came to be filled with signs of a desire for transcendence and spiritual renewal, articulated by various revisionist voices calling for a restoration of conventional moral codes and traditional cultural values. These events cannot be fully understood within the conventional framework of a nationalism whose primary concern is with the discourse of the nation-state and the formation of national identity and policies vis-à-vis other national and international actors, most importantly in Japan's case, the US. Although US–Japanese relations have played a very important role in the rise of *nihonjinron* and beyond (a subject I discuss at length in the following chapters), the problematic state of Japanese society and discourse cannot be seen in isolation from the breakdowns in the realms of subjectivity and the social imaginary[4] that were induced by the manifold of changes flowing from the historical progression of modernity.

Since its encounter with the West in the mid-nineteenth century, Japan has never been at ease with its position in the modern world, and Japanese identity has been constantly reproduced in the context of its love-hate relation to its powerful other, the modern West. Modernization for the Japanese was much more than a series of incremental adaptations of Western institutions and technologies; instead, it entailed a voluntary participation in an alien game played by what Meiji intellectuals called 'the logic of civilization,' in which the Japanese accepted the task of struggling to overcome their Western-defined inferiority. As was the case in many non-Western societies, the process of Japanese modernization brought with it an influx of Western ideas and institutions – most importantly, the capitalist market economy and the universal nation-state system – as well as the imperative to 'progress' towards a higher state of civilization that was to transform Japanese society and its people in a particularly modern mode. Once national security was confirmed by Japan's victory in the Sino–Japanese (1894–5) and the Russo–Japanese (1904–5) wars, and also the negative effects of Japan's near blind pursuit of modernization began to be visible in the 1910s and 1920s, the images and desirability of 'things modern', however, came under serious scrutiny. Japanese intellectuals began to imagine 'Japan,' formerly a sign of shame, as an ideal place free from the present troubles. These calls for a return to 'Japan' were a product of the desire for an alternative time and place outside the 'logic of civilization' and the progressive history of modernity, a nostalgia for an imagined past and a utopian hope for an alternative future. Those projected hopes and desires necessarily recalled the troubled 'origin' of Japan's encounter with the modern West as well as Japan's continuing difficulties in coming to terms with the modernly configured world, its distinct spatial and temporal schema, and the rationalized mode of human existence. In this sense, it was not at all surprising that the slogan formulated by Japanese intellectuals – just after the start of the war in Pacific, – a slogan that both rationalized the war as Japan's world-historical project to open up a new epoch beyond the modern age and proclaimed Japan's mission to liberate Asia from Western domination, was 'overcoming modernity.' From the point of view of 'overcoming modernity,' 'Japan' was located in an ambiguous position between the West and Asia, both assuming itself to be a part of the spiritual virtue of Asia while equally playing the role of an imperial power attempting to put Asia under its control by reducing 'Asia' to a rhetorical site grounding Japan's counter-hegemonic revolt against the modern West.

Contemporary nationalist angst, like that of Mishima, often takes as its target what nationalists describe as the postwar amnesia, the way Japanese postwar history began by conveniently forgetting Japan's troubled prior relation with the modern and adopted instead the modern developmental trajectory. Under the US occupation and in the throes of the initially strong reaction against the wartime regime, postwar Japanese intellectuals and the populace at large predominantly supported the collaborative project of the Japanese state, supervised by the General Head Quarter, to transform Japan into a capitalist and liberal democratic society. Given the priorities of rebuilding a war-torn society and consolidating popular efforts in the creation of a democratic society, it is hardly surprising that this reinstallation of the modern was not initially subject to any serious criticism. At the same time, however, the historical choices Japan made at this juncture had the effect of exaggerating the discursive divide between the 'pre-' and the 'post-war' eras, a divide that both demonized the past as the grave mistake of a group of wrong-headed elites and simultaneously exempted the majority from their own historical responsibility. Moreover, these factors served to preserve the old rhetorical ground upon which Japanese nationalists had previously called for a return to 'Japan' as an imagined alternative to the existing/modern world. Rather predictably, therefore, in the context of a visibly deteriorating physical landscape and the waning of conventional values induced by rapid socio-economic changes in the 1960s, anti-modernist, reactionary and nationalist voices once again surged to the fore. Figures like Etō Jun and Shimizu Ikutarō, who in the previous decades had located themselves in the liberal progressive camp, now adopted a nationalist stance, although their brand of nationalism was very different from that promoted by the pro-American conservative elites who constituted the postwar Japanese political power base and who endorsed, much like US Republicans, a strong state. Unlike these elite conservatives, whose logic was largely opportunistic and inconsistent, the more Leftist and culturally inclined Japanese nationalists of the 1960s were largely concerned with the declining cohesion of society (what they saw as the loss of the 'moral–cultural foundation' of the Japanese nation) in the face of the commercial forces that were then transforming Japan into an advanced industrial society.

Any discussion of so-called 'national foundations' must contend with the spectre of *Kokutai* (literally, the 'national body'), the wartime ideology and supposed embodiment of a timeless Japanese cultural essence often linked to the emperor as the symbol of Japanese unity. Despite its disagreeable connotations, one should be wary of rejecting the notion outright, for that would be to risk foreclosing a possible path for mutual understanding and an abdication of one's duty to examine the non-obvious and to subject it to critical scrutiny. Following the lines of the *Kokutai* narrative, Mishima, in his 1968 *Bunka Bōei Ron* (*In Defense of Culture*), written a couple of years before his suicide pact, declared that 'Japanese culture' was the founding basis of the Japanese nation. Like many other nationalists both before and since, Mishima articulated his frustration with modern democratic Japan in terms of the weakening of the emperor system:

> in order for cultural totality, continuity and the subject to find a value-in-itself . . . one must expect that all particular events taking place on the edges of Japanese culture derive their meaning from this value-in-itself. However, the central function of the emperor system was lost

under the Meiji Constitution by being increasingly confined in a Western style constitutional monarchy which, as it matured, abandoned its cultural function. We must return to the true character of the emperor as a cultural concept, as the only value-in-itself that can assure the totality of a varied, wide-ranging and inclusive culture.[5]

As a 'value-in-itself,' the emperor is here defined as the cultural centre and symbolic authority of the Japanese nation, that which supposedly endows the territorially bound and culturally defined national space with a sense of unity of purpose and shared meaning. In Mishima's (and other nationalists') view, this cultural space is virtually incompatible with the modern political system of governance by a rational and codified set of laws. As many contemporary critics have pointed out, however, this formulation is flawed; for rather than Japanese cultural particulars being incompatible with its Constitution, it is those aspects of Japanese experience that cannot be reduced to rational legal codes and governmental structures that have come to be labeled 'Japanese culture.' In this sense 'Japanese culture' is constantly recreated in terms of what is excluded from the modern institutional structure. As I further discuss below, at the heart of the fuzzy logic of nationalist thought is a fervent, counter-modern desire – what Eagleton has described as the 'revolt of the senses against the tyranny of the theoretical'[6] – to protest and transcend the inscriptional forces of enlightenment reason that are encroaching upon the realm of the empirical and transforming it in their own design. In modern Japanese history, this anti-modern revolt has most often been expressed in calls for Japanese identity in which the aesthetic desire cultivated by the inscriptional violence of the modern is confused with the desire for national identity.

The question why such confusion has so often been the case and has been constantly replicated in modern Japanese history is a legitimate one. To solve this conundrum, close attention must be paid to the structure and formation of the spatially bound territory called 'Japan.' In a nutshell, the modern nation-state of Japan is something more than the governing structure of the state, which could conceivably exist beyond a specific time and space; rather, it arose in a particular historical context to constitute a *hegemony*, a structurally and symbolically (albeit loosely) unified space wherein various material and non-material forces interact in a structurally coordinated manner.[7] By successfully balancing itself in this structured system encompassing the political, economic, socio-cultural and subjective spheres, and by representing the popular will, collective hopes, a sense of unity and the promise of future prosperity, the modern nation-state acquires legitimacy, the moral and cultural foundation upon which its hegemonic power is 'appropriately exercised' without overt coercion. Moreover, this modernly configured national space provides a historical site for the identity formation of its members. They become, in effect, predisposed to a particular mode of subjectivity by speaking the national language and 'living' the meanings ascribed in it and socialized by the particular values and codes of behaviour reigning in the national space. While such national configurations do not mean one is determined by one's upbringing, it is worth recalling that the modern nation-state, the modern age's only workable form of collective human organization, took shape in tandem with the quintessentially modernist notion of culture that assumes the 'totality, continuity and . . . [the presence of a] value-in-itself,'[8] a value without which the nation-state cannot easily sustain either its internal order or its territorial boundaries. In this sense, one cannot simply ridicule Mishima's preoccupations as stemming from a tortured self's impetuous search for the symbolic meaning of the nation; for the general well-being of the national space does affect the subject, and Mishima's despair and nihilism were both symbolic and symptomatic of the state of Japanese society. Indeed, as I argue in a later chapter, the timing of his suicide coincided with the end of progressive politics in postwar Japan, and signalled the exhaustion of the idea or hope that channelling popular will into politics was possible. This end might also be called the death of 'nationalism,' in as much as Takeuchi Yoshimi and Yoshimoto Takaaki saw 'nationalism' as something very close to a popular political movement, and Maruyama Masao, thought to be a thoroughgoing modernist, similarly associated it with what he called the popular ethos. Underlying this loss of a viable political channel between the state and society, was a transformation in the mode of national hegemony, an overall shift in the governing mechanism of the state brought about by the maturing process of capitalism and a growing technological sophistication that introduced a manifold of changes in the social milieu, in relations of production and in imaginative capacities.

Thus, instead of witnessing a continuous upsurge of romantically inclined evocations of 'Japan,' as was the case in the 1960s, the Japan of the late 1970s and 1980s discovered a different way of formulating its national identity. Emerging in the context of Japan's nascent high-consumer culture, and tending to reflect its international economic successes, this new form of identity was characterized by the so-called 'postmodern' cultural attributes of lightness, fragmentation, and stylistic sophistication freed from the burden of representing meaning and content. So intense was the expansion of this consumer culture that many foreign observers wondered if there were a Japanese subjectivity sufficiently fortified to resist its penetration into the mental and physical landscapes of the country. In this context, 'Japan' came to be defined, first by foreigners (mostly Western), and later by the Japanese themselves, as a cultural entity lacking the modern notion of the autonomous subject and thus one not only aiding and abetting the proliferation of fetishism, snobbery and aesthetic stylization but one actively encouraging it.[9] This link between 'Japan' and 'postmodernism' arose from the intersection of a Western fascination with an imagined exteriority fused with its own fears of the unknown; and the link was forged in such a way as to exaggerate the difference between the Western self and the Japanese other and to thrust aside the material aspects of the cultural moment, interpreting them instead in terms of Japanese cultural traits.

The other side of these nihilistic and optimistic characterizations of Japanese identity, so much in accord with the flourishing consumer culture of the 1980s, was constituted by the rise of *nihonjinron*, the discourse of Japanese uniqueness in which the Japanese made themselves the principal object of inquiry. The development of *nihonjinron* demonstrated that the 'romantic' desire for identity and meaning of the previous decades had not simply disappeared, but had been reshaped in a new historical context where, it was felt by many, constituting an empirically grounded subjectivity was difficult. While *nihonjinron* was initially motivated by Japanese curiosity about themselves, it became increasingly infused with bitterness and frustration as American Japan-bashing gathered momentum, and eventually developed into a breeding ground for narcissistic and exclusionary nationalist voices. It was on this ground that historical revisionist claims began to emerge denying the fact of Japan's World War II invasion of Asia. These contrary cultural inclinations of 'postmodernism' and *nihonjinron* together constituted a bifurcated manifestation of the troubled state of Japanese modernity in the 1980s.

Although the Japan of the 1980s was relatively successful in coping with this state of cultural disjunction, largely because its international economic successes and booming domestic consumption, the situation was soon to change in the 1990s. As commercial penetration into the realm of subjectivity advanced far beyond that seen in the previous decades, accelerated by the expansion of the high-tech information based economy, the subjective imaginary became a preferred area for profit extraction. This led to a condition in which the formation of individual identity became for many in the 1990s manifestly more difficult, and signs indicative of a subjective breakdown were often expressed in violent outbursts, the most explosive of which was the murder campaign unleashed by the religious cult group, *Aum Shinrikyō*. As discussed in a later chapter, this and other kinds of violent eruptions were manifestations of an acute quest for meaning in response to the seemingly endless flood of commercial signs that has permeated and suffused the realms of subjectivity and the social imaginary with notions of fragmentation, disembodiment and ambiguity. Curiously, in the troubled cultural context of the 1990s, nationalism, which in one form had died out in the late 1960s, returned in another form as culturally inclined declarations of national identity, particularly in the works of Fujioka Nobukatsu and Katō Norihiro. While this new form of nationalism sought, like its predecessors, to reconstitute the moribund national hegemony by grounding the meaning of life in the nation, the possibility of challenging the elite power of the Japanese state was almost completely foreclosed and thus instead it often followed elite initiatives seeking to unite the nation against imagined external (and sometimes internal) enemies. Although, as I argue in later chapters, these 1990s national identity claims were quite diverse, indeed often mutually contradictory, and arose from completely different political and intellectual streams, nevertheless each of the new nationalist writers' distinct narratives seemingly contracts and converges towards a single point called 'Japan,' in a mode disturbingly similar to the wartime amalgamation of discourses that took place under the sign of the emperor (*Kokutai*).

Main objectives and assumptions

The main theme of this book is the intimate but often understated relationship between nationalism and modernity, or more precisely, how modernization and the formation of the modern nation-state, which became a universal task of humanity from the late nineteenth century onward, have played a subtle but important role in constantly recreating a sense of, and a desire for, national identity in modern Japanese history, and why that is so. In the following chapters, I critically examine various assertions of Japanese national identity in twentieth century academic and fictional texts by analysing their contents and underlying motivations and by tracing their gestations in specific historical contexts. The problem of national identity has largely been approached in past scholarship in terms of its spatial configuration as the mutual and simultaneous determination of the (Western) self and the (non-Western) other. In this book, I have set myself the challenge of historicizing and materializing what has largely been contained within conceptually and spatially oriented approaches by incorporating into the study of national identity formation its temporal dimension, i.e. the historical progression of modernity. Following Adorno and Horkheimer's formulation in their *Dialectic of Enlightenment*, I view modern history as the dialectical processes of the outward expansion of enlightenment reason and the institutional forces which restructure and transform the meaning and content of human life, and the simultaneous formation of reactionary responses seeking to resist such transformations. Adapting this temporal frame, I approach the problematic of Japanese national identity not only in the light of Japan's inclusion into the Eurocentric modern world, but also within the dialectic of modernity, the penetration of modern forces and the way societies and individuals cope, or fail to cope, with the intensifying and incessant transformation to which they are subjected.

I attempt to do this by gathering together fragments of modern experience and the imaginary as recorded by some of the best minds of prewar and postwar Japan, with an awareness that they have simultaneously been circumscribed and conditioned by the particular concerns, hopes, and problematics that have increasingly and inescapably occupied writing subjects as socio-historical beings. In this formulation, I assume that knowledge, often viewed as being rational, apolitical and existing in a relation of autonomy vis-à-vis its historical context, is indeed inspired and often constituted by extra-rational and extra-discursive motivations and conditions often expressing the inarticulate but immanent voices present in society at large at a given time. Readers might find in this approach some resonance with what Fredric Jameson has called, referring to Althusser's notion of an 'absent cause,' the 'figuration' in history that 'can never emerge into the presence of perception,' but that 'find[s] figures through which to express itself in distorted and symbolic ways.'[10] In tracing Japanese responses to the maturing process of modernity as reflected in knowledge production, I attempt to elucidate some of the forms such 'distorted expressions' of an 'absent cause' have taken in twentieth century Japan, and how such expressions have increasingly found a home in the immanent figure of the Japanese nation, the 'body' onto which a manifold of inarticulate hopes and desires are projected and reified. It is the presence of these extra-rational aspects in nationalist discourse that makes their texts excessive and aesthetically inclined; and however distorted their calls for an impossible identity are, they simultaneously point to the limitations of rationalist discourse and demonstrate against its representative scheme by bringing back 'things excluded.' This last point leads us to investigate further the relation between the modern historical dialectic and knowledge production, and especially the production of that knowledge that arises from the limits of representation and seeks to give full expression to human experience.

Presumably, the inability of human beings to fully grasp their experience is the universal condition that gave rise to the necessity to speak and think in the first place. However, at certain historical junctures, the limitations of language itself are more acutely felt than at other times; there, conditions conspire to induce a writing strategy that makes extensive use of an 'aesthetic awareness,' resulting in a situation which can be described as the 'aestheticization of knowledge.' Viewing the developmental path of both prewar and postwar Japanese intellectual productions in the context of the historical dialectic of modernity, one notices a gradual fragmentation of the subject and the social imaginary developing in tandem with an equally gradual shift from political and intellectual movements based on enlightenment values to movements based on romantically inclined values accommodating extra-rational aspects. That is to say, as modernity's project of redesigning society and individuals intensifies, the resultant disturbances incurred in the realm of subjectivity and the social imaginary incline individuals towards an existentially inclined mode of cognition expressed, for example, in criticisms of realist epistemology and progressivist notions of history, in a greater appreciation of the value of beauty as opposed to that of reason, and in an extensive use of ambiguous categories loaded with emotional freight. This can be most clearly seen, perhaps, in Japanese postwar history when an initially strong commitment to the ideal of enlightenment values and the modernist developmental path was witnessed under the US occupation, and then gradually waned over the subsequent decades. It was during the 1960s especially, when the effects of rapid economic growth were fully felt and an increasingly formalized politics excluding the popular ethos became more fully entrenched, that a romantic resurgence occurred in knowledge production, expressed in terms of an intense yearning for the absolute (in popular novels), a desire to recover a lost 'nature' (often in the form of the traditional family and ideals of femininity), a condemnation of the Americanization of Japan and its subsequent loss of native spirit, and so on.

By situating the debate on this dialectical terrain between the penetration of the rational and institutional forces and the aesthetic responses to them, I seek to relocate the problematic of Japanese national identity on another theoretical terrain, namely, the changing modes of national hegemony and the social imaginary. In accordance with my analytic perspective viewing the modern Japanese nation-state as a hegemony, I view twentieth century Japanese history in terms of hegemonic formation, transformation and breakdown. The progression of modernity differently affects the distinct spheres of hegemony (e.g. the state, production relations and the discursive), while changes incurred in them are conditioned and coordinated in such a way as to balance and sustain national hegemony as a whole. Given its malleability and reflexive nature, the sphere of the discursive, in particular, with subjective cognition and the social imaginary as its parts, tends to play the role of mediating and absorbing the materially and institutionally introduced structural changes in an 'effort' to sustain national hegemony, albeit naturally, within the range of its limit. In this sense, the above described aestheticization of knowledge is not merely a reaction to rational structuring forces but attains significance as a defence mechanism, sustaining national hegemony and helping the subject adjust to transformations by depicting a renewed hegemonic reality in accord with the structural changes he or she undergoes. As the penetration of modern structuring forces intensifies, and as the fragmentation of the subject and the social imaginary advances, however, a point is ultimately reached at which hegemony can no longer be sustained, giving rise to more and more vocal calls for the recovery of national identity, the remedy at hand for rehabilitating the fragmented social imaginary and the moribund hegemony.

'Japan' as the aesthetic construct of the modern universal world

The rise of the modern Japanese state was triggered by Japan's traumatic encounter with its powerful other – the modern West – in the rough seas of the mid-nineteenth century colonial competition among Western powers. With the arrival of four US gunboats led by Commodore Perry in 1853, Japan was pressured into an unequal commercial treaty with the Americans after over 200 years of isolation, and similar treaties with the English, the French, the Dutch and the Russians soon followed. Trade with the West commenced in earnest in 1859, however, during the 1860s Japan experienced years of turmoil and menace in which the Japanese state was exposed to the dangers of internal collapse and Western colonization. International trade caused enormous confusions in the local economy and induced a series of rebellions throughout the nation on the part of angry peasants (*hyakusho ikki*) and the urban lower classes (*uchikowashi*). In 1861, a Russian fleet attempted to occupy Tsushima Island but was forced back by the concerted efforts of the locals (despite little support from the central government) and the timely pressure asserted by the arrival of the English navy.[11] In these same years, a restoration movement against the Edo *bakufu* arose, mostly among the lower-class *samurais* of Satsuma and Choshu, which, under the slogan of '*sonnō jōi*,' 'revere the emperor, expel the barbarian,' gained momentum in a political atmosphere charged with the sense of an acute external threat.[12] In this context of intensifying and widening social unrest, the *bakufu* was coerced into 'voluntarily returning' governing authority to the imperial court (*taisei hōkan*), and the Restorationists took power in 1867.

The Meiji restoration was initiated in 1868, and from the very beginning it embodied the mixed intentions of establishing a strong, modern state in order to secure national autonomy, and a democratic nation in order to liberate society from the feudalistic socio-political system. This modernization project entailed the wholesale restructuring of the nation's political, economic and socio-educational institutions under the aegis of a centralized national governing authority. Recognizing the urgent need to adapt foreign ideas and institutions, the Japanese elites undertook a rhetorical campaign to convince the populace. One of the leading intellectuals of this enlightenment movement and a convinced pragmatist, Fukuzawa Yukichi adopted in his well-known 1875 work *Bunmei-ron no Gairyaku* (*Introduction to the Theory of Civilization*) a rather crude universalist and teleological view whereby history developed from a state of barbarism to one of civilization (*bunmei ichigenron*); further, as Fukuzawa portrayed it, following the Western imperial model was not only inevitable but desirable for the Japanese. In the early Meiji years, Japanese participation in this 'alien game' was often depicted in terms of future-oriented, hopeful and optimistic visions for change, and a great deal of energy was invested in motivating the populace towards the ideological project of national construction, as the common slogans of the time attest – *bunmei kaika* ('join civilization'), *wakon yōsai* ('maintain Japanese spirit by adapting Western technology'), *fukoku kyōhei* ('build a rich nation and strong army').[13] To embrace modernization, however, was also to pursue the goal implicit in the universal narrative of 'civilization,' and that meant, among other things, accepting a lesser identity in the international political representational scheme as a non-Western other.

To the degree that modernization in Japan was simultaneously experienced as Westernization, the state-led political project entailed a voluntary cultural displacement, a willed attempt to overcome the inferiority imparted by Europe and assumed in Japan. It can be argued that to interpret the alienation and disembodiment accompanying modernization as a cultural displacement, as Japanese intellectuals have repeatedly done, is something of a misconstruction. And there are good reasons why this is often the case, since the modern Japanese nation-state had its historical origin in precisely the moment of Japan's traumatic encounter with the West, and since both the discourse of the Japanese nation-state and that of modernization were constituted in the context of an acute awareness of the presence of the West. At the same time, however, the separation of these discourses is really only possible in rational analysis; in experience, cultural displacement is part and parcel of the experience of modernization, and it is for this reason that cultural identity has emerged as a critical issue in Japan and elsewhere. In other words, the discursive confusion of the historical origin of the modern Japanese nation-state, modernization, and cultural displacement, represents much more than a lapse in critical thinking; it also makes visible the hegemonic power of the modern universal world in which universality is achieved through the subsumption and conversion of the unique temporality and spatiality of different cultures and peoples. This is to say that the narrative of civilization establishes its universality by fixing the plurality of different cultures and peoples into a linear succession of human developments, relegating heterogeneous cultural identities to the status of less-than-Europeans, shadow existences under the Western hegemonic gaze.[14] To make the issue even more complicated, the awareness of one's 'culturally specific experience' is largely generated by the very denial of such specificity, by one's inclusion in the modern universalist world and by one's internalization of the perspective of universal civilization through the experience of modernization. Once this internalization has been made, 'culture' opens itself up as a counter-hegemonic site for the articulation of resentments against the universalist inscriptions of the modern West, while simultaneously constituting a hegemonic gaze of its own.

Equally problematic is the fact that this sense of cultural displacement has been constantly regenerated in Japanese discourse since the nation's encounter with the modern West. This was particularly so because during the initial stages of modernization the traditional categories of Japanese intellectual activity were reconfigured to establish a 'modern Japanese knowledge' in correspondence with the Western division of disciplines. As Karatani Kōjin has observed, some intellectual and artistic fields, such as Chinese medicine, Japanese literature, and Buddhism, were either abolished or replaced by their Western counterparts, with the latter being henceforward regarded as the only '"proper"' academic subjects.[15] The field of visual art was a curious exception to the general subordination of native disciplines to Western ones, for the Japanese themselves realized that the domain of art was recognized by the West as something valuable in itself.[16] In the mid- to late nineteenth century, Japanese traditional arts (and indeed, East Asian arts as a whole) were 'discovered' by Westerners searching for new aesthetic possibilities and sources of inspiration as well as a potential way out of the discomfort engendered by the rationalist artistic and philosophical traditions as they had developed since the Renaissance. Asian arts, it was felt, would help rejuvenate Western culture with novel aesthetic forms and alternative intellectual and moral principles.[17] This Western recognition of the beauty of Japanese art had a deep and important impact on the formation of Japanese national identity in aesthetic terms, and particularly its development as an advocate of counter-hegemonic revolt against what was perceived as the tyrannical imposition of Western reason.[18]

It was, then, no mere coincidence that the politico-cultural space of Japan made unintelligible by the universal discourse of the modern West sought to express its unrepresentable identity in aesthetic terms. Despite their entirely different motivations and interests, the Japanese sense of cultural identity awakened by the encounter with the modern West and the Western appetite for Japanese art as a precious and exotic commodity found a meeting place in the realm of the aesthetic. Indeed, it is worth pondering the fact that the universality of reason, ethics, and modern institutions were the exclusive property of the 'superior West,' whereas subordinate Japan was only allowed, or, perhaps better said, encouraged to assert its identity in cultural, particularist, and aesthetic terms. If the particular characteristic of the aesthetic category lies, as I argued above, both in its capacity to foster and nurture counter-hegemonic aspirations, and in its synthetic comprehension of the two ends of modern dualism, then it is perhaps understandable why modern Japanese intellectual production had a particular affinity for it. Indeed, all talk of 'Japanese thought' as such, claiming for itself the status of culturally specific ideas, draws heavily from these properties of the aesthetic. It is in this context that we ought to view Japanese romanticism, for example, which undertook a persistent re-evaluation of things Japanese, mostly in cultural and aesthetic terms, both as a reclamation of things displaced by the modern West and as a forward-looking, hopeful vision of how things could be in an alternative future when the limitations of the modern were overcome. In this sense, 'Japan' itself as a politico-cultural space became an aesthetic construct of the modern universal world, designated and designed by the imaginary scheme of the superior Western powers and 'voluntarily' internalized by the subordinate Japanese.

The structural relations in force here are worth looking at more closely. The universalist framework of the contemporary world in which the national identity of non-Western nations is formulated arises out of the synchronic sphere of Western universal hegemony, leaving only the contents of the particular identity in question to be filled in by the experiences of cultural particularity. Thus, in the Japanese case, Japanese national identity comes to itself, as it were, from out of the hegemonic process in which Japan's 'true particularity' is denied by virtue of Japan's incorporation into the universalist representational schema as the other of the West. Here lies the dilemma of modern Japanese identity: Japanese identity as such is only articulable in universal terms, as a sameness-in-difference, as a difference and a distinction vis-à-vis the assumed universality of the West. As Sakai Naoki argues,

> Japan is defined as a specific and unitary particularity in universal terms: Japan's uniqueness and identity are provided insofar as Japan stands out as a particular object in the universal field of the West. Only when it is integrated into Western universalism does it gain its own identity as a particularity. In other words, Japan becomes endowed with and aware of its 'self' only when it is recognized by the West. . . . [The Japanese cultural particularists'] insistence on Japan's peculiarity and difference from the West embodies a nagging urge to see the self from the viewpoint of the other. But this is nothing but the posing of Japan's identity in Western terms which in turn establishes the centrality of the West as the universal point of reference.[19]

The parameters of the dilemma, then, are such that Japan as a culturally unique space is authorized by, dependent upon, and mediated through the universal gaze of the West; and this sense of being marginalized by universal representation cultivates in the Japanese a 'nagging urge' for a self-knowledge that can only be obtained by adopting 'the view point of the other.' Moreover, this attempt to define Japan as culturally particular space was, as I have argued, approved in advance by the West's appreciation of Japanese aesthetics as a valuable exterior commodity. The cultural particularity of the people confined within the bounds of the Japanese nation-state became, then, a symbol of the unity of the Japanese political-cultural organization in the modern hegemonic world system that transformed Western notions of ethnic hierarchies into a geographically based array of cultural differences.

Not to be forgotten in this context was Japan's ambivalent attitude to Asia during the course of its modernization. In some ways Japan's attitude was at first characterized by universal revolutionary hopes in solidarity across national boundaries; later, however, it increasingly gave way to belligerency and righteous justifications of state-imperialistic expansionism. Early Japanese liberals, like Ōi Kentaro and his fellows Asianists, advocated a policy of *kō-a-ron* (support Asia), based on universalist humanist values, and thought seriously about exporting democratic revolution to Korea and other parts of Asia. Other liberals like Fukuzawa (in 1885) called instead for *datsu-a-ron*, 'depart from Asia,' a view that was later employed in arguments advocating Japan's imperialist entitlement to prey upon its less advanced neighbours. The Sino–Japanese war (1894–5) combined aspects of both these policies in as much as Japan both supported revolutionary segments of Korean society against the Korean feudal government (allied with the Chinese) and embraced a hardening of attitudes towards Asia along imperialist lines. It was during these years that the possibility of unlimited economic access to Korea and competing with the Western powers over Manchuria and beyond proved irresistible to the Japanese, a prospect secured by the Russo–Japanese war of 1904–5. Japanese victory in the war consolidated Japan's imperial ascent and proved to the world that the nation had succeeded in the demanding task of modernization. One of the by-products of the victory was that it brought the understated racial dimension of the Eurocentric universalist system out into the open, manifest both in the growing 'yellow peril' hysteria in the West and in a series of newly inspired anti-colonial movements in parts of Asia. It was also in these years that the art historian Okakura Tenshin, in his 1903 *The Ideals of the East* (written in English), attempted to relativize the universalist narrative of the West by claiming that Asia possessed a distinct universal value of its own and by upholding the notion of the 'oneness of Asia' based on the Asian value principles of harmony and non-conflictive coexistence of contradictions.[20] Although Okakura intended his work to be a critique of both Western and Japanese imperialisms, it was instrumental in constructing 'Asia' as a site of counter-hegemonic resistance; by portraying the 'oneness of Asia' in aesthetically inspiring terms, Okakura inadvertently inspired the subsequent Japanese Pan-Asianists who were to furnish the Japanese imperialist state with the rhetorical inventions necessary to its narrative of resistance against Western imperialism. Indeed, the notion of 'oneness' was employed to rationalize Japan's annexation of Korea in 1910, and later Pan-Asianist movements carried out a tacit depoliticization of Japan's encroachment in Asia by couching 'Asian unity' in the morally charged terms of an idealized fraternity. Thus, parallel to the aesthetic construction of 'Japan' by the West's universal narrative of civilization, 'Asia,' too, was subject to a construction – by the Japanese counter-narrative of a universal Asia in which Asia was fixed by the Japanese hegemonic gaze and held submissive to its power.[21]

Underlying this ambiguity in Japan's attitude vis-à-vis Asia is the peculiarly dualistic role modern nation-states play in the hegemonic configuration of the modern world. While universalist international codes uphold the necessity of cooperation among nations to foster peace and stability in the world order, each nation retains control over its own military capacity to destroy others. Similarly, while enjoying widespread currency in the international arena, the suasion of universalist moral codes and the discourse of international human rights often halts at the various national borders. In both of these instances, the limits of the international are justified on the grounds of the autonomy of the sovereign nation-state vis-à-vis its own subjects and other states. Moreover, international economic institutions uphold the principle of free-trade over state protectionism on the grounds of mutual benefit and an equal playing field for all parties, while the socio-economic well-being of the populace is left entirely to the responsibility of each nation-state. Naturally, these limitations allow stronger global economic actors enjoying the advantage of mobile capital and technology to freely cut across national boundaries and to operate in places where local societies are struggling to foster their own industries. From a structural point of view, the dual regime of universal, international economic institutions and particular, sovereign nation-states works to conceal the structural contradiction of the modern world configuration and to reproduce its hegemonic violence. It is this structural violence that gives rise to the counter-hegemonic protests of those at the margins of the order, protests often formulated and expressed in cultural, religious and other aesthetic terms. By means of this structural dualism, problems rooted in the modern world configuration itself are passed onto the nation-state to be dealt with, and this constitutes a heavy burden, especially for those nations in the process of modernization. For this reason the questions of culture and identity, if they are to be addressed in their full amplitude, must be located in direct relation to this dualistic structural make-up of the modern world; failing to do so, one tends to neglect the problematic historical heritage of the modern universal world altogether and to uncritically accept the systemic power relations that favour the politically and economically powerful.[22]

Moreover, this arbitrary boundary between the universality of political and economic institutional frameworks and the autonomy of the sovereign nation-state imposes particular difficulties on non-Western nation-states in the process of modernization, difficulties that tend to manifest themselves in cultural and national terms. As the Japanese experience exemplifies, the non-Western nation-state has been burdened with the contradictory task of reconciling political and economic modernization, a process inescapably entailing the importation of modern technologies, institutions and values that constantly remind one of their foreignness, with the state's own attempts to establish national hegemony under the symbolic unity of the unique culture common to its peoples. In Japan, the state's principal means of foreclosing dissent and counter-acting potential resistance to its modernization project was the promulgation and dissemination of the ideology of the 'family-nation,' all the while simultaneously advancing modernization as rapidly as possible in order to free itself from the threat of Western domination. This dilemma of modernization was noted by the Japanese modernist writer Natsume Sōseki (1867–1916):

> Japan was running a race with Western history; only by reaching the Western nations' advanced stage of development could it regain cultural autonomy and control of its own destiny. And yet Japan could

be truly independent and self-respecting only if it were no longer impelled from without (*gaihatsuteki kaika*), no longer compelled to borrow from the West, no longer forced to follow an already broken path rather than a self-determined course (*naihatsuteki kaika*).[23]

Given the structural contradictions of modernity I have laid out, Sōseki's observation cannot be dismissed as the mere product of one Japanese intellectual's obsession, the result of a false juxtaposition between 'Japan' and the 'West,' for 'modern Japan' was in fact constituted on the basis of a denied cultural autonomy. By the same token, however, what Sōseki calls the pursuit of, or desire for, 'a self-determined course' cannot in any realistic sense be asserted as a possibility, because, as Sōseki knows full well, the desire for such a self-determined course is itself the product of the awareness of its very impossibility. The hegemonic violence of modern universalism operates by locking the subject, or rather the *national subject*, into this conundrum and tormenting him or her with an awareness of its closure. Obviously, this state of suspension is not easy to sustain.

Modernization and the transformation of national hegemony

From the early Meiji era, the Japanese state seems to have been well aware of the crucial importance of capturing the undirected emotional forces released in the masses by the processes of modernization and harnessing them to the goal of securing national hegemony. From early on, it attempted to articulate these forces in a narrative of the 'family-state' in order to consolidate its symbolic power. By 1890 the compulsory daily recitation of the 'Imperial Rescript on Education,' a paean to the Japanese nation as the extended family of the emperor, was standard practice throughout the national public education system. In the Rescript, loyalty to the emperor as the living representative of the mythic forefathers of the Japanese was described in no uncertain terms as one's 'ancestral duty.'

> Our Imperial Ancestors have founded Our Empire on a basis broad and everlasting and have deeply and firmly implanted virtue; Our subjects ever united in loyalty and filial piety have from generation to generation illustrated the beauty thereof . . . should emergency arise, offer yourselves courageously to the State; and thus guard and maintain the prosperity of Our Imperial Throne coeval with heaven and earth.[24]

In the Rescript and its recitation we have a potent image of the state's formal project of creating a national superstructure by 'inventing' a national mythology that would harness popular sentiment and a communal sense of morality. The ideas contained in the Rescript foreshadow a number of similar ideas that were later disseminated in the 1930s wartime ideology of *kokutai* – literally, 'national body,' or 'national polity' in a more standard translation – and it is for this reason that the Rescript is often identified as one of the roots of Japanese militarism. However, we should not elide the very different historical contexts of the two periods in question, contexts in which the same mythology was given an entirely different political function. In the late nineteenth century, the Japanese state was in the process of hegemonic formation, seeking to establish a working mechanism for absorbing a relatively dispersed society under its authority. To do this it had to create a workable link between the array of modern institutions ('structure') and their guiding principles ('superstructure'), and to consolidate national hegemony in negotiation with the existing local powers.

In her illuminating study of the modern Japanese emperor system, *Japan's Modern Myths: Ideology in the Late Meiji Period* (1985), Carol Gluck charts the intensification of the Japanese people's subjugation to ideology from the 1890s to the war years. Recognizing the significance and the difficulties inherent in 'the process of establishing a national ethos on a changed and changing social setting,' Gluck argues the Japanese state rose to hegemony through the use of tactics that were both 'rigid and flexible' and which allowed it to extend its ideological grasp deep into the everyday life of its subjects.

> The oligarchs, the bureaucrats, and their ideologues, realizing that some explanation was necessary to secure the cooperation of the people through the rigors of economic development and international expansion, created a state orthodoxy around the figure of the emperor and then imposed it upon the people. The orthodoxy was rigid and flexible at the same time. While its rigidity worked to prevent effective opposition by equating dissent with disloyalty, its vagueness enabled it to adapt its injunctions to different needs, so that sacrifice in war and savings accounts in peace could both be justified in terms of the same national myths. By moralizing and mystifying the nature of the state, politics was depoliticized.[25]

Although one might quibble with Gluck's extension of the term 'ideology' to include the articulation of the guiding principles of everyday life ('imposed,' as she says, 'upon the people'), Gluck's narrative of the intensification of state ideological control is well argued and her analysis of numerous contemporary social and intellectual texts is both insightful and cogent. I do want to question, however, her conclusion that that deepening ideological process led to what she calls the 'ever increasing power of the state,' for, in so far as the Japan of the 1930s is concerned, the Japanese state was in fact far from consolidation, and was, if anything, in the throes of an increasingly acute hegemonic crisis.

The Japanese Ministry of Education's 1937 pamphlet, *Fundamentals of Our National Polity* (*Kokutai no Hongi*), published in the year Japan invaded China, appears to suggest, both in its content and by its popularity, that the state was successfully increasing its grip upon the populace. Despite clearly exhorting the people to be ready for self-sacrifice in the coming 'total war,' the final sales of the booklet were in the neighbourhood of 2 million copies, a surprising figure at the time, and immensely outnumbering the initial print run of 300,000.[26] Opening with a condemnation of enlightenment values and the causes of the 'ideological and social evils of present-day Japan,' the *Fundamentals* concludes with a proclamation of Japan's 'mission' in world civilization to provide a synthesis between Eastern and Western ideas:

> The various ideological and social evils of present-day Japan are the result of ignoring the fundamental and running after the trivial, of a lack of judgment, and a failure to digest things thoroughly; and this is due to the fact that since the days of Meiji so many aspects of European and American culture, systems, and learning, have been imported, and that too rapidly. As a matter of fact, the foreign ideologies imported into our country are in the main ideologies of the Enlightenment that have come down from the eighteenth century, or extensions of them. The view of the world and of life that forms the basis of these ideologies are a rationalism and a positivism, lacking in historical views, which on the one hand lay the highest value on, and assert the liberty and equality of, individuals, and on the other hand lay value on a world by nature abstract, transcending nations and races. Consequently, importance is laid upon human beings and their groupings, who have become isolated from historical entities, abstract and independent of each other. It is political, social, moral, and pedagogical theories based on such views of the world and of life, that have on the one hand made contributions to the various reforms seen in our country, and on the other have had deep and wide influence on our nation's primary ideology and cult . . .
>
> Our present mission as a people is to build up a new Japanese culture by adopting and sublimating Western cultures with our national polity as the basis, and to contribute spontaneously to the advancement of world culture. Our nation early saw the introduction of Chinese and Indian cultures, and even succeeded in evolving original creations and developments. This was made possible, indeed, by *the profound and boundless nature of our national polity*; so that the mission of the people to whom it is bequeathed is truly great in its historical significance.[27]

The notion employed here of 'our national polity,' or *kokutai*, was based upon a similar notion in the late nineteenth-century Rescript, in which the Japanese people were conceived as the direct descendants of the imperial family, ruling from time immemorial. In the middle section of the pamphlet, various attempts are made to evoke a sense of responsibility to the family, to the local representatives of each agrarian community, and to the emperor at the summit of the hierarchy in which ethical and ideological structures were merged. In essence the *Fundamentals* duplicates the content of the Rescript, with the only real addition being the above quoted opening passage advocating Japan's 'cultural mission' in clearly anti-modernist and ideological terms. The passage criticizing enlightenment ideas still reads relatively well, and captures the unresolved problems of modernity that we still face today, albeit in a different historical context.

What appears to be odd, at least from the present vantage point, however, is the leap of logic between the diagnosis contained in the first passage and the remedy in the second, the leap assuming that the solution to all the ills of modernity the nation had undergone since the Meiji restoration would be what the *Fundamentals* calls 'total war.' The reasons why this 'odd logic' was so widely 'accepted' cannot be reduced to the 'efficacy of ideology,' and in order to fully understand the *Fundamentals* and its reception, one must first account for the transformation that the Japanese society and people had undergone since Meiji and the crucial changes that had been effected in *the modality of national hegemony*.

The process of erosion whereby instabilities in the structure of the national hegemony were gradually magnified as modernization progressed, unleashing sources of conflict and differentiation, is not easily articulated back into the state's founding myths, nor into the frame of the legal and institutional order. In the 1930s, the familiar rhetoric of the 'family state' was advanced as a remedy for the general unease of a society plagued by multiple breakdowns in various spheres of life, an unease that many Japanese intellectuals of the time expressed as an acute sense of 'homelessness' and inner void. While the old family myth was recalled and pressed into active service in the 1930s, its function in the new context was no longer merely to provide an 'organic link' between the state and the popular ethos; instead, it was employed to fill in the wide-spread social and subjective void, to mask grave historical facts, and to transform them into a hopeful vision of a glorious future. Here, if we are to speak of 'nationalism' we should distinguish this version from varieties rooted in simple expressions of one's attachment to the nation as a common polity wherein some sense of community is still intact. What characterized Japanese national hegemony at the historical juncture of the 1930s was the exhaustion of the links formerly capable of absorbing and channelling popular sentiments back into the national hegemony as its source of legitimacy. It was only in this context of the troubled relations between knowledge production and the subject, on the one hand, and between knowledge and the historical world, on the other, that the emperor mythology could play the potent ideological role of transcending the historical ills generated by modernity in a vision of a 'true Japan' existing in an alternative time and space outside of modernity. To repeat, the move towards 'mythological transcendence' in wartime Japan cannot be satisfactorily understood within conventional notions of nationalism or state ideological manipulation; to do that we need to enlarge our theoretical frame to include consideration of the universal problematic of modernity, the historical configuration that it designed, and the growing significance of the aesthetic as a site of counter-hegemonic response to it. In the following paragraphs, I provide a brief sketch of prewar modernization from the 'Romantic turn' around the turn of the century to the years leading towards the war, as a way of preparing the background for my analysis in Chapter 2 of the intellectual ferment of the 1930s and the 'aesthetic solution' that developed out of it.

Similar to the process witnessed in Europe, Japan also was initially inspired by enlightenment ideas, and in that inspiration a wholesale borrowing of Western ideas, technologies and institutions was accommodated. In Japan, however, the process of modernization was much more intense than in the West, almost 200 years of modern Western development occurring in a matter of 50–60 years. Once the initial threat of Western colonization had abated and the goal of 'catching up with the West' was felt to have been more or less achieved, especially following Japan's victory in the Russo–Japanese war (1904–5), and once the negative manifestations of modernity, such as rural poverty, alienation, egotistical competition in the capitalist economy, and rising social tensions, became increasingly visible, modernization in Japan began to lose its lustre and came to be seen as the source of unwanted Western influences. In the socio-historical sphere, the Japan of the 1910s and 1920s can be described in terms of a deepening of the dialectical process of modernity between the progression of modern forces and the social responses of political resistance. As universal education and the extension of political representation advanced, democratic consciousness, including demands for civil rights, flourished, particularly in the 1910s and 1920s during the period of the so-called 'Taishō Democracy.' In the socio-economic sphere, Marxist influences awakened Japanese labour to its organizational rights, and rural agrarian and urban labour movements subsequently developed, forcing landlords and management classes to recognize the right to collective negotiation for the first time in Japanese history. As the Japanese economy faltered throughout the late 1910s and early 1920s, new developments arose in response: the Japan Communist Party was formed in 1922, inspired by the 1917 Bolshevik Revolution, social unrest grew in scale and intensity in both the rural and urban spheres, and right-wing organizations sprung up to counter the Leftist movement.

In the cultural and discursive domains, the deepening process of modernity brought about a gradual weakening of the rigour initially accompanying the adoption of the Western model, and the search for an alternative national trajectory developed in tandem with romantically inclined intellectual and cultural attitudes. Broadly speaking, post-1905

Japanese intellectual trends followed a course of growing aestheticization and increasingly sharp challenges to the enlightenment notions of transcendental reason, the rational and autonomous subject, and the linear-progressive unfolding of history. These challenges were made either by idealizing the object of inquiry, as exemplified in the development of folk studies and Asianism, or by depoliticized interpretations of social and artistic texts as in literary and social criticism. Around 1910 the literary circle known as *shizen-shugi* – literally 'naturalism,' but often closer to a form of spiritualism – emerged, at the same time marking of the emergence of the modern Japanese subject who objectified nature and was aware of his or her displaced self. Concurrently, a growing interest in and concern about the disappearance of rural customs, thought to be carriers of the Japanese cultural tradition, gave rise to the field of Japanese folk studies (*minzoku-gaku*).[28] The same decade also saw the growing popularity of Asianism as a discourse conceiving Asia either in depoliticized terms or in pragmatic terms directly linked to the colonial enterprise of Japan's increasing political encroachment in Taiwan, Korea and later, China. Simultaneous with these developments was the growing dissemination of intellectual ideas from the intellectual class to the educated populace at large who by and large viewed the advent of modern subjectivity and the social transformation wrought by modernization as nothing less than the dehumanization of the individual, the erosion of the communal fabric and morality, and the spread of spiritual decay.

By the 1930s, with the radical downturn in world economic growth, Japanese society began to manifest the stark signs of a general crisis: a heightened atmosphere of social unrest and social confrontation led by Marxist-directed social movements; the military occupation of Manchuria; an increasing incidence of violent fascist attacks against the democratic regime; and a widespread mood of anxiety, yearning, uncertainty and desperation. In the domain of knowledge, romantic trends reached their apogee, in the period immediately following the state's suppression of the urban and rural Leftist movements in the mid-1930s, with the sophisticated intellectual productions of Watsuji Tetsurō's aesthetic account of Japanese socio-cultural foundations, Nishida Kitarō and his Kyoto school's notion of Japan's world-historical project, and Yasuda Yojūrō and his Japan Romantic School's anti-modern aestheticism lauding the lost beauty of Japan. These socio-economic, intellectual and cultural conditions, which had developed within and in reaction to the deepening process of modernity, together prepared Japan for its descent down the ideological path towards the Greater East-Asia Co-prosperity Sphere, 'total war,' and 'overcoming modernity,' the ideological complex recounting Japan's world-historical mission to liberate Asia from Western domination. With the opening of the Pacific War, many Japanese intellectuals, Rightists and Leftists, expressed their profound sense of joy: the Japanese state had recovered the 'organic link' with its people.

In summary, we may say that modern knowledge and the universalist and rationalist principles embodied in modern political institutions and the capitalist economy gradually brought modern Japanese national identity to a point of self-consciousness, awakened precisely in the perception that it was in the process of disappearing. To complicate matters, this reactionary awakening of national identity was simultaneously a process in which the modern Japanese subject was constituted and, tormented by a sense of loss, seized by the anti-modern desire to transcend its inner displacement. In the dialectical process of modernity this reactionarily generated Japanese aesthetic desire was articulated as a lament for a lost unity with nature, the totality of being, and 'things Japanese,' which is to say, the cultural tradition designating the particularity of Japan that, it was felt, modern universalism denied. In this, the term 'Japan' became a catch-all, empty signifier designating all things lost to modernization. Clearly important to this development was what I have called the immanence of the counter-hegemonic impulse in modern Japanese national identity, inscribed from the beginning in the encounter with the modern West. This impulse would come to play an important role in the later formulation of Japanese national identity as a being-in-opposition to things modern and Western, and seemingly predisposed the nation to articulate its ultimate form of identity in aesthetic terms, as it did in the years leading to the Pacific War. It bears repeating: what gave content to this form was an inarticulate, and often revolutionary (albeit depoliticized and aestheticized) desire cultivated in the process of modernization – a desire to go beyond the modern, to transcend the Western, externally imposed, universal and synchronic structures of capital, reason, and the lesser identity of the other. From within the optic of this counter-hegemonic ideal, the Japanese in the years leading up to the war were on a course to realize their self-defined identity; having fully embraced the aesthetic imagination, they were on the very brink of breaking free from all the ills of modernization.

2 'Overcoming modernity'

Towards an aesthetic politics of identity

> ... in the grip of such a radical irony, even I in some instances wanted to imagine a revolution. As *Kokugaku*-like ideas became increasingly pronounced in Yasuda's writing, a complete rejection of all political realism and all situational analysis came strongly forward, leading him to insist with a desperate intensity on the destruction of scientific thinking. It was almost like an accelerating premonition of the defeat and coming catastrophe.
>
> Hashikawa Bunzō, *Nihon Rōman-ha Josetsu*

> Behind the mask of peace the poison of civilization spreads ... In those battlefields the rise or fall of the Japanese people will depend upon the clarity of their insight and resolution to drive away all delusions and upon the ineradicable fearlessness of their belief. Rather a war of kings than the peace of slaves!
>
> Kamei Katsuichirō, from the symposium 'Overcoming Modernity'

Introduction

As Japanese society came to be fully permeated by the various effects of modernization during the first few decades of the twentieth century, the subjective terrain of the individual underwent a thorough transformation from 'premodern' to modern dualistic mode. In Chapter 2, I seek to outline the Japanese experience of modernity from the turn of the century to the period leading up to and including the Pacific War, by tracing a sense of the contradictions about modernization as reflected in the works of those Japanese intellectuals who 'discovered' their modern subjectivity primarily in a romantically inclined mode. Faced with the powerful intrusion of modern forces that were radically transforming the picture of the world and the self, as they knew it, these intellectuals, both as representative voices of society and as writing subjects conditioned by the particulars of their time, thematized and struggled with the problematic of modernity in its many senses. In what immediately follows, I trace the emergence of the modern Japanese subject in the urban literary movements that flourished between Japan's two imperial wars and the early 1930s. Throughout the Taishō era (1912–25), with the intensification of the dialectical struggle between the encroachment of modern material forces and the varied responses to them, the deepening of modernization was accompanied by a series of subtle but decisive changes in subjectivity and the relation between the self and the world mediated by language, changes which naturally entailed some fundamental transformations in the mode of discourse as well. During this time, many writers felt that language was betraying them, that the satisfactory expression of their inner selves and social conditions was being foreclosed. Two literary streams – proletarian literature and avant-garde modern literature – emerged, both striving, despite their very different ways, to situate themselves and define their opposition to the increasingly difficult political conditions and the discursive opacity of the time. From our distant perspective, these two streams represent both a maturation of and a resistance to the abstract and disembodied modern subject.

The second section of this chapter examines the role played by the work of three prominent intellectuals who were extremely influential in the mid-1930s, the period of so-called 'cultural renaissance': Watsuji Tetsurō, Nishida Kitarō and Yasuda Yojūrō. In the heightened political tensions of the early 1930s, aesthetic discourses became an important source feeding political aspirations to overcome the contradictions of the modern and a key defining characteristic of Japanese cultural identity. This aesthetic turn of the mid-1930s prepared a common ground for the unification of the fragmented, dispersed and conflict-laden Japanese socio-discursive space, and nurtured the burgeoning vision of a Japanese-designed, alternative modernization trajectory, in which the aesthetic was placed above reason. As I discuss in the third section, this aesthetically based, alternative worldview was fashioned into a political project in the opening months of the Pacific War; as participants of the 1942 symposium 'Overcoming Modernity' were to argue, the failed experience of Japanese modernity might be redeemed and the ideal of a Japanese (and Asian) cultural beauty might be realized – by means of war. An examination of the developmental path of knowledge during the period in question suggests that the category of aesthetics, conventionally seen as apolitical, was in fact highly political in nature. Or, rather, it was precisely when the aesthetic imagination came to be formulated in depoliticized and dematerialized terms that it became a powerful ideological instrument, as was the case in those troubled years when the contradictions of modernity were all too visible. The last section gathers together the threads of the previous arguments in light of Japan's troubled experience with modernity, in which an anti-modern, anti-Western, and aesthetically oriented identity formation crystallized out inspirations and forces that were undeniably modern, in order to broaden our perspective beyond the conventional notions of 'nationalism' and 'Japanese identity.'

The emergence, maturation and crisis of the modern Japanese subject in urban politico-cultural movements

As the Japanese economy matured, entering into a stage of heavy industrialization by the end of the Russo–Japanese war, its wholesale socioeconomic transformation was accompanied by a great concentration of wealth and the creation of large underclasses, both of which were to generate dissent and resentment. In the context of the nation-wide expansion of public discourse led by a nascent print culture, a large emergent educated class became aware of the various social problems, as well as the limitations and contradictions of democracy at large ('democracy' was often pronounced '*demo-kurushii*,' literally 'yet painful,' an ironic comment on the hard life of the populace).[1] The Taishō era (1912–25) was indeed 'democratic' in the original sense of the word, inasmuch as the populace brought itself onto the politico-historical stage. The era began with an outburst of dissent when large numbers of anti-state demonstrators surrounded the diet and demanded that politicians act on behalf of the interests of the majority. The ideal upheld in this popular movement, so-called *Taishō demokurashii*, was rather modestly expressed by popular opinion leader and intellectual Yoshino Sakuzō in his conception of *minpon-shugi*, more of the compromise between people's rights and the sovereign state's right than a pursuit of the rule of the subject as such.[2] As the voices of dissent became louder, the Japanese state began making clear assertions of its authority, starting with the arrest and execution in 1910 of twelve politically active writers who were accused of 'conspiring to assault' the emperor. In short, the decade following the end of the Russo–Japanese war, or the early Taishō period, was characterized by the maturation of Japan as a modern nation-state, both in terms of its socio-economic development and its politico-cultural awareness, opening up an era of dialectical struggle between the populace and the state-elite coalition.

These material and conceptual changes accompanying the progression of modernization gave rise to changes in consciousness reflected in a new literacy movement referred to as *shizen-shugi* ('naturalism'), commonly understood today as an attempt to depict life 'realistically,' a movement which grew particularly strong in the years following the Russo–Japanese war. Since the Meiji romantic literary movement's project of establishing modern subjectivity continued, *shizen-shugi* in the Japanese literary context turned out to be a highly inconsistent amalgamation of various elements: an attempt to discover truth in life; a disdain for fiction in favour of personal confession; an inclination for the description of factual observations; an adherence to realism based on individualistic ideas and concerns; a negation of universal truth and morality, and so on.[3] Referring to its overt inclination for describing the everyday and its strong tendency towards personal confession, Ishikawa Takuboku, a romantic poet and critic, concluded in 1910 that in an age when 'self-assertion lost its direction and exit,' and when, hardly able to establish itself in a meaningful way, the subject simply replicated the forms of private-ownership in the capitalist economy, *shizen-shugi* was little more than a debilitated literary movement.[4] From the beginning the movement was in danger of failing to introduce a scientific analytical perspective capable of objectifying given historical conditions, and indeed, its static, flat description of the ordinary gradually deteriorated into a literature that either indulged in personal confessions completely isolated from the social and historical (c.f. *shi-shōsetsu*) or became an overt affirmation of sensuality as a fundamental aspect of human existence (cf. *tanbi-shugi*).[5]

Seen from a different perspective, Hasumi Shigehiko, a contemporary Japanese theorist, characterizes *shizen-shugi*'s rise to popularity as a marker of the death of realist materialism. Hasumi sees the central importance of this new literary movement as a shift away from broadly conceived literary realism (*shajitsu-shugi*) based upon observation with the 'analytical eyes of the intellect' to a stance that attempts to detect greater truth with 'spiritual eyes,' in which intellect and emotion are supposedly synthesized.[6] Hasumi is concerned with the state of subjectivity that created and popularized this somewhat mysterious notion of 'spiritual eyes.' In his reading, the notion of 'spiritual eyes' is to be seen in conjunction with the emergence of modern dualistic subjectivity/perspective and the reactionary response of the writing subject who, concerned with his/her internal split, was desirous of overcoming the state of dualism. As Karatani Kōjin has argued, it was the romantic novelist Kunikida Doppo who in the 1880s first reflected in writing the subtle relation between language, interiority and object, in his depiction of 'landscape' as an external object.[7] Kunikida's 'discovery of landscape' can be seen as a marker of the emergence of a certain kind of interiority, that of the modern subject who came to view nature as the reverse-side reflection of the self alienated from nature. Moreover, not only did Kunikida view 'landscape' from a modern perspective, but he later also 'discovered' the common man thrown into a mysterious nature which could not, he thought, be exhausted by human knowledge. 'Because mankind exists in a dialectical relation with a mysterious and graceful natural world,' Kunikida remarked in 1908, 'the ordinary life of the individual in the world became an extremely important phenomenon to me.'[8] This acute sense of the boundary between interiority and exteriority and the growing awareness of the subject as alienated from the objective nature-world were pre-conditions for the rise of *shizen-shugi*. In other words, the 'spiritual eyes' of *shizen-shugi* was a reactionary response of the modern dualistic subject to the intrusion of the inscriptional forces of modern (and Western) epistemology, a device by means of which the subject hoped to nullify the effect of the newly grafted inscriptions and to 'recover' an integral self free from the sense of alienation.

What Hasumi identifies as the core problem of the *shizen-shugi* movement was its dependence upon ambiguous formulated dualistic conceptual schemes, which as they circulated came to be taken for granted. In this movement, argues Hasumi, the discursive terrain was reshaped by erecting as key categories the opposition between 'life' and the 'material,' for example, wherein 'life' meant the emotional aspects of human existence as opposed to the cold-blooded scientific rationality which governed the 'material' world.[9] It followed, then, that for the *shizen-shugi* movement a 'solution' to the dehumanizing effects of modern rationalism could be sought by synthesizing emotion and spirituality with the objective/ scientific/'material' aspects of knowledge by means of the insight of the 'spiritual eyes,' and by doing so, *shizen-shugi* discourse secured the primacy of the former over the latter.[10] One effect of creating this hierarchy of ambiguous categories was to undermine reason and objectivity as inferior literary principles, and to make meaningful literary debate governed by objectivity and reason increasingly difficult; or rather, one might say it was the very rise of this anti-rationalism that allowed *shizen-shugi* to prevail.[11] In short, with *shizen-shugi* taking the upper hand in championing 'life' and humane emotions over 'materiality' and scientific rationality, Japanese literary discourse of the early Taishō era turned towards anti-rationalism and equivocity and constituted a discourse 'indulgent of ambiguity and indifferent about distinguishing differences from identity.'[12]

Hasumi sees these inclinations in the *shizen-shugi* movement as a widespread tendency in the entire discursive sphere of the Taishō era, the intellectual and public discourse of which was increasingly adopted a highly problematic mode that operated more to mask real issues than reveal them. He observes that the rampant coining of various '-isms' during the period ultimately came to define the issues at stake, rather than vice-versa, and, lamenting the state of discourse that allowed these '-isms' to represent the common concerns of society at large, claims that:

> Starting with '*shizen-shugi*' and '*minpon-shugi*' (literally, 'people-centrism,' the Japanese notion of democracy), not to mention Souda Kiichiro's '*bunka-shugi*' ('culturalism'), Abe Jiro's '*jinkaku-shugi*' ('personality-ism'), Tanaka Oudo's '*tettei-kojin-shugi*' ('thorough individualism'), Takamure Itsue's '*shinjosei-shugi*' ('new feminism'), and even '*shakai-shugi*' ('socialism') and '*museifu-shugi*' ('anarchism') were proposed as nothing more than those kinds of 'problematics,' and it is extremely difficult to find any occasion for a 'critique' in this context.[13]

In as much as this speech mode of abstract 'problematics' replaced the real issues and their complex historical context by abstract and generalized '-isms' designated images vaguely understood but widely-accepted, it was no longer concerned with concrete objects of analysis.[14] In Hasumi's words:

Choosing unity over division, and identity over difference, as its suitable context, and continuing to indulge with 'problematics' by letting the subject float in the realm of ambiguity, the 'Taishō-esque' speech naturally does not need to describe or analyze a concrete object in order to sustain itself.[15]

As we can see, the abstraction and 'aestheticization' observed in our discussion of folk ethnology and Asianist discourse were not unique to those knowledge domains, but also ran through the literary movements of the late Meiji and Taishō eras, reflecting the troubled state of contemporary intellectual and public discourse that indulged in the circulation of imagistic signs de-linked from concrete objects. This self-sustaining mode of discourse unconstrained by historical facts/objects perpetuated an attitude of indifference to the world outside of itself, and prepared the discursive ground for the free construction of 'rural folk' and 'Asians.' As the sense of politico-historical urgency grew from the late 1910s onward, however, the *shizen-shugi* movement, unable to provide means for satisfactorily reflecting social problems and/or revealing truth, gradually lost its appeal, and gave way to a proletarian literature movement that prioritized political issues over artistic concerns on the one hand, and the *shin-kankaku-ha* (neo-sensualism) movement strongly influenced by the rhetorical style of the avant-garde arts, on the other.

In the context of the deepening contradictions of modern capitalist development and two epoch-making historical events on the international stage, World War I (1914–18) and the October Revolution of 1917, Japanese society of the late 1910s also entered a period of turmoil characterized by intensifying conflicts. The increasing hardships and miseries that characterized the lives of the lower classes, especially during the severe economic recession in the years following World War I, led to a series of desperate protests, including the Rice Riot of 1918 that involved one quarter of the entire population. Moreover, the success of the Russian Revolution showed that an alternative vision to the previously undoubted capitalist developmental path was possible, and voices calling for fundamental structural reform of society arose. Inspired by the French anti-war movement *Clarté* and the new vision of structural change in light of acute social contradictions, an internationally affiliated Leftist intellectual forum was established in 1920 by a group of young Japanese intellectuals under the leadership of Komaki Oumi, giving birth to the journal *Tane maku hito* (*The Sower*). The publication of *Tane maku hito* marked the origin of the proletarian literary movement in Japan, gathering together various contributors including anarchists, liberals, socialist poets, and some foreign intellectuals, activists and artists.[16] At the same time, the emergence of popular resistance posed an ethical and political challenge to intellectuals and artists; the increasing involvement of art in politics placed them in a serious dilemma that was most tragically manifest in Arishima Takeo's suicide, one that the *shin-kankaku-ha* writers, albeit to a lesser degree, were to face constantly.[17]

Tensions between the organized labour movement and state oppression further intensified in the 1920s, increasingly exposing the entire society, including the literary community, to the political battle for reform. The decade opened with Japan's first large scale organized strike (1920), followed by the establishment of a Japan Communist Party (1922). These developments were soon met by a series of oppressive state measures and brute violence, including the arrests of Communists, the murders of proletarian writers (1923), and the outlawing of revolutionary ideologies by the notorious 1925 Public Peace Maintenance Law (*Chian ijihō*), followed by the 1926 Labour Dispute Conciliation Law (*Rōdo sōgi chōtei hō*).[18] It was in this tense climate that the Great Kanto Earthquake struck on September 1, 1923, one of the worst urban catastrophes in human history.[19] The quake took 70,000 lives and left over 1,300,000 homeless, and the subsequent three-day firestorm virtually destroyed half of Tokyo. The shock of the quake and its aftermath went much further than the immediate damage. The advanced technological and materially wealthy society that symbolized for many Japanese the modern urban life of which they were so proud, proved vulnerable and powerless in the face of such a natural disaster; and with this realization there arose a deep disillusionment with the previously unquestioned belief in 'the modern.' Moreover, in the aftermath of the destruction and confusion caused by the earthquake, indiscriminate attacks on Koreans and large-scale assaults against labour activists and proletarian writers were orchestrated. These assaults included the arrest, torture and murder of Ōsugi Sakae, a prominent anarchist activist, and Itō Noe, his partner and a women's movement activist, in the hands of military police, as well as the murder of ten labour activists by the army (the Kamedo Incident).

Under great pressure from the state in the aftermath of the Great Kanto earthquake, *Tane maku hito* virtually dissolved, but it was soon followed by another proletarian journal, *Bungei sensen* (1924), and its institutional body, the Japan Federation of Proletarian Arts (*Nihon puroretaria bungei domei*), in 1925. While maintaining itself as an intellectual coalition accommodating writers of diverse political and intellectual standpoints, its manifesto clearly announced a shift of orientation from the former broadly-based intellectual forum to a more directly proletarian one.[20] Within a year, however, the Association lost a group of anarchistic members after their leading theorist, Aono Suekichi, published an article emphasizing the significance of the political role of literature and calling for a greater commitment to it. Aono's article argued that it was 'the collective activity of the socialist proletarian artists to enlighten the non-conscious (*shizen seichō-teki*) proletarian artists to have a conscious aim, to have the consciousness of socialism.'[21] Generally speaking, the developmental path of proletarian literature from this time on increasingly adopted a Marxist political agenda that tended to limit and subordinate literary themes and ideas to their pedagogical effects upon the society. This radicalization of proletarian literature was the other side of the coin of the increasingly limited space granted to artistic and literary freedom in the general swing of national politics to the right. Under such conditions insistence on artistic freedom could no longer be a progressive gesture, but rather instead risked creating an indifference to the political foundation of free expression. Following this breakdown of the broader intellectual coalition, the Association was divided in 1927 between those who strictly followed the dominant ideology of the then-outlawed Japan Communist Party (*Fukumoto*-ism) and those who chose to do otherwise, with the latter establishing a new group, the Federation of Labour–Agrarian Artists (*rōnō geijutsuka renmei*), which in the same year further split into two groups.

Those writers who chose to pursue a modern literary career outside of the Marxist-proletarian path found their home in a new literary movement called *shin-kankaku-ha*, literally 'neo-sensualism.' Rejecting the conventional literary methods of the day, *shin-kankaku-ha* was inspired by the emerging new artistic forms during the European interwar period and avant garde art movements, and has been described as a Japanese 'syncretism of Futurism, Cubism, Expressionism, Dadaism, Symbolism, Constructivism, Surrealism.'[22] The *shin-kankaku-ha* group emphasized the ability of the scenes to uncover the truth of the times, and held the conviction that elaborate descriptions of phenomological reality could disclose what literary realism was unable to effect. One of the leaders of the School, Yokomitsu Riichi, depicted modern man as a tragic figure who, having lost organic unity with his own body, had been deformed and reduced into a replaceable part of an abstract machine, a fragmented being whose feelings were under surveillance by his own self-consciousness.[23] By depicting the psychological and sensual breakdown of contemporary man, Yokomitsu, argues one critic, was able to portray the deeply alienated state of the modern Japanese subject, crudely stripped of his self-worth and dignity.[24] To portray this deformed subject, Yokomitsu abandoned the conventional literary realist notion of depth, believing that the truth of his times was better captured by a description of surfaces. Launching 'a defiant battle with language' and experimenting with the demolition of the key conventional conceptual categories of interior/exterior, form/content and surface/depth, Yokomitsu's endeavour entailed some risky epistemological implications.[25] This comes out clearly in a 1927 essay:

> Words are a surface (*gaimen*). Words that make an interior (*naimen*) echo forth more strongly are words that shine more brightly. For this reason I love words – the surface that shines brighter. . . . Form is nothing more than the arrangement of words whose meaning comes through rhythm. Without the form of this arrangement of words, can there possibly be content? That one might discern the content of what has

been written through looking at the form is the illusion of readers; the form itself is the content.[26]

Determined to accompany the incessant forward movement of the modern to the end, even at the cost of its worst effects, Yokomitsu sought to give a positive value to the active acceptance of the apparent loss of meaning as the condition for living in the challenging new age.

Unlike Yokomitsu, Kawabata Yasunari, another leading figure of the *shin-kankaku-ha* group, never came anywhere near abandoning notions of 'the interior' and 'content,' but instead was implicitly critical of other members of the School, claiming that a new literary movement 'would never emerge from those who put too much trust in a language that could not reach the depths of the soul.'[27] For Kawabata, language was nothing more than an instrument for representing that which lay beyond itself, namely, spirituality. In a 1926 essay he writes:

> As for novelists, those who turned their deep gaze to reality went as far as to go beyond it. In other words, they glimpsed the depths of the soul, and their observations and expressions are rather sense-oriented [intuitive] ... *Kankaku-ha* does not only mean a fine description of subjective phenomena; rather, it is an intuitive method and a supreme spiritualism.[28]

Kawabata believed in the intuitive ability of the senses to exceed the power of words and to regenerate meaning; for him, intuition was the means of overcoming the limitations of conventional insight and the constraints imposed by its faith in rationality. One can see in these writers' reflections, the difficulties faced by literary movements after *shizen-shugi*; despite their seemingly opposite reasons, both Yokomitsu and Kawabata championed the senses over meaning and rationality as means to a greater breadth and depth of expression. In a nutshell, *shin-kankaku-ha* could be seen as a response to the increasingly felt difficulties of articulating lived experience with language, and the necessity of exploring other means of expression outside realism. In other words, the emergence of *shin-kankaku-ha* points to an aggravated disjunction perceived in the relation between the subject, language, and this historical world, and to an attempt to 'resolve' this disjunction by ascribing to the senses a greater ability to reveal truth.

The July 1927 suicide of the talented novelist Akutagawa Ryūnosuke at the age of thirty-five had a tremendous impact not only upon intellectual circles but also upon society at large. In his will, Akutagawa explained that he had been driven to suicide by a 'vague anxiety about the future.'[29] Partly because of this ambiguous reasoning, his death came to be seen as symbolic of the atmosphere of Japan in the late 1920s, as his obituary from a major newspaper noted: 'Seen from a broad perspective, everything is a shadow of its time. The sharp sensitivity of a novelist always detects the agony of our time most quickly, just as the peak of a mountain receives the first beam of the sun at dawn.'[30] Amongst his contemporaries, Akutagawa's suicide was variously interpreted as either a 'completion of his art by death,' 'the defeat of a petit-bourgeois novelist,' or 'proof of the powerlessness of the intellect' whose 'aesthetic absolutism' followed the path of its own self-destruction.[31] This sense of closure and the deepening loss of hope and meaning overwhelmed the Dadaist writer, Tsuji Jun, for whom the damage inflicted on his era was beyond repair, and to whom life itself became nothing but disgust. In is 1929 prose-poem *Despera* (*Despair*), he wrote:

> The age rushes along, the flow of the currents of thought surge upon us and are greedily sucked up by the fresh minds and instincts of the new age. Stemming the tide through base and absurd methods is even more pathetic. One might better surrender, helmets removed, the rotting bourgeois castle.[32]

According to Tsuji, bourgeois culture had reached a state of decay in which every introduction of new ideas was merely a matter of stylistic change, a 'changing of idols,' and was thus no longer capable of engendering any new insights.[33] Unlike Kawabata or Yokomitsu, however, Tsuji was unable to find refuge in the search for the senses/spirituality beyond language; instead, he fell into a bottomless despair, dying relatively young. By the late 1920s Japanese society was visibly divided, riddled with tensions and signs of suppressed violence, and the literary movements of the time, both modernist and proletarian alike, had to fight hard to secure an increasingly narrow space for creative activities in a climate fast sliding towards a total war.

The year of Akutagawa's suicide also witnessed a number of significant political and economic events: the first signs of a chronic financial depression, the first large scale arrests and torture of labour activists, the emergence of the first military cabinet led by General Tanaka Giichi, and the dispatch to China of the Japanese army in preparation for the full-scale assault to come. In 1928, in response to the intensification of the Communist Party-led political and labour actions, the Japanese state launched an unprecedented crackdown, arresting over 1,000 activists (the 3.15 Incident), sending shockwaves through the proletarian writers' community and society at large. Thanks to the efforts of the leading Marxist literary theorist, Kurahara Korehito, pro-Communist Party factions were brought together to form a united coalition, giving birth to the All-Japan Federation of Proletarian Arts (*Zen Nihon Musansha Geijutsu Dōmei*; NAPF). Its journal *Senki* gained an influential public voice and its circulation reached over 20,000, publishing novels by young talented writers such as Kobayashi Takiji and Tokunaga Sunao, as well as literary criticism on various themes central to the proletarian arts, including Kurahara's influential article 'The

Passage for Proletarian Realism.'[34] In the climate of burgeoning political oppression, leading figures of the organization, such as Kurahara, Kobayashi and Nakano Shigeharu, became members of the much-weakened Communist Party (1929–31), increasingly advocating a communist art.[35] To strengthen its political role in the arts, the NAPF was dissolved and reorganized in 1931 as the Japan Proletarian Culture Federation (*Nihon Puroretaria Bunka Renmei*; KOPF), practically functioning as the surrogate of the moribund Communist Party.

When the repressed violence of the late 1920s became fully overt in the early 1930s, the acute sense of anxiety that had in the previous decade largely been limited to intellectuals began to diffuse throughout the class of educated Japanese and society at large. The road to state militarism was opened up by the occupation of Manchuria in September 1931 and the establishment soon thereafter of the puppet state of Manchukuo. These years were also marked by a series of fascist terrorist attacks, including the assault on Prime Minister Hamaguchi Osachi (November 1930) and the assassinations of the Minister of Finance Inoue Junnosuke, the industrialist Dan Takuma (the Ketsumeidan Incident, February 1932), and Prime Minister Inukai Tsuyoshi (the 5.15 Incident, May 1932), which marked the *de facto* end of democratic politics in Japan. In the face of worsening economic conditions, the labour movement adopted a more radical, Soviet-influenced line, a development that was met with increasingly brutal state violence. Following the mass imprisonment of Communist Party members in 1930, the state began targeting Leftist intellectuals, and the 1933 murder of Kobayashi Takiji, a promising young proletarian novelist, deeply shocked the left. In these anxious times, what one writer described as the 'ether-like substance that had come to fill the intellectual vacuum' gave currency to the phrase 'Shestovian anxiety' (*Shesutofu-teki fuan*), taken from the 1934 Japanese publication of Lev Shestov's *Dostoevsky and Nietzsche: The Philosophy of Tragedy* [1903] which had sold thousands of copies.[36]

Laying the ground for the 'national body' (*Kokutai*): 'cultural renaissance' (1933–7) and intellectual discourse of the mid-1930s

With the end of the war in Manchuria in August 1933 and the *de facto* Chinese acceptance of Japanese rule, a relatively stable political climate ensued, a brief period rich in intellectual production known as the period of 'cultural renaissance' (*bungei fukkō ki*, 1933–7) in which literature was 'liberated from politics.'[37] The same year also saw the breakdown of the Leftist agrarian tenant and Marxist labour movements, and the *tenkō* or 'ideological conversion' of intellectuals from Marxism (broadly defined) to more culturally oriented positions. The *tenkō* was triggered by the imprisonment of two leading Marxists, Sano Manabu and Nabeyama Sadachika, and the publication of their repudiations (while they were still in prison) of the Japan Communist Party for its blind pursuit of a Soviet-style Communism.[38] While Sano and Nabeyama's repudiations could be interpreted as attempts to reshape Communism as a universal progressive movement and make it accountable to the particularity of Japanese culture and history, it appeared that such rationales hastened the dissolution of Communism. Over the next two years, 90 per cent of Japanese Communist party members followed suit.[39] Born immediately out of the breakdown of the Marxist movements and the dissolution of the Japan Federation of Proletarian Literature (NALP), and in the midst of 'Shestovian anxiety,' the 'cultural renaissance' movement was by and large a safe means of reasserting literary freedom in the form of the depoliticization of culture. In these years the issues of artistic autonomy and political resistance, the problem of the subject, and the question of a return to tradition were subject to lively debates in a number of newly established cultural magazines.[40]

It was during this brief period that a 'humanization of philosophy' took place, by which I mean that many scholars attempted to incorporate a more profound sense of the existential dilemma and agony of the contemporary subject into the previously dominant philosophic currents of Marxist materialism and modernist rationalism.[41] The most influential prewar social sciences and humanities scholars, including the philosopher Nishida Kitarō (1870–1945) and the anthropologist/ethicist Watsuji Tetsurō (1889–1947), were no exception to this nascent aestheticization. Many works of this period, in their attempts to incorporate the existential into 'crude formal scientism,' submerged objective scientific categories and the materialist aspects of Marxism in favour of what were called the 'humane' moral categories and existential aspects of Marxism.[42] Moreover, these 'humanized' philosophical concepts coalesced around the archetype of *kokutai*, a concept essentializing 'the nation' as equivalent to 'the people,' as an alternative temporality and communal space outside modern progressive history. The constitution of this foundation for a Japanese essence was, however, both a departure from the historical and an internalization of history (and thus its erasure as an exteriority). Driving these new developments was the nascent omnipotent discourse of 'Japan.'

On the literary front, 'the period of cultural renaissance' (*bungei fukkō ki*) was marked by the 'conversion' (*tenkō*) that took place when many writers abandoned their previous positions as either Marxists or modernists and increasingly embraced 'the artistic sensibility of indigenous Japanese culture.'[43] Kamei Katsuichiro, then a member of the executive committee for NALP, published an article in 1933 called 'Return to the Homeland' in which he laid out the problems he had with NALP and other factions of the proletarian literary movement.[44] The problems Kamei identified in proletarian literature were basically twofold: the question of autonomous subjectivity, of literature taking account of its full political responsibility, and that of the exclusion of cultural and ethnic specificity by Marxist and universalist literary schemas.⁴⁵ Confronted by the dilemma of literary autonomy and political responsibility, Hayashi Fusao, who coined the term 'the period of cultural renaissance,' vehemently defended what he called 'the completion of the internal world of the author.'⁴⁶ In this inward turn, not only was literature to be freed from politics, but socio-historical and material relations were seen as being absorbed into and subordinated to the subjective world of artistic creation. In the climate of increasing oppression and confusion, Hayashi's questions fundamentally shook the *raison-d'être* of NALP, and it rapidly declined until it dissolved altogether in 1934.

Founding essence – Watsuji Tetsurō's aesthetic community

Watsuji Tetsurō, an influential and respected prewar Japanese thinker whose work I discussed earlier, was highly critical of the positivistic epistemology of separating the subject from the object (and of man from nature) and the linear progressive notion of history in modern/Western scientific knowledge. In one of his most representative works, *Climate and Culture (Fūdo: ningengaku-teki Kōsatsu*; 1935), Watsuji rejects the conception of an autonomous subject thrown into the objective environment, and advances in its stead his concept of *fūdo*, or 'climatological features,' as an alternative temporal and spatial scheme designating 'a structural constituent of human existence,' in which each local human organization defined itself according to its own unique terms of development in evolution.⁴⁷ Watsuji's ambition was to reconceive the Heideggerian notion of mankind as a temporal existence within the spatial terms of *fūdo*.⁴⁸ According to Watsuji, the predominance of temporality over spatiality in Heidegger's thought arises from a bias for the individual subject (his being as *Dasein*), and because of Heidegger's failure to articulate human existence as *both* individual *and* social. Watsuji's interest in spatiality over temporality, however, is curious, particularly when one notes that spatiality was easily linked to Japan's sense of geographical isolation and uniqueness, whereas a focus on temporality would likely suggest a universalist historical narrative in which Japan was seen as backward and less civilized. By viewing human history as a part of a bio-evolutionary grand developmental scheme, Watsuji negates the political component of human existence and proposes a peaceful, harmonious human space as an extension and complement of natural space.

Watsuji's attempt to incorporate 'humanity' into what he saw as disembodied and objectified mathematical space was made possible by synthesizing the modern conception of the rational, individual subject and a notion of spatiality as the embodiment of human collectivity, a 'synthesis' privileging the latter at the expense of the autonomy of the former. This trade-off can be seen, for example, in the following passage:

> A man lives and dies. Despite the continuous process of the death of the individual, mankind lives and human relations continue. Human existence incessantly continues by incessantly ending. The 'existence for death' in the perspective of the individual is the 'existence for life' from the stand-point of society. . . . It is from the union of climate with history that the latter obtains its flesh and bones. If spirit is to be defined in opposition to materiality, history cannot be conceived solely as a self-realization of spirit. Only when spirit, as self-active being, is a subject which objectifies itself, in other words, only when it includes such a self-active physical principle, does it realizes itself as history. This, what might be called 'self-active physical principle,' is what I mean by *fūdo*.[49]

The all-encompassing collective and corporeal subject of the 'spirit' was envisaged by Watsuji as unfolding in a Hegelian fashion in which the self-motivated movement of 'history' would be revealed.

The price for this corporeal conception of *fūdo* was the absorption of the materiality of history into spirit, a nullification of the dialectical tension between two mutually irreducible components of existence, and a confirmation of the predominance of the social whole over the individual part.

Watsuji's nullification of the historical and his downgrading of the rational and autonomous subject became much more manifest and poignant when he applied his pseudo-scientific 'method' to the question of collective ethics. In his *Ethics as the Study of Humanity* (*Ningen no Gaku Toshiteno Rinri-gaku*; 1934) and *Ethics* (*Rinri-gaku*; 1937, vol. 1), his criticism of Marxist materialism and liberal institutionalism went a step further. In these works, Watsuji attempted to overcome the problem of subject/object duality by humanizing and aestheticizing social scientific inquiry through the application of a concept of 'mankind' (*ningen*) developed in his earlier works. He insisted that the Japanese conception of mankind should not be taken to mean 'person'/'man' as it is often used in modern commonsense. Rather, as is indicated by the two Chinese characters constituting the term – the first of which signifies 'person,' the second 'between' – mankind has to be understood as a relationally and contextually shaped being, born and raised within the sphere of human relations which embodies local bio-cultural specificity.[50] Watsuji argues, somewhat tautologously, that '*rinri wa jinrin no ri*,' that is, 'ethics ("*rinri*") is the logic ("*ri*") of the moral ways of mankind ("*jinrin*"),' defining ethics as already and always embodied in the social relations normally held between Japanese people, and thus boldly equating ethics with the social status-quo.[51] By interpreting semantic signification as social reality, and/or equating 'what ought to be' with 'what is,' the critical space for the rational moral subject and for debate on universal ethical standards was foreclosed. In short, by dehistoricizing and idealizing Japanese social relations as inherently ethical, Watsuji constructs an idealized narrative of an incarnate moral community as a truth in itself beyond the reach of objective, 'scientific' analysis that was in his mind inferior.[52] Such an idealized ethical community became a central constituent of *kokutai* fundamentalism, tacitly masking existing social injustices, and clearly serving to prop up the *de facto* control of those who exercised power.

By representing Japanese social relations in these moral-aesthetic images and in the same gesture exhorting the Japanese to fulfil their duty, Watsuji's narrative subjected the Japanese people to the objectifying power of the nascent discourse of Japanese essence. The problem here concerns not only the particularity of the individual absorbed into the 'harmony' of the social whole, but more importantly, the epistemological violation that equated an *image* of the Japanese with *the people as historical beings*. Watsuji's project of overcoming the exclusion from theory of the collective experience of people – the 'dehumanization' he found so loathsome in modern Western knowledge – in the end amounted to advocating the subjugation of the people to his pre-existing truth of a timeless and harmonious society devoid of political and historical processes and practices. The 'realization' of this idealized moral and aesthetic community in *kokutai* would mean overthrowing the system of representation by discursive mediation without which no subjectivity or intersubjective meaning could possibly be constituted. This attempt to discard representation and to 'overcome' the perceived insurmountable gap between meaning (representation in language) and being (existence itself) is the form in which the recurrent problem of modern Japanese identity manifests itself, and is closely linked with a desire to transcend the Eurocentric configuration of the modern world and resistance to the universalization and rationalization of culturally specific lived experience.

The world historical project – Nishida Kitarō's 'place of nothingness'

If Watsuji's contribution to the formulation of official war ideology consisted in laying out the foundations on which the theory of Japanese essence was to be built, the contribution of Nishida's late work was to provide the meaning of Japan's struggle on the world-historical stage. Nishida Kitarō is widely acknowledged as the first Japanese philosopher who, under the influence of German idealism, attempted to constitute 'Eastern philosophy' in terms of Western philosophical categories and methods. Nishida's contribution to the war ideology is difficult to evaluate, particularly because of the depth and erudition of his thinking, its strictly reasoned principles, and its objective methods and clearly defined concepts, elements that are particularly characteristic of his works of the 1910s and 1920s. However, in the context of historical turmoil and the transformation of the discursive modality discussed above, his philosophy from the mid-1930s onward began to show some problematic signs. One can note, however, even without these powerful contextual influences, that Nishida's philosophy had certain aesthetic and transgressive features even in its early stages, for his central thematic is an inquiry into the ontological status of knowledge. Crudely put, his challenge to the universality of Western philosophy opened up a space in which an equally universalist claim for Japanese philosophy was made possible; and Nishida's challenge was to later authorize the Japanese vindication of themselves as displaced 'others' in a way similar to how Heidegger 'contributed' to the subsequent alliance between a stream of German idealism and Nazism. This 'potential' latent in Nishida's thought was realized by his Kyoto School disciples from the late 1930s onward.

One of the basic concepts of Nishida's early philosophic work, developed in his *Study of the Good* (*Zen no Kenkyu*, 1911), is 'pure experience' (*junsui keiken*). 'Pure experience' designates a form of 'direct knowledge' that could not be doubted, a state of 'knowing subject' prior to the operation of self-reflective consciousness. It also designates a metaphysically conceived ground out of which the distinctions between the subject and the object, act and meaning, and being and value are produced as effects of the operations of the conscious mind.[53] In Nishida's system, this 'unity' of antinomies in 'pure experience' is referred to as 'self-definition of the predicate' (*ippansha no jiko-gentei*), a concept perhaps analogous to Heidegger's 'Being,' which, while encompassing all existence, cannot be defined by anything other than itself. For Nishida, omnipresent, primal non-being is called 'the place of nothingness' (*mu no basho*).[54] Nishida uses these concepts to demonstrate the limited conditions of rational knowledge, to point out that intelligibility can only be derived from the founding basis, the presence of unintelligible non-being. By articulating the conditions of rational knowledge in this way, Nishida relativized the universality of Western ontology as one of many possible forms, and established in Japanese philosophy the primacy of the key concepts surrounding 'the place of nothingness.' It could be said that Nishida's philosophy lies within the idealist – aesthetic tradition in that reason and the senses are seen as united in 'pure experience,' a unity made possible by blurring the Kantian boundaries between the realms of the cognitive, the moral, and the aesthetic.[55] Moreover, since Nishida's philosophical system is monistic, it does not allow one to think in terms of dynamic process without importing notions that would self-differentiate the predicate.[56] In the developing historical context, this monistic structure would eventually internalize its exterior and swallow the historical world into its totalizing system.

Continuing to deal with a metaphysical conception of the world, Nishida's work in the mid-1930s began to show some signs of 'reification' in which 'pure experience' began to be conceived as sharing the same ground as the historical world.[57] In his earlier conception, what he called 'the contradictory self-identity' (*mujun-teki jiko dōitsu*), Nishida revealed the impossibility of an identity between the individual and the collective because the willing subject was conceived of as an existence exterior to the realm of being/intelligibility, and thus irreducible to the collective. Since Nishida saw the world in terms of the infinite, the 'identity' of the part (the individual) and the whole (society) was only possible by a discontinuous logical and ontological 'leap' effected through the agency of an imaginative power.[58] However, over time, Nishida's 'absolutely contradictory self-identity' came to be seen by his students and his readers as a relation equating the part and the whole in a more literal sense, and the contradictions between the subject and the object, the individual and the collective, and thought and action were often interpreted as united in being itself. Nishida himself seems to have somewhat endorsed this misinterpretation of his complex metaphysical system, as the following passages from his 1938 'The Problem of Japanese Culture' ('Nihon bunka no mondai') suggest:

> To reflect on the traces of our several thousand years of cultural development centering on the imperial court, I think it is fair to conclude that it was an endless repetition of the creative process that transformed what is created into what is creating, as a contradictory self-identity of the oneness of the whole and the many of the particular. What constitutes the subject as the oneness of the whole has changed in the course of history into various forms. . . . However, *the imperial court has located itself in the position of the world defining itself as a contradictory self-identity between the oneness of the subject and the many of the particular, beyond these various forms of the subject.*[59]

Even discounting the increasingly strict censorship and political pressures, it is hard to defend Nishida's submerging here all historical and dialectical contradictions, his abolition of the distinction between being in history and the other of 'nature,' and his explicit equation of the Japanese imperial court with the essence of the Japanese people.[60] It is not difficult to see that the imperial court thus conceived could easily be taken as the symbolic figurehead of Watsuji's aesthetic-moral community of the Japanese.

Moreover, once the Pacific War had begun, Nishida's writing predictably accommodated itself to the rhetorical lines of the official war doctrine by interjecting the *kokutai* narrative into his narratives of world-historical (philosophical) development. In 1943, Nishida wrote a government sponsored pamphlet, extolling the Greater Asian Co-prosperity Sphere, possibly hoping that his emphasis on a morally grounded rule in Asia might be reflected in state policy. In the booklet, 'Sekai chitsujo no genri,' ('The principles of the World Order') Nishida argued:

> As a result of the development of science, technology and economy, each ethnic nation-state has come to enter an intimately linked single international space. To face this new challenge, there is no other way than for each nation to construct a universal world by recognizing the historical task of each and overcoming the limitation of the self while indefinitely submitting to its culturally given particularity. This is why

> I call the contemporary age the age of world self-awareness of the ethnic nation-state.... In such a universal world, each ethnic nation lives a unique historical life of its own, while simultaneously being united in the singular universal world with each their own distinct task. This is the ultimate Reason of the historical development of mankind, and is simultaneously the principle of the new world order demanded in today's world war.[61]

As the passage makes plain, Nishida's vision of the world is an ultimately 'holistic' one in which each nation-state is simultaneously conceived as an embodiment of its 'local tradition,' as well as a system 'surpassing itself' to constitute 'the universal world.' In other words, both holism (priority of the whole over the parts) and atomism (that of the parts over the whole) are simultaneously denied and affirmed, 'synthesized' into a kind of 'absolutely contradictory self-identity.'[62] Needless to say, Nishida's 'reified' conceptions were taken up by members of the Kyoto School and articulated in explicitly political and historical dimensions with which Nishida himself was somewhat uncomfortable.

The works of Watsuji and Nishida provided the theoretical repertoire from which the arguments of the Kyoto School and the state *kokutai* ideology drew their fundamentals. By the mid-1930s, the discourse of *kokutai* had already matured under the influence of the ethnological study of the agrarian folk (*minzoku-gaku*) and the development of a revolutionary agrarian movement (*nōhonshugi*) in the early 1930s. Adding to these developments, Watsuji's contribution in the mid-1930s was to extend his initially agrarian based foundationalism to the national scale in his notion of the aesthetic community of the Japanese, a community in which the all too evident rural–urban gap was smoothed over. In this extension, it was no longer the rural agrarian population alone who were objectified, now the entire Japanese populace were idealized as equal members of the aesthetic community, a notion implicitly linked to the folk-*nōhonshugi* ancestral paradigm in which all subjects were as if the children of the emperor. Similarly, Nishida's statements about the 'world-historical role of Japan' were from the mid-1930s on added upon and read in the general discursive context of the Pan-Asianist ideological narrative emphasizing 'Japan's mission' to liberate Asia from Western domination and the creation of an alternative order based on 'Asian' values and cultural traditions. In the political and discursive context of the late 1930s and early 1940s, Nishida's notion of the 'place of nothingness' (*mu no basho*) and Watsuji's aesthetic representation of the moral Japanese community were linked together, in a broad ideological narrative that identified the people as the collective embodiment of a Japanese cultural essence, attaining the state of 'contradictory self-identity.' Regardless of Watsuji's and Nishida's own positions vis-à-vis various bastardized versions of their ideas, they both tacitly played a role in contributing to the development of the official war ideology and the cogent critiques of the modern West that had become part and parcel of it.

'Japan as irony' – Yasuda Yojūrō and the Japan Romantic School

The Japan Romantic School (*Nihon Rōman-ha*) was established in 1935, principally by the efforts of Yasuda Yojūrō, Kamai Katsuichirō, Hayashi Fusao, and Jinbo Kōtarō. Although each of the members of the Japan Romantic School had their own preferred themes and distinct methods, it is possible to extract a common thread binding them together: a romantic adoration of classical Japanese culture as an expression of disdain for those aspects of modernity that Japanese society had internalized. For the Japan Romantic School, the Japanese national trajectory centred on modernization and the adoption of Western ideas and technologies in order to maintain Japanese cultural autonomy was a contradiction in terms. In his ironically entitled prose-poem 'Return to Japan' ('Nihon e no Kaiki,' 1938), Hagiwara Sakutarō lamented Japan's reckless pursuit of material growth in the name of progress and its neglect for the preservation of the cultural and spiritual homeland.

> Once when we drew a 'picture of the West' in our minds, dreaming of an illusory utopia across the sea, our hearts were filled with the hope and passion of youth. Now this illusion has vanished and after looking in every corner of the world, we see that the true homeland is nowhere else than in our native land Japan. Moreover, in this homeland we see the vanished picture of the West everywhere in an ugly fashion, operating steam and electric trains and constructing ugly buildings. We have lost everything.[63]

This bleak vision of inner loss, anxiety, and groundlessness was shared by most Japanese intellectuals of the time, regardless of their ideological differences, and was the ground on which the Japan Romantic School took root. This 'discovery' of a Japanese essence in the state of absence – 'the lost past' – and mental landscape preoccupied with a sense of groundlessness and existential agony tells us a great deal about the nature of Japanese identity and its subsequent path of development in the years leading towards the war.

The members of the School were fully aware of a sense of deadlock: not only was the contemporary imagination exhausted, they thought, but further knowledge would be powerless to arrest this process of decay. To their minds any attempt to surpass the rationality of modernity could only propose another rationality, and, as a form of reason, continue the same assault on the tradition of beauty.[64] Noteworthy to this view was an underlying eschatology of history that saw the Romantic movement as the final stage of modernity and the consummation of Marxism. In his Japan Romantic School manifesto, the School's acknowledged leader, Yasuda Yojūrō, described the School as a 'self-conscious' and 'decadent' literary movement aware of its own irony, that is, of adorning the beauty of Japanese culture all the while contributing to its destruction:

> The literary movement of the past several years is an archetypal example of how the 'intellect' repeats the same corruption, being unable to escape a fixed pattern of pursuing one rationality after another. In such times, if there must be a literary movement aware of the form of its own corruption, the Japan Romantic School is perhaps it, the only one of its kind. This overly self-conscious literary movement, thus, is decadent enough, even by today's standards – the last movement to decorate the decline of our modern era.[65]

As Hagiwara's prose-poem makes clear, the School's condemnation of the modern was merely the other side of a quest for an alternative temporality/spatiality outside the modern, an outside that the members of the School saw as – and here lies the import of 'poetry,' 'Asia' and 'Japan,' in all their beauty – a potential means for transcending history.[66] However, given that they were also aware of the impossibility of reconstructing such a lost beauty, this alternative vision of time and space remained a retreat into an imaginative refuge. Although not all members of the School actively resorted to irony, for those who did embrace it irony emerged as an attractive intellectual stance; for irony 'sustains contradictions and makes paradox a productive principle' by purposely disturbing categorical oppositions such as destruction/creation, self-aggrandizement/self-sacrifice, war/peace and past/future.[67] Yasuda's work was perhaps the most successful in combining aestheticism with irony, and his invention of an ironic romantic language, neither poetry nor prose, was passionately received by many young intellectuals tired of the hopelessness of politics but still radical and revolutionary enough to pursue ideal visions. His use of romantic irony can be understood by focusing on three of its closely related components: aestheticism, anti-realist epistemology, and ironic consciousness.

Since Yasuda valued ancient Japanese court culture as the ultimate form of grace and beauty in life, the modernizing path followed by the Meiji state could only be viewed with contempt. In his well-known *Japanese Bridges* (*Nihon no Hashi*, 1936), Yasuda championed the beauty of the Japanese artistic tradition by describing how sad and beautiful it is. Like Motoori Norinaga, the eighteenth century founder of Japanese native studies (*kokugaku*), Yasuda elevated to predominance the values of emotion (*jyō*) and beauty (*bi*) from out of two traditionally conceived sets of value principles – intellect (*chi*), will (*i*), emotion (*jyō*); and truth (*shin*), good (*zen*), and beauty (*bi*). He praised Japanese bridges for their fragility and simplicity, compared to the more lofty constructions of the West and China; for Yasuda, Japanese bridges were embodiments of *mono no aware*, the pathos of things, the consummate aesthetic value of the sad and beautiful.[68] Underlying Yasuda's particular sense of beauty is the superiority of negativity (as *feminine*) as the ontological ground of both intellect (*chi*) and truth (*shin*) and as something both beyond and inclusive of them.[69] Yasuda, by placing beauty above and beyond reason, attempted to create a superior knowledge of the Japanese, beyond the limitations of what he thought was the modern and Western. His challenge, however, was 'not [simply] to replace reason with emotion [as earlier romantics had done] but to maintain the fiction of rationality as the ironic condition of modern Japanese culture.'[70] In this the romanticism of the Japan Romantic School distanced itself from the intimacy with nature and the yearning for a return to it that had characterized the early Meiji romantics. To some degree, the School even championed the sophisticated aesthetic consciousness capable of detecting, interpreting and creating beauty, not merely in objects, but above all in the expression of an artificial and decadent self-consciousness.[71]

There is an important epistemological implication in Yasuda's ironic aestheticism, one that was directly linked to the School's ridicule of the modern and the rational. According to Yasuda, the School's 'new knowledge' derived its ultimate strength from its violation of a fundamental function of knowledge: it abandoned its function of representing, either literally or metaphorically, the historical world. Yasuda points out that, 'the basis of the Japan Romantic School has become a realism called Japan as irony, or the irony of a free Japan that has simultaneously maintained destruction and construction.'[72] In this ironic scheme, the conventional relation between nature (i.e. the objective world) and consciousness is reversed, and, as Yasuda openly states, truth in nature becomes fictitious while fiction as a subjective and intentional act 'gains practical truthfulness.'[73] In this 'consciousness of fiction,' in which consciousness was given as the ground of truth, the objectivity of the socio-historical world existing outside human consciousness was subordinated to, even repudiated by, the imagined beauty of Japan.[74] By virtue of this epistemic distortion, Yasuda's irony opened up an ambiguous imaginary space, alternative to the one based on reason and ultimately ungraspable by realism. Yasuda described this space as the 'Japanese reality' denied by Western rationality, and as a realization of the 'non-knowledge of the Japanese people,' a knowledge that was freed from the burden of representing the historical world that was for Yasuda nothing but a hegemonic project of the modern West.[75] Interestingly, Yasuda describes the Japan Romantic School as 'a bridge of the night [*yoru no hashi*] leading to the next dawn,' the dawn which would supposedly follow the dismal final years of modernity.[76] However, despite appearances, Yasuda's bridge was not really a hopeful vision of the future but rather a symbol ironically expressing the anxiety that nothing was certain after the end of decadence.[77] In short, Yasuda's attempt to overcome the impasse of materialism and historicism by adopting an archly ironic stance came at the cost of replacing the real world by fiction: the idealized imaginary space of beauty no longer sought to relate to the historical world.

Not only did Yasuda create a knowledge de-linked from history, but his thought displaced the historical subject by advocating an aesthetic consciousness passionate for decay in which the historical subject was to be destroyed by decadence and self-negation. Yasuda condemned the Marxist and nativist writers of his time for their lack of 'passion for decay,' the active promulgation of irony and decadence that, for him, was the only way to save Japan and the Japanese from further corruption. In another context, however, this 'passion for decay' was realized in a more literal manner. Referring to the war years when he willingly followed Yasuda's aesthetic narrative, the critic Hashikawa Bunzo recalls the passionate desire of one of his friends to end his life as 'a decaying corpse in a tropical jungle with a copy of the *Kojiki* [an eighth-century collection of national founding myths] in his hands.'[78] Similarly, another critic has argued that Yasuda's language 'killed people,' or more precisely, that by 'promising them the highest moment of aesthetic satisfaction' it 'made people feel that they did not mind dying.'[79] In his 1939 'The Ruins of Asia' ('Ajia no Haikyo'), two years after the Japanese military invasion of China, Yasuda painted the following poetic vision:

> I burn with my passion as a poet for the national task of today's Japanese. During the past several years Japanese romanticism has been expressed as the passion of the Japanese, and these are the days that must be determinedly recorded in our history. As I was dwelling on the irresponsible idea that I would no longer care whether we won or lost the war, a thought occurred to me in the rare view of a thunderstorm that rushed upon the military base at Chōkako, blackening all in a sandy windstorm. Being spurred limitlessly, we might have to sacrifice all our life force for the sake of the surge of that life force itself. I think works of art expressing Asian life and emotions have always been permeated by a feeling for the tragedy of life.[80]

One imagines that Yasuda's attraction for people like Hashikawa and his friend stems from Yasuda's ability to evoke a powerful aesthetic vision of what was primarily a dismal and bloody matter – i.e. Japan's invasion of China and the mass murder of the Chinese. His ambiguous language, neither poem nor prose, and his vivid description of the black sand-storm radically transcends the historical state of events into an image of sublime beauty – the war and the glorious self-sacrifice to the life force itself. Although Yasuda speaks here in a metaphorical language completely exterior to the realm of history, such powerful appeals to the imagination capture the very essence of the romantic moment. Indeed, his advocacy of the 'passion for decay' was literally replicated in the rash behaviour of many young men who during the war willingly sacrificed themselves on countless battlefields – *without irony*.[81]

Hashikawa has analysed the Japan Romantic School doctrine into three key components: Marxism, German romanticism, and the aestheticism of Edo native studies (*kokugaku*). By Marxism he means a radical revolutionary impulse, albeit completely depoliticized and dematerialized, and a desperate pursuit of the absolute and the universal.[82] Recalling his own experience at the time, Hashikawa thinks that the School's aestheticism was a crystallization of 'a kind of radical anti-imperialism,' a 'regression and explosion of revolutionary feelings alienated from politics towards beauty,' and a desperate attempt to transcend the ills of the historical world.[83] He argues that the School's irony was an inversion of materialist realism that took the form of an aesthetic absolutism under historical conditions where political revolution was felt to be no longer possible. According to Hashikawa's interpretation, it was Yasuda's completely depoliticized *kokugaku* aestheticism that accelerated the radical desire for transcendence, and in this sense, the depoliticization was in fact highly political:

> However, in the grip of such a radical irony, even I, in some instances wanted to imagine a revolution. As *kokugaku*-like ideas became increasingly pronounced in Yasuda's writings, a complete rejection of all political realism and all situational analysis came strongly forward, leading him to insist with a desperate intensity on the destruction of scientific thinking. It was almost like an accelerating premonition of the defeat and coming catastrophe.[84]

When Hashikawa speaks of 'an impulse that tries to vertically ascend to the potential of the ego by rejecting the limitations of realism in reality,' he puts in his own words Yasuda's heightened sense of the 'passion for decay' sublimated into the essence of Japan – Japan as 'sad and beautiful.'[85] Hashikawa's war experiences and his reflections on them seem to indicate a reification of Yasuda's irony as a historical experience, driven by a desperate passion for the transcendental absolute which took the form of an aesthetics of death. According to Hashikawa the aesthetic is a principle deeply embedded in the Japanese cultural tradition, and one which, he believes, remains the most effective political ideology to date.[86]

With his aesthetic absolutism, irony and anti-essentialist transcendalism, Yasuda's work sought to transcend all the ills of modernity by placing them on the level of imaginary. To characterize Yasuda's discourse as one of aesthetic violence, does not, however, mean to suggest that it bears ultimate responsibility for all that was to come. On the contrary, the developmental path of Japanese intellectual discourse, at least since the 1910s, had been continuously seeking to heal the perceived injury done to Japanese subjectivity by attempting to incorporate aesthetic aspects (e.g. 'spirituality'), and that aesthetic current had developed hand-in-hand with the objectification of the rural folk and Asian others. By virtue of his literary style, Yasuda perhaps most successfully articulated among his contemporaries what Japanese intellectuals, consciously or not, had been striving for over the past decade or so: namely, the possibility of going beyond the limitations of language and obtaining a spirituality and an intimacy of being that would supposedly restore the unity of Japanese life thought lost to modernity.

The war as spiritual renewal: overcoming the modern West

The intellectual thrill – December 8th, 1941

The intellectual climate of the late 1930s was one of a profound hopelessness, reflecting the bleak inner landscape inhabited by most Japanese intellectuals of the time, regardless of their ideological differences. That dark state of mind and discourse, however, was immediately reversed on December 8th, 1941 – the moment war was declared against the Western allies. Kawakami Tetsutarō (1902–64), a Leftist literary critic, explained how this moment came over him as an 'intellectual thrill' and how that powerful 'emotion' crystallized the previously diverse and fractious medley of Japanese intellectuals around the common slogan and sentiment of 'overcoming modernity.'

> If we are allowed to describe it in the following way, we [the participants of the 1942 symposium of 'overcoming modernity'] have not necessarily lived uniformly in our history running from, say, the Meiji era. That is to say, each of us has viewed that historical time from a different angle and lived differently. *However, especially since December 8th, our emotions have been in unison, formed into an identical shape.* This unison of the shape cannot be effectively described in words – and this is what I call '*kindai no chōkoku*' ('overcoming modernity'). However, in this discussion, I think *we can work backwards from this shared emotional shape*.[87]

Kawakami, in his article entitled 'Glorious Day' referring to December 8th, also expressed a sense of spiritual renewal in terms of joyful excitement.

> I cannot help feeling happy that I now truly enjoy a refreshed mind (*karatto shita kimochi*). In retrospect, the words 'gray clouds of the Pacific' themselves had long been in a state of putrefaction. With the opening of the war, it might not be precise to describe the clouds as having cleared, but my true feeling is that it is almost accurate to describe them as having cleared. How muddy and displeasing a confused and dismal peace is, compared to the purity of the war![88]

Kawakami's sentiment was shared by many of the then progressive or politically 'neutral' intellectuals of the time. Inspired by the same event, an editor of the journal *Literary Art* (*Bungei*) organized a special issue entitled 'The Will to Fight' ('*tatakai no ishi*'), a phrase drawn from a journal published in Moscow reporting of Soviet writers' resistance to the German invasion.[89] Statements by eighteen writers of various positions were cited, unanimously expressing their support for the war and praising the Japanese state's decision as evidence of Japanese fearlessness vis-à-vis the West (Ō-Bei).[90]

Referring to the same moment, Takeuchi Yoshimi (1910–77) noted how relieved he felt to be liberated from the deep sense of guilt he had felt since the 1937 Japanese invasion of China. In his 'The Great Asian War and Our Will to Fight' ('Daitōa senso to warera no ketsui,' 1942), he passionately expressed the excitement and pride he felt at the moment:

> History has been made. The world has metamorphosed overnight. We have seen this with our own eyes. We have witnessed the trajectory of a beam of light as if it were a rainbow, trembling with strong emotions. We have felt something explosive, indescribable feelings that filled our hearts. On December 8th, the day Japan declared war, the determination of all Japanese nationals burned as one. It was refreshing. Everyone thought that things are all right now, walked with their mouths shut, and exchanged warm intimate looks with fellow citizens. There was nothing to be said in words. The history of national creation flashed back in our memories all at that moment, and things were all too obvious, no explanation needed.[91]

The war proved to be a historical turning point, for previous military aggressions against Asian neighbours obtained justification in the new historical context as a part of Japan's struggle for self-determination against Eurocentric hegemony, as 'the liberation of Asia' from centuries of Western domination. Takeuchi's passage goes on to vividly describe how this recovery of moral legitimacy restored satisfaction and 'intimacy among the Japanese people.' The opening of the *Nichibei senso* (the US–Japanese war) allowed many Japanese a chance for spiritual renewal, a renewal in which they could once again live with purpose, their emotions in concord with their actions, a chance to live a morally justified and meaningful existence no longer threatened by the self-destructive spiritual suicide advocated by the decadents.[92] In other words, the nation-state as a moral community was expressed and embraced on December 8th as a recovered experience of the totality of life beyond the rational calculation of consequences.

This climate of exhilaration must be seen as the reverse side of the coin of the larger socio-cultural climate of the time, wherein the ubiquitous 'grey cloud' of decadence and the sense of guilt and inertia were effectively transcended by the advent of war against the Allies. The rest was done by the 'intellectual thrill': the previous dismal historical narrative was rewritten into a new grand aesthetic narrative and a new vision of hope. The groundwork for this alternative discourse had been prepared for over the previous decades and it was completed when a fully-fledged epistemological assault on representation was carried out in the period of the 'cultural renaissance' when the 'aestheticization of philosophy' and the notion of 'Japan as irony', freed thought from historical and material constraints.

The 1942 symposium of 'Overcoming modernity'

No event more dramatically symbolizes the ultimate end point of the prewar Japanese intellectual crisis than the 1942 symposium of 'Overcoming modernity' ('*kindai no chōkoku*'). The symposium was organized by Kawakami Tetsutaro, supported by the then leading Leftist literary circle Literary World (*Bungakukai*), in the year following the opening of the Pacific War. According to the participants, the intent of the symposium was to define the historical significance of the coming war as an opening up of a new historical epoch based on the traditional virtues of Japanese culture. In real terms, however, the discussion was much more modestly focused on a reevaluation of the Meiji government's historical trajectory guided by Fukuzawa Yukichi's pragmatic adaptation of the theory of universal civilization (*bunmei ichigen-ron*). In his opening remarks, Kawakami set the tone of the debates to follow by formulating the current crisis and imaginary dead end of Japan in terms of a tension between the modern and Japanese tradition, in his words between 'the blood of the Japanese that truly motivates our intellectual life' and the 'Western knowledge that has been superimposed on Japan.'[93] The discussions attempted a 'critical rethinking' of the modern, and it was largely agreed that long neglected traditional Japanese cultural and religious values must be revitalized in the era to come.

Thirteen leading intellectuals from various fields participated, including novelists, philosophers, art specialists and historians. Despite the differences among them on specific issues, they can be roughly grouped into three factions, representing distinct philosophical and political positions: the Literary World circle, the Kyoto School of philosophy, and the Japan Romantic School (*Nihon Rōman-ha*).[94] As Kawakami himself later admitted, however, the symposium was less than a success because there was little consensus among participants on how to define the modern in the first place. Some equated the modern with the Western, juxtaposing it to 'the Japanese,' while others objected that Japan had already become modern and that the general frame of the symposium was thus wrongheaded. In terms of remedies to the current crisis, many advocated a revitalization of traditional Japanese culture, while a few took a rationalist position insisting that the modern could only be overcome by means of the modern.⁹⁵ Indeed, so varied were the views of the participants that debate became nearly impossible, and as a consequence the symposium closed with no joint statement or agreement. However, beyond this matter of the differing points of view lay the much deeper problem of the attempt to alter the meaning of the war on a conceptual level rather than aiming at altering the historical conditions of the war. In this sense, the symposium was much more a symptom of the Japanese intellectual predicament than an intellectual forum wherein the crisis of modernity as such could be debated and resolved.

Of the three factions, the Kyoto School's position was the closest to the official war ideology as laid down in such state propaganda tracts as *Fundamentals of Our National Polity* (*Kokutai no Hongi*) and *The Duty of the Subject* (*Shinmin no Michi*). What set the Kyoto School apart from the other two factions was its general appreciation of the achievements of the Meiji state and the state's pursuit of *bunmei kaika* following 'the logic of civilization.' Critically assessing the problem of the modern, Nishitani Keiji (1990–), a member of Kyoto School, identified the most serious ill effect of Japanese modernization as the loss of religiosity brought about by Western science; this loss, he argued, could only be overcome by a return to the 'traditional Japanese spirit' embodied in *kokutai*.

> Our present national life is fundamentally defined by our tradition, that is, the spirit of the nation embodied in the ethno-social community [*minzoku*], in the historical practice of tradition from the ancient era. Faced with the current challenge of our time to create a synthesis between the worlds of religiosity and national morality, we must exert our moral energy from the bottom of our national life, because the potential of creating such a synthesis ultimately depends on the presence of this traditional spirit in national life.⁹⁶

As the following passages make clear, his glorification of 'moral energy' and 'traditional spirit' were conceived as instrumental means towards the consolidation of national unity and the state's mission to create a self-defined Asian order.

> The task our country now faces is, needless to say, the establishment of the new world order and the construction of Greater Asia (*Daitōa*). The reason a concentration of national power, particularly a strong moral energy, is now required is so that we may realize this task. Naturally the construction of Greater Asia must not mean the acquisition of new colonies for Japan, for this new world order must create an order of justice. Although this is a world historical necessity, its necessity is given to our country, because our country rose to be the only non-European power and is thus now faced with a task of confronting Anglo-Saxon domination in Asia.⁹⁷

As these passages demonstrate, the School's narrative is marked by sweeping generalizations and the linking of a whole series of diverse issues belonging to different realms and levels of concern in a rather singularly patterned manner – such as the problem of the modern, the issue of Japanese cultural tradition, the question of the socio-political order of Japanese society, and the historical–political state of Asian nations.

The dispositions of Nishitani and other members of the Kyoto School were overflowing with a metaphysical jargon that deeply irritated the other participants. Kobayashi Hideo (1902–83), probably the most respected literary and social critic of the entire Shōwa period, did not conceal his annoyance with their abstractions, describing them as lacking 'the sensuality of Japanese language.'[98] Kobayashi remarked to Nishitani that if one wanted to create Japanese philosophy, one must do so in a manner accountable to the language by thinking and articulating ideas in 'proper' Japanese. For Kobayashi, the Kyoto School style and mode of thinking distorted the temporal and spatial specificities of Japanese cultural and empirical life by crudely subordinating them to the metaphysical and universal prerogatives of reason. Building on this critique, Kobayashi also rejected the Kyoto School's implicit historical progressivism, and sought instead to advance an alternative conception of time, obtained in an aesthetically fulfilling moment, outside and beyond linear homogeneous time.

> When we are struck with awe and respect, there is no temporality or progress, Where history appears as a classical past, the place where artists create their objects, there becomes no time or progress since that is the place where they experience the old masters' achievements as their modes. Even to the average person, the experience of the admiration of classical art teaches that. That is our everyday experience.[99]

Beauty, Kobayashi emphasized, could not be contained in nor understood by the progressive conception of time, and thus aesthetic subjectivity, he argued, was the only existence capable of realizing the full potential of life in a specific time and place in history.[100] By emphasizing an aesthetically conceived temporality, Kobayashi implicitly criticized the spatialized form of Hegelian history in the Kyoto School's world historical narrative.[101] In doing so, however, Kobayashi privileged the creativity and will of the individual over the objective socio-political structure, and thereby sought to convert the powerlessness of the former vis-à-vis the latter into a vision fusing artistic freedom with the richness of tradition.[102] While attracted to romantic aestheticism and its critique of universal reason, however Kobayashi, recognizing the inescapability of the modern and rejecting any simple solution drawn from an opposition between the modern and the traditional, remained firmly in the camp of the Literary World circle.

A more reckless departure from rationalism towards romantic aestheticism can be seen in the thinking of Hayashi Fusao (1903–75), a former

Communist and a member of the Literary World circle, who later became a member of the Japan Romantic School.[103] In harsh tones Hayashi condemned Japan's pursuit of *bunmei kaika* modernization, arguing that the pursuit of modernization had only led to Japan's subordination to the West:

> I think that *bunmei kaika* is an adaptation of European culture since the Meiji Restoration and in consequence a subordination to Europe. To view it from an international perspective, the Meiji restoration was the last resistance of the East against the West and its fine successes. India was defeated and so was China, but Japan alone has stalled the bounding Western wave. Thus in order to survive and to compete equally with Europe, we had to adapt the pragmatic utility of European civilization. *Bunmei kaika* has meant the adoption of a practical culture that has no substantial cultural essence to it. Then, in the Meiji 20s (i.e. 1906–), a revolt against such a culture began calling for a return to the root as opposed to the pragmatist *bunmei kaika* culture.[104]

Kamei Katsuichirō (1907–66), one of the core members of Literary World, advanced a similar charge against *bunmei kaika*, although, unlike Hayashi, he was fully conscious that the modern was already at least a part of Japanese culture. Kamei instead emphasized the importance of recovering what he perceived the Japanese had lost, namely religious belief, in order to fill the current spiritual vacuum in the hearts of the Japanese.

> Looking back at the past from the present, I, who was educated in the period of Taishō and Shōwa and experienced various problems of our thought, identified the fundamental weakness in the fact that we have lived in the era of a lack of belief. Or, we can describe it as the tragedy of human beings who are persecuted by the gods ... if I ask myself what bright light has emerged out of this confusion and misery since *bunmei kaika*, I can only vaguely answer an upsurge of desire for belief in the gods and the spirits (*shinfutsu*). Not an interpretation of religious belief but a belief itself.[105]

Contrary to Hayashi and Kamei, Nakamura Mitsuo, a modernist critic, exemplified the rationalist position of Literary World proper.

> The true fundamentals of the spirit of 'modernity' or the consent of the modern spirit, came to be within our reach. But I think unless we understand the truth of the modern spirit, we can hardly conceive of overcoming modernity. From this perspective, I think the characteristic of the modern – the modern since the Renaissance – can be grasped as the era in which the human mind was thrown into an unknown order.... The existence of god, and things such as nature, can no longer be unconditionally believed in: one has to test one's own

belief in god.... Human minds are thrown into and forced to live with such an unknown order and that has been causing various confusions.... *The true essence of the modern is a state of mind in which we are exposed to the unknown, and in that constantly attempting to discover the new; in this sense, the true modern has just arrived in contemporary Japan.*[106]

The critical difference between the view presented by Hayashi and Kamei and that presented by Nakamura is their understanding of the status of the modern subject: while the former conceived the advent of modernity as a process of the destruction of subjectivity, the latter saw modernity as a process of its maturing. Hayashi and Kamei saw the intrusion of modern rationalist discourse as responsible for a disturbance of the previous subjecthood assumed to be free from self-critical interrogation, and targeted modernity as the cause of this upheaval. Nakamura, for his part, understood subjectivity as a state of being haunted by a constant intrusion of the unknown, resulting in a lack of solid foundations; yet he also believed that what many of the other participants viewed as the 'traditional' was a reactionary product of the modern. He saw the rhetorical conflation of the modern and the Western, thus, as intellectual dishonesty and did not speak of locating the idea of 'overcoming' in a historical narrative of the declining West and a rising Japan. However, after the above early statement, he remained largely silent and unsupported.

Generalizing from the diverse positions of the Japan Romantic School, we can identify some characteristic features presented in the symposium: an eschatological vision of history and a disdain for those aspects of the modern internalized by Japanese society. These two attitudes can be seen in the following passage by Kamei, in which he views prewar Japanese society as having reached a point of self-destruction and the war as holding out the potential for renewal.

> In the background of the present war, another war is going on. We see it in the pressure of a civilization moving relentlessly ahead with an apparently natural force of persuasion; in our trust in the machine and all the maladies and debilities of the spirit this brings in its wake; in the self-destructive behaviour of people who have lost all sense of moderation. It is uncertain whether we will perish in this fight or be saved, but at least when we count our victories in the visible war, let us not deceive ourselves into thinking that this deeper war, hidden to the eyes, is a mere fantasy.[107]

Pointing to 'another war' of far deeper significance, Kamei's idealism conveys the image of a quest for spiritual renewal founded directly upon the war as a historical event. With this elevation of the 'spiritual war' over the historical one, Kamei came to a notorious conclusion: peace was merely a state of spiritual decay.

The illusion of 'peace' that victors often carry around with them glosses over this abysmal war. . . . Behind the mask of 'peace' the poison of civilization spreads. More frightening than war is peace. . . . The present disturbances are a war in the name of that abyssal war. In those battlefields the rise or fall of the Japanese people will depend upon the clarity of their insight and resolution to drive away all delusions and upon the ineradicable fearlessness of their belief. Rather a war of kings than the peace of slaves![108]

These passages demonstrate something more than the anti-modern strain of the Japan Romantic School's thinking, represented by Hayashi's condemnation of *bunmei kaika* and Kobayashi's challenge to logocentric reason on the basis of 'life' as lived experience. In addition to the aesthetic categories of sense experience, spirit, intimacy and beauty over and above reason, the core position of the Japan Romantic School cannot fully be represented without taking into consideration the epistemic inversion of the real and the imagined, as Kamei's words in the above passages demonstrate.

Another core aspect of the Japan Romantic School, the notion of irony, was barely reflected in the discussion, due to the absence of Yasuda Yojūrō, the leading figure of the circle. The essential position of the Japan Romantic School, as most clearly exemplified in the writings of Yasuda, negates not only the historical path taken by modern Japan, but more importantly rejects the modernity of the Japanese.[109] Yasuda saw the self and its statements as futile, as well as perhaps all talk of 'overcoming modernity,' for the most part, from his romantic and ironic point of view, all positive assertions were only worthy of ridicule. And yet Yasuda's romantic irony was a thoroughly modern consciousness and shared with Nakamura a wholesale rejection of foundation seeking, i.e. of any and every notion of Japanese cultural essence. On this account, the idealized romantic narratives of Hayashi and Kamei had more in common with the Kyoto School and state *kokutai* essentialism than Yasuda's romantic irony, and their ambivalent position is a peculiar 'synthesis' between the Japan Romantic School's aestheticism and *kokutai* fundamentalism – the position perhaps most widely accepted in intellectual and popular discourses of wartime Japan. In short, Japanese wartime ideology was a highly fragmented amalgam of mutually contradictory ideological streams that nevertheless functioned together to consolidate the Japanese state's war effort.

Takeuchi Yoshimi, an influential nationalist intellectual, has critically reassessed the significance of the symposium, interpreting it as an attempt by prewar intellectuals to transform the top-down war ideology into a bottom-up struggle for self-determination.[110] He argues that the members of Literary World tried to co-opt the state militarist ideology by formulating an alternative ideology, and for that purpose made use of the 'explosive power' of the Japan Romantic School that stemmed from its sharply anti-statist position, its romantic irony, and its eschatological vision of declining modernity.[111] In my view, however, this interpretation gives too much credit to a symposium which was as much a manifestation of the troubled state of intellectual discourse of the time as it was a constructive effort by intellectuals. Triggered by the feelings of unity resulting from the excitement of creating a new historical narrative of revolt against the West, the symposium, rather than being an intellectual project, was a product of a lapsed intelligence, a whitewash of the brute politics of the war and ultimately an affirmation of the Japanese war ideology.

It is noteworthy that with the advent of the 'intellectual thrill' at the opening of the war, the ironies of the Japan Romantic School's negative statements of identity and anti-statist postures were easily discarded and replaced by the state *kokutai* ideology, the idea of a corporeal communal space, and positive assertions of Japan's identity and mission on the world-historical stage. As soon as this representative transformation took place, irony was turned into history; an ironically formulated 'bridge of the night' (*yoru no hashi*) came to represent the historical hope of leading the nation to 'the next dawn' and was occasionally embraced by passionately radicalized Japanese youths. From this point forward, the Kyoto School's vision of Japan's mission in the world and the Japan Romantic School's aesthetic absolutism began their infamous collaboration as the twin complements of a powerful war ideology, with the former rationally and the latter aesthetically motivating Japanese subjects to play their designated parts. Most importantly, the 'grand historical project' was a product of the breakdown of domestic political movements; it served as a mechanism for tacitly redirecting the bitterness and dispiritedness that had resulted from the failure to resist fascism onto the external enemy, as well as for projecting once-shattered hopes onto an idealized 'Asia' as Japan's spiritual home. In a paradoxical way, political radicalism in Japan was perpetuated in the war effort and blinded itself to the brutal military violence it waged against Asians.

Beyond representation, beyond history – the rise of the sublime aesthetic subject

The historical events undergone by Japan in the late 1930s and early 1940s, including its military aggression against Asia and its declaration of war against the West, are most often claimed to have been driven by Japanese 'nationalism,' or more crudely, by a fanatic expression of Japanese 'national sentiments.' However, what took place during the period in question was much more complex than the category of nationalism can adequately explain, for Japanese military expansionism in Asia was not driven by nationalism but a form of internationalism motivated to create in 'Asia' a single political unit, supposedly representing a racially and culturally common identity. This expansionary movement was fed by Pan-Asianist ideological rhetoric together with a fundamentalism centring on the essence of the Japanese nation. Moreover, the intellectual developments that ultimately constituted – albeit unintendedly – the official war ideology were only partially the product of the 'national sentiment' of being grounded in one's sense of homeland; rather, they were in large part mediated by an awareness of the loss of such a homeland, and it was this sense of homelessness that called forth the romantic and ironic phantom of 'Japan.' Instead of limiting our understanding of what precipitated total war to the conventional notion of nationalism, I propose to broaden our scope to view it in light of the various problematics that accumulated in the maturing process of Japanese modernity, and especially in relation to the effect that the emergence of modern subjectivity had upon the relations between the self, language and the world outside. As modernization was a total process of transformation involving complex changes in the entire human lifesphere of political, economic, cultural-discursive, and subjective and inter-subjective relations, establishing workable linkages among these spheres and constituting a stable mode of hegemony throughout the process of historical transformation was a challenging task indeed.

The victories in Japan's two imperial wars were not only markers of Japan's success in achieving modernization, they also marked a turning point in perspective from a forward-looking, future-oriented one to a romantically oriented, regressive one. During this period Japanese intellectuals 'discovered' their modern subjectivity, most often with a sense of loss and alienation that inclined them towards the recovery of 'things lost.' These were the conditions in which the *shizen-shugi* literary movement arose, and, as can be seen in its notion of 'spiritual eyes,' it was laden with hopes of countering the dualistic state of selfhood and overcoming what appeared to be rationalism's dehumanizing effects. In other words, *shizen-shugi*, and the Taishō discursive space at large, was permeated by the reactionary desire of Japanese intellectuals to counter the agitation they felt as a result of their experience of modern subjectivity, and they responded by attempting to incorporate extra-rational components into the rational discursive order, i.e. by aestheticizing that order. The motivating force behind the aesthetic currents in post-1905 Japanese discourse was the perceived discrepancy, opacity and void of subjectivity, perceptions which grew in strength as modernization advanced. The first inscription of this transcendental gaze of the modern subject was imprinted upon Japanese intellectuals in the first decade of the twentieth century, and its maturation in the 1910s and 1920s further unmoored them from their empirical bases. It was from this point forward that modern Japanese literature began its long search for ways of comprehending the fragmented self and the disintegrating word, and as that search proceeded a growing sense of the limitations of language was felt and an increasing tendency to experiment with extra-realist epistemological methods was seen.

On the other hand, modern Japanese subjectivity was also significantly shaped by the introduction of Marxism into intellectual circles, and its

58 *'Overcoming modernity': aesthetic politics of identity*

dissemination to urban workers and rural tenant farmers resulted in the establishment of various local unions and other forms of collective organization, for the first time in Japanese history. By the late 1920s the cultural and discursive conditions of Japanese society were in a state of profound disarray, suffering from an intensification of state oppression against powerful resistance organized along Marxist lines in the urban and rural sectors on the one hand, and a wide-spread sense of existential anxiety on the other. Following a series of economic crises and the state's severe assaults upon the Leftist movements in the early 1930s, both of which deeply shocked the entire society, Japanese critical thought took a clear 'aesthetic turn' in the period of the so-called 'cultural renaissance' (1933–7), in which the notions of the primacy of reason, progressive and universal history, and the rational autonomous subject came to be vehemently challenged. As discussed above, Watsuji challenged the universal progressive notion of history by conceiving of a geographically determined temporal/cultural space in which a culturally defined human behaviour formed the basis for an aesthetic-moral community of collectively embodied subjects. Likewise, Nishida 'historicized' his previously metaphysical categories of the 'place of nothingness' and the 'absolutely contradictory self-identity' into essential features of Japanese cultural identity. It was also in this period that the Japan Romantic School emerged, a literary circle grounded in an ironic self-consciousness and aestheticism that valued the traditional beauty of Japanese culture above all else. In Yasuda's view, the current state of Japan was nothing more than that of 'irony,' a modernity sick to the core, and he advocated the strong medicine of accelerating the process of decay as the only remedy by which an imagined beauty of the 'true Japan' might be realized.

Kevin Doak suggests that the problematic of the Japan Romantic School needs to be seen in the context of the 'dilemma' inherent in representation itself; that is, while '[r]epresentation always aims to make the subject or presence present to itself . . . there always remains a separation between language and what it purports to represent.'[112] This uneasy relation between representation (meaning) and its object (being) was the crux of the 'problem of the modern' that Japanese intellectuals of the post-1905 era had struggled to overcome. By virtue of standing in a privileged position outside history, a strategy many Japanese intellectuals flirted with and increasingly embraced, one would instantly know that such unity between meaning and being was only possible by transcending history in the realm of the imaginary and subordinating the former to the latter. While neither the writing subject nor his/her works are produced outside of a given historical context, it does seem that, consciously or not, Japanese intellectuals from the Taishō period onward, and most explicitly in the period of 'cultural renaissance,' moved in a direction that allowed for the creation of an alternative system of representation and the rise of this impossible, yet intensely desired, presence. In spite of the irony that characterized the

Japan Romantic School, which explicitly denied the possibility of identity and instead endorsed an ironic distance, the subsequent conversion of the members of the School suggests that they desired a foundation for the perceived lost selfhood just as much as did the earlier romantics.

Moreover, this ironic subject paradoxically 'called for' an artificial and absolute identity in order to fill in its inner void; and from the mid-1930s to the opening of the war, this problematic played itself out in the creation of an alternative system of representation outside and beyond the modern, a system in which, it was hoped, the Japanese could 'realize' their deprived cultural essence. One should note here how quickly and painlessly the ironic position was discarded in favour of recovering the totality of life during the moment of the 'intellectual thrill' at the opening of the Pacific War, and how effortlessly the critical distance between the war rhetoric and the recognition of the fact of the war was transcended by most Leftist intellectuals.

Not only did the emergent modern Japanese subject-perspective generate an internal split in the Japanese self, thus giving rise to a desire to unify that dualism, it also expanded outward in such a way as to affirm the Japanese self by exercising its epistemic power over its others, transforming their unique temporal and spatial differences into inferior states of itself. As H. D. Harootunian has argued, in the early Taishō era the newly established field of Japanese ethnology transformed the rural folk into an object of social inquiry in which the Japanese countryside and its rural population served as an imaginative space for the constitution of an archetypal Japanese identity (i.e. *jyōmin*).[113] This image of Japanese cultural tradition was then put into political movement by *nōhonshugi*; rural villagers were mobilized, by internalizing an urban and ideal depiction of themselves, to turn the images into an actual politico-cultural order.[114] It was out of this transformation that the Japanese state rose itself to an overarching position as the national, political, and spiritual authority, uniting all internal divisions within local villages under the sign of the emperor. Thus, by virtue of fixing the countryside in its vision, modern and urban Japanese subjectivity created a nationally homogenized space under its universal gaze. By the mid-1930s, when Watsuiji's notion of the moral–aesthetic community of the Japanese and the state's *kokutai* ideology had erected themselves upon the ancestral (and implicitly rural) foundation, the urban–rural split had been overcome. With the erasure of internal diversity within Japan, the modern Japanese self turned its gaze towards Asia, and began ascribing to Asians arbitrary, ambiguous and often contradictory images. As Stefan Tanaka has shown, in Japanese Asianist and Pan-Asianist discourses Asian peoples were depicted both as worthy of great admiration, since they dwelled in Japan's ideal home, and as backward nations needing assistance, a characterization that was used to justify Japan's leadership in Asia.[115] In other words, the modern Japanese self could not constitute itself without objectifying these internal and external others, against which the Japanese self affirmed its superior identity. As the discourse of Asia developed into Pan-Asianism, Asians came to be understood, talked about, and dealt with in Japanese hegemonic discourse as mere signs, stripped of their historically specific attributes.[116]

In addition to being driven by its internal void and instability, therefore, the modern Japanese subject was also driven by the necessity for self-affirmation vis-à-vis its others, and in this sense, the aestheticization of rationalist discourse in the post-1905 period was simultaneously a process constitutive of modern Japanese national identity. Thus remedies for the ill effects of the modern were formulated in aesthetic terms and the discursive space of the 1920s and 1930s became increasingly aestheticized, not only as a response to the alleged limitations of modern rationalism, but also because the aesthetic was the realm in which the essence of Japanese culture was thought to lie. Envisaging an alternative vision of the future grounded on the value of the aesthetic, was not only an attempt at a counter-hegemonic revolt against the modern West, whose core value principle was seen as reason, but also an attempt to revitalize the 'Japanese way of life' by creating an alternative cultural space governed by the conventional Japanese values that would allow the nation to locate itself outside the hegemonic gaze of the modern West. The unified expressions of these two efforts were plainly visible in the intellectual productions of the mid-1930s as discussed above: Watsuji's redefinition of history in anti-materialist terms and his idealization of Japanese society as an aesthetic community; Nishida's reification of the 'place of nothingness,' and the Kyoto School's interpretation of the war as Japan's world-historical project; Yasuda's wholesale rejection of modernized Japan in favour of the beauty of its ancient court-culture; and so on. All grounded themselves, in one way or another, on images of 'Japan' as a place of beauty, a principle superior to reason; and all, appealing to the power of the aesthetic imagination, pointed to the desirability of an alternative world order outside the modern. In this sense, aesthetics offered a means of cultural redemption for those Japanese intellectuals who felt the nation's temporal/spatial specificity was being rendered untenable by Eurocentric, universalist and rationalist modern subjectivity.

In light of these factors, the historical development of post-1905 Japan cannot satisfactorily be explained by the category of nationalism, principally because the category of identity does not adequately comprehend the scope of the problematic of the modern subject. The modern subject, or perhaps more precisely the modern *perspective*, defines the world with a particular set of temporal and spatial assumptions and values. The lack of an ontological basis, and thus the desire for self-knowledge that characterizes the modern perspective, compels it to outwardly expand the scope of its hegemonic gaze and thus to affirm the superiority of itself through the creation of 'objective others.' On this account, the question of identity should be seen in terms of a dialectic between the expanding modern universal/hegemonic perspective and the inevitable encounter with its own limitations, i.e. the resistance of its others, including, in Japan's case, the 'Asians' and 'things empirical' it attempts to objectify and transform. The difficulty of discussing the question of *identity* in this sense, is in part derived from the fact that the significance of its process-oriented meaning – the developmental process of the modern subject and its inherent tendency to *identify* the body with consciousness (or being with meaning) – is bestowed on a noun form alone, *identity* as essential attribute of the self. In this conflation of meanings, the problematic of identity as a universal problem of the modern subject yearning for a unity of its divided self becomes subsumed under the sense of identity as the specificity of the national subject. However, despite the clear distinction between these two meanings of 'identity,' the two are in fact closely intertwined in the historical process of modernization because the experience of groundlessness, or the 'discovery' of an insurmountable gap between being and meaning, is constantly generated and invariably interpreted as a loss of 'identity' as shared cultural essences. While the problematic of a cultural particularist desire for identity has gained much attention in recent years, the universality of the problematic, the dematerialization of the self coupled with the aesthetic desire for 'identity' and the aestheticization of discourse, often escapes critical engagement. This oversight has resulted in articulations of the problematic of Japanese national identity in terms of a desire for a lost cultural tradition

The aforementioned distinctions notwithstanding, discussions of identity cannot simply sweep the phenomenon of common cultural traits under the rug of universality, either. And here lies a further difficulty of the subject. Granting that the characterization of any culture is a difficult and vexing issue, there may be additional difficulties in describing the 'content' of Japanese identity, given its tradition of negative formulation and lack of a clear and persistent shape. One might want to follow the critic Asada Akira's suggestion here that the core ideological strength of Japanese identity lies not in any definable form of cultural essence, but rather in its depiction of 'Japan' as an absence of identity, as an empty 'container' that can be filled with desirable contents as they are identified at each given moment.[117] Seen in this light, the Japan Romantic School's romantic irony and aesthetic principle perhaps best encapsulated this negative essence in the modern period, providing an empty container in which various ideological fragments could be accommodated regardless of their contradictions. Moreover, some components of the Japan Romantic School's aestheticism – the negation of the content of the self as a pure form, a preference for indeterminacy over a defined ideal and meaning, and situating the ultimate form of beauty in death – had particular affinities with some of the self-negating and suicidal narratives of previous eras, including the ethical principle of *Bushidō* and the ideal form of unity between forbidden lovers found in death. The common link between the

62   *'Overcoming modernity': aesthetic politics of identity*

School's appreciation of the passion for decay and the romantic notion of sacrifice for a higher goal in the earlier narratives, was an idea of aesthetic absolutism in which the value of life is inferior to the beauty of death. Of course, the wartime ideology was not articulated on the basis of such negative principles alone; an amalgamation of various related ideological components, including the positive rhetorical formulation of Japanese identity as part of *kokutai*, was necessary before aesthetic absolutism could be fused into the state war ideology. Moreover, despite the anti-modern rhetoric, obsessive attempts to articulate the 'lost identity' of tradition, Japan (the desire animating the 'cultural renaissance' movement) were themselves features of modern subjectivity. This paradoxical nature of the aesthetic and negative formulation of modern Japanese national identity needs further elaboration.

Despite its rhetorical position of denying the existence of any subjective will to construct the objective world, it is essential to see in romantic irony the hidden presence of a subject, a subject that locates itself above and beyond all historical contingencies, that is, a pure consciousness elevated to the status of absolute Subject. Consider, for example, the subject implicit in the following passages:

> I am speaking as a spectator . . . as an audience, I think it would be more interesting if the Germans won the war and it is a hope of mine, I who have been concerned with such realizations of a culture in history. Moreover, it appears to me that the gods always direct history towards the path that makes it more interesting.[118]

> Even if this war [the Sino–Japanese war] ends up a draw, Japan has made a world-historical expedition. When I stood at Yellow River flowing through Manchuria, I, for the first time, felt the significance of the Japanese continental policy in world history . . . Speaking from this theoretical position, I imagine now that *even should the war end in a draw, it is truly a grand romanticism.*[119]

Hashikawa Bunzō has argued that the ironic subject 'infinitely postpones determination of the self [identity],' and that by virtue of abiding in this state of suspended subjectivity the ironic subject exempts itself from making any ethical judgements.[120] Having departed from the material, politico-historical world for the realm of the aesthetic imaginary, the romantic ironic subject is dehistoricized and barred from making any appropriate links between the material/historical world and consciousness. In this solipsistic realm, in which the self-expression of a narcissistic consciousness has become equivalent to the world, and in which the empirical subject or the 'materiality' of the subject not reducible to consciousness is erased, the lofty omnipotence of consciousness disposes of such 'objects' at its will. By dissolving the historical subject in this way, romantic irony entitles the 'objects' of this pure absolute consciousness to 'live' in a world of unreal beauty, freedom and indeterminacy, unhindered by any material constraints. In this alternative discourse, even war becomes a means of achieving absolute beauty, the sole concern of aesthetic consciousness.[121]

By virtue of being possessed of this absolute consciousness, the romantic ironic subject exempts himself from falling into the state of being an 'object.' As Karatani Kōjin argues,

> the absolute consciousness of romantic irony is an affirmation of the superiority of the transcendent Self that stands above and is contemptuous of all existing things that are finite and empirical. It rejects all purposes, and thus rejects Hegelian dialectics. If one does anything, it is not for meaning or reason. However, it is not nihilism; contrarily, it discovers meaning in the self-consciousness that seriously plays with meaningless things, being fully aware of their meaninglessness. There is no possible defeat in this position, since it assumes defeat from its beginning. That is to say, irony is an absolute victory by accepting absolute powerlessness.[122]

It is hard to imagine how an act of sacrifice could emerge from such an ironic subject, since they had already given up everything. The sacrifices exhorted by the state war ideology were thus instead invoked by the seductions of the foundational narrative of *kokutai* in combination with the rhetorical 'world historical' reason of the Kyoto School, the two streams of Japanese thought that merged with the romantic irony of the Japan Romantic School in the 'thrill' of 1941. In this consolidation, the romantic stance took on a foundation and essence for itself, and thus ceased to be ironic. Thus, in order for the historical subject to willingly sacrifice himself/herself, that is, in order for the ironic subject to ascend to the status of the transcendental self and to reach out as an exemplary model to the greatest number of subordinate subjects, it had to undergo a metamorphosis from a negative to a positive identity.

Since this discourse of the ironic subject was not governed by the authority of meaning or reason, but instead by beauty and indeterminacy, assertions of difference no longer entailed differing political and moral positions. As exemplified by Hayashi and Kamei, the shift of position from Marxism to the Japan Romantic School, and then to a quasi-*kokutai* fundamentalism, no longer constituted a 'conversion' defined in terms of rational grounds for belief; instead, the grounds for such justified beliefs having been annulled, a shift from one position to another (however antithetical) was merely a matter of taste, style, or rhetoric. As seen above, this nullification of reason and the ascendance of the aesthetic were the central impetus behind the mid-1930s 'cultural renaissance,' and the means of which the aesthetic subject/consciousness was able and authorized to transcend representation and history. This absolute aesthetic subject shares a great deal of similarity with what Philippe Lacoue-Labarthe and Jean-Luc Nancy have called the 'eidaesthetics' of the German Jena Romantics. As Martin Jay writes:

> This quasi-religious metaphysics of art is responsible for an absolute notion of literature, whose task is the overcoming of differences, contradictions, and disharmonies. Although implicitly challenged by a counter-impulse they call 'romantic equivocity,' the telos of eidaesthetics is the closure of a complete work produced by an omnipotent subject, who realizes the Idea in sensual form. Jena Romanticism's desire for poetic perfection is thus derived from an ultimately metaphysical project, which has political implications as well.[123]

Contrary to what some have suggested, then, the rejection of essence and foundation in the Japan Romantic School did not hinder the rise of fundamentalism. Rather, it prepared the 'groundless ground' from which *kokutai* fascism would emerge by engendering an ever greater desire the 'identity' in the negation of its possibility, totalizing the role of (ironic) consciousness vis-à-vis history, and imbuing the radical romantic sentiments of the entire younger generation with its sublime aestheticism.

In short, the aesthetic obsession which runs through Japanese intellectual productions from the late 1920s through to the war must be seen as an essential part of the maturing process of modern Japanese identity. In their efforts to define and 'recover' a 'lost' Japanese identity in 'its own terms,' Japanese intellectuals followed a path that promised to free them from what they felt constantly threatened Japan's unique cultural/ethnic temporality with erasure: by constructing an alternative time and space beyond the modern. By resorting to the category of the aesthetic as supposedly superior to reason, and by employing irony as a principle for the new discourse, however, Japanese intellectuals launched an epistemic assault on 'realist' representation that allowed them to conceive the war as a world-historical project of 'overcoming modernity.' In elevating ideal images of an 'unrealized' Japan over the actual historical Japan, prewar aesthetic representations of modern Japanese identity inaugurated a radical epistemological leap in which the impossible problem of the modern was 'resolved' on the level of the aesthetic imaginary by creating an alternative system of representation. However, such an attempt to resolve historically grounded problems necessarily entailed a departure from the reality of the historical world, a leap into the imaginary. Moreover, grounded in a 'passion for decay,' the attempt to create an alternative system of representation and identity gave rise to a self-destructive imperative in which self-sacrifice was seen as the ultimate realization of Japanese cultural essence.

The maturing process of modern Japanese identity and its increasingly manifest crisis, therefore, need to be seen at the intersection of the universal problematics inherent in the modern disembodied/transcendental subject and the national status of the Japanese as Western others in Eurocentric modern international discourse. The very fact of the emergence of modern Japanese subjectivity was rationalized (if not often experienced) as the erosion of Japanese cultural foundations, while the outward expansion of this same universal perspective 'exported' cultural disfiguration to other Asian nations. By defining its identity in aesthetic and hegemonic terms, the sublime subject of wartime Japan subjugated reason and the historical/empirical to its gaze. It is this absolute, transcendental aspect of Japanese identity that undeniably confirms its modern constitution.

Conclusion

In conclusion, I would like to outline five propositions central to an understanding of Japanese identity in the universalized modern world. Together they constitute a theoretical frame for my arguments about postwar Japanese identity in the chapters to come.

First, it is not entirely satisfactory to address Japan's military expansion and internal socio-political and cultural transformations in the 1930s solely within the framework of nationalism, particularly when we note that the 'internationalist' and expansionary inspirations of the Japanese state were grounded in notions of a common 'Asian' culture and race. Moreover, contrary to conventional wisdom, the ideology of Japanese expansionism was not driven by simple national sentiments but the more complex formulation of an anti-foundationalist rhetoric, a desire for identity mediated by an acute awareness of its impossibility. What lay beneath the anti-modern, anti-Western cultural particularist claims made by Japanese intellectuals in the discussion of 'overcoming modernity' was this sense of the loss of identity in their encounter with 'the modern,' inseparably mingled with a notion of 'the hegemonic West.' The desperate attempt to 'recover' a lost identity took form as an alternative and reactionary discourse of recreating a lost temporality – Japanese 'cultural particularity' – in which images of 'Japan' antithetical to the modern/West were central.

Second, the attempt to lay claim to a lost identity issued in the creation of an alternative representational schema in which the centrality of reason was replaced by that of beauty. This was the inspiration behind the aestheticizing trend in philosophy during the period of the 'cultural renaissance' in which such anti-modern philosophical projects as Watsuji's nullification of universal progressive time, his rejection of the rational atomistic subject and universal ethics, and Nishida's doubts about the epistemological grounds of universal reason were formulated. These attempts to construct a highly idealized world not only provided basic foundations for the state's *kokutai* ideology, but also cultivated discursive conditions that separated Japan and the Japanese from the historical world by spatializing temporality, collectivizing the subject and grounding cultural essence in place.

Third, the most powerful force driving the construction of this alternative representational schema was the anti-essentialist, anti-foundationalist romanticism of the Japan Romantic School which radically departed from dialectical thinking and embraced instead irony and aestheticism. It was by means of this kind of knowledge that the ultimate, transcendental images of Japanese identity were created and that the notion of the modern subject, history and reason came to be enveloped in and subjugated to an absolute consciousness elevating beauty above truth and morality. Under the influence of Yasuda's romantic irony and his anti-materialist glorification of the beauty of defeat, Japanese politics came to be expressed in aesthetic terms, whose ultimate form was the 'aesthetics of death.' Despite its anti-state stance, this aestheticized radicalism seeking a transcendence of the political in effect contributed to the state war effort by motivating large groups of young men towards voluntary sacrifice in the name of *kokutai*.

Fourth, the Japanese attempt to 'overcome the modern,' the ultimately disastrous project of constructing an alternative representational schema, was brought to maturity, therefore, by a combination of *kokutai* fundamentalism as embodiment of Japanese essence (proposition two above) and an anti-foundational aesthetic absolutism (proposition three) expressed in terms of a revolutionary and formless desire for transcendence. The collaboration of these seemingly contradictory currents shaped the constitutive process of modern Japanese identity in the two distinct meanings of the word: cultural essence and the elimination of the gap between being and meaning. By virtue of interpreting the rise of modern Japanese consciousness as a 'loss' of cultural identity, Japanese intellectuals formulated a notion of modern Japanese identity as an aesthetic mode antithetical to 'the modern.' With the advent of an aestheticized identity taking form in *kokutai* identity, political radicalism was absorbed into an aesthetic absolutism that the Japanese state–militarist machinery mobilized into a project of 'overcoming modernity.'

Finally, the disembodied, absolute, self-negating subject of *kokutai* emerged out of the collapse of the empirical subject in the era of the 'cultural renaissance.' This degeneration of the empirical subject and the discursive structure 'coincided' with a shift in political focus from a critique of the internal power structure to, following the failure of domestic political movements to challenge state power politics, a critique of the external international hegemonic hierarchy. In this shift, the energy previously directed towards domestic revolutionary struggle was transformed into a political project of aestheticization that, in a spirit of decadence and irony, freed Japanese intellectuals from the dismal spiritual malaise of the historical. In the period immediately following this shift, revolutionary radicalism came to be articulated in the form of an aesthetic absolutism, a depoliticized 'politics' that found extreme expression in the 'aesthetics of death' as the most direct, radical and pure act of realizing one's spirituality.

3 Uneasy with the modern
The postwar revival of the modern and the return of dissent

> Through the previous eras of left wing movements, fascism and war, and the more recent days of democratic revolution – through these periods of hope, despair, and hope again; of light, darkness, and light again – what I discovered was humanity as beautiful yet ignoble, ignoble yet beautiful. I learned to recognize pettiness in the great, and greatness in the petty. Recounting this journey will help to somehow define the substance of our 'second youth.'
>
> Ara Masato, 'Dai ni no seishun'

> I don't deny that the day brought me something like relief or loss at the realization that all was over. My moral attitude towards war, however, checked that thought right away. I remember feeling an uncomfortable self-hate as I seemed to espy a rift of falsity in my awareness of war and death. From the following day on, I was tortured by a sense of guilt I experienced as one who happened to have survived. I was not certain why I felt guilty; but the largest portion of that guilt seems to stem from the fact that I had driven myself idealistically toward death, convinced that the moment of Japan's surrender would be the moment of death. I was embarrassed that that thought now exposed its miserable corpse.
>
> Yoshimoto Takaaki, 'Takamura Kōtarō'

> August 15 was a humiliating event for me. Humiliation to *the nation* and humiliation to *myself*. . . . We, either as *minzoku* or as *individuals*, seem to have faced August 15 like a bunch of fools. Compared to Korea and China, this is unbearably shameful.
>
> Takeuchi Yoshimi, 'Kutsujyoku no Jiken'

Introduction

The end of the war and the beginning of the occupation ushered in a new era and a spiritual renewal for the Japanese nation, not by 'overcoming modernity' as wartime Japanese intellectuals had imagined, but by installing democratic institutions and values. Postwar Japanese discourse rewrote Japanese political history by reviving the overthrown 'modern' political order and discursive climate and by taking up the previously abandoned modernist path. In the years immediately following the cessation of hostilities this revival of modern ideas and institutions was generally welcomed by all segments of war-torn society; indeed, few opposing voices, if any, were raised to the modernist trajectory, and US soldiers were seen as liberators by the general public. That liberation was brought to Japan by the victorious US occupation force could be seen as ironic, but this irony went largely unrecognized, or was conveniently overlooked, in the dominant intellectual discourse of the time. In some ways this negligence probably helped the nation effect a rapid transformation from a military to a democratic regime, as well as enabling the creation of a common consensus about the desirability of 'democratic revolution.' Seen from a longer-term perspective, however, it now appears rather unfortunate that postwar Japanese intellectuals did not make a more concerted effort to come to terms with the past by critically examining the nation's troubled relation with modernity, and elected instead to overthrow its shadow by simply condemning Japanese cultural tradition as the cause of the problems and to condemn it as a 'feudalistic remainder.' Given these factors, it was hardly surprising, then, that the Japanese postwar democratic revolution stumbled when US foreign policy changed at the beginning of the Cold War. Indeed, once the initial celebratory period of liberation had passed, the postwar modernist trajectory was subject to a number of revisions, its enlightenment assumptions were subject to harsh scrutiny, and, within less than two decades, 'the problematic of the modern' returned to the centre stage of Japanese intellectual discourse once again.

In the first section of Chapter 3, I attempt to unearth what lies beneath this uneasy relation between Japanese society and the postwar modernist democratic trajectory by looking at intellectual discourses in the years of political turmoil between 1945 and 1960. Following this section, I then sketch the intellectual and political climate in the years immediately following the war, with particular focus on the following three issues: the policy guidelines of the Supreme Commander for Allied Forces (SCAP) that defined the general frame of the postwar political trajectory; the cleavages and general problematics identified in that trajectory by the new opinion leaders of the literary discourse; and the early postwar works of Maruyama Masao which perhaps best represent the consensus of informed opinion at the time and were the guiding theory for the revival of the enlightened national trajectory. This initial trajectory was soon overshadowed, however, by changes in US occupation policy in the late 1940s reflecting the beginning of the Cold-War regime. The second section of Chapter 3 then discusses the changing political and intellectual climate from the time of the so-called 'reverse course' in the late 1940s and the early 1950s, to the popular protests against the renewal of the US–Japan Security Treaty in 1960. During these years, while there was a groundswell of popular consciousness and a consensus for democracy and peace that culminated in the anti US–Japan Security Treaty movement (Anpo), the largest democratic protests in Japanese history, the realization of Japan's postwar modernist trajectory was frustrated by state power politics backed up by the US military. The last section of this chapter deals with the vigorous and fundamental criticisms of the enlightened democratic project that surfaced in the second postwar decade, when, in the years following the disappointing experience of the anti-Treaty movement, such criticisms were widely popularized. I focus particularly on the works of Yoshimoto Takaaki and Takeuchi Yoshimi that eloquently articulated the problems inherent in the notion of political enlightenment and called into question Japan's uncritical acceptance of the postwar modernist path from the standpoint of national self-determination and the everyday life of the people.

Back to the modern: ideas and the political climate of early postwar Japan

SCAP's role in postwar democratic reform

Shortly after the signing of the Potsdam Declaration (July 1945), all American prisoners of war and some Japanese political prisoners were released and the political and military institutions that had formed the infrastructure of the wartime regime were dissolved. The Allied occupation forces, however, went much further than simply demilitarizing the nation; they launched a grand experiment of transplanting Western democratic institutions into Japan in an effort to forestall the possibility of Japan's re-emergence as a threat to the West. By ambitiously furnishing Japan with a nearly complete basic institutional framework for liberal democracy based on a party representative system, the democratic reforms promulgated by the Supreme Commander for Allied Forces (SCAP) framed the terms in which postwar Japanese history, and indeed all the spheres of postwar Japanese social life, would be seen. As a first step towards the establishment of a democratic polity, the major political parties – Liberal, Socialist and Communist Parties – were established as representative of the people by the end of 1945, and universal suffrage inclusive of adult women came into place. The Japanese Imperial Court, which was believed to be at the core of the prewar social order, was maintained by reducing the status of the emperor to a cultural symbol in a manner similar to a constitutional monarchy. In January 1946, emperor Hirohito made a public speech renouncing his divinity and thus officially ending his role as the sovereign subject directly representing the Japanese people. In the same year, aiming at a radical redistribution of rural incomes, SCAP enforced the major land reforms and dissolved many large corporate-capital enterprises that, together with the war sympathizers, who had formed the *de facto* prewar government, were expelled from all public offices. With the arrival of the new Constitution in May 1947, SCAP-led installation of modern, democratic institutions was largely completed.

While the establishment of these democratic institutions was planned by and executed under the authority of SCAP, the long-term task of making these institutions work was left to the Japanese people. Victor Koschmann has pointed out that the Potsdam Declaration, whose guiding principle was 'the classical liberal view of democracy,' in the sense that it 'tasks society with ensuring the freedom and equality of all its members who are understood to be rational, individual agents endowed with formal rights,' was curiously lacking in philosophical content.[1] The vaguely liberal philosophical standpoint of the Declaration was evident in its universalist and humanist language emphasizing the values of 'individual liberties,' 'human rights' and other liberal institutions, all assumed to be unproblematically applicable to the historically and culturally particular postwar Japanese context. This rationale was exemplified in such phrases from the Declaration as: 'The Japanese people shall be encouraged to develop a desire for individual liberties and respect for fundamental human rights . . .'; 'Democratic political parties, with rights of assembly and public discussion, shall be encouraged . . .'; and 'The judicial, legal, and police systems shall be reformed as soon as practicable to conform to the policies set forth . . .'[2] In other words, what was normally assumed to be present in order for liberal democratic institutions to be in effect was somehow thought to be in the same instance instituted by the proposed institutional mechanism. In a sense, this meant that Japanese society was left with the task of making its socio-cultural content conform with the bestowed legal and institutional form, that is, forming the nation based on a given state model, rather than forming the state on the basis of the specificity of the nation. This was the path postwar Japan was to pursue under the guidance of the occupation forces.

The difficulties of launching such a demanding task were not underestimated by SCAP. Indeed, SCAP's awareness of these difficulties stands out clearly in a number of public pronouncements made by General MacArthur during the occupation, for instance in his 'Message to the Japanese People on the First Anniversary of the Constitution' (May 3rd, 1948). The discourse is framed around the twin poles of the enlightenment ideals of civilization and progress, and 'the resolute will of the people':

> One year ago your new constitution became the supreme law of the land, and the cause of human freedom advanced as a mantle of personal dignity thereby fell upon every Japanese citizen. The people turned their eyes toward the dawn of a higher concept of life, heralded by a charter which provides the design for a political and social edifice resting upon the pillars of liberty.
>
> Adapted from the experience of the ages, this charter embodies the most enlightened advance in the concept of human relationship which

civilization thus far has been able to evolve, and as it now stands it lags behind none in form, substance, or in progressive thought. But the written word alone gives only indirect protection to the rights and privileges which it ordains. Such protection resides actually in the resolute will of the people in whom the sovereign power dwells.[3]

The 'Message' notes several times over that progress has been made 'in the reshaping of Japanese life to conform to Japan's constitutional mandates,' while emphasizing that the principles of the charter alone are insufficient and that the 'immutable' 'concept of human freedom' now must be translated into 'living actuality.'[4] Along this line of ideas, it calls upon the 'spiritual strength of the people,' their 'growing consciousness of public responsibility,' and the vital role of a 'free, responsible and courageous press … in order that the people wherein sovereignty rests may make sound political decisions with minds uncorrupted by slanted, distorted or false propaganda.'[5]

In the same collection of US State Department papers housing this speech, Section XII, entitled 'Political Education,' introduces the rationale for democratic reform in Japan in a tone of guarded reserve concerning its potential:

> Governmental and political reforms are inevitably bound up with the problem of political education. It is evident that a new Constitution and legislation required to implement it, however enlightened, will ultimately prove ineffectual unless broadly based on popular understanding and support.[6]

In order to foster understanding and support, SCAP put the Japanese mass media under a strict regimen that included direct control of the press and radio, prepublication and prebroadcast censorship and even a ban on information about the censorship system itself that kept the public 'almost totally uninformed and unaware of the practice,' as well as promoting a series of initiatives disseminating information on radio, in the press, and through posters about the new constitution, legal protections and individual rights.[7] The aim of these efforts, in the words of the report, was 'to awaken' the people:

> It is imperative, therefore, that all measures be taken to insure the permanence of the democratic structure being erected in Japan, a structure that can only be established on the solid foundation of an informed citizenry. An awakened people, conscious of their sovereignty and fully aware of their privileges and responsibilities as members of a democratic state, represent the only real insurance against the possibility of eventual perversion by aggressive and unscrupulous extremists of the objectives achieved during the Occupation.[8]

The democratic experiment was from the beginning handicapped by a number of factors: a lack of thorough US commitment to Japanese reforms, SCAP's lack of resources, personnel and appropriate knowledge of Japan, and thus a lack of scrutiny vis-à-vis the implementation of reform measures.[9] More importantly, the nature of the reforms was framed and circumscribed by the US geo-political interest in transforming Japan for the purpose of possible future benefits, and indeed by the end of the decade, many of the reforms would be rolled back or blunted by new legislation in the context of the advent of the Cold War.

This US-centred perspective set the tone for Japanese postwar social reconstruction and the Japanese postwar intellectual discourse, inclining them both towards a democratic reformation of society along liberal democratic lines based upon enlightenment values. A further result was the general neglect of those issues that fell to the outside of US interests. Instead of a coming to terms with the various problems that had been accumulating in the nation in the years leading up to and including the war, the end of the war saw a proclamation of Japan's liberation from the oppressive military regime and a general jettisoning of the prewar intellectual heritage that had raised so many doubts and questions about the modern Japanese national trajectory. Moreover, because the predominant focus of the postwar political process was directed towards issues of US–Japanese concern, postwar Japanese intellectual discourse has largely and boldly understated Japan's wartime military expansionism in Asia. This bias has strongly influenced the status quo interpretation of the Pacific War in Japan, a narrative which until this day tends to focus on Japan's tragic experiences at Hiroshima and Nagasaki and emphasizes Japan's commitment to peace – a narrative that Andrew Barshay has described as 'liberation and victimization,' and one which has bluntly failed to come to terms with Japan's war responsibility to Asia.[10]

Cleavages in early postwar literary discourse

Although some nationalistically inclined contemporary Japanese intellectuals have attempted to portray the first years of postwar Japan as a defeated society bristling under the oppressive yoke of the US occupying forces, this is a highly misleading picture.[11] Many Leftist intellectuals have retrospectively claimed that the occupation constituted the greatest period of freedom in postwar Japanese history because the oppressive state war machine which had harassed and tormented them for over a decade had been dismantled wholesale. Honda Shūgo, for one, characterized the time as one in which 'both emptiness (*kyodatsu*) and limitless expectations swarmed above the intellectual barren (*shisōteki haikyo*),' a state in which Japan's near complete material destruction paradoxically opened up a freedom of the imagination and was closely associated with utopian hopes for reconstruction.[12] Freed from the strict wartime political controls and censorship, a number of new Leftist journals, such as *Shin Nihon Bungaku, Kindai Bungaku, Tenbō, Sekai, Sekai Bungaku, Gunzō*, sprung up. Two of these journals played an especially significant role in early postwar intellectual movements: *Kindai Bungaku* (*Modern Literature*) and *Shin Nihon Bungaku* (*New Japan Literary Review*). While *Shin Nihon Bungaku* pursued a democratic literary politics along the lines of proletarian literature and Communist Party guidelines, *Kindai Bungaku* on the other hand pursued a more inclusive and broader intellectual–cultural agenda along generally liberal lines and was rather tolerant of various notions of the autonomy of art from politics. These two journals largely defined the initial frame of the main problematics to be dealt with in the early postwar intellectual discourse.

The degree of influence that Communism enjoyed both in political and intellectual spheres in the immediate postwar years is somewhat difficult to grasp from today's standpoint. The Japan Communist Party (JCP) was given credit as the sole organization to have resisted the war and the state militarist regime, perhaps because most of its leaders, unlike other oppositional figures who either remained silent or passively followed the war regime, had been imprisoned throughout the war. The *Shin Nihon Bungakukai* (*New Japan Literary Society*) was formed in 1946 by former proletarian writers led by Kurahara Korehito under the auspices of the Communist Party. Kurahara had published a two-part article in the *Tokyo Shinbun* in November 1945 that was a sort of Communist literary manifesto for postwar Japan.[13] Framing his discourse largely along the lines of the prewar proletarian literary movements, Kurahara, strongly influenced by Marxist–Leninist epistemology, located literature in the superstructure of a base-superstructure model as a didactic medium. Looking back on the literary discourses of prewar Japan, Kurahara saw the intimate relationship between state political oppression and the anti-realist literary inclinations that had surfaced in the 1930s when writers had increasingly retreated into the realm of the 'subjective.'[14] On the basis of this analysis, Kurahara emphasized that it was important for literary work to convey a sense of the material world and to situate the writer vis-à-vis the general state of social life:

> First of all, writers must recover the element of reality that has been missing from literature, and reproduce within literary works the true circumstances and voice of the people. They must restore to literature its artistic value by accurately and vividly portraying the reality that has been distorted in the past ... it is first necessary that our writers should know reality, and in order to know reality they must live and fight with, and share the happiness and misery of, the people.[15]

This call for 'the element of reality' was derived from Kurahara's literary realist epistemology and was a core element of the *Shin Nihon Bungakukai*'s historical materialist position in which the distinction between 'the subjective,' ideas and cultural elements, and 'the objective,' the economic structure, was assumed.¹⁶ The last sentence of the quotation gives evidence of Kurahara's view that writers were not only to play a role in guiding politico-cultural transformations but also that they were leaders of socialist revolution, and as such it was their intellectual duty to 'live and fight with the people.'

Kurahara's 'manifesto' urged Leftist intellectuals to form an alternative literary circle, *Kindai Bungaku*, committed to the full expression of subjective creativity.¹⁷ The founding members of *Kindai Bungaku* – Honda Shūgo, Hirano Ken, Haniya Yutaka, Ara Masato, Yamamuro Shizuka, Sasaki Kiichi and Odagiri Hideo – were all in their thirties, substantially younger than the core members of *Shin Nihon Bungakukai*; most of them had experience in the prewar anti-militarist Leftist movements and some of them were imprisoned as a result. The leader of the circle, Honda Shūgo, wrote a counter-manifesto to Kurahara's in which he presented his objections to the idea of the writer's 'selfless devotion' to the goal of social transformation. In the opening passage of 'Geijutsu, rekishi, ningen' ('Art, History, Human') published in the first issue of the circle's journal in January 1946, Honda, referring to the literary achievements of Tolstoy, wrote:

> Simply put, I think there is no other way, in a literary sense, than for *petty-bourgeois* and intellectual writers to unabashedly remain *petty-bourgeois* and intellectual writers, in order to live and struggle together with the people. The works of Tolstoy, especially the early half of his works, are extremely aristocratic. And yet, these works reach out to the realm of eternity. *Petty-bourgeois* and intellectual writers can also make some meagre contribution to humanity. To do so, however, there is no other possible way for them than to be honest to the inner necessity of *petty-bourgeois* and intellectual writers themselves.¹⁸

Honda himself was a proletarian literary critic and respected Kurahara's devotion to the prewar proletarian movement, although a sense of guilt about his failure to resist the war made his objections to *Shin Nihon Bungaku* cautious and weak. A more outspoken voice expressing the common emotional landscape of the circle, perhaps shared by many educated Japanese, was that of Ara Masato, whose 'Dai ni no seishun' ('The Second Youth') Honda published in the second issue of *Kindai Bungaku*, convinced it would make the journal famous.¹⁹ Ara's 'often dramatic, flamboyant style' of writing, exploiting juxtapositions and ironical reversals of meaning, was seen as an optimistic (or for some, even opportunistic) celebration of a hopeful vision of the future, albeit in a heavily ironized tone for which he and the circle were later criticized.²⁰ Despite these problems, *Kindai Bungaku* nevertheless secured an open intellectual space in the early postwar era, becoming a literary forum for the advancement of a broadly defined democratic movement outside the literary realist movement informed by political goals. It engaged the major issues and the immediate concerns of the educated Japanese of the time, such as the question of the intellectuals' war responsibility, the relation between politics and literature, and the role of subjectivity.

The main issues of disagreement between the two literary circles were clarified in the first issue of *Kindai Bungaku* when Kurahara was invited to a round table with five members of the journal's editorial board. One of the central issues of debate concerned the difficulties of representing 'the people' and the political responsibility of writers. For example, in objection to Kurahara's party-line literary project, Sasaki Kiichi claimed that literature is 'not just a matter of objective reality ... but of the human spirit which confronts that reality'; a similar concern was raised by Haniya Yutaka who wondered whether it might not be the case that the 'new politics' of the postwar era would soon make unreasonable demands upon literature.'[21] In response, Kurahara emphasized that writers had to incorporate in their work the interests and concerns of the people as a way of reflecting the objective historical reality of the times.[22] These points of view clearly reflected different conceptions of what literature should be: from *Kindai Bungaku*'s perspective, *Shin Nihon Bungaku*'s historical materialist position – exemplified by Kurahara's insistence that the writer 'align one's subjectivity with real historical developments' and his statement that 'a writer has to move as closely as possible to the standpoint of the people' – was 'insufficiently sensitive to the human, subjective dimensions of history and creativity.'[23] For the *Kindai Bungaku* circle literature was not something which could be programmed, but rather something 'residual' in the historical development of the world, something 'aesthetic' as Honda claims, in the sense that it remained outside 'the political.' On the other hand, from Kurahara's perspective the *Kindai Bungaku* circle was preoccupied with defending the autonomy of the realm of free expression from politics; for Kurahara, the expression of subjective experience without a reflection of the 'objective reality' failed to come to terms with the problems of the prewar literary movements that had increasingly forced them into the corner of a subjectivism isolated from the outside world.

These two expressions of differing concerns and positions can be seen as contributing to the wealth of postwar literary discourse and the question of the priority of commitment to politics or literature. However, the debate was somewhat unproductively fuelled by the tendency of both parties to juxtapose literature and politics along the lines of a 'subjective' versus 'objective' opposition, and some members of *Kindai Bungaku* denounced the politically inclined literary stance of their antagonists, pointedly criticizing their devotion to social causes. In his criticism of what he saw as *Shin Nihon Bungaku*'s pedantic project of 'literature for people,' Ara Masato argued that the writing subject could only represent his or her own experience: the expression of 'various elements of our inner self,' he claimed, '... should be the starting point of literature.'[24] Ara emphasized that it was through an investigation of the self rather than through observation of the people that the writer 'will connect in a literary sense with the people.'[25] This in itself was a respectable point, but Ara went further, denying any progressive potential for the literary subject altogether by arguing that 'political activity could occur only as an extension of self-centredness, not at its expense,' and comparing *Shin Nihon Bungaku*'s adherence to the Party policy-line as equivalent to the wartime 'blind worship' of the emperor.[26] With this wholesale negation of political agency in literature, Ara reconceived 'humanism' as the egoistic pursuit of self-interest, going so far as to claim that 'Petty bourgeois egoism itself shows love for the people and amounts to the highest humanism.'[27] Even granting the possibility of locating the moral ground of the subject in his or her interiority, rather than in the social and external, as Ara might have intended, his affirmation of egoism troubled many and invited pointed counter-criticisms.[28] Nakano Shigeharu, for one, countered that the notion of an absolute literary freedom at the expense of political commitment, and especially Ara's explicit advocacy of egoism, rendered the content of *Kindai Bungaku* writers' democratic manifesto doubtful and demeaning. In his series of critical essays 'hihyo no ningensei,' published in the early issues of *Shin Nihon Bungaku*, Nakano highlighted three symptoms of what he saw as the emergence of a reactionary literary trend – the attempts to forget and forgive the war, the prevalence of 'carnal literature,' and the 'erotic literature' that separated the realm of amorous relations from the greater concerns of humanity – implicitly critcizing the position taken by *Kindai Bungaku*, and especially those of Ara and Hirano Ken.[29]

Beyond these two leading literary groups, there were others who remained relatively unaffected by the powerful historical and intellectual currents of the time and continued to focus on their own interests. These figures, often grouped together as the *Burai-ha*, included writers such as Dazai Osamu, Sakaguchi Ango and Oda Sakunosuke.[30] The literary critic Okuno Takeo recalled in 1982 the early postwar literary scene when he and many other young writers passionately read the *Burai-ha* writers' work, finding in them 'true words which could not be found in other writers and intellectuals'; in Okuno's recollection they were able to put into words what many anonymous youths of the time were feeling.[31] According to Okuno, these 'true words' were often to be found in the silence, or the sense of shame and modesty that characterized writers like Dazai who refrained from participating in any of the then current literary debates.[32] What won Okuno's trust was Dazai's sensitive perception of Japan's unconditional surrender as leaving him 'feel[ing] ashamed to the extent [that he] could not say anything.'[33] Interpreting Dazai's increasingly self-destructive inclinations as a reflection of a deepening despair in the face of the intellectual dishonesty and corruption of the times, Okuno reflects that:

> Although Japan had accepted the shameful unconditional surrender, the essence of the Japanese had not changed in the slightest. Far from

a human revolution, they were unchangingly clinging to stingy and ugly egoism. And the leaders [of the war] and the intellectuals were far from being ashamed; they continued to shamelessly and happily write and talk about their ideas and activities with no hesitation, trying to ride the tide of the times. These words and actions germinated and circulated on their own, whereas those who remained in silence, out of a deep sense of shame, sorrow, and pain, struggled in a desperate search for a new birth.[34]

Putting aside the question of to what degree Dazai's inclination for self-destruction was related to the postwar sense of intellectual and politico-cultural malaise, it was nevertheless the case that, as Okuno suggests, many of those who reflected deeply on their experience of the war remained silent or sought to answer questions about it in more reflexive and uniquely personal ways rather than hastily jumping onto the band wagon of occasional issues raised according to the demands of the times. In this context, the *Burai-ha* writers were perhaps truer to their convictions in not being bothered to justify their positions and instead 'practising' the freedom of literature from politics rather than discussing it.

Recalling the early postwar years, Honda, the leader of *Kindai Bungaku*, self-critically wrote in 1982 that the members of the circle largely refrained from reflecting on the presence of the occupation forces and the international power politics that provided the basic framework for the postwar Japanese democratic revolution. As a result, he reflected, the *Kindai Bungaku* circle was overly optimistic and confident about the democratic potential of postwar Japan, as if they themselves were in charge of the matter.[35] Honda stated that he later felt a deep sense of shame and regret when he realized that 'what had eliminated the oppressive pressures [of the wartime regime] was not the efforts of the Japanese,' and that his self-critical awareness of the true realities in the early postwar years was 'far too insufficient.'[36] What Honda retrospectively came to understand was the significance of the American occupation policy in the current of postwar literature, the fact that previously suppressed creative energies were shaped within the framework it provided and channelled towards democracy and the peace movement. Certainly, it would be unfair, however, to denounce the early postwar intellectuals all together a quarter of a century later, for such criticisms are safely situated in a privileged position outside the historical context of the times and its particular limitations. Our task, then, is to analyse the context in which the majority of postwar Japanese intellectuals failed to detect the presence of an external political agenda behind the rhetoric of democracy they uncritically accepted as their own.

The postwar 'democratic revolution' and its critics: Maruyama Masao and the 'old liberals'

In contrast to the leaders of the prewar and wartime intellectual discourse, largely philosophers and literary critics, the intellectuals who played a central role in the early postwar discourse were social-scientists, many of whom were conscious of the immediate impact of their theories upon current issues. These postwar intellectuals, who together were called the 'modernists,' irrespective of their diversity of orientations and their self-designations, included Ōtsuka Hisao, Kuno Osamu, Shimizu Ikutarō, Umemoto Katsumi, Mashita Shin'ichi, and, perhaps the most influential of the group, Maruyama Masao. These Leftists, like their literary counterparts, could be broadly categorized into Marxist and liberal camps; however, they could also be seen as a single group since they shared the common goal of a democratic national trajectory inspired by enlightenment ideals, and since the commonly accepted notion of 'democratic revolution' implied a sense of solidarity.[37] In order to better evaluate the possibilities and limitations of the democratic revolution led by these progressive, popularly supported intellectuals, one needs to examine the substance and underlying assumptions of the modern enlightenment ideas they upheld in the early postwar era, as well as the various objections raised against them. For this purpose I will discuss in the following sections, first, the main ideas and assumptions of Maruyama Masao's Enlightenment Project because they perhaps best exemplify the then leading theory of 'democratic revolution,' both in terms of its content and the powerful influence it was to have, and second, the ideas of the 'old liberals' who largely maintained in the postwar period their prewar positions, against the tide of the times.

Maruyama Masao and his Enlightenment Project

Many of his contemporaries have expressed the exhilaration they experienced upon first reading Maruyama Masao's 'Chōkokka shugi no Ronri to shisō' ('The Logic and Psychology of Ultranationalism'), written during the war and published in 1945.[38] The lucidity and cogency of Maruyama's analysis of the causes and the mechanism of Japanese wartime 'ultra-nationalism' had an enormous impact upon the early postwar intellectual scene, and played a decisive role in shaping intellectual orientations in the early postwar political trajectory. Maruyama himself was aware of his leading role in what he saw as the enlightenment mission of the intellectual, and his determination arose from his experience of the war. Referring to the role Fukuzawa had played in Meiji Japan, Maruyama argued:

> If Japan should properly develop as a modern nation, some leading intellectuals have to carry out the daunting task of awakening in the

Japanese masses, who had known until then nothing other than passively obeying the existing political order, and their active subjective status as members of the nation. In so awakening, the intellectuals would help them internalize the national and political environment, which used to be seen as the external, into their individual political consciousnesses.[39]

This description of the intellectual's role in guiding the masses towards national enlightenment is one expression of Maruyama's self-defined task of initiating and stewarding the postwar Japanese democratization project, a project intended to transform the nation into a new social organization governed by the rule of the law and democratic institutions, and constituted by publicly responsible citizens.

In his celebrated article on Japanese 'ultranationalism,' Maruyama identified as the essential feature of its rise the failure to create the preconditions for democratic institutions and the lack of a democratic subject who understood, supported and enhanced a democratic social order. More specifically, he saw the core defect of modern Japanese society as lying in the inadequate separation of spiritual and political authorities; that is, unlike the European political systems that had grounded a separation between moral principles defined by law and the sovereign state as their executors, such a separation had never been clear in Japan.[40] Maruyama believed that this lack of separation in Japan had resulted from a failure to establish both a distinction between the public and private domains, a distinction necessary for the proper operation of a democratic system, and a set of objective legal criteria and political procedures existing above and beyond the state, unaffected by its arbitrary exercise of power.[41] The task of establishing the socio-cultural pre-conditions for a workable democracy had, he believed, never seriously been attempted in modern Japanese history, even during the time of the 'people's rights' movements, and given this lack of democratic foundations, it was inevitable that these movements would later be subsumed under the notion of national rights. Maruyama argued that it was a decisive mistake not to 'combat first and foremost the ideology of "loyalty" ("*chūkō*" *kannen*),' by which was meant feudalistic personal relations; having failed to do so, he thought, the freedom of the autonomous subject guaranteeing the state's 'formal/institutional adequacy' (*keishiki-teki datoosei*) could never be established.[42]

By eschewing this critical process of democratic state formation, the prewar Japanese state ultimately ended up reifying political and moral authority in the figure of the emperor as the sovereign subject, a reification, Maruyama believed, that lay at the core of prewar ultranationalism:

> The reason that the activities of the state are not subject to moral criteria beyond the state is ... because absolute value is thought of as being reified in the sovereign subject itself. That is because the

sovereign subject is thought to be 'always and everywhere the ultimate manifestation of truth-morality-beauty.' ... Such a standpoint can also be explained as the imbrication ('*sōgo inyū*') of morality and power. Where state sovereignty is the ultimate source of morality and political power, and the two are immediately united into one, morality is not internalized by the subject, and thereby, it [morality] is constantly driven toward authoritarianism.[43]

In this system, Maruyama observes, both acts of state and human relations are determined by those directly above one in the hierarchy, and the system as a whole is structured by an oppressive chain of command from superior to inferior.[44] Maruyama saw in this system a remainder of the feudalistic human relations that had been deeply ingrained in the consciousness and behaviour of the Japanese populace. He characterized wartime Japanese power as a 'system of irresponsibility,' in the sense that there was no ultimately identifiable location of responsibility, since the actions of individuals were based solely on loyalty to one's immediate superiors instead of to objective moral criteria. Even the emperor, the supposed centre of power in wartime Japan, argues Maruyama, was exempt from responsibility, because what authorized his power did not stem from his person, nor from the loyalty of the people, but rather was rooted in the unbroken imperial reign of his predecessors.

These findings led Maruyama to conclude that a Japanese civil society could only be created on the basis of a rational and autonomous subject who, having internalized universal moral principles, thinks and acts to further democratic goals. For Maruyama, one of the most disturbing aspects of the Japanese war experience was the manner in which the populace perceived the war, as if it were something that had befallen them like 'fate,' beyond their control and against their will.[45] He argues that this sense of popular passivity, people seeing themselves as having absolutely no control, no power to affect, and thus, no responsibility over historical events, was the cause and the manifestation of prewar Japan's ultimate failure to establish a strong democratic social order. It was this lack of political agency in the prewar Japanese subject that had permitted the 'system of irresponsibility' to rule. From this past experience of failure to come to terms with the modern – i.e. the triumph of ultranationalism – Maruyama unhesitatingly drew the conclusion that if Japan were to become modern and democratic it would first be necessary to transform the core of the 'system of irresponsibility,' that is, ultimately, to alter the mind-set of the Japanese populace from a feudalistic mode of passive obedience to a rational, autonomous, and progressive one. To this end, Maruyama, drawing from the Meiji enlightenment philosopher and politician Fukuzawa Yukichi, elaborated an ideal model of the modern enlightenment subject, his indispensable intellectual contribution to the postwar Japanese project of democratic revolution.

As Maruyama himself acknowledged, it was the enlightenment ideas of Fukuzawa that had the greatest influence on his early formation. In his 1947 article based on a reading of Fukuzawa's ideas, 'Fukuzawa ni okeru "jitsugaku" no tenkai,' Maruyama lauds Fukuzawa's identification of 'the secret of the stagnation of Eastern societies in the lack of mathematical understanding and the autonomous mind' and his emphasis on the necessary inculcation of these traits as a means of overcoming the stagnant socio-political condition.[46] Maruyama interprets Fukuzawa's emphasis on mathematics and physics, unlike the conventional emphasis on ethics, as being of central import to modernizing Japan since he also believes that 'the greatest task in Japanese modernization is first and foremost the question of understanding the "spirit" of civilization,' or the 'spirit' that produced modern science.[47] In his critique of the philosophy of the *ancient régime*, and by extension that of an ethnically oriented Japanese studies, as subjective and static, Maruyama advocates the fostering of a modern subject capable of objective thinking:

> When man becomes aware of alienation from the social environment surrounding himself, he for the first time finds himself confronting objective nature *unmediated* by the subjective. The individual's becoming autonomous from society is simultaneously nature becoming autonomous from society, and that constitutes the establishment of objective nature, a purely *external* nature which is free from all subjective value imputations. It is only the mind that becomes aware of its *subjectivity* vis-à-vis the environment that separates 'law' from 'norms,' and liberates 'physics' from the control of 'morality' (*dōri*).[48]

What Maruyama emphasizes here is the need for the Japanese to go through this epistemological and ontological transformation in order to live and act as modern subjects who have internalized the dualistic conception of 'subjective' and 'objective.' It is this dualistic world view that Maruyama identifies as the necessary precondition to avoiding 'reification and inertia (*wakudeki*) in politics,' the very tendency that Japanese society must overcome to make democracy work.[49]

Justifying this modern epistemological position entails a belief in the presence and desirability of the transcendental perspective as a value in itself, as something one should strive to obtain. Clarifying the difference between 'the spirit of civilization' as manifest in scientific thinking, and that of 'ethics' in the *ancien régime*, Maruyama, opting for the former, argues that this choice must also entail a revolutionary change in 'the way thought permeates life.'[50] Interestingly, Maruyama lauds Fukuzawa's modern version of pragmatism as progressive, productive and rigorous for resisting the 'eas[y] compromise with "reality,"' unlike conventional pragmatism (*jitsugaku*), which 'constantly pulls back from its theoretical advances by comparing them with "reality."'[51] He goes on to characterize Fukuzawa's pragmatism as completely opposite to the attitude that adheres to the vulgar everyday routine; it was something that must be continuously regenerated by the *power of the imagination* motivated to overcome such everyday routine by opening up the unknown future. To put it paradoxically, therefore, it is the incessant forward movement towards 'abstract,' which the philosophy of the *ancien régime* avoided more than anything, that was thought [by Fukuzawa] to be a guarantor of a *superior* unification of life and philosophy.[52]

One can vaguely sense behind the Fukuzawa–Maruyama version of pragmatism an optimistic belief in rationality and science as if only they were capable of providing the possible means for guiding society and the individual towards the realization of a greater good.[53] Indeed, the ideal modern man as envisaged by Maruyama is, adapting Fukuzawa's vision of an 'entirely new human-type,' 'an energetically struggling human type (*huntou-teki ningen*)' who 'consistently organizes his everyday life based on foresight and planning, and is untiringly motivated to opening up new frontiers of life through trial and error.'[54] Left outside of Maruyama's discussion is any sense of the possible down-side of such an ideal type and society, that is, the potential negative consequences of transforming an empirically based and culturally specific life into an abstract society embodying the 'spirit of civilization' under its transcendental gaze.

The dualistic subject and society that internalizes 'the spirit of civilization,' characteristics Maruyama thought were the necessary preconditions for democratic revolution, have significant implications for our understanding of the difficulties experienced in established liberal democracy in Japan, and raise as well the question of its adequacy. As Victor Koschmann argues, Maruyama's view of liberal democracy strikes a curious chord with SCAP's reform policies and universalist value assumptions: Maruyama's liberal notion of freedom is 'sought through a process of self-discipline, or self-legislation, focused on the nation-state,' a process that seeks to effect a segregation of 'the private world of desire from the public world of reason,' as well as that of 'family and civil society from the state' and 'the realm of the female from that of the male.'[55] In this dualistic reconstitution of the life sphere under liberal democratic society, 'interests and desires should be introduced systematically' in each appropriate domain so that they are 'mediated and adjusted in [such] a manner' that state institutions can channel them in a predictable and controllable fashion.[56] In this way, the state's autonomy from society as well as that of individuals from the state can be simultaneously achieved, and as Maruyama argued in his 1943 work, the relation between the two becomes one in which 'the nation (*kokumin*) links itself to the state by the spontaneously made decisions of each individual,' while affirming the integrity of civil society, or the nation, as a whole.[57] This mutually autonomous, albeit systematically linked, relation, then, is mediated by the twin mechanism of the subjugation of the state to objectively codified law and political and institutional procedures, on the one hand, and the subjugation of the subject to the transcendental state authority, on the other. In liberal democratic society, therefore, '"nationalism" and "individualism" were not ... contradictory but were rather complementary aspects of a coherent political approach' (here Maruyama echoes Fukuzawa), wherein individuals are bound together as a nation under the transcendental gaze of the state that also functions as the ultimate guarantor of individual freedom.[58] It is noteworthy that this emergence of a transcendental national perspective was simultaneously constitutive of a closure that segregated Japanese national subjects from all other subjects and objectified Asian subjects under its imperial gaze. As many have noted, criticism of this aspect of the Japanese hegemonic view is absent from Maruyama's analysis.[59]

While Maruyama's dualistic conceptions of society and the subject point to the limitations of his liberal notion of democracy, a more appealing side of his thought can be found in his conception of democracy as a revolutionary processes of pursuing a utopian goal. Maruyama conceived democracy as the continuous effort of making history, or 'an eternal revolution,' to be carried out by the subject motivated to improve his or her condition by partaking in politics as a responsible citizien.[60]

> The parliamentary representative system is an institutional expression of democracy under certain historical conditions. However, the system which perfectly embodied democracy has (and will have) never existed, neither in the past nor in the future, and one can only talk about democracy in terms of more or less. In this sense, 'an eternal revolution' is precisely apposite to the term democtracy.[61]

In this conception, democracy is always in the process of creating and adjusting itself to an ever changing set of social circumstances and demands, and the subject is the principal and active participant in its definition, expression, and constitution. This notion of democracy as 'eternal revolution' came from Maruyma's analysis of his own experience of 'ultra-nationalism' (*chōkokka-shugi*), and makes him both an enlightenment modernist and revolutionary, a theorist and an activist, as indeed he was. At the same time, however, and as his critics later charged, Maruyama did not cast his critical eyes on the darker side of 'the modern,' nor did he entertain doubts about his assumed opposition between the modern and the traditional, with the former linked to democracy, freedom, and rationality, and the latter to nationalism, oppression and emotionalism. One wonders whether the 'feudal remainders' that he identified as being the root cause of Japanese ultranationalism were themselves in part products of modernization, and whether and how democratic revolution could continue once the modern itself came to be seen as problematic.

Dissenting voices of the 'old liberals' and the Kokoro group

Although the modern enlightenment perspective dominated the early postwar intellectual discourse, there were some contesting groups of intellectuals who by and large maintained their prewar cultural particularist positions and voiced their dissent at the tenor of the times. These intellectuals, many of them referred to as the 'old liberals,' took issue, from a number of differing vantage points, with the general climate of the postwar era because it appeared to them to have uncritically and opportunistically embraced the universal narrative of modernity. What particularly upset them was the way the question of war responsibility was dealt with by those Communists who urged a purge of politicians and intellectuals who had 'contributed' to the state war effort, producing a list of 1,600 'war criminals' that included local school teachers and government officials.[62] Another unfortunate incident in these years was the retroactive condemnation of all the intellectuals affiliated with the prewar Japan Romantic school (*Nihon Rōman-ha*), and most notably Yasuda Yojūrō (once seen as a figure of genius), as fascist collaborators who had endorsed 'aesthetic absolutism.' Beyond these events, however, the 'old liberals' had some fundamental disagreements not only with the modernist-led democratic revolution but also with the enlightenment ideas of a rational and autonomous subject and the progressive view of history which they saw as inhuman and alien to the Japanese cultural context.

Fukuda Tsuneari, for one, scorned the postwar trend of Leftist progressivism as groundless because it had resulted not from internal interrogation and political struggle but as a result of the external political conquest and the erasure of the past:

> There is no continuity between prewar and postwar Japan. Insofar as there is no continuity, there is no progress. Progressives, from their perspective, would want to call it a revolution; but in fact, there was only conquest. It is in their replacement of conquest with revolution and in finding that progress that their complacency and self-indulgence are manifest. However, was not the most important task for us to find continuity by bridging the gap that conquest created, or differently put, to incorporate the pseudo-revolution by the conquest into [an internal process for] progress? The Japanese progressives, however, left this task to the conservatives alone, or rather, they committed the mistake of thinking that to accept this task was itself a conservative act.[63]

Postwar Japanese conservatives were not as politically right-wing as they were often thought to be, but in view of the fact that their prewar political position was nearer to the centre or even to the left, as Fukuda argued, they were called the 'old liberals.' Although the variety of their positions is not reducible to a right/left spectrum, they were liberals in the sense that their prewar opposition to the state's ideological manipulation of the people, as well as their anti-political and anti-statist views, remained unchanged in the early postwar context. Fukuda protested against what he saw as the opportunistic transformation of intellectual orientation from anti-modern to pro-modern, vehemently arguing that it silenced opposing voices and made the necessary process of coming to terms with the past more difficult, and thereby planted unnecessarily the seeds of a future reactionary anti-modernism.

Among these 'old liberals,' however, there was a sub-group who were more specifically interested in protecting the cultural particularity and lived experience of Japan, and in their arguments one can see a continuity with the pronounced culturalist and aesthetic focus of prewar intellectual discourses. These intellectuals included Watsuji Tetsurō, Tsuda Sōkichi, Yanagida Kunio, Yanagi Sōetsu, Tanizaki Junichirō, Takamura Kōtarō, Shiga Naoya and others, many of whom came together in 1948 to establish the first major postwar conservative journal *Kokoro* (*Heart*). They strongly opposed the atomized notion of the modern subject, and while accepting and championing a notion of the unique individual in the realm of artistic creation, the majority rejected individuality on a political level, emphasizing instead the continuing significance of culturally and linguistically defined inter-subjectivity. In general, these scholars found both the Marxist conception of the state as a system of hierarchical power and the liberal institutional conception of the state as a governing mechanism legitimated by the Constitution, too abstract and lacking in a fundamental linkage connecting the individual with the social whole.[64] An anti-institutional conception of inter-subjective human organization, combined with a vision of society as a community sharing a common cultural, linguistic and historical background tied the *Kokoro* intellectuals together. Given their culturally based understanding of nation, they ultimately rejected the pursuit of enlightenment ideals, and the notion of a transcendental universal principle which lay at its core; these they saw as nothing more than impositions of a foreign logic and foreign institutions that would, they felt, seriously undermine the integrity and the autonomy of the native socio-cultural order.

These notions of society were perhaps best exemplified in Watsuji Tetsurō's attempt to redefine the concept of 'human.' Watsuji, one of the most influential philosophers of the 1930s and 1940s, re-read the two Chinese characters composing the Japanese character for 'human' (normally read as *ningen*) as *jinkan*, in order to highlight the meaning of 'human' as being 'between individuals.' As mentioned in Chapter 2, for Watsuji the Japanese socio-cultural system was built upon a network of human bonds integrated by traditional values and the neo-Confucian family code of respect for parents, harmony between spouses, solidarity among brothers, and so on. Modern subjectivity and democracy were for him nothing but the destruction of this ethico-cultural order, and its replacement by alien conceptions of time, space, and self would necessarily create internal divisions and conflicts. Moreover, in the postwar era Watsuji maintained his prewar view of the Emperor as not only the symbolic representative of the cultural unity of the Japanese people, but also as the highest moral authority of the nation. In a 1946 discussion on the radio (the only place his work could be publicized after being refused by all the major newspapers and journals), Watsuji declared his support for maintaining the Imperial Court System (*tennosei*) as the nation debated its dismantling. In order to establish the sovereignty of the people, he claimed, there was no need to destroy the Imperial Court System, because the sovereignty of the people is one and the same as the Emperor's sovereignty.[65] Moreover, he argued:

> That sovereignty resides in the people does not mean that each individual has a sovereign power. It means that the common will of the people, that is, the total will (*soui*) of the people is the highest authority of the nation. In that case, the question of how to formulate the total will of the people and how to express it becomes of crucial importance.[66]

For Watsuji, this total will cannot be formulated nor expressed by any other means than by the Emperor. Criticizing the legal scholar Sasaki Soichi's 1947 work that confirmed an inevitable change in the quality of *kokutai* (the national body) under the new Constitution, Watsuji defended the Imperial Court by arguing that the legal and institutional systems would not by themselves create a nation without the 'national body' (*kokutai*) that makes the system work. For Watsuji, the emperor's prewar role as the centre of the fascist state's ideological and political power was an accidental and rather exceptional event viewed from the perspective of the Imperial Court's long history of peaceful rule since ancient times. Underplaying the war responsibility of the Imperial Court, Watsuji attempted to avert any fundamental change in either the political or spiritual significance of the 'national symbol.' Watsuji's passionate and obstinate determination to protect the emperor system from change was shared by many members of the *Kokoro* circle. This firm anti-individualist and anti-institutionalist stance was, one assumes, a manifestation of their fear of losing the sense of communal unity which was integral to their own sense of identity, and thus their conservative, anti-political attitude was permeated by an intolerant rejection of the idea underlying the democratic process, that of mediation, negotiation and compromise among conflicting values and interests.

What is curious about the way 'old liberals' opposed both the revival of the modern and the subjectivity upheld by the liberal progressives and the Marxists was their grounding of their opposition on a concept of the 'human.' It is noteworthy that the word in Japanese for 'subjectivity' – *shutaisei* – has as many negative connotations, i.e. 'antisocial' and 'selfish,' as positive ones, i.e. autonomous, and self-controlling. In addition, in Japanese academic discourse the epistemological separation between the subject and the object is not as nearly well grounded as it is in the Western metaphysical tradition. The word 'human' ('*ningen*') was elected by the *Kokoro* intellectuals to designate the collectively oriented humane subject as opposed to the atomized rational subject. This value-difference was also reflected in the Japanese interpretation of the word 'history.' In his 1952 work 'Rekishi no gaku ni okeru "hito" no kaifuku' ('The recovery of the "Human" in the Study of History'), Tsuda Sōkichi, an outspoken *Kokoro* member, railed against the modern conception of history as an anti-human destruction of the lived experience of people inside history. As the following passage demonstrates, Tsuda conceived 'history' as 'the process of human life' in terms quite distinct from what is commonly understood by the term in the scholarly community of the West.[67]

> To know history is to replicate the concrete process of human life experience into one's consciousness as concrete as it is ... the method of writing history must be a description of history as it is known, that is, it must be a concrete description of the process of concrete life experience as it is. To write history means to replicate and describe history in its making from one moment to another in the way it is made, *by standing in the position of the one who participated in that process*.[68]

In this relativist and contextualist account of history as a recording of an insiders' 'lived experience,' the analytic representation of 'history' by an observer outside the historical process does not qualify as true or valid. According to Tsuda, such 'scientific history,' the history written in the modern social sciences, reduces and depreciates human experience into a set of scientific laws governed by causal relations in a present-centred and linearly reductive temporal scheme. Describing his version of 'history as human-centered' and contrasting it with what he sees as the social scientific, mechanistic version of modern history, Tsuda calls for 'a recovery of the "human" from the destruction by a mechanized civilization and social life' that is, he feels, imminent.[69]

> If [historians] lose a sense of self and 'humanity' (*hito*), by being overpowered by mechanical civilization and thus treating human life in a mechanical manner, or by losing control to the forces of the mass and being carried away into the current trend, history cannot be [properly] understood nor described. In order to recover the 'human' in the study of history, historians must first recover 'humanity' in themselves.[70]

Undergirding Tsuda's criticisms of an 'anti-human' and 'social scientific' notion of history is his firm rejection of the enlightenment metaphysical assumptions of linear progressive time, positivist epistemology separating man from nature, and logocentrism subordinating concrete experience, the senses, and beauty to reason. These elements of modernity, Tsuda believes, are the means by which a corrosive rationalism penetrates the harmonious human community operating in a traditional mode of temporality under the guidance of traditional values. From a modern perspective, on the other hand, Tsuda's 'history' is beyond rational discourse's critique, and his socio-cultural community would inescapably conflict with the authority of universal moral codes and the operation of democratic institutions. In this sense, Tsuda's position, together with that of most of the other *Kokoro* group members, represents a renewed form of cultural particularist resistance to universalism. One wonders whether Tsuda believed that the creation of an alternative democracy in which native discourse was not subordinated to transcendental moral authority was possible. By virtue of conceiving historical experience outside of modern ideas and rejecting its subordination to modern institutions, Tsuda attempted to maintain the unique temporal and spatial order of Japan in a manner similar to the prewar romantics who had fixed the native cultural space in an idealized mode.

It should be noted that Japanese intellectuals of different political positions did enjoy a brief period of (relative) collaboration, sharing the common goals of peace and democracy in the immediate postwar years, albeit never being completely at ease with one another. However, this short 'honeymoon period' came to an end by the early 1950s, when the Japanese power elite – backed by the US anti-Communist foreign policy initiatives that signalled the advent of the Cold War – consolidated itself. Thus, these first fundamental challenges to the enlightenment discourse did not really emerge in full force until a decade later when, as I discuss in the last section, a critical analysis of the war, nationalism, and the early postwar democratic trajectory were undertaken in the broader frame of Japan's experience of modernity as a whole. In the context of the rapidly changing politico-cultural climate of the early 1950s, however, cleavages between groups began to enlarge, increasingly opening up a space for the initially suppressed voices to reemerge.

From the 'reverse course' to the Anpo movement: the end of 'democracy from above' and the rise of popular movements

The 'reverse course'

The course of the postwar Japanese democratic trajectory was overshadowed by the increasingly anti-Communist policies adopted by both the Japanese government and SCAP in the course of 1947. SCAP's initial stance towards Marxism and Communism was one of tolerance, regarding them as major forces contributing to the dissolution of the wartime political-social order. In the context of the growing tensions of the Cold War regime then taking shape, however, US occupation policy clearly shifted to an anti-Communist stance that would dramatically circumscribe the democratic national trajectory and its potential in postwar Japan. One of the pretexts for the acceleration and consolidation of this anti-Communist turn was internal to Japanese society. Despite the newly implemented labour laws guaranteeing freedom of collective organization and bargaining, SCAP's labour policies were gradually tightened up out of fear that a rapidly building momentum in the popular labour movements would lead to disobedience against the authority of the elites and the Japanese government, upon which foundation SCAP's rule was ultimately based. Prime minister Yoshida Shigeru's anti-labour stance, and especially his 1946 new year's speech condemning the general strike, led by the Communist Tokuda Kyūichi and the labour activist Ii Yajiro representing 6 million workers, planned for February 1st, 1947, accelerated the protests; a political movement began to take shape seeking to establish an alternative 'people's government' under Communist and labour union leadership.[71] Up until this point SCAP had 'suggested' that the general strike be called off; now it adopted a hard line against the movement: MacArthur issued an order prohibiting the strike and Ii was imprisoned after he was forced to make an announcement on the radio calling off of the strike.[72] This recognition of the threat that the workers posed gave birth to a coalition between Japanese elite politicians and SCAP that established the model of mainstream postwar conservative politics along the lines of a liberal, pro-US, pro-capitalist, 'democratic' national trajectory. This was the first major suppression of the Marxist and Communist inspired and guided popular movement.

The anti-Communist political climate that reigned from late 1947 (or arguably earlier) to the beginning of the 1950s was commonly described as the 'reverse course' (*gyaku kōsu*). It was accompanied by a series of regressive state policies – the prohibition of strikes and peaceful demonstrations, intervention in union activities, the expulsion of public figures associated with the Japan Communist Party (JCP), and so on – that generated an intense fear throughout Japanese society that dictatorship would return to postwar Japan. In accord with the staunchly anti-Soviet policy of the Truman Doctrine, the alliance between Japanese conservative politicians and SCAP began to forge the outlines of post-occupation, US–Japan relations in the image of Japan as a 'fortified bulwark against Communism.' In tandem with this development, the persecution of those who had previously been condemned as war collaborators was relaxed, and signals were given that Japan was headed towards an unabashedly pro-US, post-occupation era. Following the execution of seven war criminals in December 1948, several Class A war criminals, including Kishi Nohusuke and Kodama Yoshio, were released under the second Yoshida government, with many of them allowed to return to their public posts. In the tense atmosphere surrounding the formation of the People's Republic of China in late 1949, General MacArthur's New Year's speech of January 1950 indicated America's intention of creating the *keisatsu yobi tai*, literally the supplementary policy force, contravening Article Nine of the Japanese Constitution explicitly prohibiting the possession of military armaments. As political tensions heightened in the run up to the Korean War, which broke out in June 1950, Japanese society was put under an extremely strict security directive prohibiting all political meetings and demonstrations. In the following year the US–Japan Security Treaty was signed under the mantle of the San Francisco Treaty as a condition for Japan's political independence. In short, with its new geo-political interests, and the opening of the Cold War and the growing fear of communism in Asia, SCAP-led democratization and demilitarization of Japan was cut short and virtually reversed.

After having enjoyed immense popularity among Japanese labour activists and intellectuals during the early postwar period under more tolerant occupation policies, Japanese Marxism and Communism suffered a number of devastating setbacks in the late 1940s. In response to the forced layoff of 300,000 workers under the Dodge Line policy in 1949, the JCP called for the establishment of an alternative workers' government; the government responded with an open Red Purge in which twenty-four members of the JCP were expelled, a nearly fatal blow to the JCP. Just as they had been in wartime Japan, Communists were once against the favourite target of conspiracies and humiliations by the state and state-sponsored extreme right-wing groups. In August 1949, for example, five Communists were mistakenly sentenced to death after being charged with conspiracy to overturn a passenger train in Matsukawa, Fukushima prefecture; after over ten years of exhausting court cases, it became clear that not only were the accused innocent but that the entire Matsukawa incident was staged by the police.[73] Although conspiracies against Communists received considerable public attention and support from Leftist intellectuals, overall, the state was able to effect its plan of associating Communism with danger and criminality. Moreover, heeding the guidelines of the Cominform, the JCP leadership responded to these oppressive measures by taking a more radical and aggressive stance against US imperialism, a move that frightened the public and ultimately hurt the popularity of the Party.[74] The initially strong support that the JCP had enjoyed began to wane, and the thirty-five seats they had won in the Diet elections of 1949 were reduced to zero in 1952, leading to a serious fragmentation of the Party into various radical and moderate factions. When in 1956 Khrushchev disclosed the violent repression that Stalin had deployed in the USSR, the JCP was decisively shaken and Marxist–Leninist Communist idealism in Japan virtually came to an end. Altogether, these incidents inflicted irreparable damage on the JCP, and Marxism by extension, and resulted in an erosion of its credibility and former status as the most reliable ideological leader of the postwar democracy movement.

The political events of the reverse course also fostered some regressive developments in the postwar Japanese intellectual scene, one of which was the breakdown of the coalition among progressive Leftists. In the increasingly hostile political climate, some liberal intellectuals challenged the theoretical assumptions of Marxist–Leninism for its tendency to be intolerant of other ideas. Odagiri Hideo, a member of *Kindai Bungaku*, argued in a 1954 work that this intolerance was derived from the totalizing systemic character of Marxist thought, which had internalized the scientific world view as part of its theory and had united a particular set of moral values with the scientific-analytic method.[75] In addition, the politically charged climate engendered a new type of conservative – known as the 'realists' due to the primacy of their assumption that states were locked in an international geopolitical power struggle – who utilized a powerful anti-Communist rhetoric not only against the Marxists but equally against non-Marxist Leftists, condemning them as 'Communist sympathizers' and 'traitors to democracy.' The 'realists' argued that an absolute conception of peace was politically naive and unrealistic, since from their perspective peace would only be possible under certain political conditions. The outbreak of the Korean war in June 1950 particularly disrupted many Leftist intellectuals and their collective efforts for world peace, awakening in the minds of some the desirability of a Japanese self-defence force and bi-lateral security arrangements as the sole means of survival in the Cold-War regime. Koizumi Shinzō of the *Kokoro* group, for one, explicitly supported the 'realist' position taken by the Japanese state and argued in his 1952 '*Heiwaron*' ('Theory of Peace') that if Japan wanted to secure peace, it had no other choice than to rely on US protection from a potential attack by Russia.[76] To counter such 'realist' calls for the 'protection of democracy from Communism,' Maruyama responded by arguing that there was not yet an established democracy to be protected in Japan, and such defensive thinking merely reinforced a conservatism that would foster a climate compliant to the status quo powers. Maruyama condemned the rhetoric used in these polemics as attempts to demolish the progressive Left altogether by associating it with the negative images of 'Communism'; in his words, 'the practical danger of totalitarianism in Japan lay [not in Communism but] in the rhetorical attempt to oppress and weaken Leftist progressivism as a whole.'[77]

On the other hand, the reversal of political and intellectual trends induced an awakened sense of crisis in the postwar democracy and peace projects that developed into a large-scale popular civil movement calling for world peace. Responding to UNESCO's (United Nations' Educational, Scientific and Cultural Organization) Stockholm Declaration of June 1948 affirming world peace, sponsored by European intellectuals concerned with the mounting tensions between the US and the USSR, Japanese intellectuals issued their own version of the declaration under the leadership of

Yoshino Gensaburō, the editor of *Sekai* (*The World*).⁷⁸ The joint statement published in *Sekai* was signed by fifty-five leading intellectuals, including conservatives like Watsuji Tetsurō and Tsuda Sōkichi, as well as those from the progressive Left, such as Maruyama Masao, Nakano Yoshio, Kuno Osamu, Tsuru Shigeto and Shimizu Ikutarō.⁷⁹ The popularity and rigour of the peace movement was expressed in, for example, the 6,400,000 signatures gathered in support of the statement and in the formation of a circle (and a journal) of concerned intellectuals (*Heiwa mondai danwa kai*). The movement was also fuelled by the 1949 publication of an emotionally powerful collection of excerpts from the diaries of young men killed in the war (*Kike wadatsumi no koe*); these publications inspired a number of grass-roots peace movements and the popularization of the notion that Japan ought not to repeat the mistakes of the past. While firmly opposing the 'realists'' arguments, many peace advocates suffered from the weakness of being unable to ground their claims in a theoretically convincing way apart from the obvious ethical standpoint and popular support, especially after the demise of the popular labour movements and the weakening of the Marxist–Communist doctrine which had offered a concrete trajectory for popular governance. Kuno Osamu, for one, in his 'The Logic of War and the Logic of Peace,' argued that all wars, including national self-determination and anti-colonial struggles, were illegitimate, and called for 'passive resistance' to the logic of war and violence and for links with other progressive movements.⁸⁰ This absolute repudiation of violence seemed to represent the symbolic limitation of a movement operating on the basis of universal humanitarian ideals within the liberal pluralist frame. On this basis the peace movement won widespread popular support, and gained a renewed momentum when twenty-three Japanese fishermen were contaminated with radiation in the 1954 American hydrogen bomb experiment in the Bikini Islands (the 'Lucky Dragon incident'). Shortly thereafter the Japanese anti-nuclear movement mushroomed, garnering 32 million signatures to the *Sekai* initiated joint statement, and an appeal was issued to the International Peace Council.⁸¹

The 1960 Anpo movement

These popular peace movements were the precursors to the 1960 struggle against the renewal of the US–Japan Security Treaty, commonly known as the Anpo movement, the largest democratic movement in Japanese history. In addition to reiterating the provisions of the original Treaty signed at the time of Japan's independence, which included an agreement with respect to a continuing US military presence in Japan, the new Treaty obliged Japan to take an active military role in 'mutual cooperation' with the US 'against a common threat' to either US or Japanese territory.⁸² The content of the new Treaty, thus, clearly contravened Article Nine of the Japanese Constitution renouncing all military involvement and armaments. The vast majority of the Japanese were strongly against any form of rearmament, and movements to uphold the spirit of the Constitution gained momentum. Most intellectuals, including many of the *Kokoro* group, objected to the 'realists'' rhetoric in favour of the arms race and nuclear deterrence, arguing that building up more armaments in order to reduce the potential threat of armed conflict was contradictory in terms, and only generated more causes for a higher intensity conflict. Notwithstanding the overwhelming public opposition and protests from various segments of society, however, negotiations towards the signing of the Treaty were prepared by the cabinet of Kishi Nobusuke, a former Class A war criminal released during the reverse course years, and signed in Washington in January 1960. The Diet's ratification of the Treaty was forced through parliament on May 19th, 1960 (the day before Eisenhower's planned visit to Japan) in the absence of the protesting opposition and under the protection of several thousand police.[83] Beyond public objection to the Treaty itself, the Kishi government's high handed tactics in ratifying the new Treaty, not only betraying popular demands for peace but also bluntly violating the democratic spirit and procedures, outraged both intellectuals and the populace at large. Criticism of the Treaty and the Kishi cabinet came not only from the Leftist opposition but also from 'conservative' politicians within the Liberal Democratic Party (two conservative parties – the Liberal Party and the Democratic Party – had united in 1955), including Ishibashi Tanzan and Miki Takeo. To give representation to these protesting voices, a national congress on the Anpo issue (*Anpō Jyōyaku Kaitei Soshi Kokumin Kaigi*) was formed under the leadership of the Japan Socialist Party (JSP) and the United Labour Front (*sōhyō*) uniting 134 labour and civil organizations.[84] The congress called for a worldwide, pacifist, non-military alliance in which, they envisaged, Japan would act as a neutral advocate of international peace. To counter this ground swell of popular sentiment, the state resorted to a covert campaign of violence and intimidation against the populace: gangs of right-wing thugs broke up demonstrations and harassed peaceful participants. Six months after his speech condemning US imperialism, the US–Japan Security Treaty, and the possession of nuclear weapons, and in the midst of his extensive efforts to re-establish diplomatic relations between Japan and China and to unite the then divided JSP, the newly elected JSP leader, Asanuma Inejiro, was assassinated in October 1960 by a right-wing youth.

The Anpo movement clearly had a crucial significance far beyond the US–Japan Security Treaty negotiations: it was a fundamental test for the young and maturing Japanese democracy. Progressive intellectuals, such as Maruyama, Shimizu, Kuno and Takeuchi, played a significant role as opinion leaders, participating in demonstrations and presenting their ideas both in the press and in public speeches. The intellectuals' passionate calls for action were a manifestation of the heightened sense of urgency and tense expectations of the times. Maruyama, stressing the necessity for

94 *Uneasy with the modern: the postwar revival*

political involvement on the part of the intellectuals as well as the populace, especially addressed himself to those inclined to remain distant observers, including the members of *Kindai Bungaku* (*Modern Literature*).

> to decide is to literally *cut off* this unlimited thought process at one point. Only by cutting it off, can decision and thus action be born... To live between the contradiction of recognition [theoretical analysis] and decision making [political action] is the fate of we humans who are not gods. I think to live as humans means to actively accept this fate and to take responsibility for that act.[85]

Similarly, Shimizu calling for immediate political action from the populace, aimed at making politicians directly responsible to the people, and claimed: 'If a large crowd with a petition in their hands gathered in Tokyo and surrounded the Diet building in many layers ... there would be born a form of political power that nothing could obstruct.'[86] Protesting government policy, Takeuchi, then teaching at Tokyo Metropolitan University, went a step further and, resigning his professorship, he began planning the establishment of a government alternative to the existing Diet system that would be run by the 'people themselves.' In a tone charged by urgency, he wrote:

> Democracy or dictatorship, that is the only crucial dividing point we face today. What is not democracy is dictatorship, and not dictatorship, democracy. There is no in-between. It is necessary to decide one's attitude on this sole issue at this point. One must not mix this with the question of the Security Treaty. The debate between those who are for and against the Treaty is meaningless. Such debate can be done once dictatorship is defeated. For now, all Japanese nationals should gather together their power in order to defeat dictatorship.[87]

Unlike Maruyama and Shimizu, who continued to place their trust in liberal democratic institutions, Takeuchi located the core of the problem in the fact that, having been established within the frame provided by the US occupation forces, postwar Japanese liberal democracy had turned into a system of conservative elite politics. Abandoning this system, he believed, would allow an alternative, more participatory democracy with a greater representation of popular will to arise. Takeuchi's posing of the question of the form of political representation was indeed critical; however, it remained largely at the margin of the mainstream arguments and agenda of the movement.

The scale of and degree of solidarity in the Anpo movement demonstrated a gradual maturity of democratic consciousness in postwar Japan in that popular expression of political demands had permeated into wide segments of society in a little over a decade. On the other hand, however, the movement also demonstrated clear limitations in that it did not seek to fundamentally challenge the elite power structure.[88] The political outcomes of the Anpo-struggle fell far short of the expectations of many; apart from the dissolution of the Kishi cabinet and the cancellation of Eisenhower's visit to Japan, the movement did not prevent the renewal of the Security Treaty, nor did it produce any meaningful plans for systematic amendments to policy making procedures. What was clearly revealed in the course of the movement and the government's responses to it was the operation of *Realpolitik*, the fact that the allied power of the US and Japanese elites appeared to be beyond the reach of popular political pressures. The failure of the Anpo movement generated, consequently, a deep sense of disappointment and powerlessness; in its aftermath many Japanese intellectuals tended to turn their attention to an internal self-interrogation, directed their recriminations at the leaders of the national congress, the JSP, the JCP, the United Labour Front (*sōhyō*) and other intellectuals, and even began to evince distrust of democratic institutions altogether. These overly critical, pessimistic, and misdirected reactions have been taken by some as revealing the intellectuals' and the public's poverty of experience, vision, and tactics, as well as their naive conception of democratic struggle. Compared to the more desperate struggles for survival that characterized the years immediately following the war, the Anpo-movement clearly reflected, as one critic has pointed out, a rapidly growing 'middle-class mentality not prepared to endanger their livelihood or take serious risks on behalf of the cause.'[89] Indeed, Japanese society in the second half of the 1950s was undergoing a transformation, led by the booming economy (*Jinmu keiki*), that fostered a wide-spread consumerism and a cultural climate personal self-interest and material wealth. While rising prosperity helped to raise the level of consciousness of many, and thus contributed to the constitution of a broad base of popular support for the Anpo-movement, these same socio-economic changes also steered many others away from more serious political commitment and gradually transformed the nature of 'democratic revolution' itself. Overall, the apparent failure of the Anpo struggle marked another turning point in the national postwar trajectory; the political centre of the Japanese democratic movement had shifted from the Leftist coalition of the Marxist-led organized labour movement and the enlightenment/liberal pursuit of democracy to a popular civil movement sharing a minimum common denominator; now, in the wake of Anpo, many were already turning away from politics to the sphere of private economic life.

The decline of the Enlightenment Project

The legacy of the 1960 Anpo struggle was serious intellectual confusion, loss of direction in political movements, loss of belief in postwar democracy and a distrust of abstract political principles and institutions in favour of direct action. After the 1960 defeat, Maruyama and other postwar leaders faced constant challenges from opponents who came to see the enlightened democratic ideals the progressives had advocated as bankrupt. Critics argued that the progressive Leftists tended to see Japanese culture and nationalism too critically, from an elitist perspective, and that they tended to overlook the weaknesses embedded in enlightenment values themselves.[90] According to these critics, this overly critical view was derived from the enlightenment's absolutist opposition of modern versus traditional and rational versus irrational in which one pole was preferred while the other was an obstacle to be overcome. Due to this one-dimensional understanding of the modern, critics argued, the enlightenment-inspired struggle for abstract ideals was bound to fail when it encountered historically given limitations beyond the control of individuals; and due to their idealist stance, the critics claimed, Maruyama and other progressive modernists had no other option than to maintain their position in increasing isolation from the rest of the world.[91]

Maruyama gave the enlightenment project a much greater significance than his critics did, and his pursuit of the universal goal of transforming society and the subject was passionate and consistent with what Kuno Osamu has described as his 'puritan strictness.'[92] For Maruyama, wilful effort in the process of the struggle was valuable in itself and could not be judged by its consequences, as Maruyama's well-known response to the criticism that his idealism was illusory implied – he stated that he would rather 'commit [himself] to an illusion of postwar democracy than to the reality of the Great Japanese Empire (*Dai Nihon Teikoku*).'[93] Awareness of the limitations of theory with respect to historical outcomes made Maruyama into a pragmatist of a kind, and it was on account of this awareness that he refrained from the attempt to unify theory and practice that is often implied in the rigid interpretation of the Marxist notion of *praxis*. Regardless of his intentions, however, Maruyama's intellectual enlightenment notion of democracy seems to have lost its capacity to channel popular sentiment towards democratic goals as Japanese society in the late 1950s came to be dominated by a growing middle-class mentality and its interest in continuing political struggle began to wane.

As the critic Matsumoto Ken'ichi has pointed out, sometime in the 1960s Maruyama himself came to accept the end of his project for democratic revolution, a recognition manifest in his 1972 work, 'Rekishi ishiki no "kosō"' ('The "Old Strata" of Japanese Historical Consciousness').[94] In it, Maruyama identified three key temporal notions by which the Japanese conception of history had traditionally been defined: *naru* (history as a natural process of becoming), *tsugi* (history as a succession of discrete, causally unlinked events in the greater whole of flux), and *ikioi* (the natural creative dynamic as the driving force for history). Together these three notions constituted 'history' conceived as the unfolding sequence of naturally motivated events without subjective intervention, or as he expressed it: '*Tsugi tsugi ni nariyuku ikioi.*'[95] Seen from this 'historical' perspective each moment is ahistorically totalized in the present, reason and truth are made relative and inconsequential to each moment, and the world appears as a kind of nihilistic series of events governed by *nariyuki*, the uncontrolled natural process.[96] Maruyama concluded that this optimistic and relativist notion of history was deeply embedded in Japanese culture and language, that it ultimately fostered a contemplative subject devoid of any active notion of agency, ability or obligation to participate in the making of history, and that it thus inclined the Japanese people towards a resolute subordination to naturalistic orders and a tenacious resistance to the acceptance of universal reason, truth and morality.[97] The 'Old Strata' reflects, perhaps, Maruyama's disappointment with the over two-and-a-half decades of struggle for democratic revolution in Japan. Indeed, over the course of the 1960s Maruyama increasingly withdrew from political activism into more purely academic activities, and during the heyday of the late-1960s student movement he came to be seen by generations of younger activists and intellectuals as a representative of the status quo, elite academic system.

In Maruyama's view, the enlightenment values he championed had ultimately failed to penetrate into the problematic historical consciousness running through the Japanese native cultural orientation and thus the realization of democratic goals was foreclosed. From the above analysis of the Anpo movement, however, his assessment could be contested at least on two counts: the uncritical appropriation of the notions of liberal democracy and enlightenment values by Japanese society and, relatedly, the uncritical acceptance of externally introduced institutions reflective of the international hegemonic power system. The establishment, by foreign agents, of modern, democratic institutions in a society in which they did not historically arise was bound to produce some structural difficulties. What was at stake here was how could 'foreign' enlightenment values and institutions be successfully grafted upon a 'native' socio-cultural foundation – i.e. a community of subjects and ideas – and integrated into people's everyday discourses and practices.[98] How could the sense of historical continuity, integrity and cohesion of a given collective human organization be maintained during such a transformation, especially when the 'foreignness' of the ideal to be established was continuously perceived, or more precisely, the pains and difficulties that the transformation gave rise to were felt to be and understood as an intrusion of things foreign and the loss of things native? To put it differently, in order to successfully transform the 'native' political institutional order, cultural values and subjectivity, would not some ideological invention or translation be necessary, bridging the gap between the 'traditional' and the 'modern,' so that the agent(s) of modernization would no longer be seen as simply 'foreign'? These questions remained outside of Maruyama's and the other liberal leaders' theoretical field of operations. To complicate matters, the postwar democratic revolution was from the beginning closely linked with, or rather initiated by and developed within the scope of, SCAP's occupation policy. As argued above, this seemingly obvious fact became clear to many only when democratic initiatives were frustrated by changes in US occupation policy and the renewal of the US–Japan Security Treaty. These changes awakened an awareness of the rule of US geo-political power, in alliance with the Japanese state elites in Japan: standing firmly in opposition to the Japanese workers and the populace, the state decisively weakened the credibility of the liberal/enlightenment stance, especially when the question of the international hegemonic hierarchy, which had indeed impeded postwar Japanese democratic movements, remained unanalysed.

It was in the second postwar decade that two original thinkers emerged, Yoshimoto Takaaki and Takeuchi Yoshimi, whose alternative proposals for the future democratic national trajectory were conceived in terms of a bottom-up popular movement, rather than as a top-down enlightenment project. In the section immediately following, I discuss the works of these two intellectuals in some detail since, by proposing fundamental criticisms of modern enlightenment discourse, they were the precursors of the romantic movement of the late 1960s. Each addressed a number of critical questions to the modernist Japanese national trajectory, questions that had been neglected in the optimism of the early postwar era. The questions put forth by Yoshimoto Takaaki centred upon the issue of the accountability of democracy. Could it be, asked Yoshimoto, that the conception of democracy itself is in need of substantial modifications, modifications that would take it beyond the limitations of the liberal universalist and enlightenment vision, in order that democracy be more reflective of the voices of the populace and be accountable to the cultural specificity of the Japanese? By rejecting the 'abstraction of modernism' and the 'external imposition' of a political ideal in favour of a vision of democracy grounded in the concrete experience of the people, Yoshimoto opened up a set of complex problematics bearing on the difficulties of modernization and democratization for a non-Western society. The questions posed by Takeuchi Yoshimi centred on whether democracy could be treated solely as a 'domestic problem,' or whether it was necessary to set it within the greater framework of the international power hierarchy. Arguing that modern enlightenment political theory had failed to take into account the question of the international power structure which conditions the domestic polity, Takeuchi located the historical difficulties encountered by the modern Japan in context of inherent problems in the modern hegemonic world. Both authors posed serious challenges, not only to the modernists' uncritical commitment to Eurocentric rationalist values, but also to the trajectory pursued by postwar Japan; in doing so they reopened for the postwar Japanese intellectual scene the forgotten problematics raised by the wartime symposium of 'Overcoming modernity.'

Challenges to the enlightenment and a return to concrete place: the politics of the masses and ethnic self-determination in the modern universal world

Yoshimoto Takaaki and the independence of the masses (taishū no jiritsu)

Unlike Maruyama, who had awaited Japan's defeat with bated breath, for Yoshimoto August 15th was an experience more humiliating and dispiriting than liberating. For those committed to the cause of the war, the uncritical revival of and the popular support for modern institutions and ideas was like setting the clock back, and particularly hard to swallow. Like some of *kokoro* intellectuals, Yoshimoto was critical of postwar intellectuals trends that dismissed the prewar debate altogether, and in a series of works published in the late 1950s he severely criticized both progressive modernists and Marxists. Yoshimoto saw Japanese progressive modernism a kind of 'pseudo-avant-gardism' that opportunistically rode the tide of the times, while Japanese Marxism, he thought, tended to be either a rationalization of personal resentments against war collaborators or a soothing of guilt-complexes through the act of accusation. He argued that both camps had failed to address the fundamental problematics involved in popular resistance as expressed in the realms of art and culture, problematics such as the difficulties of interpreting and expressing popular ethos/sentiments in the medium of mass culture and of organizing and mobilizing popular resistance.[99] Although a general distrust of postwar intellectuals permeates Yoshimoto's work in a way similar to that of the 'old liberals,' Yoshimoto was clearly a modernist in his progressive revolutionary intent to transform Japanese society. However, in contrast to Maruyama's enlightenment position, he sought to do so by affirming aspects of Japanese culture as the concrete historical base on which a Japanese democracy was to be established in its own terms.

Under the influence of Kobayashi Hideo, Yoshimoto was critical of the 'humanized Marxisms' as exemplified in Umemoto Katsumi and Mashita Shin'ichi, and especially of the way they included the subjective will in the process of the structural determination of capital.[100] Yoshimoto found the attempt to incorporate subjectivity into materialist theory, a task commonly identified by postwar Marxists as among the most urgent, irrelevant since he believed the subject was locked into historically and materially determined social conditions beyond his/her will. Concluding that the subjective will in revolutionary struggle is a function of the structural determination of material relations, Yoshimoto reasons that attempts to reconcile the two are not only a theoretical misapprehension but detrimental to the organization of resistance. This conception of the relation between subjective will and historical structure was derived from Yoshimoto's reading of the Gospel of Matthew ('Machiusho Shiron,' 1954), in which he sees what he calls a 'deeply pathetic hatred' as motivating the early Christians' challenge to an all powerful, oppressive Judaism:

> [t]he author of the Gospel of Matthew must have gained his inspiration from the oppressive order and the bloody conflict with Judaism. Regardless of the content of the doctrine, the primitive Christians just needed to conquer those Jews.... If there is any method which can be used to justify this extremely aggressive pathos and their dismal psychological hatred, it is the introduction of the concept of the absoluteness of the relation.[101]

Yoshimoto is not entirely uncritical of the resentments of the oppressed who, in attempting to overthrow the system to which they are subjugated, tend to erect an equally oppressive alternative structure of their own.[102] However, Yoshimoto ultimately redeems the resentments of the primitive Christians as a legitimate force of counter-hegemonic struggle in a conflict-laden history as a means by which such subjective struggle seeks to overcome objective restraints. For Yoshimoto, what motivates this self-determination of the collective subject is the 'absoluteness of the relation' (*kankei no zettaisei*), the objective historical structure against which human subjects strive in an effort to take control of their own lives.

In his well known critique of Maruyama ('Maruyama Masao Ron,' 1962), Yoshimoto portrays Maruyama as 'strange creature,' a being too lifeless – 'endowed with only a nervous system' – to be called a thinker but too vivid a critical consciousness to be called a scholar.[103] Yoshimoto denounces Maruyama's modernist theory as 'stainless,' too perfect, lacking any sense of either the everyday or the 'bloody vision of history,' the product perhaps of a social theorist 'remaining too long and too static inside his office.'[104] With respect to Maruyama's endorsement of the Hegelian conception of history – i.e. the rationalist view of world history as the unfolding process of the world spirit – Yoshimoto is critical of what he sees as Maruyama's purposeful neglect of the 'bloody side' of Hegelian history, while adapting its teleological conception of historical progress to suit his democratic ideal. What annoys Yoshimoto most is Maruyama's abstract rationalism by which, according to Yoshimoto, he stands outside the concrete socio-historical ground of his times, viewing Japanese society and the Japanese people from a 'superior,' modern, objective and objectifying perspective.

> When Maruyama rationally approaches the objective world as the subject of his study, the world begins to have rational features. And then, when I approach Maruyama's rationally conceived world, then I feel something inside me solidifies, as if I had been strung up on a gallows (*shimeki ni kakerareru*).[105]

What Yoshimoto is protesting against is Maruyama's 'cold-bloodedness,' his merciless objectification of the everyday experiences of life – and the traditional cultural ethos Yoshimoto sees as residing in the concrete.[106] Moreover, by virtue of adopting this 'superior perspective,' one Yoshimoto believes is alien to Japanese socio-cultural space, and by acting as self-sufficient agents promoting democracy, Yoshimoto claims Maruyama and the modernists have become servants of the interests of the Japanese elites.

Yoshimoto's criticism of the modernist enlightenment position stems from his analysis of the causes of the prewar fascist social system, what he calls ultra-nationalism, an analysis quite different from Maruyama's. Criticizing Maruyama for blaming the Japanese cultural orientation, Yoshimoto argues that the roots of prewar Japanese fascism are not to be found in the Japanese tradition, but, on the contrary, in the destruction of that tradition and the resulting loss of identity among the populace uprooted from their traditional agrarian ways of life. These uprooted, identity-stressed masses were vulnerable to the attractions of ultranationalist mythology and its promises of articulating in cultural terms their sentiments and transcending them into a higher morality.[107] In Yoshimoto's diagnosis, the breakdown of the prewar Japanese left – both liberal and Marxist – and that subsequent triumph of ultranationalist ideology followed precisely because Japanese intellectuals failed to create a social theory grounded in the specific experience of the populace. In his 1958 work 'Tenkō Ron' ('Theory of Ideological Conversion'), Yoshimoto argued that the large scale ideological conversion of prewar Leftists of agrarian fundamentalism, which were themselves later subsumed in *kokutai* ultra-nationalism, came about not so much as a result of the Japanese state's oppression or ideological manipulations but as a result of the intellectuals' failure to articulate in their theoretical schemes popular sentiments. As a result, the majority of the population was excluded from potentially revolutionary movements, while most of the intellectuals ended up in total isolation from the populace.[108] If one wishes to understand the *raison d'être* of prewar ultranationalism, argues Yoshimoto, one has to objectify the conditions under which, and the ways in which, the communal ethos of *taishū*, i.e. 'mass nationalism' as distinguished from the nationalism of the intellectuals, came to be positively articulated. The exclusion of mass national sentiment from the theoretical vision of the modernists constitutes for Yoshimoto a form of elitism; it reflects the theorists' blindness, laziness and/or arrogance, and has only been reinforced in postwar social theory. He thinks that unless they strive to include that mass sentiment, Japanese intellectuals are bound to repeat the same mistake of formulating an abstract nationalism that in effect subjugates the masses to the power of elite ideology.

To be sure, Yoshimoto is far from being a simple romantic who yearns for a return to traditional life. He asserts that popular expressions of the mass ethos do not tell one much about the true state of popular national sentiment because they are, he believes, already represented, and as such removed from what he calls the 'original image of the masses' (*taishū no genzō*).¹⁰⁹ In his 1964 work 'Japanese nationalism' ('*Nihon no nashonarizumu*'), Yoshimoto argues:

> the true fact of the popular experience of nationalism and their understanding of it cannot be represented. One could infer that this is why the masses cannot appear themselves on the historical stage as anything but a virtual image, despite the fact that at all stages of history they have been its driving forces. However, there is one way of making this representation [of the original image of the masses] to some extent a real image; we can begin doing so only by examining our own life and thought experiences as members of the masses, or by the 'internal investigation' of ourselves.¹¹⁰

Taking up his own suggestion, Yoshimoto analyses popular poems and other popular art forms as a signpost to the identification of the 'original image of the masses.' Although a fully satisfactory resumé of Yoshimoto's works is far beyond the scope of this chapter, some introduction to his basic ideas concerning popular literature would be useful here. In Yoshimoto's reading, what is usually regarded as a straightforward expression of national sentiment in late Meiji (1900–19) songs thematizing war and national pride is not an indication of a swelling 'nationalism,' but instead gives evidence of a healthy relation between the state and society, effectively linked by popular national sentiment. According to Yoshimoto, what was more problematic was the disappearance of these national themes and sentiments, a disappearance that tended to call forth abstract and/or artificially manufactured replacements. Yoshimoto saw this happening in the 1920s and the 1930s, when a widespread consumer materialism and disbelief in national goals practically wiped out the pre-existing mass nationalism. In the early Shōwa era (1925–), Yoshimoto notes that the focus of popular poems and songs is reduced to a mere reproduction of representational techniques, nearly completely detached from national sentiment and the everyday concerns of the populace. What he highlights in this analysis is how 'images of the masses' in popular discourse operate as a kind of barometer measuring the degree to which functional linkages between the state and society are present. Yoshimoto concludes that what the weakening of those links and the concurrent loss of identity – both collective and individual – signify is that ground upon which ultranationalism would rise was being prepared, the ground on which the Japanese state superimposed its own phantom definition of Japanese identity as *kokutai*.

Learning from the past, Yoshimoto attempts to construct a theory that accounts for the silent masses (*taishū*) – those, he thinks, who resist enlightenment – and specifically their autonomy as a group, as opposed to the modernists' project of creating a modern subject through some form of institutional or cultural education. Yoshimoto sees the only hope for postwar Japanese democracy in the ability of the *taishū* to remain 'independent' (*jiritsu*) from such ideological manipulations of the elites, including both progressive and conservative intellectuals, and in a social theory that supports the masses in their struggle to advance their own causes on their own terms.[111] He argues:

> If there is a way for [the blue-collar] workers to surpass the 'avant-garde' [intellectuals and artists], that will come only when workers achieve independence in their everyday lives by rejecting the 'avant-garde' ways of communicating and rationalizing their lives with their own logic. If there is a way for a fish-wife to surpass Mrs. X, a pseudo-intellectual member of the PTA, it is not when she clings to an ideology of peace and democracy, but when she successfully ideologizes the issues involved in selling fish, cooking rice, bearing and raising children.[112]

In this passage, however, Yoshimoto seems to idealize images of the everyday as the essence of the *taishū*, confusing the question of the concreteness of life with that of economic class. For Yoshimoto, the everyday activities of the household (e.g. 'cooking rice') are the activities of blue collar workers and their wives in opposition to the rational, abstract ideas (e.g. 'avant-gardism' and 'democracy') identified with the educated middle class. However, the obvious fact that middle-class Japanese have everyday lives just as much as the lower classes seems to escape him. By virtue of this idealized representation of the *taishū* as the imagined bearers of a Japanese cultural ethos, Yoshimoto transforms the *taishū* into a bulwark against the penetration of the modern, the institutional, and the Western. Moreover, by including the non-rational aspects of life (i.e. the everyday) in his representation of the *taishū* and by conceiving of the *taishū* as his intellectual and political base, Yoshimoto aestheticizes class politics in as much as his conception binds political motivation to the aesthetic desire to overcome the insurmountable gap between life (content) and representation (form). Underlying this attempt is Yoshimoto's antipathy to modern dualistic epistemology and the rational institutional mediation of collective life which he sees as nothing more than an imposition of alien values upon 'the everyday.' This inclination is closely akin to that running through Tsuda's, and the other *Kokoro* intellectuals', conception of history.

There is a further aspect of Yoshimoto's critique that needs discussing. Yoshimoto's anti-rational epistemic position is related to the 'poetic' style of his writings (it is not insignificant that he began his career as a poet), a style that radically elides the boundaries between the aesthetic and the analytic, the creative and the scientific. Thus, the place his work occupies in Japanese intellectual discourse is highly ambiguous, politically speaking. On the one hand, Yoshimoto's populist theory clearly incorporated some of the progressive aspects of Marxist social theory, for example the attempt to motivate the populace towards social transformation. Indeed, by the late 1960s Yoshimoto's work had become incredibly popular, as much for his populist consciousness as for his penetrating analytical insights, provocative argumentative style, and uncompromising challenges to his contemporaries. During the wave of radical student activism demanding self-government of the universities that crested in the late 1960s (*Zenkyōtō undō*; see Chapter 4), Yoshimoto became something of a charismatic figure. On the other hand, progressive as it may be, Yoshimoto's anarchistic vision of democracy centring on an idealized and aestheticized notion of the collective subject (*taishū*) and his prioritization of the concrete decisively undermined the heuristic aspect of the modern enlightenment position, and in effect contributed to a revision of the initial postwar democratic trajectory founded on the notion of the rational autonomous subject. In his critique of Maruyama's notion of a universal ideal of mankind and in his desire to base progressive politics on the concrete life of the *taishū*, Yoshimoto romanticized the modernist revolutionary project with his own version of mass politics, a formulation that contradicts the institutional aspects of modern progressivism. Moreover, despite his Leftist political activism, Yoshimoto's notion of *taishū* populism had something in common with the *Kokoro* group's cultural particularism: while for the *Kokoro* group the antithesis of objectifying reason was the 'human,' for Yoshimoto it was the everyday of *taishū*. In effect, then, Yoshimoto's powerful works furnished an ideological platform whereupon cultural particularism and conservatism intolerance to modern rationalism could intersect with radical activism, and from which modern progressivism could be challenged.

This ambiguity in Yoshimoto's work curiously parallels the popular political movement, the *Zenkyōtō* student rebellion, that marked another turning point in postwar Japanese political history. While the 1960 Anpo movement was led by a coalition of intellectuals from various modernist positions, the late-1960s student movement targeted the liberal progressives as elitists and despised enemies. During the course of the 1960s, the concept of democratic revolution, carried out by a rational subject, guided and mediated by enlightenment ideals and democratic institutions was replaced by a notion of popular democracy characterized by direct action, an appreciation for concrete experience and emotions, and a sense of collective identity. This 'popularization' and 'aestheticization' of politics coincided with the rise of mass society that resulted from the rapid economic growth that began in the mid-1950s and whose effects were acutely felt in the 1960s. Disappointed by the failure to produce concrete political results and the socio-economic structural changes society had undergone in the 1960s, the Japanese democratic movement opened itself to the embrace of anti-rational, anti-institutional and anti-enlightenment inclinations, decisively turning its back on early postwar modern progressive ideals. In attempting to repair the rift between theory and political practice, Japanese intellectuals in the 1960s in effect contested Maruyama's democratic enlightenment project, and allowed passion, action (often violent), and collectivity to take priority over the rational, the institutional, and the individual. In other words, the *pathos* that in the early postwar period Maruyama and the other modernists' had criticized had returned in force to challenge their authority. It should be emphasized that this returning *pathos* did not emerge as a simple recovery of the conservatism of the old liberals, but was mediated by a form of radical progressivism which found the weakest spot of the postwar Japanese democratic movement and placed its pressure there. However, the somewhat euphoric populist politics typically advocated by Yoshimoto would itself come to be seriously challenged in the 1970s when, in the face of the rapid intrusion of commercial and technological forces into the realms of subjectivity and intersubjectivity, populist images of collectivity became difficult to sustain.

Takeuchi Yoshimi and the question of national self-determination

Like Yoshimoto, Takeuchi Yoshimi refused to alter the basic position he had taken before and during the war, and continued his efforts to delineate the problems involved in the Japanese experience of modernity that had been largely abandoned by postwar intellectual discourse. For Takeuchi, the wartime 'overcoming modernity' debates were an attempt to face up to problems that a modernized Japan could not avoid, problems – he described them as historical *aporia* – whose relevance was in no way diminished in the postwar era.[113] In his view, the ultranationalist political and intellectual regime was an inevitable consequence of a non-Western Japan's reckless attempts to fit into the Eurocentric world by adapting *their* ways, attempts that fostered in Japanese discourse a schizophrenic world-view marked by a division between the modern and the traditional Takeuchi insisted that the fifteen years war had to be disassembled into two distinct phases or aspects representing Japan's imperialist aggression against Asia and Japan's resistance to the Western power. According to Takeuchi, the latter aspect could not simply be dismissed altogether as part and parcel of the former, since the struggle for national self-determination was an inescapable process that every non-Western nation had to undergo in order to establish itself in the context of the Eurocentric universalist discourse backed up by the military strength of the West. In Takeuchi's thinking Japan had still to come to terms with the long and difficult task of self-determination in that world, a challenge he saw as being more seriously thought through and successfully undertaken by other Asian nations, most notably by China.

For Takeuchi, to reduce the problem of prewar Japan as stemming from characteristics of the Japanese cultural tradition, as Maruyama and other modernists had done, was both highly unsatisfactory and bound to be an explanatory failure since it had not taken into account the historical context of Japan's encounter with the modern world, nor the structural constraints it faced. Thus, to condemn the 'ultra' aspect of prewar nationalism and to ignore popular national sentiment was not only meaningless but also masked the hegemonic violence of the modern West that had awakened Japanese ethnic identity and brought about the formation of the modern Japanese state in the first place. Takeuchi argues:

> It is necessary to condemn the system of power under Japanese fascism which awakened this ethnic consciousness from its sleep and utilized it by transforming it into ultra-nationalism; but it is incorrect to suppress even a simple nationalist sentiment for that reason. The latter has a legitimate voice to be heard. It is a voice that is rooted in an unceasing desire to recover an original shape of the human images that were deformed by modernism.[114]

Similar to Yoshimoto, Takeuchi understands that the prewar manipulations of *kokutai* fundamentalism were made possible by a prior alienation in which 'the initially simple sentiments of the people,' finding no other means of expression, 'were taken up and twisted by the authorities who absorbed them into their militarist and imperialist system.'[115] On the other hand, Takeuchi radically differs from Yoshimoto in that he locates the root cause of the problematic in the historical context of the expansion of the modern hegemonic world, a context in which the question of ethnic self-determination cannot be reduced to the internal tension between the modern elites and the communal masses. For Takeuchi, the encroachment of modern universalist logic into Asia was nothing but a tragedy because with its advent Asian peoples were left with an impossible choice between either accepting the Eurocentric definition of themselves as less than European or embarking on a desperate campaign of resistance against an enemy whose military superiority was overwhelming. In Takeuchi's view, Japanese ultra-nationalism was an inevitable result of the fact that the energy of the populace, which ought to have been channelled into resistance against the domination of the modern and the Western, was instead gathered and harnessed in the campaign of imperialist expansion against Asia.[116]

According to Takeuchi, the expansion of the modern world was an amplification of a particular perspective, created and developed in Europe, which was obsessed with a self-defining identity struggle and which 'barely manages to sustain itself in the incessant tension of recreating itself.'[117] Takeuchi saw this essential characteristic of modern Europe in the global expansion of capitalism and various missionary movements, a simultaneous development both in terms of the metaphysical (spirit) and the material (capital):

> Capital demands the expansion of the market, and the missionaries are convinced of their task of expanding the nation of God. They try to be themselves by an incessant tension [to become themselves] ... They cannot sustain themselves in any other means but in that dynamic. This is what is called the spirit of capitalism; it grasps [and realizes] its being in the expanding temporal and spatial trajectory.[118]

It was this dynamic drive of European self-realization that transformed the rest of the world according to its own design; that is to say, with the ascent of this perspective to supremacy emerged the modern universal world which defined and subsumed peoples outside of itself under its universal gaze. Subsumed under their expanding and objectifying gaze, 'the East,' in its resistance to it, was made captive to the temporal and spatial scheme defined by modern Europe. Takeuchi claims:

> Through resistance, the East has modernized itself. The history of resistance is that of modernization, and there was no modernization which has not been mediated by resistance. Europe has affirmed its victory in the resistance of the East, in its process of including the East in world history, and that was rationalized as the cultural, ethnic, and productive superiority of Europe. The East has affirmed its defeat in the same process. The defeat was a result of the resistance, for there is no defeat without resistance. Thus, the continuation of resistance is that of defeat. Europe has advanced forward step by step, and the East withdrew backward step by step, and this withdrawal was accompanied by resistance. When this advancement and withdrawal was rationalized by Europeans as the progression of world history and the triumph of reason, and when that effect was internalized in the East in the continuing sense of defeat in their resistance, their defeat became decisive.[119]

Thus for Takeuchi modern history is the developmental process of the simultaneous self-determination of Europe and the resistance of the East, in which process the latter transforms itself as the negative half of the former and thereby, in his words, 'accepts the defeat.' In this scheme, the configuration of the modern world is a process of spatial homogenization and temporal synchronization according to the dynamic modality internal to Europe's obsessive desire for self-definition, by means of which the universals of 'truth,' 'history' and 'civilization' are established for all.

Takeuchi remained doubtful as to whether enlightenment ideals could indeed serve their heuristic function of guiding the Japanese populace towards the creation of a new social order without coming to be seen as merely foreign ideas that could be disposed of at will. Critical of the early postwar modernist paradigm for its uncritical acceptance of the benefits of universalism and its blind trust in a rationalism that, he thought, the postwar 'modernists' hardly understood, Takeuchi argues:

> For me, what is frightening is rationalism's belief that all can be analyzed [by its objectifying gaze]. Or, rather than the belief in rationalism itself, what is truly frightening is the irrational will to power behind rationalism that authorizes its belief. And that seems to be something European to me . . . I was anxious that many Japanese thinkers, writers and the like, with the exception of a few poets, did not feel as I feel, that they were not afraid of rationalism, and moreover, that what they were calling rationalism (including materialism) does not by any means appear to me to be rationalism at all.[120]

Although he did not reject modernist goals for progress, Takeuchi believed that any social movement, if it were to be inclusive and effective, must be substantially grounded in the social and material reality of the Japanese. For Takeuchi, the *minzoku* (*Volk*) was a potential counter-concept to the hegemonic expansion of modern Europe and its rationalist spirit; it could serve as a basis for resistance, and through it Western values and institutions could be redefined and transformed into forms that would be accountable in the Japanese historical context. Takeuchi criticized the postwar modernist paradigm for its opportunistic demonization of 'the blood-spattered issue of *minzoku-shugi* (ethnic nationalism),' a demonization that merely served, he thought, to abort the potential for creating a self-determining resistance.[121] Understanding the emergence of the prewar ideology of *kokutai* as an antithesis to the modern rationalist pragmatism pursued by the Meiji oligarchy, Takeuchi thought that some form of 'synthesis' between the modernist rationalism and the popular antithesis should be sought if Japan was to pursue an accountable modern trajectory.[122]

Convinced that abstract ideas had to be grounded in the social body, Takeuchi called for the establishment of a new literary genre that would include aspects of both the liberal modernist literature of *Kindai Bungaku* and the Marxist *Shin Nihon Bungaku* – what he called 'national literature' (*kokumin Bungaku*) as opposed to modern literature. This, he thought, was a means of nurturing a politically reliable subject capable of the tasks at hand. Explaining his rationale for this project, he declares:

> To define human beings as free individuals or as bound to their class is itself a necessary task at some point. However, Japanese proletarian literature, just like any other stream of modern Japanese literature, was not immune from making the hasty assertion that such an abstract portrait of the human being delinked from the concrete grasps as if the whole of human existence. Forgetting the original task of literature, to save the whole [of human existence], [modernist proletarian literature] attempted to capture the whole with a part. One must say that it is only natural that neglected voices of pain demanding the recovery of a total humanity emerged from a dark, forgotten corner. Ethnicity is rooted in this dark corner.[123]

This statement does not mean that Takeuchi was either a simple advocate of the 'logic of place' or an ethnic nationalist hostile to others; on the contrary, he was fully aware of the impossibility of positive expressions of ethnic identity as such. In fact, he clearly acknowledges that ethnicity is fundamentally reactionary and empty:

> The problematic of ethnicity is of such a nature that it emerges as a problem when it is neglected: the consciousness of ethnicity arises by oppression. Even if it joins forces with other elements as it later advances itself into an ethnic movement, in its birth, it is not unrelated to a demand for the recovery of humanity. While ethnicity does not surface unless it is oppressed, its potential for emergence is always immanent. It is impossible to keep ethnic consciousness forever dormant by the imposition of a one-dimensional [ideological] force by avoiding our efforts to recover the lost humanity.[124]

This 'romantic' conception of *minzoku* as a site for struggle, combined with his vision of the resistance of 'the other' – what he often calls 'the East' – as an eternal struggle for self-determination, leaves one with the impression that Takeuchi could find his 'home' only in a deep despair.[125] And in a certain sense this impression would be correct. Despair, as Takeuchi conceives it, can never be grasped by the optimism inherent in modern progressivism and rationalism, for such a 'sentiment' would only appear to modern rationalism as an obstacle to be overcome.[126] Takeuchi seems to be the sole postwar Japanese intellectual who, figuratively speaking, attempted to bear the full weight of the sense of loss in the Japanese self, the feeling of cultural dislocation and alienation from the familiar time and place that resulted from the violent decontextualization accompanying the penetration of the universal discourse of the modern West.

Seen in this optic, the problem of prewar and postwar Japan for Takeuchi was not that of the insufficient internalization of modern subjectivity and institutions, but rather the slavish acceptance of an externally defined identity and of the universally given historical trajectory without any sense of resistance. Takeuchi attributed this lack of resistance to the essential orientation of the Japanese cultural and intellectual tradition which lacked an internally defined and intrinsically rooted sense of the self, and therefore, which could not engender a self-motivated struggle to create history out of resistance to the external imposition of power. Takeuchi compares these 'lacks' to a form of 'slave consciousness' in which independence is unknown because dependency is so deeply ingrained in consciousness that the subject does not even notice its slavery. Further, he argues that this attribute is uniquely Japanese and sets the Japanese apart from both 'the East' and 'the West.'

> I am doubtful that Japanese culture has had any experience of independence in its tradition, and for that reason, I think there has been

no real sense to feel the state of independence. The Japanese might have never received what comes from outside as a pain and in resistance. Those who do not know the taste of freedom satisfy themselves with an illusory notion of freedom. A slave is a slave by thinking that s/he is not a slave. I wonder if the pain of 'being awakened' is irrelevant in Japanese culture.[127]

It is because [in Japan] there is no resistance [against Europe], that is, no desire to maintain the self (a lack of identity). The lack of resistance demonstrates that Japan is unlike the East [East, or Asia, for Takeuchi is a symbol of resistance], and the lack of a desire to maintain the self demonstrates that Japan is unlike Europe. In other words, Japan is nothing.[128]

While this lack of subjectivity did discourage the Japanese from originating movements to create modern history in their own terms and trajectory, Takeuchi points out that it also contributed to the breath-taking rapidity of Japan's modern economic transformation. That is to say, having willingly adopted the place of the non-European other, modern Japan has taken full advantage of its own lack of identity and resistance; while enjoying the 'flexibility' to adapt foreign technologies, ideas and institutions on a superficial and instrumental level, it has never been able to truly accept the principles underlying them. Speaking ironically, Takeuchi claims that this is a paradox in that 'what appears to be the most progressive is simultaneously the most regressive.'[129]

Critical of the modern universalist world view and its progressive conception of history, Takeuchi attempts to forge an alternative path to the blind pursuit of the 'logic of civilization.' For Takeuchi, Japan's path to modernization has been a mistake that deprived the Japanese of the potential realization of their own identity rooted in their ethno-cultural and historical specificities. This suppression of particularity, he thinks, was what ultimately led the Japanese towards *kokutai* fundamentalism as an expression of revolt against a modern West that Japan had in some fundamental way already embraced. Had the Japanese chosen an alternative, revolutionary path towards self-determination and modernization, as some other Asian nations had, this would not have been the case. Thus, Takeuchi lauds the Chinese pursuit of their own national trajectory, believing they had found a means of overcoming the dilemma of modernity by advancing towards the establishment of a unique cultural and ethnic identity of their own. Based on this understanding, Takeuchi conceives 'Asia' as a 'method,' a possible historical path for transcending the contradictions of the universal modern world and the ethnically and culturally specific nation-state.[130] In this theoretical scheme, the universality of the modern West and its hegemonic discourse is relativized by the counter-hegemonic discourse of 'Asia.'

Evoking the category of 'Asia,' however, takes us directly back to the prewar overcoming modernity debates, in which Pan-Asianist internationalism collaborated with *kokutai* fundamentalism, and in which images of the Japanese cultural tradition were projected upon the geographic space outside of Japan.[131] Given that ethnic particularity, as Takeuchi himself argues, can have no positively formulated expressions, his romantic call for national self-determination runs the risk of providing a site for the articulation of a Japan-centric perspective that pays little heed to the perspectives of others. One also has cause to question the 'third path' Takeuchi saw China taking vis-à-vis modern Europe – was China really free of the problems he saw as besetting Europe? If a counter-hegemonic struggle against the modern constitutes the modern subject in resistance, could not the same struggle be operative within the frame of the modern, and ultimately be visited by the same problems?

Conclusion

Postwar Japanese history began with the reinstallation of the modernization and democratization project that had been derailed by the prewar regime without, however, Japanese intellectuals coming to terms with the prewar questioning of the modern. Indeed, it appeared as if the postwar regime, the general intellectual climate, and socio-political discourse all experienced a 180-degree about face, from the previous order based on *kokutai* to a democratic and liberal internationalism guided by the US occupation forces. A series of sweeping democratic reforms were implemented by SCAP that tossed the ball, so to speak, into the Japanese court, and the pressing issue then became how to root democracy in Japanese society at the deepest level, how to foster the democratic subject who thinks and acts as a socially and politically responsible agent, and how to translate democratic principles into a living actuality. Maruyama Masao, the godfather of postwar progressivism, assumed the intellectual leadership of the postwar social transformation by articulating the theoretical foundations of 'democratic revolution' upon a belief in the rational autonomous subject as the agent of social democratic transformation. With the onset of the Cold War and the so-called 'reverse course,' however, the initial confidence and optimism in the project stumbled when faced with a growing awareness of the brute force of international power politics behind the increasingly oppressive policies of the Japanese state. Generally speaking, however, throughout the period of political turmoil from the end of the war to the early 1960s, postwar Japan witnessed a high tide of mass political participation that peaked in the Anpo movement of 1960.

The failure of the anti-US–Japan Security Treaty movement led to a sense of political fatigue, frustration, and intellectual confusion, and marked a turning point in the postwar social and intellectual developmental path. It was in this context of failure that Yoshimoto's and Takeuchi's critiques of the modern came to acquire a far reaching significance. Seeking to overcome the impasse of the postwar democratic movement, Yoshimoto attempted to include the notions of 'concrete place' and 'empirical life' in his theoretical scheme as the basis for socio-political struggle. Similarly, Takeuchi highlighted in his theoretical formulations the long-neglected notion of *minzoku (ethnos)* as a counter-hegemonic 'site' in the struggle for self-determination and opened up the question of nationalism in direct relation to the postwar democratic trajectory. What distinguished their efforts from the earlier postwar criticisms of the enlightenment theorists was the fact that they both produced alternative visions of social struggle precisely by centring their arguments upon what had been discarded and degraded in the enlightenment theories: the concepts of everyday life, concrete experience, nation and ethnicity, and international hegemony. By attempting to overcome the modernist impasse in this way, however, Yoshimoto and Takeuchi renewed the potential of the national developmental trajectory at a very high cost, for they opened the door to an aestheticization of politics formulated in terms of the popular struggle for the independence of the masses (*taishū no jiritsu*) and the self-determination of the Japanese *minzoku* in the hegemonic international order. While these intellectual endeavours satisfied the needs of the changing context of the times, their overall result was to effect a shift over the course of the 1960s from an enlightenment-led national trajectory to a romantically inclined, popular participatory movement. This is the subject of Chapter 4; but first, a brief point.

One important change that surfaced in this 'romantic turn' was a re-evaluation of the role theory was thought to play in (the analysis of) history, a re-evaluation that can be seen as evidence of an epistemological shift in the way the subject was to relate to the objective/historical world. For both Yoshimoto and Takeuchi, the principal import of theory lay in its guiding function, its role as navigator to the helmsman in the collective transformation of the historical world and existing social relations. Maruyama, on the other hand, believed that given the imperfections of human knowledge and one's consequent partial understanding of the world, the best theory could do was to play a heuristic role by providing a vision of Utopia towards which transformative struggle would be directed. These different conceptions of the relations between theory and practice, or, more precisely, the desired relation the subject takes in the historical world, partly corresponded to the thinkers' different experiences of the war. While Yoshimoto and Takeuchi were fully involved in the debates leading up to, and surrounding the historical meaning of, the war, Maruyama throughout those years was critical of such activities, and maintained a cool distance. It is worth asking in this context whether the various responses to the question of modern subjectivity in postwar Japan were ultimately informed by personal attributes, especially by each of the principal participants' susceptibility to the allure of transcendental reason. Although the question of what underlies one's inclination for or against enlightened rational subjectivity is beyond the scope of this work, what is clear is that in the wake of the Anpo failures, Maruyama's enlightened project of 'democratic revolution' was substantially weakened and the alternative conceptions of Yoshimoto and Takeuchi rose to the fore.

4 The age of rapid economic growth and romantic resurgence

Mass society and the erosion of popular politics and the social imaginary

Introduction

In July 1956, a Japanese economic white paper (*keizai hakusho*) declared the end of the postwar era after consecutive years of steady economic growth had brought back the satisfaction of basic needs and a sense of security to society. By the early 1950s, food rationing and price controls were largely eliminated, and in 1954 the balance of payments turned to a surplus for the first time in the postwar period. It could be safely said that the Japanese economy as a whole had fully recovered from the devastation of the war by the end of the 1950s. Such rapid development was naturally accompanied by broad changes in people's everyday lives and the cultural orientation of society. Widespread electrification of household tasks became the norm in the mid-1950s, and the possession of consumer electric goods became for many an identifying mark of the promised boons of 'middle-class life.' The arrival of television in 1953 was perhaps the most symbolic event, foretelling the coming age of mass culture. Ishihara Shintarō's 1955 novel *Taiyō no kisetsu* (*The Season of the Sun*) could be seen as another cultural indicator of the times, representing and reflecting conditions and the desires of the younger postwar generations who celebrated youth, the body and a leisurely lifestyle, and challenged conventional moral codes and parental authority. Less visible but concurrent with these material and cultural changes was the postwar structural transformation of society which gave rise to a new social reality and system – what some Japanese intellectuals have described as the emergence of 'mass society' – in which the means of social control operates through the homogenization of culture and an intensive use of mass communications. In the face of these radical societal changes, memories of the war and the political climate of the early postwar era quickly faded.

Quite apart from changes in the political and ideological realm, dealt with in the previous chapter, then, the decline of the progressive leftism that had peaked in the 1960 Anpo struggle was undergirded by the materially driven societal changes whose effects began to be increasingly evident in the second half of the 1950s. In the aftermath of the Anpo fiasco, a new form of conservatism led by LDP (Liberal Democratic Party) Prime Minister Ikeda Hayato came up with a highly successful rhetorical strategy, the 'official ideology' of rapid economic growth. With little hesitation, new conservatives painted an overtly optimistic picture of the coming age of prosperity that would supposedly guarantee the greatest 'happiness' for all, and in doing so successfully gained a broad-based support from a populace weary of politics. Leftist intellectuals, Marxists and liberals alike, completely failed to articulate any strategically sound plan in the rapidly changing socio-economic and discursive context, and instead, 'Leftist voices' in the 1960s came to be increasingly represented by the 'romantic,' 'mute' and aesthetically inclined expressions of political actions and ideas. These same 'romantic' inclinations were even more manifest in creative writings produced in the decade, when currents of thought articulating societal concerns and the pains experienced by the writing subject emerged in response to the ever intensifying systemic control to which the populace was becoming subjugated. Such 'romantic' expressions of an alienated subjectivity represent the other side of the coin of the optimism of the new conservative 'economism'; in the social and discursive conditions of the 1960s progressive causes had lost both their means of expression and a sense of goals to be achieved, and now could only be expressed in aesthetic terms, largely by turning one's eyes to the subjective interior and interrogating 'what went wrong.'

The political and discursive terrains of the 1960s could thus be characterized by two opposed politico-ideological trends: a conservative technocratic politics based on a depoliticized bureaucratic rationalism and a radical leftism standing squarely against the establishment. What lay beneath the visible opposition between the two, however, was the emergence of a particular mode of social hegemony that accompanied the emergence of corporate capitalism. The structural transformation to this mode of social organization entailed a series of far-reaching effects in Japanese society, encompassing all spheres of life accessible to the subject. As a result of this wholesale transformation, not only was the conventional political opposition between right and left made meaningless, but politics itself was made impossible in the sense that popular political concerns could only be articulated outside the public and political domain, and that such subjective expressions were increasingly laden with a romantic yearning to recover 'things lost.'

The age of optimism: economic growth and mass consumer society

The emergence of the new Conservatives

In the wake of the 1960 Anpo rallies the ruling Liberal Democratic Party (LDP) was faced with the challenge of restoring a popular trust badly shaken by the largest democratic protests in modern Japanese history. Attempting to recapture popular support, Prime Mister Ikeda Hayato, who replaced Kishi Nobusuke, strategically proclaimed a populist policy centring on economic growth, promising to double incomes within ten years. Article Three, the most important of the Ikeda cabinet's nine policies, reads:

> We will take full advantage of the current state of our economy, which has reached levels of growth unprecedented in history. We will maintain growth without inflation, and increase the GNP by more than twice the current level within ten years. In this way, we will encourage everyone who has the will and ability to work to fully realize their full potential, so that we as a nation can reach the same level of income and standard of living in the future as Western societies. For those less fortunate or unable to work, we will attempt to realize full employment and promise a welfare state.[1]

The emotional appeal behind this economic policy was clearly intended to bolster a weakened government legitimacy by setting up a new national goal and to divert popular disaffection away from real concerns towards the aspirations for a better economic life. In this rhetorical move, the individual's pursuit of a better life is presented as a national goal in which government plays the leading role of gathering together the efforts of all individuals to achieve that goal. In his electoral speech, Ikeda pitched his message of economic optimism and the mutual benefits of self-interest in easily accessible and emotionally appealing language:

> Ladies and gentlemen, I am sorry to disturb your work, but please listen to me for a moment. I am going to tell you a story about how your pay will be doubled. Recall the hard situation we faced with the defeat in the war, out of which ashes we have managed to reestablish ourselves. We no longer stand in queues for rationed food. Our lives have seen tremendous improvements compared to those days. Some say our economy is not yet good enough; but it will get better with your own effort. . . . It is you who will carry out this challenging task, not me. We will work hard together with you.[2]

Despite Ikeda's 'populist' rhetorical tactic of depicting his government as the servants of the people's will, his cabinet was fundamentally conservative, a distinct kind of conservatism from previous versions, one adopting a neo-liberal ideological agenda, in which market forces were to play the central role in national politics.

Indeed, the shift in focus from politics to economics, initiated by the Ikeda cabinet, marks a departure in postwar Japanese history as the beginning of an apolitical, technocratic, functionalist approach to politics. As his response to the press interview upon becoming prime minister clearly shows, politics for Ikeda was a matter of meeting targeted economic forecasts, a matter of instruments and executing policy:

> Politics is the art of improving the living standards of people, and of creating satisfactory social welfare. To double incomes within ten years means an economic growth of 7.2 percent per year. Our record of growth over the past five years is over 9 percent, and there is nothing wrong with estimating that we will have the same growth rate in the near future.... The task of a politician is to do that with confidence.[3]

Needless to say, there was no trace of the early postwar years' hopes and concerns for a 'democratic revolution' in this new vision of politics-as-economy, nor any sense that this radical change in Japan's developmental trajectory was an issue worth discussing. The primary concern of this politics was to create a climate and social infrastructure wherein the market could freely operate with little hindrance from Leftist ideology and people, and to minimize the state's responsibility of mitigating the possible negative effects of such market-driven development policies. The American influence on the Ikeda cabinet's technocratic politics can be noted in several areas. First, following the renewal of the US–Japan Security Treaty and the wave of popular civil disobedience in 1960, the US sent Edwin Reischauer, a well respected historian of Japan and ambassador to Tokyo in 1961.[4] In conjunction with Reischauer's appointment, W. W. Rostow's *The Stages of Economic Development* (1960) was introduced to a circle of prominent Japanese social scientists, bolstering Reischauer's anti-Communist modernization theory, according to which Japan's economic developmental trajectory was accepted and encouraged as beneficial to the US national interest. Along these lines, moreover, mainstream Japanese political economy was shaped in a realist, positivist and pragmatist mode affirmative of US hegemony in Asia.[5] This realist advocacy for US hegemony was the other side of the new conservative, technocratic politics of the Ikeda cabinet.

Rather obviously, this type of positivist politics favoured those who were better educated, pragmatically oriented and had better access to power. Despite the promises of a welfare state in the LDP's policy Article Three, the LDP had no intention of redistributing wealth. This can be seen, for example, in the interview on social welfare policy that Ikeda gave soon after being elected prime minister:

> On the matter of low-income welfare (*seikatsu hogo*), medical security (*iryō-hoshō*), unemployment insurance (*shitsugyō hoken*), old age pensions (*fukushi nenkin*) and so on, it is more important to encourage people to stand on their own two feet than to give them money with thoughts

of salvation for the poor ... We are not going to make large increases in the budget for social welfare right away. However, this year we have decided to hospitalize tuberculosis patients and the mentally ill with government money.[6]

Contrary to its pre-election rhetoric, the Ikeda government assumed that structural reform of the existing domestic politico-economic order was unnecessary, and felt no moral responsibility to support the disadvantaged. The ideology behind this anti-welfare policy seems to belong to the order of value assumptions beneath the rhetoric of 'self-help,' i.e. since poverty is not socially caused but is rather a lack of effort and ability on the part of particular individuals, they, thus, are fully responsible for facing up to the social conditions they find themselves in. In addition to a lacklustre welfare policy, the new political trajectory explicitly favoured large business corporations as the engines of growth, at the expense of smaller enterprises. Many have pointed out that Ikeda was able to rise to the leadership of the LDP only with strong support from the financial giants, the business conglomerates which had mushroomed under the system established during the prime ministry of Yoshida Shigeru. The Ikeda cabinet was located at the centre of the same power network as these major financial-business groups, which also enjoyed strong connections with the mass media.[7] That is to say, with the election of the Ikeda cabinet with its new political trajectory centring on economic growth, the door towards the concentration of Japanese capital was thrown wide open: the financial conglomerates began their rapid ascent, an exclusive hierarchical system linking elite businesses to the financial and political system was consolidated, and the conglomerates consolidated their dominance in the subsequent Sato Eisaku cabinet.[8]

In short, the new conservative trend was economic-centred, pacifist, positivist and elitist, and their ideological and political tools – rational choice theory, *laissez-faire* economics, and political realism – replaced the old ideals of progressive leftism, without much resistance. With its optimism and appeals to a better life, Ikeda's policy of doubling incomes (*shotoku baizō keikaku*) did manage to capture a broad-base of support among the ideologically and politically fatigued public. By correctly reading the changes that society was undergoing and tacitly articulating the demands of the populace in appealing ways, the new conservative policy successfully manoeuvred the LDP to a position of legitimacy as the nation's ruling party.[9] Moreover, it is noteworthy that this new conservative trajectory attempted to incorporate aspects of nationalist rhetoric, not in cultural particularist terms, as the old conservatives had done or wanted to do, but in a renewed assertion congenial to economic success. In 1963, Ikeda introduced another new policy, that of 'creating people' reflecting the need of the economic engine of big business:

> Creating people is the foundation of the creation of a nation. Creating people means fostering those who create themselves by moral self-examination. The role of the government is to enhance the climate of human creation in each sphere of life, such as the household, schools, and work places, and to improve the environment and conditions for that purpose.[10]

This ambiguously defined policy sought to revitalize the links between personal identity and that of the nation, to forestall the growing sense of frustration with the negative effects of the government-promoted economic growth policies and the all-too-rapid social change that accompanied them. In June of the same year, Ikeda ordered the Ministry of Education to formulate a series of moral guidelines for the nation entitled 'Image of the ideal Japanese' (*Kitai sareru ningen zō*, issued January 1965); as pointed out by many, it is not at all clear in whose terms this ideal moral accomplishment is conceived, since the Japanese title is phrased in the passive voice and lacks a subject.[11] The guidelines begin with a description of the highly technologically oriented state of present society as inevitable, and emphasize the need for the Japanese to be apt and open to the challenge of 'internationalization' without losing their sense of national identity. In order to foster this international–national identity, the guidelines paint a picture of the 'model' Japanese individual as one capable of playing a multiplicity of roles, as an individual, as a member of a family, as a member of society and as a member of the nation, and competent in combining traditional cultural virtues with the ability to adapt new skills. Emphasis on the family and the nation raised the suspicions of many Leftists that the paternalistic state of the prewar era might again be on the rise. However, the overall effect of the guidelines and the policy of creating people did not have as much impact as the conservatives had hoped nor the Leftists had feared.

With the successful articulation of the new conservative ideology in the mid-1960s and with the solid backing of the increasingly powerful business and financial groups the material ground of new conservatism was solidified. In 1963, 92 per cent of all goods sold in Japan were not subject to trade restrictions or tariffs, and in the following year Japan joined the OECD as an internationally recognized developed nation. In 1964 a bullet-train service with a maximum speed of over 200 km/h was initiated, and the Japanese were fascinated with it as a symbol of national economic success. When the Tokyo Olympic Games opened the following October, Japan occupied the centre stage of the world for two full weeks, and was able to project an image of confidence as the newest member of the world's leading industrial nations. On average, Japan recorded a 10 per cent annual growth in GNP throughout the 1960s, with average nominal incomes increasing by 12.2 per cent (real incomes increasing by 5.9 per cent), breaking the myth that full employment was impossible.[12] In fact, Japan was happily plagued by a shortage of labour, and that, together with the various entertaining attractions, motivated many of the younger generation of the rural poor to migrate to the big cities. In 1968, Japan's GNP surpassed that of West Germany, putting Japan in the position of second most productive nation, behind the US. By the end of the decade the identifying symbols of Japanese middle-class life were upgraded from the TV, the refrigerator and the washing machine to the air-conditioner, the automobile and the colour TV set. In addition, university enrolment dramatically increased throughout this period and continued to rise into the 1970s: from 10.3 per cent in 1960, to 17.0 per cent in 1965, 23.6 per cent in 1970 and 34.2 per cent in 1975.[13]

In the wake of the Anpo struggle, there was a strongly felt need among Leftist politicians and intellectuals that a cogent answer to the growing ideological vacuum was necessary; the time was ripe to rearticulate a new set of concerns and policy alternatives. However, in the face of the new conservative initiatives, the JSP, and Leftist intellectuals in general, were demoralized and in disarray, and failed to come up with meaningful new political or economic strategies to counteract the LDP's new conservatism. Moreover, in the rapidly changing socio-economic context, the ideals of peace, democracy and freedom inherited from the earlier progressives became little more than empty slogans, or worse, could be turned to the conservatives' advantage if inflected to mean peace and prosperity in private life, free economic competition and freedom to pursue self-interest.[14] One JSP member, Katsumata Seiichi, later recalling the strategic failure of the JSP at the time (and, indeed, throughout the 1960s), remarked:

> After the resignation of Kishi . . . Ikeda appeared and said nothing on Anpo nor on Constitutional reform. He only talked about tolerance and patience as his principles, and doubling incomes as his key policy. This directly contributed to the collapse of the left. The LDP had fashioned this change of pace very well. . . . That is what I regret now.[15]

> In the stable period of economic growth in the 1960s . . . the LDP achieved great success in battling the problems of the double-structured economy [the combination of agrarian and industrial economies], in achieving full employment, in increasing real incomes, etc. The reason for the stagnation of the JSP lay in its weak strategy under such conditions.[16]

While some of the fault for the collapse of the Left may be placed at the doorstep of the JSP, the failure to articulate a new Leftist ideology was partly due to their reluctance to address issues of nationalism and identity, which in their analysis were identified with the causes of the prewar disaster. Their weakness on these issues hindered them from creating a progressive alternative to the conservatives, one able to re-establish democratic links between the government and the populace.[17] Conversely, it was the conservatives who during the period of rapid economic growth tacitly articulated to the uprooted a state-initiated corporate nationalism capable of conjoining the pursuit of personal interest and home-centred values.[18] As a result of these failures, the JSP ended up in principle passively following the LDP policy trajectory; the strange situation then arose in which Leftist intellectuals largely spoke about social and economic policy in the same terms of reference as the new conservatives. With this shift, postwar Japanese democracy was reduced to a formalized process of negotiation, universal peace watered down to a more quotidian version, and the labour struggle to a ritualized and corporate unionism.[19]

Emergence of the new Left

It was during this same mid-1960s period, however, that a new form of popular Leftist activism arose, triggered by protests against the Vietnam war. The impromptu gathering of individuals who began calling for 'Peace in Vietnam!,' 'Vietnam for Vietnamese!' and 'Stop the collaboration with US aggression in Vietnam!' is commonly known as *Beheiren*, the Peace in Vietnam Committee. Having no clearly defined membership or organizing principles, nor a central office or hierarchically organized command structure, *Beheiren* was cemented together by a strongly shared and vaguely defined feeling. When Oda Makoto, a leading and charismatic figure of the group, remarked that 'I do not clearly know what *Beheiren* is,' but 'I know it at its core,' he gestured to the nature of the group's nexus as being based upon a spirit of spontaneity that emerged and developed outside formal institutional structures.[20] In many ways *Beheiren* was the antithesis of conventional organized Leftist politics, which tended to subsume the diverse abilities, volitions and needs of its members to its uniform organizational goals along ideological lines. Learning from the limitations of the Anpo movement, *Beheiren* claimed to be a new kind of civil movement that relied upon self-educated individuals actively seeking greater political understanding and participation by situating and integrating their everyday lives in the contexts of international and domestic political causes. As Oda claimed:

> The movements of the early 1960s were based on a passive beneficiary mentality, which attempted to protect the small happiness that the participants as citizens enjoyed in daily life; those movements arose when people felt their everyday peace was under threat. . . . The civil movement today, however, has come to understand the fact that peaceful everyday life itself, what we had attempted to protect in the early 1960s, was used for justifying Japanese contributions to the Vietnamese

war, for cutting Okinawa off from Japanese jurisdiction, and for supporting the US–Japan Security Treaty and the system of which it is a part. The citizens of 1960 shouted 'Follow the Constitution,' 'Protect the democratic parliamentary system.' *Beheiren* and other civil movements today, however, acknowledge regretfully that the very Constitution does not apply to Okinawa, and the postwar peace has only been established by excepting Okinawa from its jurisdiction.[21]

Oda, who was born in 1932, saw Japan's indirect participation in the Vietnamese war as a challenge to the beliefs and values he had acquired in his postwar education, and he came to the conclusion that the political movements of the 1960s demanded greater education in and awareness of the complexity of the issues that faced society. In a difficult age where actions quickly became routine, Oda attempted to take responsibility for confronting the hypocrisy of the status quo in which the 'everyday peace' was maintained and enforced in tandem with the politics of brute power. In doing so, Oda made it the condition of his own politics to walk the tightrope between being a writer and a knowing subject and being an activist. Many young people admired Oda's combination of activism backed up by a broad, critical and international knowledge, and saw him as a representative of the younger generation.

It is noteworthy that *Beheiren*'s unique tactic of linking its members' everyday lives to international politics was actualized in part by incorporating aspects of festivity into popular political action and by building upon networks of friends. Thus *Beheiren*'s news letters, for example, served as a communal forum encouraging members to express and exchange their views on current issues as well as to expand their human networks. The political demonstrations that were *Beheiren*'s main activity were not only political expressions of discontent, but also forms of self-expression and interpersonal communication, building and affirming solidarity with others. Commenting on this social and even 'pleasurable' dimension, Oda remarked that

> I encourage people to form a movement to tour Japan with demonstrations. This is half joke and half serious. *Beheiren* in Urawa goes to Kyoto for a demonstration in support of *Beheiren* in Kyoto. Of course, they can see temples in Kyoto on the way. Or conversely, *Beheiren* in Kyoto can learn about the urban conditions at the edge of Tokyo by joining the Urawa *Beheiren*'s demonstration.[22]

> *Beheiren*'s demonstrations have the function of mutually confirming the existence and the will of the people themselves, above and beyond the value of their political acts of demonstration. And I can add another function: to provide a place for people to exchange information and experience.[23]

In Oda's conception, then, the strength of *Beheiren* is based upon the active incorporation of these enjoyable by-products and the participants' own ends into the protest movement, insofar as they would enhance public education and advance *Beheiren*'s political goals. In this sense, a tactical change in popular participatory Leftist movements became manifest in the shift from the Anpo-era movements to one like *Beheiren*, more adapted to the awakening mass consumer/information society characterized by the material affluence and individualistic cultural orientations of the new middle-class.[24]

Beheiren was also proud of its active form of political participation distinct from the mere voicing of objections; they gave sanctuary, for example, to US deserters, helping them seek asylum in Sweden. As Oda claimed: 'It is important to know that we object to the Vietnam war, but members must realize that expressing our objection in concrete action is even more important.'[25] This shift of emphasis from intellectual discussion to direct action, or from theory to practice, reflects another criticism of conventional Leftist politics. Distinct as it may be from the old style, *Beheiren*'s politics of action as self-expression, by failing to establish a common ground with the conventional left, in some ways contributed to the further undermining of the existing formal political parties and unions. Moreover, *Beheiren*'s incorporation into political expression of a radical attempt to liberate desire and the senses, thus challenging the petit-bourgeois moralism of the conventional left, flirted with the risk of overstating the participatory aspects of demonstration as a political action and purpose in itself.[26] In short, *Beheiren*'s new left politics was circumscribed by, and formulated within, the emergent socio-economic conditions of the mass consumer/ information society; in this sense it did not seriously challenge the status-quo, all the while serving as a counter-ballast for the grounding of the nascent neo-conservative right. Thus, the new political battle lines between the new right and the new left were drawn by subordinating politics to the given socio-economic and cultural climate. This in turn reflected, after the great structural changes society had undergone, the overwhelming potency of the new structural configuration, for beneath the optimism shared by the ideologies of the political right and left alike lay the middle-class lifestyle of personal consumption and leisure that had quietly effected the depoliticization of society.[27]

A more radical movement arose among university students when the Ministry of Education attempted to intervene in university affairs as part of its greater project to subject university education to greater bureaucratic control. By the mid-1960s, many isolated student groups, each struggling at a particular university for diverse causes (e.g. against the separation of the teachers' programme from the other faculties, tuition increases, and the introduction of university-wide examinations), coalesced in September 1969 into a nationwide student union called *Zengaku Kyōtō Kaigi*, the Joint Struggle Committee, or *Zenkyōtō* for short.[28] The coalition came together during a phase of large increases in university enrolment (particularly among young women) and matured into a movement first at Tokyo University, later spreading elsewhere and involving formerly '*non-pori*' (non-political) student masses.[29] Together with *Beheiren*, the *Zenkyōtō* movement was often referred to as a new left movement because of its progressive, non-sectarian and anarchistic stance against elitist technocratic/bureaucratic control. Unlike *Beheiren*, however, *Zenkyōtō* did not rule out violence as a means of political resistance against the establishment, and while *Beheiren* took a self-affirmative stance, the ideological undertone of *Zenkyōtō* was a strict self-negation, viewing the principal enemy as the 'imperialism inside oneself.' Developing under the influence of the mid-1960s Chinese cultural revolution, the *Zenkyōtō* movement could be seen as a moderate version of a Japanese cultural revolution, focused specifically on revolutionizing the consciousness of the intellectuals who thus were placed in the position of having to choose between self-confinement in the 'ivory tower' and participation in the movement by descending to the streets.[30] Although *Zenkyōtō* bore some similarities with radical student movements in other advanced societies (the influences of Sartre and Mao, for example), its development did not follow the conventional pattern of ideological and cultural importation from the West.

Particularly significant among these struggles were two incidents which both took place in 1968, one at Tokyo University, Japan's top-ranked university, and the other at Nihon University, a university long known for being a bastion of conservative elite power. The *Zenkyōtō* uprising at Tokyo University initially began as a protest by medical students seeking the abolition of the highly exploitative medical intern system, but, in response to the administration's calling in the police force in the face of its inability to handle the students' demands, the protest quickly escalated to occupying parts of the campus, including the Yasuda lecture hall, the symbolic centre of the university.[31] The student-occupied areas were called the 'liberated zones' (*kaihō-ku*), spaces supposedly free from authority's bureaucratic control, until the police put an end to the rebellion by force after a six months' strike and occupation. The *Zenkyōtō* struggle at Nihon University was triggered by a financial scandal in which 3 billion yen went missing from the administrative budget; outrage ran high when it was alleged that the money had been used for the university president's private purposes, campaign donations to LDP politicians, and slush funds for right-wing groups.[32] In pitched battles against squads of right-wing students from the faculty of physical education and local thugs employed by the administration, the *Zenkyōtō* students closed the university behind barricades, and demanded the resignation of the rector. When the police arrested the leading figures of the movement, the rebellion was effectively broken and quickly died. Compared to the Tokyo University revolt against bureaucratic control, the Nihon University *Zenkyōtō* rebellion was much more similar to conventional democratic struggles against the elite power-establishment, in that it faced a corrupt administration and was marked by an adversarial politics with clear goals.

One notable feature of *Zenkyōtō* progressivism was its emphasis on radical and direct action, its acceptance of violence as a legitimate means of fighting oppression. *Zenkyōtō* radicals armed themselves with helmets, wrapped their faces with towels, and wielded wooden batons or iron pipes as a means of expressing solidarity and their will to fight. These tactics certainly reflected the growing distrust of formal party-line politics and a recognition that 'the Japanese capitalist and increasingly imperialist society will be restructured not by any parliamentary or electoral means but ... [by] revolutionary struggle which alone can work such a transformation.'[33] As Yamamoto Yoshitaka, the leader of the Tokyo University *Zenkyōtō* group and author of *The Rebellion of the Intellect* (*Chisei no hanran*, 1969), remarked, the cause of the *Zenkyōtō* uprisings was 'not because discussion was lacking, but because discussion was not to generate any solutions.'[34] Yamamoto claimed that the barricades were an active political statement demonstrating the movement's outright rejection of 'the university as a factory' for the production of the servants of capital, mere cogs in the wheel of authority.[35] At the same time, the *Zenkyōtō* radical revolutionary inclination brought, in effect, a climactic end to the postwar Japanese progressivist and Leftist movements, and created an intellectual legacy that further entrenched the distrust of a rationality that was increasingly associated with elite oppression and bureaucratic power. These anti-rational and progressive features were combined in *Zenkyōtō* with an intense self-interrogation and self-negation, in which students were exhorted to question the meaning of their own existence in a bureaucratized, mass-consumer society.[36] It was the task of students to find a way to *engage* with history, in full recognition of their responsibilities as well as the hypocrisy of being an elite university student and intellectual-to-be. Clearly linked to Sartre's understanding of the role of the intellectual, in the context of Japanese student radicalism these ideas were fused with Yoshimoto's notions of pathos (*jyōnen*) and the independence of the masses (*taishū no jiritsu*).[37]

One critic has remarked that the *Zenkyōtō* movement also reflected an age of troubled subjectivity in which, for many of the younger generation, one's sense of self could only be confirmed by violence and radical action, in which resistance, not negotiation, was the sole means of affirming one's identity.[38] Indeed, many ex-*Zenkyōtō* members later recalled that their true motivation for action and violence was a sense of physical satisfaction and pleasure quite apart from their theoretical rationalizations. The movement offered its participants a place to test their ideas, to express and display a unique political practice, and to share with their peers a similar political identity and ideals.[39] In some ways, the members of *Zenkyōtō* willingly confined themselves in an imaginary container and masochistically put themselves under an oppressive pressure as a means of affirming their identity.[40] In this sense, the *Zenkyōtō* movement was several steps removed from civilian types of Leftist activism like *Beheiren*, for while the members of *Beheiren* affirmed themselves simply by liberating their senses, the members of *Zenkyōtō* had to deny themselves in order to affirm their identity. *Zenkyōtō* radicalism was in a sense quite logically derived from the structural changes Japanese society was undergoing and their resultant effects upon subjectivity, under which conditions educated individuals could no longer affirm political consciousness and rehabilitate identity by simply liberating their senses, but instead needed to construct and then reify an imaginary oppressor (e.g. the elite establishment). In other words, over the course of the 1960s the increasing opacity of the enemy and the increasing internalization of systemic control in effect increasingly linked one's political and personal struggles to forms of anarchistic self-negation.

One might view the *Zenkyōtō* movement and its goal of creating an anarchic commune as a rebellion against the invisible power and control that operated through technical rationalism, the state bureaucratic machinery, and the abstract knowledge that alienates the individual from his/her daily life. The rise of the *Zenkyōtō* movement demonstrated the extent to which the ideal–typical content of the rational autonomous subject, the principal agent of the early postwar democratic revolution, had been undermined and replaced by a romantic, collective and agonized notion of the subject. In this change, the previous enlightenment-oriented democratic movement was transformed in a collective and aesthetically inclined romantic mode, with possibly the most progressive autonomous segments of society (the students) as its main participants, who now became the dominant actors representing the voice of mass society, the middle class *taishū* (masses). Given that *Zenkyōtō* radicalism lacked an effective organization for achieving its goals (which were not clearly defined), and once the moment of resistance had reached its peak it naturally, and rapidly, deteriorated into conflicts among extreme radical factions alienated from the student masses, as exemplified in the 1972 Asama villa incident. Overall, mass political movements in the 1960s – from the Anpo struggle to *Beheiren*, and then on to *Zenkyōtō* – reflected a general slide towards the breakdown of Leftist popular politics. Although initially very broad and popularized, 1960s Leftist politics as a whole became increasingly confined to smaller and smaller segments of the population, a process of marginalization that would be symbolic of the coming decade in which Japanese society became almost completely lacking in any popular means of participatory political expression.

Romantic resurgence: desire for identity, beauty and meaning

Not only did prosperous material development mark a departure from the postwar era, but the rapid socio-economic and cultural changes produced from the late 1950s onward also had a tremendous impact upon the internal state of the subject. In part because of the Leftists' failure to articulate new political programmes and ideas, but more substantially because of the fundamental transformation taking place in the relation between the human senses and their means of expression – i.e. language – there emerged in the inner landscape of individuals an increasing sense of discontinuity. Voices articulating this disjunction and a resultant sense of void, variously expressed according to the way each author encountered problems in their daily lives and the subjects of their concern, were often to be found in the field of creative writing, and sometimes in culturally and aesthetically inclined academic writings. For example, these expressions protesting against a perceived sense of closure, excessive rationality, Westernized lifestyles, American cultural hegemony and the loss of tradition or the sense of beauty, could be broadly categorized as 'romantic.' Together they tend to set a revisionist inflection on the previous enlightenment discourse and democratic revolutionary trajectory. In this section, I depict some of the romantic currents that emerged in response to the socio-economic and cultural transformations of Japan in the 1950s and 1960s, transformations in which the realm of subjectivity and discursive meanings were subjected to serious disturbances. I focus on the emergence of four preferred sites for thematizing and expressing these often inarticulate voices, sentiments and concerns: the realm of sexuality as the antithesis of political hopelessness; the breakdown of the family as a symbol of 'nature'; the increasing assertion of the relativity of truth, morality, and history in international political settings; and the domains of culture and aesthetics as areas in which a desire for transcendence was articulated.

Individuals in struggle: sex, politics and desire for the absolute

Marking a stark contrast with the rosy images of the age as one of economic wealth and democracy painted by the new conservatives, two celebrated young writers of the late-1950s took up as their themes the sense of closure and the frustration with a formless enemy. Both Ishihara Shintarō and Ōe Kenzaburō expressed a widely felt vague sense of anxiety, irritation and powerlessness:

> We ... cannot participate in politics in real terms in any way.... Real politics is so far away from where we expect the concept of politics to be, or perhaps it can be said that politics already exists in a different realm altogether.[41]

> We are stagnant. The conceptual map of the Japanese of the 1950s is marked by stagnation. This stagnation is not for the intellectuals alone; it seems to be spreading to industrial sites, fishing villages and agrarian villages as a harmful disease, a fatal one.[42]

The two authors are often seen as opposites in terms of their writing style, sensitivities, political positions and concerns. While Ishihara's main characters are typically active, reckless, masculine-type youths, searching for sexual pleasure and attracted to violence, Ōe's feminized youths look inward, untiringly self-interrogating their frustrated political desires and feelings of powerlessness, which often find their only means of expression by mutating into sexual desire and its fulfilment. Nevertheless, the two authors' late-1950s works share a striking similarity in a persistent underlying tone of a sense of confinement, of being enclosed inside walls from which there seems to be no escape.

The emergence of Ishihara in the postwar Japanese literary scene came as a shock to the literary establishment, and Ishihara's abrupt rejection of the familiar postwar themes and sensitivities split the selection board of the prestigious Akutagawa literary prize into passionate supporters and outraged opponents. Ishihara's work was seen as representing a new generation, and as a result received constant and intense media attention. His 1955 debut novel *Taiyō no kisetsu* (*The Season of the Sun*), later made into a film, was an unprecedented bestseller, and Ishihara was lionized by the mass media as a popular star. A new subculture imitative of the young protagonists in the novel was created; the so-called 'sun tribe' hung around the fashionable yacht harbours of the Shōnan coastal area sporting a hairstyle called the 'Shintarō cut.' In part because of the sensation associated with his debut, Ishihara was subject to much harsh criticism for his explicit disregard of the concerns of the older generations (principally their preoccupation with the war), as well as for a seeming lack of moral sensitivity in his celebrations – of the masculine body, of an idle life-style, and of egotistical sex – that boldly gave voice to the 'mood' of the nascent mass consumer culture. As the critic Etō Jun has pointed out, however, the greatest value of Ishihara's literature lay in his desperate pursuit of 'reality' and 'the body' which, as he attempts ever more intensely to hunts them down, flee from him ever more, leading him more and more to a recognition of their opposites, the elusive nature of the world and one's body.[43] Etō sees this paradox as representing a nation-wide, ongoing process in the Japan of the late 1950s and 1960s; for Etō, Ishihara's agony symbolizes the age of postwar romanticism in which an inversion of 'reality' and illusion was rapidly progressing.[44]

Indeed, contrary to the optimistic, indulgent, and even hedonistic impressions of Ishihara's works given in the mass-media, his core theme is much more closely associated with the futility of action and a sense of powerlessness. Ishihara repeatedly gives his male protagonists the task of breaking down what he and they call 'the wall': in his 1956 novel *Shokei no heya* (*The Execution Room*), for example, Ishihara conveys this sense of powerlessness in the voice of one of his main characters:

the world is suffocating just as if it were confined in a small room. We are gradually worm-eaten in this enclosed room. I do something to jump out of here, do what I want until I am completely exhausted. I do not have time to think whether that is the best way to do it, and even if you think, nobody knows what is. There is something I want to break down by hitting my entire body against it; but I do not know what and where that something is.[45]

This character desperately and recklessly hurls his body against the invisible enemy surrounding him, with little success, as though impetuous explosion and self-destruction were his sole weapons. In his *Kiretsu* (*The Cleavage*, 1956–7), Ishihara portrays another character, who, struggling against the formless, ambiguous world, attempts to grasp the essence of things through sex. After a momentary resolution of the conundrum of his existence and the 'reality' he so desperately desires to possess, 'the cleavage' returns as a sinister abyss that throws the protagonist into an all too familiar place of prohibition and anxiety.

> Desiring to quench the thirst in the midst of fulfiling each other, Akira was repeatedly telling himself.
> 'I am now possessing what I wanted.'
> At the same time, just a step beyond that ecstasy, he continuously felt that that vague unknown anxiety, an anxiety he always felt, was opening up its crack, waiting for him to soon fall into it.[46]

This character's desire for transcendence takes the form of a quasi-religious quest to encounter something greater than his trivial existence, something that, he feels, would provide him with a meaning in life, something that would help him to discover an identity in his indeterminate self. In Etō's reading, the protagonist's anxiety stems from an acute feeling of 'cleavage' in Ishihara himself, an unbearable sense of the abyss between the author's interior self and his 'body,' and between himself and 'reality.'[47] Interpreting Ishihara's inclination to reject all self-determinations/restrictions (*jiko-gentei*) and determinations of the world as his 'distinct stoicism,' Etō writes:

> [what was original in Ishihara's manner of encountering 'the cleavage' was] his exertion of a stoicism to sustain himself in a kind of pure state of 'suspension' by refusing any form of self-determination and any attitude of determining 'reality.' Most likely, Mr. Ishihara himself wants to say that he wants to keep himself in the pure state of 'potential,' rather than 'suspension.'[48]

Referring to *Shokei no heya*, Etō sees Ishihara's extensive use of aimless violence as a representation of the author's 'mental aphasia,' his awkward relation with words. Despite the fact that he is an accomplished writer, there is, argues Etō, something hopeless and impossible in his relation to language: '"words" lead him either towards literature or politics, but at that very moment he collapses in the direction of a double muteness – sex and violence.'[49] This collapse is inevitable insofar as he is loyal to his stoicism, wanting to remain in the pure state of 'suspension' and to maintain his rejection of all self-determination by means of reducing his being in a singularly logical manner. In Etō's reading, the state of muteness Ishihara symbolizes represent the alienated Japanese youth of the late 1950s, who in general 'did not have any means of expression other than [using] their own bodies, which were thus reduced to self-purposive objects (*jiko-mokuteki-ka shita karada*).'[50] However, this stance, was later abandoned as Ishihara matured and came to accept the terms of the world.

Contrary to Ishihara's inclination to ignoring the past, Ōe described his generational position as 'one who came late,' born too late for the war and for the early postwar progressive leftism. Like Ishihara, Ōe also thematized the situation of his time as being caught in a state of suffocating confinement.[51] Ōe expresses depicts a sense of powerlessness in the tragic and comic existence of Japanese males who, as a sexual men (*seiteki ningen*), seek to attain a sense of totality and satisfaction by indulging in sexual ecstasy. In Ōe's definition the sexual man constitutes the antithesis of the political man (*seijiteki ningen*):

> A political man firmly and coldly confronts, and fights against, the other; he either destroys the other or erases the other from his own system and makes the other abandon being his other. . . . A sexual man, on the contrary, neither opposes nor confronts his other. Not only does he not have a firm and cold relation with the other, but to him the other does not fundamentally exist. Also, he himself cannot be an other to any other being.[52]

Many of Ōe's protagonists are sexual men who voluntarily confine themselves behind the walls imposed by the superior other, often taken to mean society as an oppressive mechanism. Focusing their attention on the attainment of ecstasy by enslaving themselves to the imaginary in the world of sex, Ōe's sexual men never bother to break through the imaginary wall and confront others. Or, to put it differently, abandoning the possibility for struggle is what constitutes a sexual man, the man whose attention is diverted by his quest for satisfaction in the comfort of being protected from the intrusion of the senseless outside of the political/historical world.

Ōe sees postwar Japan as a nation filled with sexual men, particularly in the period following the renewal of the US–Japan Security Treaty, where peace and prosperity were guaranteed by US hegemonic protection. In Ōe's view, it was the loss of a tension with the outside world, a loss that resulted from the awareness that the pursuit of being political men was both meaningless and impossible, that transformed the Japanese politico-cultural space and rendered it complacent:

> I think that beneath the atmosphere filling contemporary Japan with a sense of peace and comfort lies the shadow of sexual men like unborn babies, men whose self-complacency leaves them lacking in fighting spirit and fretfulness. I view contemporary Japan as a nation of sexual men, indulging in peace and comfort by being dominated and subordinated to a mighty America. I see difficulties and anxieties burdening the progressive political activists in this nation; an overpowering wall stands against them. In the country of sexual men, political men can be nothing but outsiders, not only powerless but also funny and tragic.[53]

These works of Ōe and Ishihara share a number of factors that critics have related to the legacy of Japan's defeat in World War II: the symbolization of a threat to existence in the form of confinement, a self-consciousness endangered by some politico-cultural structure which has annulled 'politics,' and even a symbolic castration of Japanese masculine identity. The directions in which these thematics are developed, however, are quite distinct: while Ishihara's protagonists focus on blind acts of struggle to affirm their existence, Ōe's characters focus on internalized reflections of the world, constituting a total, albeit enclosed, sphere of feelings.

In his *Seventeen* (1961), a story he felt compelled to write soon after the assassination of the JSP leader Asanuma Inejirō in 1960, Ōe depicts the intimate link between masculine sexuality and the convoluted expressions of desire for identity suppressed in the typical sexual man. The main character of the story is a teenager named Seventeen who, agonizing over his lack of confidence and failure to win respect from others, is depicted as a habitual masturbator in search of a strong guiding principle to provide a solid architecture for his ambiguous sense of self. By finding this principle in right-wing beliefs, he liberates himself from his stifling anxieties, and transforms himself into a solid, manly right-wing youth. What makes this transformation possible is what Seventeen calls the armour of the emperor, a sign of the absolute to whose authority he subjugates himself.

> Stones and trees do not have anxiety, cannot fall into the state of anxiety. By discarding my own desire, I became a stone and a tree of the emperor. There is no longer any anxiety in myself, into which I could fall. I feel I can go on living lightly, feel that a once so complicated and incomprehensible world has become so nice and simple.[54]

By acquiring a clear goal and a purpose in life, the young man feels he has exchanged his troubled identity for a new strength as a manly right-wing terrorist. This acquisition of self-confidence mediated by a submission to the emperor, can be read as a parable of the generation of post-1960

Japanese men whose confrontation with others takes the form of a submission to a greater other. That is to say, rather than confronting overpowering others like US hegemony and the Japanese elites, the main character finds contentment, confidence and superiority in a readily available source, by terrorizing ordinary citizens with threats of senseless and brutal right-wing violence.

Moreover, by self-denial and unification with the absolute moral-political being – i.e. the emperor – the main character attains a 'sexualized' political potency mediated by the eroticism of the 'manly act' of self-sacrifice.[55] This can be seen, for example, in the following self-affirmation where the protagonist, realizing the very sight of him puts fear into the hearts of a group of on-looking office girls, awakens to his new status as a right-wing thug:

> Yes, I am right-wing. I shivered as extreme joy suddenly struck me. I have touched my truth; I am right-wing! . . . I felt a new self, one who does not become nervous or blush when stared at by others . . . I felt I had just shut out others' eyes from the sight of a weak and timid myself which is now covered by strong armour. The armour of the right-wing! . . . I felt a spiritual delight similar to sexual arousal in the fear I saw in the hearts of those girls where warm blood is rushing fast.[56]

Eroticism, in this account, operates in the domain where the protagonist affirms his righteousness by displacing the other, by virtue of equating his self-images with an absolute symbol through which he attempts to transcend his limited existence. Simultaneously, however, the protagonist's self-affirmation demands his submission to, and even self-sacrifice for, the absolute symbol. Seventeen's sacrificial passion for the ultimate ideal of the nation is portrayed as essentially operating by means of the same mechanism as the abandonment of the self in sexual pleasure.

> I will discard my personal soul filled with fear and jump into the great smelter of the pure emperor. After that arrives a never ending heaven only permitted to a few select men, an eternal orgasm that comes and lasts forever, as if that is the state of normality. The moment is eternal, death will be absorbed into it, transforming nothing, a zero change. At the moment I stabbed the Chairman, I jumped into the four-dimensional world of heavenly delight.[57]

Critic Isoda Kōichi sees in Ōe's works a critique of those Japanese intellectuals, both right and left, who tried to play the role of 'political men,' but who, in fact, ignored their actual relations with others and lived politics as the object of eroticism, and who were thus akin to the 'sexual men' who attained ecstatic release in a world devoid of others.[58] In Ōe's view, the sexual man is a problematic and representative figure of his generation, a figure who must struggle to establish an identity of his own in a society where moral absolutes and political goals are increasingly vacuous, and, in this sense, the sexualized expression of politics is an attempt to redeem a lost politics from the genuine power domains. In a desperate attempt to establish one's identity, the damaged link between oneself and the world, and that between the past and the present, Ōe's contemporary youths are vulnerable to surrendering themselves to ideas and symbols that are all too readily available, thereby rapidly enhancing their own sense of power but in a short-circuited way.[59]

By largely thematizing the problematics of the war and nationalism as internal reflections or psychological and emotional effects of their characters, both Ishihara and Ōe have been subject to the criticism that they demonstrated little sense of the historical context of their times. One critic suggested that both authors had willingly confined themselves behind a wall of self-consciousness and had passively submitted to the current of the time.[60] In my view, however, both Ishihara and Ōe provide us with a precious record, otherwise unrecorded, of the internal landscape of the younger generation in the late 1950s and 1960s. Their depictions of the muteness of political protest, the loss of political direction, and the absence of moral principles and ideology, all of which they were largely critical of, allow us a glimpse into the darker side of the conservative discourse's rosy picture of rapid economic growth, as well as at the severe limitations it imposed on the articulation of political thought and action. Despite the initial similarities of their problematics, however, the two authors have subsequently taken quite different paths in their explorations of overcoming powerlessness. Ishihara, having already won nation-wide popularity as a novelist, turned to a political career and ran as an LDP candidate for the Upper-House in 1968, winning by a huge margin of 320,000 votes, and subsequently became the Minister of the Environment in 1976 at the age of 44. Ōe, on the other hand, continued his creative activities, matured as a novelist through a period of struggle with the question of the family, especially with the relation to his disabled son as dealt with in his *A Personal Matter* (1964) and *Teach Us to Outgrow our Madness* (1969). Many critics have felt that Ōe finally broke away from his previous focus on psycho-sexual descriptions towards a more open spirit reflective of an active relation between the self, society and the world at large in his 1967 *Man'ei gannen no futtobōru* (translated as *The Silent Cry*).

The breakdown of the family: changing gender roles and reactionary responses

One of the most thematized subjects in the literature of the 1960s was the disintegration of the traditional family, as exemplified in the works of Kojima Nobuo (*Hoyo Kazoku*, 1965), Shōno Junzō (*Seibutsu*, 1960; *Yūbe no kumo*, 1965), Yasuoka Shōtarō (*Umibe no kōkei*, 1959; *Hanamatsuri*, 1962) and

Shimao Toshio (*Shi no toge*, 1960). The popularity of the family as a novelistic theme (revealingly, most often in the works of male authors) was closely related to the breakdown of the traditional family system, and typically these family novels are concerned with the value conflict between the sexes and the resultant difficulties of maturation for children (most often assumed male) in such an unstable environment. With the emergence in the postwar period of new values that often exacerbated conflicts between the sexes, and with the collapse of the extended family into the nuclear family, the traditional Japanese family system suffered a serious erosion that altered both the role ascribed to each family member and the dynamic of husband–wife relations. The ratio between arranged and free marriages (the former made up three-quarters of early postwar unions) was reversed in the second half of the 1960s; sexual pleasure, conventionally suppressed, came to be publicly affirmed as an individual right, and its segregation from reproduction made possible by the birth-control technology that in effect advanced the equality between the sexes.[61] Reflecting these changes, the 'family novels' no longer concerned themselves with oppression in the stable and traditionally sacred sanctuary of the family, but moved on to an exploration of the territories of conflict, distrust, confusion and despair. The focus is on the inner struggle of the individual, most often a male protagonist, especially in terms of challenges to their sexual identity and their struggles to find a meeting point with their wives in the context of increasingly ambiguous gender role models.[62]

In his 1967 *Seijuku to soshitsu: Haha no hōkai* (*Maturation and Loss: The Destruction of the 'Mother'*), Etō Jun interprets the process of modernization as a destruction of the relation between the mother and the male child. Etō, one of the most celebrated postwar literary critics, became known for his harsh criticisms of the romantic-subjective literary trends of a group of authors who, he felt, had abdicated their socio-political responsibilities as intellectuals by advancing what Etō called 'slave thought.' In *Maturation and Loss*, however, Etō himself takes a romantic turn, from a champion of modernization to a defender of traditional cultural values, by diagnosing the fundamental change in family structures as the root cause of then current Japanese socio-political problems. *Maturation and Loss* largely focuses on two contemporary family novels: *Umibe no Kōkei* (*The View of the Sea*) by Yasuoka Shōtarō and *Hōyō Kazoku* (*The Embracing Family*) by Kojima Nobuo. As he notes in his afterword, Etō was motivated to write *Maturation* when, upon returning from the US, he was struck by the far-reaching influence of American cultural goods and images on Japanese culture and the Japanese psyche. He was particularly concerned with the penetration that was rapidly altering the representation of the Japanese mother, the figure for Etō who lies at the core of traditional family relations and the sexual relations between men and women.

Contrasting mother–child relations in America (here he uses Erik Erikson's *Childhood and Society*) with those in Japan as reflected in Kojima's and Yasuoka's novels, Etō attributes the fundamental difference between the two visions of the mother to the Japanese lack of a sense of the self as a singular, independent being. That is to say, for Etō, Japanese family relations are at their core based on the realm of physical sensuality (*nikukan-teki na sekai*), initially between mother and child but later extended to the relation between spouses. Etō writes,

> the relation between Shunsuke and Tokiko [the husband and wife of Kojima's novel] has been maintained by the desire to recover a natural relation between the mother and the child, rather than by the ethical relation between the husband and the wife. This is because there is no other value standard outside the existence or non-existence of the intensely intimate emotional bonds between mother and child. Needless to say, to desire the sensual bond of the mother–child relation in the husband–wife relation is *incestuous* [in English in the original]. Through sex, Japanese men attempt to discover the mother; in sexual pleasure, they try to be enfolded within the safe haven of the mother's breast. This might be understood as the impulse to assimilate an extra-familial relationship into the world of blood ties. In other words, Miwa Shunsuke's freedom has no other criteria but pleasure–displeasure: it is a freedom in which others never appear.[63]

The tragic destruction of the mother in Kojima's novel is told from the perspective of the male protagonist, Shunsuke, who desperately attempts to defend the traditional image of the mother from erosion by projecting his ideals upon his wife, Tokiko. Tokiko, on the other hand, wants none of this, and treats Shunsuke contemptuously for his failure to satisfy her modern, Westernized images of happiness. Commenting on this gender gap, Etō writes:

> The powerful presence of the mother, forever alive in the hearts of Japanese men, is surprising. It continues to persist and has even been strengthened by the introduction of the modern school system into agrarian society, when modernity began to threaten the relationship between mother and child. The increasingly influential power of the mother in modern Japan is perhaps negatively correlated with the weakening of images of the father. Simultaneous to the establishment of the school system, the father became something to be ashamed of for many a mother and child. . . . Since mother and child share the same value system which sees the father as embarrassing, the figure of the mother is usually behind the success of the son. Although he will probably not encounter the enfeebled father until he himself is old, at marriage the image of his wife will be superimposed upon the image of his mother.[64]

Etō goes on to connect these notions of the role that masculine and feminine figures play in the narrative of the self to the process of Japanese modernization. Modernization, for Etō, is a process of maturation (*seijuku*) attained only by trading off the natural realm of sensuality (*nikukan-teki na sekai*) laying at the core of traditional family relations and the sexual identity of the Japanese male, in favour of abstract democratic values – i.e. freedom, justice and a sense of citizenship.

This conception of a trade-off between modernization and the mother-as-tradition is not uncommon in modern Japanese literature; it can also be seen in a popular novel by Takahashi Kazumi in which the main character Kiyoshi survives by literally sacrificing his mother. The mother for her part pleads with him: 'Please eat me, eat my flesh. . . . If I die, my soul with my flesh will enter your body, and will protect you. . . . After all, you and I are one from the beginning.'[65] This notion of the mother's sacrifice symbolizing the son's future success as a mature adult in modern Japanese society is, as one critic has pointed out, strikingly different from the Oedipal story of patricide and incest.[66] With this story of the son who ate his mother, Takahashi attempts to thematize life as a form of redemption of the eternal image of the mother.

> The love of the mother – the mother is not giving love because the child is good, nor because she expects future returns, but simply because she cherishes all living beings as they are, and this is perhaps the original form of all religious feeling. Moreover, at the same time, this is the root cause of all desire and suffering.[67]

Although this ideal mother should not be equated with living mothers, such symbolic images naturally construct a kind of allegory around the family and each of its members. Contrary to this sacrificing mother, the wife and mother in Kojima's novel, Tokiko, demands that her husband facilitate the realization of her dreams of a Westernized life and ultimately betrays her husband by having an affair with an American man. In a sense Tokiko symbolizes the modern Japanese woman who no longer accepts the traditional role and images of the mother and wife, and in whose modern view (which she passes on to her children) the father is a relic of the past of whom one can only feel ashamed.

Etō sees the essential problem of modern Japanese society as the intrusion of the other – for him, 'American influences' – that have caused the breakdown of the traditional family system symbolized by the sacrificing mother and the authoritative father, and the consequent loss of the stable cultural/familial environment in which children grow into mature adults. Etō extends his allegorical thinking to viewing the traditional family as a microcosm of society as a whole. In his thought, the traditional authoritative father is invested with additional significance as the centre of symbolic meaning, a meaning indispensable for the proper functioning of social relations.

> Society can only be constructed under God as the father. In other words, the system built upon the principles of responsibility, ethics, and contract can only exist under the gaze of God as the father. That is an order in which each individual is given a role, a system structured by prohibition and limitation. The reason that this kind of God does not manifest itself to Shunsuke is, as I mentioned earlier, largely because he is ashamed of his father after having been brought up in a modern Japanese culture that strove to erase the images of the shameful father. For Shunsuke, God, or divinity if you like, is from the beginning located in the mother and not the father. This divine mother is something animistic and sensuous compared to the fatherly god who represents the ethical. The divine mother is that which imparts a sense of ultimate happiness by limitlessly accepting the child, whereas the father can only save the child within the realm of the finite.[68]

Etō goes on to argue that when the Confucianist world system that had sustained the socio-political order of Japan fell apart, Japan ironically reached 'a new self-complacent disorder.'[69] What he means is that in the past one typically reached a state of maturity by sacrificing the mother and, backed by the firm consciousness of the paternal ethical system, wilfully fought against oppression; in the 'fatherless' society of the 1960s, however, the typical individual is in Etō's terms immature, because he or she lacks a moral foundation and is thus passively carried away by the emptiness of the times.

Etō's solution to the destruction of the mother and the disintegration of the family was to reinstall the Confucian moral order and paternal state in which the divine father authorizes all meaning. Moreover, Etō ultimately attributes the cause of the erosion of the traditional family to Japan's defeat in the war, for that defeat ultimately authorized the flood of American influences that Etō believes radically affected every aspect of Japanese culture. Indeed, Etō's later nationalistic texts blaming the US hegemonic control of Japan for all Japan's social ills, and his advocacy of a Japanese national culture were visible in his late 1960s identification of the root cause of Japanese social problems in the symbolic castration of the Japanese father by the intrusion of the modern West. Etō's contrast between the traditional setting of the individual subservient to the divine father and the contemporary setting of the divine mother certainly has some resonance to Ōe's notion of political and sexual men. Although the site of the problematic for Ōe is the identity and sexuality of individuals, both authors see the root cause of Japanese social problems in the inordinate influence of the US and its legacy of reshaping postwar Japan from within. Etō and his contemporaries saw this reshaping as taking place primarily in the family, particularly in the alteration of the husband-wife relationship, with its serious repercussions for the identity of the child and society as a whole.

Challenges to the universal: relativization of truth and spatialization of history

In the climate of the increasingly self-evident system of power politics under the maturing process of the Cold-War regime in the 1950s and 1960s, there emerged in various forms a stream of theories which came to challenge the universality of truth, justice and history. These arguments often took a political realist position assuming that the exercise of state military power in the national interest was a legitimate form of political action in the domain of international politics. Political realism itself was not a new stream of thought, and, as discussed in Chapter 3, its early versions emerged in the early 1950s in the contexts of the 'reverse course' and the outbreak of the Korean War. These earlier political realist arguments took, however, largely strategic and pragmatist viewpoints in their criticisms of the Leftist intellectuals, especially the Communists, implicitly and explicitly arguing that Japanese national interest was best advanced by following US leadership. In the decade of the 1960s, however, a new type of political realism emerged in light of the *de facto* decline of the universality of international moral codes, arguing for the relativity of truth and morality and the limited applicability of international law and institutions. One predictable outcome of such relativist claims was a reinterpretation of the status of the Japanese Constitution, as well as the meaning of World War II and its historical significance for the Japanese, that occasionally viewed the causes of the war in an affirmative light. What deserves even more attention in this development is the implicit and intimate relation between this relativist politico-military perspective and comparative civilizational theories in which history is seen in ecological, and thus apolitical and ahistorical terms. Despite their obvious differences, however, the two share deep affinities with each other, especially when civilizational and cultural particularist notions of historical relativity were rearticulated in a totalizing modern historical narrative that discarded the pragmatism of the realist politico-military perspectives altogether.

A 1961 article by Ueyama Shumpei, an influential historian, perhaps best exemplifies the above mentioned relativist political realist position. In this work, Ueyama is at pains to make an issue of the changing status of the Japanese Constitution in the changing international context. Opening his article with a condemnation of postwar Japanese intellectuals' blind acceptance of the 180° about face in their evaluation of World War II, Ueyama claims they simply adopted the Allies' partial perspective as universal:

> We initially called the war 'the Great Asian War' (*Daitōa Senso*). But from a certain time, it became a convention to call it 'the Pacific War,' mimicking the way the occupation army did. Along with that,

the evaluation of the war was also changed. That is, in the process 'imperial Japan' (*kōkoku Nihon*) came to be replaced with 'fascism,' 'evil English and Americans' (*kichiku Bei-Ei*) with 'democracy,' and 'the creation of a new Asian order' with 'imperialist invasion,' all previously held values being reversed. It was this advancement of our knowledge, the recognition of the other side of the shield of 'imperial Japan' and 'the creation of the new Asian order,' that was disclosed by virtue of these changes. It was a fallacy to interpret World War II as a territorial war between an advanced economy and late-comer capitalist economy, as a war between good and evil, between a 'peace loving nation' and an 'aggressive nation,' or between democracy and fascism.[70]

In Ueyama's view, historical understanding and moral judgement vary according to one's position, and each interpretation of the war and national history is equally partial since knowledge and truth cannot be seen in isolation from national interests which are an integral part of the discourse operating within the bounds of the nation-state. He argues that since each historical perspective is linked with a particular national authority and reflects its interests, there is, accordingly, no overarching universal truth and justice beyond nationally circumscribed politico-legal systems.

Noteworthy here is the timing and the historical context in which Ueyama advanced his claims for the relativity of truth and morality. In the same article, Ueyama manifests his great appreciation of early postwar universal idealism and the multilateral international order that were embodied in a set of legal codes, including The Atlantic Charter (1941), the Potsdam Declaration (1945) and the Charter of the United Nations (1948). Unlike some realist conservatives, Ueyama does not single-mindedly advocate the abolition of Article Nine, but instead sees the Japanese Constitution as an '*international document*' born out of the early postwar idealism in which 'the common will of the Allies,' who had gone through the catastrophic experiences of the two world wars, was embodied:

> [The Japanese Constitution] was established on the basis of the newly created international political system (the United Nations) that embodied the common will of the Allied forces who learned from the two world wars. It was the first attempt to institutionalize the international state (*kokusai kokka*), the first time in human history that fundamental revisions to the conventional logic of the primacy of the nation-state were attempted. The idea of the 'renunciation of war' in Article Nine is nothing but the logical deduction from such a new conception of the state.[71]

Ueyama's ultimate concern, however, is with the changing status of the Japanese Constitution in the face of the eclipse of those universalist ideals, the rise of the Cold War, and the new US foreign policy trajectory of pursuing its national strategic interests, as evidenced in developments like the Truman Declaration, the Marshall Plan, NATO, SEATO and the US–Japan Security Treaty, all of which, he claims, contradict the spirit of multilateralism. While appreciative of the rapid maturity of the postwar Japanese populace in protesting against this deterioration in the international climate as well as in resisting the political realists' attempts to rearm Japan, Ueyama is at the same time acutely aware of the irony that the peace Constitution has imposed a kind of rigidity on the Japanese that no longer squares with the dramatic alterations in the international context, and the visibly widening gap between the possibilities of 'subjective intention' (civilian resistance) and the overpowering influence of 'objective conditions' (military practice).[72] In this new context, argues Ueyama, both the universal historical perspective of the Allies and the pre-war Japanese perspective of the 'Great Asian War' lost their claims to absoluteness, and all historical and moral perspectives cannot but be represented as partial.

Beyond asserting relativity, Ueyama drew a direct link between power and morality, making reference to the logic of the nation-state that was so clearly exposed during events such as the Korean War, the Algerian War and the Suez crisis. Drawing upon Takeuchi's work, Ueyama claimed that what we think today to be the universally legitimate moral and historical perspective is only the result of a power imposition by strong states upon weaker states.

> Takeuchi Yoshimi criticized the Tokyo war criminal trial by saying one imperialism cannot judge another imperialism. Going a step further, I would argue that one sovereign nation cannot judge another. This is because there is no universal principle, or standard of judgment, beyond partial biases which can fairly recognize others when each sovereign nation-state insists on its own rightfulness. The history of past twenty years has demonstrated the truth of this right in front of our eyes.[73]

By this account, the reason postwar Japan shared the same interpretation of World War II as the US was due to the fact that Japan's defeat in the war allowed Americans to impose their partial truth upon the Japanese, a truth symbolized in the 'externally given' Japanese Constitution.[74] Ueyama seems to claim his and Takeuchi's positions were in concert; however, it is necessary to point out that there were some critical differences between them as well. Despite his criticism of modernism and the Eurocentric hegemonic configuration of the world, Takeuchi was equally, if not more, critical of the modern Japanese historical trajectory; he was especially critical of its failure of will to pursue a programme of self-determination, which, he believed, resulted in the imposition of Japanese imperialism on Asian nations. As I argued in Chapter 3, Takeuchi conceived 'Asia' as a 'method' by which the Japanese might critically see themselves as a part of the modern world, particularly in light of their continuing failure to appreciate the historical significance of other Asian nations. Moreover, Takeuchi's critique of the modern was presented as a necessary antithesis to the reigning intellectual climate of a modernism triumphant, while Ueyama's criticisms of modern universalism arose in the context of a critically weakened modernism, and were designed to subordinate popular democratic ideals to state power in the name of international power politics.

Noteworthy in these general trends towards the relativity of history, truth and morality, and providing part of the intellectual context for their development, was the emergence of a number of civilizational theories explicitly or implicitly encouraging challenges to universalism. Most influential among them was Umesao Tadao's 'Introduction to the Theory of an Ecological Perspective on the History of Civilization' (*Bunmei no seitai-shikan josetsu*, 1957), in which Umesao presented an alternative perspective to the modernist views of history (and especially historical materialism) based on the assumptions of a universal civilization of European origin and of a progressive history. Umesao's work took the form of a theorized travelogue based on his experiences during a six month trip to Afghanistan, Pakistan and India. As the title indicates, his view of 'history' is an ecological one in which human progress is seen as part of a greater natural development wherein history is reduced to the functional relation between human activities and the natural-geographic features of particular localities. According to Umesao, the historical progression in Japan from feudalism to modernism was a process independent from and simultaneous to that which took place in Western Europe; starting from this assertion, he went on to categorize Japan and Western Europe as being distinct from the rest of the Old World:

> The old world, including Asia, Europe, and North Africa can be categorized into two groups. The First Area includes Western Europe and Japan, and the other [the Second Area], the rest of the [Eurasian] continent located between the two ... The Second Area is the region that could not develop a Feudal system, in spite of its advantage of having given birth to all the ancient civilizations, since it suffered from the contradictions of absolute rule (*sensei teikoku*). As a result most of the region was colonized, or half-colonized, by the countries of the First Area, and the region in recent years is belatedly trying to follow the path of modernization by going through a series of revolutions.[75]

This placing of Japan on an equal ground with Western Europe in terms of its originality and degree of development, was passionately supported by Takeyama Michio and some other members of the *Kokoro* group since it constituted in their eyes a fundamental criticism of Spengler and

Toynbee's universal and Eurocentric view of history, in which Japan was reduced to a marginal culture of Chinese civilization.[76] In his enthusiasm, Takeyama reinterpreted Umesao's ecologically conceived relativism back onto the politico-historical terrain, flagrantly ignoring Umesao's notion of 'history' as a realm outside of modern historical thought, and especially outside the teleological scheme of historical materialism which the 'old liberals' and the *Kokoro* group consistently opposed.

However, the historical significance of Umesao's alternative historical view goes beyond such 'inappropriate adaptations' by some for their own political agenda; rather, as Takeuchi carefully implies, the real problem is rooted in Umesao's dematerialized and depoliticized view of history itself, in which history as a sequence of material processes contingent upon human power relations is completely eliminated.[77] Indeed, Umesao's interpretation of the development of civilizations in ecological terms is certainly reminiscent of Watsuji's 1935 work *Fūdo* (*Climate and Culture*), in which Umesao conceived the history of civilizations in the plural by translating the human processes of history into ecological terms very similar to those used by Watsuji. By lifting localities out of the context of the conflict-laden modern universal world, Watsuji reduced their histories to a series of taxonomic differences in which the critical role played by international hegemonic power was completely effaced. Similarly, by emphasizing the harmonious relation between mankind and environment, Umesao's functionalist ecological perspective of history challenges, first and foremost, the structurally and materially grounded view of history in which power relations are determinant. Unlike Takeyama and the *Kokoro* group, however, Ueyama resisted the enticing idea of Japan's status as cultural equal to Western Europe (and its implicit corollary of superiority over Asia), and did not draw any simple-minded political implications from his account for the current international setting. However, by adapting Umesao's relativist notion of history, Ueyama's political realist claims were to pose a similar challenge to the universal view of history, not in ecological terms but in political and historical terms.[78] Indeed, praising Umesao's work, Ueyama suggests that a 'synthesis' of the strengths of their works would 'improve the Marxist universalist view of history [by moving it] towards an ecological pluralist one,' and by 'understand[ing] both [historical materialism and ecological functionalism] as complementary.'[79]

Rather predictably, the ground prepared by Ueyama's political realism was the seedbed for the germination of a much more explicit affirmation of the historical meaning of World War II on the basis of the relativity of truth and morality. Hayashi Fusao, a literary critic who in prewar times was a member of the Japan Romantic School, argued in a 1963 work, 'An Affirmative Theory of the Great Asian War' (*Daitōa senso kotei ron*), that World War II was merely the 'logical outcome' for the Japanese, who were left with no other option than to develop a modern nation-state in the face of the threat posed by the Western imperial powers. Hayashi's reinterpretation of Japan's modernization path as a '100 years' war,' in which World War II was the finale, openly justified Japan's conduct in World War II as driven by hopes of liberating the Asian races, and it was brought about by the 'logical practice of modern nation-state and power politics' that the modern West introduced into Asia.[80] Pointing out that Japan was not alone in attempting to colonize Korea in the years towards its annexation in 1910, Hayashi attempted to nullify Japanese war responsibilities in Asia by emphasizing the pre-existing context of Western imperialism and Japan's reluctant participation in it.[81] Unlike Ueyama's consistently political realist argument, Hayashi's discourse was laden with strong resentments towards the universalism of the West, for example, his absolute rejection of the Tokyo War Crimes Trial and his interpretation of the opening of the Pacific War as the result of Japan's falling into an American conspiracy.[82] Moreover, Hayashi's revisionism manifest a curiously 'gendered angst' insofar as he defined and condemned pacifist postwar Japan as a 'feminization of the state':

> The current intellectual climate, which appears to be wickedly feminized, having lost its masculine character and manliness, is entirely insane. Some of the 'ideologies' that have been persecuted in the postwar era must have been indispensable for the Japanese. How can we recover what was lost [and necessary for the Japanese], in order to recover from this jelly-fish-like spineless state?[83]

> The urgent task of the day is to formulate masculine nationalism ... On what basis should we seek the formulation of Japanese nationalism? In nothing if not in the recovery of a sense of historical continuity which runs between the Japanese in the age of the Imperial Japan and the Japanese today.[84]

In these passages, the recovery of state power, which for Hayashi also means recovering a sense of historical continuity, is equated with regaining a masculine national identity. Like Etō, Hayashi seems to assume an allegorical equation between the hope that Japanese men regain their paternal authority and that of re-establishing a 'masculine' Japanese state, although in Hayashi the two seems to be far less self-reflexively mixed.

The return of the aesthetic: early calls for 'Japan'

Rapid economic growth in the 1960s and consequent changes in the sociocultural sphere brought the troubled state of the Japanese inner landscape out into the open, as well as romantic anti-rationalist currents that had been suppressed in the first decade of postwar intellectual discourse. As mentioned earlier, Japanese society became increasingly subject to a rapid change in values and lifestyles, and widespread resentment to abstract bureaucratic and technological control gave rise to an insistence upon the traditional family system, bodily sensations and nature. Similar to prewar developments, these new anti-rationalist currents criticized the Western philosophical bias for universal progressive notions of history, rationalism and an atomized self-governing subject, and called for a recovery of things which were identified as being lost. As these criticisms mounted, reactions to the effects of modernization were, once again, inseparably conflated with criticisms of the West – this time more specifically with the US. These voices of dissent were perhaps most clearly and deeply pronounced in quests for religious conviction and spirituality, reflecting the fact that the structural transformation of Japan in the 1960s entailed a marked erosion in the functional linkage between the individual and the outside world and affected the stability of subjectivity. Two streams of ideas deserve particular attention here: the anti-materialist knowledge that attempted to create a culturally accountable philosophy of society by incorporating an understanding of aesthetics and spirituality; and the complete rejection, comparable to that of the prewar Japan Romantic School, of Japanese modernism as a failed idea.

The first stream of these romantic currents was a direct response to the growing perception of an intellectual vacuum and the perceived bankruptcy of modernism and Western philosophy. Umehara Takeshi, then a student of philosophy at Kyoto university, abandoned his studies of Western philosophy in search of an alternative philosophy better suited to the Japanese cultural and historical heritage. In a 1960 work, Umehara, investigating the significance and function of Japanese laughter, developed a 'theory of emotions' (*Kanjō ron*) as a way of overcoming the logocentric biases in philosophy.[85] Umehara was especially critical of Western philosophy's assumption of the centrality of the subjective will of the autonomous subject; critically analysing its developmental trajectory from Descartes to Sartre, he strove to modify the Western notion of ethical action based upon the transcendental self. Umehara found this notion too strictly Christian, particularly in its denial of pleasure, the body, and nature, which he saw as ultimately a denial of life itself.[86] In order to overcome this Eurocentric/logocentric tradition, Umehara proposed a 'philosophy of laughter,' and from the 1960s he developed a theory of the emotions in which pleasure, the body and nature are placed beyond the grasp of philosophical reason as values in themselves. This criticism of Western philosophy naturally led Umehara to challenge those contemporary Japanese intellectuals who recklessly imported Western philosophy without making it accountable to the specificity of Japanese art and social thought. Like Yoshimoto, Umehara did not believe prewar Japanese militarism was a form of 'ultranationalism' or a 'feudal' remainder in the Japanese cultural tradition, as Maruyama had described it, but was rather a product of the suppression of everyday cultural life, upon which the wartime emperor mythology and the mythological fabrication of the modern Japanese state, was super-imposed.

He argued that Japanese intellectuals' blind worship of modern and Western ideas and their singular rejection of native culture and religion had seriously impaired their understanding of the Japanese tradition derived from the Buddhist notion of forgiveness. From this standpoint, Umehara attempted to transcend the shortfalls of a Western philosophy grounded in the overconfident belief in reason's ability to make the world intelligible, by incorporating aspects of Eastern philosophy that tended to 'simultaneously affirm the power of life and its darkness.'[87]

In making such argument, however, Umehara came to embrace precisely what he had challenged in his earlier critiques – the ideological confusion of culture and reason that was a potentially powerful political tool.[88] Underlying this change of orientation lay Umehara's increasing concern with the socio-economic and cultural state of Japan in the 1960s which, as it appeared to him, was rapidly foregoing its own past and forgetting its traditions – what he saw as the cultural alienation of the Japanese. In the introduction to his 1967 *Bi to Shūkyō no Hakken* (*The Discovery of Beauty and Religion*), Umehara explains the motivation for his change of direction:

> What is particularly forgotten in the postwar era are the values of beauty and religion. In a society which has been under the overwhelming influence of a modern European civilization, esteeming only what is rational and practical, it is quite natural that these values lose their glow day by day relative to the values of science, morality, and above all, profit. However, our ancestors valued beauty above all and various religions shaped their souls. If we are to know our own culture, then we must know our ancestors' sense of beauty and religion. In order to rediscover the true features of beauty and religion that have animated our culture, and to challenge the overpowering materialism of contemporary Japanese society, I have undertaken a Quixotic quest to recover those values necessary for the revival of our souls.[89]

Umehara's ambitious programme of 'rediscovering beauty and religion' extended itself to include calls for the creation of a new Japanese cultural theory capable of explaining contemporary Japan. Interestingly, he envisioned that this theory would be formulated in an international and 'interdisciplinary' orientation that locates Japan in a political, international, and civilizational context. In the conclusion of *The Discovery of Beauty* he argues that:

> The creation of Japanese culture and religion is the spiritual task of all future Japanese. Only those peoples who have succeeded in developing a suitable national pride within the context of the modern historical realities can hope to leave some kind of legacy for the rest of the world. The time has come for us to face up to the task of seriously reconsidering our mission on the world historical stage. How to

understand our tradition is not a trivial question. How deeply and creatively we can interpret our tradition will ultimately determine the future cultural fate of our nation.[90]

Contrary to what appears to be the inward-looking orientation of the volume, this concluding passage strikes one with its international perspective of viewing 'the Japanese' in the 'world historical stage,' and its future orientation in which generations of the Japanese are charged with the 'spiritual task' of carrying on tradition as a 'mission' that 'will ultimately determine the future cultural fate of our nation.'

Umehara continued this programme in his subsequent work, where, arguing it was a Eurocentric misconception to claim that the Japanese had no philosophy before the coming of the West, he condemns past Japanese intellectuals for their wholesale importation of 'philosophy.' Identifying ancient Shintoism and mystic Buddhism of the Nara and Heian eras (*mikkyō*, such as *Tendai-shū* and *Shingon-shū*) as the archetypes of Japanese philosophy, Umehara argued that they have continued to animate Japanese ways of thinking and living. In Umehara's conception, Japanese culture and religion was constituted by three key foundations: a naturalistic ontology of life; the centrality of the notion of purity/impurity; and an emotional epistemology and/or logic of feelings.[91] These three foundations were initially derived from and inseparably interwoven with three principles that constitute the Buddhist universe: *kokoro* (heart), *seimei* (life) and *jigoku* (hell).[92] By understanding these three foundations and three principles and contrasting them with the cultural and spiritual bases of European thought, we can, argues Umehara, for the first time seriously ask what kind of philosophy was native to Japan. As a result of Umehara's labours in pursuit of native Japanese ideas, in the 1980s a systematized field of study was established, with considerable financial and institutional support, called Umehara Japan Studies, providing the back up for his 'mission' in the 'world historical stage.'

Another noteworthy development in the 1960s was the intrusion of religion into politics. Ikeda Daisaku, the leader of *Sōkagakkai*, a sect of *nichiren* Buddhism, formed a political organization in 1955 based on religious principles, thereby uniting for the first time in postwar Japan political and religious institutions. Ikeda challenged the LDP's elitist and materialist, new conservative orientation by insisting on the inclusion of the moral and spiritual in politics, and was able to garner strong support amongst the lower strata of society for his efforts. The typical *Sōkagakkai* supporter arose from the ranks of those alienated from the rural agricultural sectors as a result of the displacements accompanying the social restructuring of the late 1950s and 1960s. In these years serious urban–rural problems developed when, lured by attractive images of urban material wealth and cultural life, there was a flood of migrant labourers to the large cities and a consequent depopulation of rural villages. Rather predictably, it was often the case that many of the displaced found no quarter within existing labour, student, or other organizations, and were isolated in an increasingly hostile and dehumanizing industrialized environment.[93] In 1964, taking advantage of the *Sōkagakkai*'s popularity, Ikeda founded the *Kōmeitō* (The Clean Government Party) aiming to challenge the current state of Japanese politics:

> the contemporary situation of Japanese politics, its poverty, corruption and decay is unbearable to watch, and nothing but a source of lament. People and politics are completely delinked from each other in today's Japan, despite its rhetoric of democracy. Political parties are influenced more by their own gains than by the welfare of the people. This is a symptom common to parties of the right and the left; in fact these parties are really a collection of various sects, and calling them sectarian politics rather than party politics is much more adequate.[94]

One particular target of Ikeda's attacks was the lack of any philosophical underpinning to the LDP's bureaucratic politics, the structure in which politics was reduced to little more than a series of policy initiatives, built upon no coherent and consistent philosophic, moral, or spiritual principles. Based on this diagnosis, Ikeda suggested that the only effective remedy to the current political state was to incorporate religion into politics, what he called *ōhfutsu myōgō*, a politics directly conducive to the welfare of the masses.

> ... *ōhfutsu myōgō* is a philosophical principle and at its core is a spirit of mercy with [the foremost purpose of] conducting politics in a manner benefiting the masses ... [It] is a politics based on mercy practiced by those who have transformed themselves by purifying their lives according to correct beliefs and a life of philosophy ... In concrete terms, our party aims to initiate a politics in which the prosperity of society and the happiness of individuals coincides ... Since our party is based on a life philosophy, we are able to resolve what policies cannot: the inner problems of the people, through the practice of religion.[95]

While many remained sceptical of this seemingly natural link between religion and politics in the amelioration of social well being, Ikeda's criticisms of the current state of the Japanese polity appealed to a substantial number of the population. Moreover, the steps he took down this road had far reaching implications for the Japanese polity in the following decades, in that the question of spirituality, or more precisely its emotional resonance, would become a central issue for the other established parties as well (as we will see in Chapter 5).

If Umehara and Ikeda had conceived of and pursued a reformist path in knowledge and politics respectively, the quest for meaning struck the novelist Mishima Yukio as a question far too radical and absolute to make him a reformist. As a precocious young writer, Mishima rose to maturity under the influence of the Japan Romantic School (he was 20-years-old at the end of the war) and his literary position on the centrality of beauty remained basically unchanged throughout the postwar era. At the end of the war, Mishima described his generation as one afflicted by the 'incurable disease of health'; according to some commentators, the postwar era represented for Mishima the loss of the beauty of death, the death that could give meaning to life.[96] Although Mishima's quest for a continuity of meaning can be said to have begun as early as the end of the war, it was not until the mid-1960s that his despair of absolute meaning became charged with nationalistic overtones. This time-lag is significant in that in it his earlier desire for meaning advanced a step further, turning it into a form of nostalgia (*nostos*: returning home, and *algos*: pain) in which the past was recalled in the context of the unbearable emptiness of the present.[97]

Once again, as was the case with Etō, one encounters a conflation of the loss of meaning and a loss of the national spirit, the remedy for the former being sought in the revitalization of the latter. Mishima's awakening nostalgia was in a sense simultaneously a discovery of the root causes of the problem of meaning in the cultural and spiritual decay of postwar Japan, which for Mishima meant the death of god, or the emperor as the spiritual centre of the Japanese.[98] Like Etō, Mishima saw a postwar trade-off in operation between spirituality and material wealth, although, unlike Etō who chose 'maturity' and to go along with the modern, Mishima's increasing bitterness led him to negate postwar Japan in its entirety. In his 1966 discussion with Hayashi Fusao, an ex-Japan Romantic School literary critic, Mishima remarked,

> I have learned that the modernists have been entirely useless for the past twenty years. The only thing they predicted that became true was the industrialization of society [without a concurrent modernization of the mentality of the people], and this is the extreme irony of history. . . . Despite the fact that modern progressivism is entirely foreign to our mentality, industrialization nevertheless advanced, and as a result a spiritual decay, an emptiness, and a nihilism became deeply rooted in our society.[99]

According to Mishima, the prosperous Japanese who survived the turmoil of the postwar years were soulless beings, whose diminished condition was symbolically represented by the emperor's demotion from a living god to a constitutional and mortal monarch. For Mishima, the emperor had traditionally served Japan not only as the ultimate symbol of Japanese culture but also as the centre of its symbolic system authorizing the meaning of life and death, and Mishima insisted that he ought to have remained as he was, for that was the only way he could fulfil his responsibility to the (Japanese) war dead.[100] The significance of the emperor as the absolute authority for truth and meaning is advanced in Mishima's (1968) *In Defence of National Culture* (*Bunka Boei Ron*):

in order for cultural totality, continuity and the subject to find a value-in-itself . . . one must expect that all particular events taking place on the edges of Japanese culture derive their meaning from this value-in-itself. However, the central function of the emperor system was lost under the Meiji Constitution by being increasingly confined in a Western style constitutional monarchy which, as it matured, abandoned its cultural function. We must return to the true character of the emperor as a cultural concept, as the only value-in-itself that can assure the totality of a varied, wide-ranging and inclusive culture.[101]

Underlying Mishima's idea here is the notion that politics is in essence inseparably linked with that which modern secularization has irrevocably undermined: the spiritual. Mishima argues that the political motivations of nations and the communal/social identity of individuals are both derived from a sense of cultural unity.

The rational and technical political system will inescapably encounter pathos as the source of politics . . . The current political system is doomed to the fate of always being torn between the two wheels of the universal reason of mankind and the deep psychological impulse of the people.[102]

Mishima despised the hypocrisy of postwar Japan and its ungroundedness: he asked ironically 'Will this nation that appears to have succeeded in Westernizing itself in terms of importing vulgar culture, someday succeed in importing the sacred?'[103] For Mishima, the emperor represented the tragic will and the last bulwark against Westernization, the lonely, shipwrecked symbol of a 'pure-Japan' and of the will that strove to salvage something from it.[104] He was equally contemptuous of himself as a survivor and 'collaborator' with the postwar hypocrisy; his ultimate yearning was, perhaps, for a revival of the awesome and the profound sense of communal bond he had experienced under the threat of death during the war, the emotional satisfaction of being protected by the ancient deities.

Clearly, Mishima's emperor was an abstract symbol embodying an idealized Japanese spirit, a far cry from the living emperor. In the postwar era, the Japanese imperial court had undergone a radical transformation in which the previously authoritative semi-divine patriarch was made over in the image best suited to the notion of the democratic sovereignty of the people under the Constitution – a sort of benign uncle of the populace. In 1958, a nation-wide sensation and mass media fever (the Michie boom) erupted when Prince Akihito became engaged to the daughter of a commoner, Shōda Michiko. Mishima was outraged at this betrayal of the imperial court's traditions, although his outrage must be seen in relation to his own intensifying sense of personal emptiness. His 1966 novel *The*

Voices of the Honoured Dead (*Eirei no Koe*), taking up the 2.26 incident (February 26th, 1936), ends with a cursing chorus of war-dead voices, unable to rest in peace, who accuse the emperor of betraying the loyal followers who had sacrificed their lives in the war. The refrain of these haunting voices is repeated over and over: 'Why has your excellency become a human being?' If one interprets *The Voices* as a justification of the 2.26 incident, Mishima's sensational suicide could be seen as an attempted symbolic sacrifice made in order to revitalize the authority of the emperor and thereby the Japanese cultural ethos.

As is widely known, Mishima committed *seppuku* (ritual disembowelment) in a manner somewhat reminiscent of one of his own stories. The main character in his novel, *Yūkoku*, is a young military officer who joins in the February 26th, 1936 rebellion of young officers against their superiors demanding national submission to the divinity of the emperor. Mishima's testament, entitled *Geki* (*Outrage*), written shortly before his suicide in 1970, expresses his outrage and disgust with the postwar peace and routine life of the 'living dead.' It could be read as a desperate plea for the sublime beauty of the life he had experienced in the war.

> We have seen that the postwar Japanese have opportunistically welcomed economic prosperity, forgetting the principles of the nation, losing their native spirit, pursuing the trivial without correcting the essential, indulging in momentary convenience and hypocrisy, and leading themselves into spiritual emptiness. Politics has been solely devoted to the covering up of contradictions, the protecting of the self, the desire for power and hypocritical ideals, while we have stood by like helpless bystanders, biting our teeth hard, passively witnessing the sell-off of our national politics over the last 100 years, deceiving ourselves about the humiliation of defeat in the war rather than confronting it – the Japanese themselves have assaulted their own history and tradition.[105]

Beneath Mishima's gestures towards the sublime beauty of sacrifice, however, lay his conviction that modern life had become an endless mechanical continuity of drudgery and routine; perhaps suicide was the only response possible to the overwhelming nihilism that had ripened within him.[106]

Bankruptcy of the old narrative: the collapse of identity and the sea of nihilism

The rapid material changes that began in the late 1950s and were nourished under the new conservative discourse of the early 1960s exposed Japanese society to a dizzying series of changes. These changes brought an end to the dualistic economic structure that had characterized Japan up until this point, the coexistence of an urban industrial economy and a rural agrarian economy, and the latter was increasingly absorbed to the former. In addition to the accelerated industrialization and the new conservative ideology which accompanied it, religious feelings that had previously been contained in the figurehead image of the emperor were un-moored and dispersed in a nascent commercial culture without spiritual or symbolic meaning. As a result, the Japanese political system, which used to have room to accommodate the imperial court system, came to rely solely on an increasingly formalized democratic institutional structure. Furthermore, as the penetration of capital advanced into the realm of the everyday, people's relation to nature, including their own bodies, was also transformed, resulting in a radical rearrangement in the domains of the senses and cognition. The adjustment to a more abstract human/nature relation was accompanied by various difficulties, including an increasingly visible gap between the realms of labour and empirical life experience, and was also reflected in human relations, including those between the sexes and family members, as discussed above.[107] These palpable changes were merely the tip of the iceberg of the structural, systemic transformation effected in Japanese society in the late 1950s and 1960s, a transformation involving, as I elaborate in the following paragraphs, a wholesale restructuring of society and the modality of its institutional operation, as well as a reorientation of people's 'mode of being,' so-to-speak, who had no other choice than to adapt as best they could to the new conditions.

To be sure, this large scale systemic transformation involving the emergence of a new social organizational structure was not unique to the experience of Japan in the late 1950s and throughout the 1960s, but a world-wide phenomenon experienced in all the industrial societies. The advent in question has been described as the emergence of the 'post-industrial society,' a notion reflected in various well-known works such as D. Bell's *Notes on the Post-Industrial Society* (1967), J. Galbraith's *The New Industrial State* (1967), and P. Drucker's *The Age of Discontinuity* (1969), among others. In the Japanese intellectual context Matsushita Keiichi's article, 'Taishū kokka no seiritsu to sono mondaisei' published in *Shisō* in 1956, pioneered a systemic theoretical framework for understanding such a structural transformation.[108] Seeking to reformulate postwar Japanese Marxism in order to strengthen its analysis of the structural problems faced by Japanese society, Matsushita's work located those problematics in the broader context of the rise of corporate capitalism.[109] Simultaneously, however, his works marked a departure from the principal thematics and concerns of postwar progressive leftism, in the sense that they shifted their focus away from the subject as the political agent of democratic transformation to a systemic analysis of the social structure itself. Let us first consider Matsushita's theoretical formulation, since it perhaps best exemplifies the strengths of this type of analysis and had a substantial impact upon the Japanese intellectual discourse of the times.

152 *Rapid economic growth and romantic resurgence*

Matsushita characterized the particular form of social organization that emerged out of the structural transformation in twentieth century industrial capitalism as a mass society. The main components of this new mass society are defined by Matsushita as: (1) a huge leap in technological ability, its adaptation to production, communication, and social organization, and the resultant changes in the life of the individual and in social operations; (2) the 'proletarianization' of a large part of the population, both middle-class and working class; and (3) the decline of the politics based on class struggle due to the leveling of society and political equalization.[110] Matsushita argues that the availability of new energy supplies (oil and electricity) and rapid technological advancement made the entire restructuring of society possible, and that entailed changes in the life-styles of individuals, in the composition of the social segments, in the mode of political participation, and in the means of state social control. At the core of these changes was the Fordist mode of production, the mechanization of production processes and the quantification of the labour force (the inclusion of unskilled labour), and the extension of the effects of this production mode throughout the society.[111] In his words:

> Corporate capitalism advances a change in the mode of production itself, that carried out by the accumulation and the concentration of capital and the advancement of technology as its agent. This change in the mode of production makes social transformation logically inevitable, through the 'systematization' and 'atomization' that accompanies the process. . . . Mass production is *social* principle – its core principle is *human* organization.[112]

Matsushita argues that technological developments used to be largely contained in production processes, but with the arrival of Fordist mass production, technology began to permeate society with a greater systematization, and thus the systemic organization and regulation of social and individual life were dramatically enhanced.[113]

This change in the mode of production results in what Matsushita describes as the 'proletarianization' of the masses, those whose previous existence as agrarian labour was overturned when they became an urban work force alienated from the traditional means of production and from the cultural and human environment of specific localities.[114] Constituted as an abstracted, mobile and commodified form of labour, 'the masses' (*taishū*), consisting of the working classes and the new middle-class (*shin chūsan kaikyū*), were the corollary of the rise of a highly mechanized, bureaucratized and technologically oriented society.[115] 'Atomized,' alienated, isolated and anonymous individuals, the masses are at the same time 'systematized' into the mechanized and bureaucratized society connected by the information disseminated from the mass media and by various institutional regulations.[116] According to Matsushita, the culture that permeates mass society, mass culture (*taishū bunka*), is very distinct from previous popular cultures since they were grounded upon the historical and cultural heritage of particular localities. In addition, the mass culture has some 'imperial characteristics' that it expands its sphere of influence by transforming and internalizing local cultures, while simultaneously incorporating aspects of the elite culture into the commercialized and homogeneous space of the mass culture.[117] In other words, the mass culture transforms distinct local cultures into a synchronic national form, suitable for consumption in a mass society. Moreover, given the loss of what Matsushita calls 'the allegorical relation between the subject and the object as assumed in classical epistemology,' mass society is 'emotionalized' (*jōchoka*), especially in the light of the alienation of labour and the destruction of the family system advanced by bureaucratic systematization. As Matsushita puts it, 'emotion (*jōcho*) accumulates within the cultural sphere of the mass society as 'irrational' energy, without being rationalized'; and this 'irrational energy' has a tendency to seek counter-hegemonic outlets for its expression of rebellion against the rationalization and bureaucratization of society.[118]

If one accepts these characteristics of economic and cultural systematization and homogenization under corporate capitalism as central features of Japanese society in the 1960s, some fundamental changes in the forms of political participation and means of control are implied. For one, the conventional Marxist notion of political participation via class struggle is subject to the challenge of maintaining its political appeal and its support base. If the working class, former counter-weight to the middle class, has now become integrated into a new middle class that constitutes, by far, the majority of society, the contradictions inherent in civil society assumed by conventional Marxists have in part been transcended. Moreover, as the structural basis for class conflict was absorbed into the diffused system of state power in the 1960s, the state's means of social control began to be exercised instead through information and mass culture, giving rise to what Matsushita calls the mass state (*taishū kokka*).[119] Mass society theorists have generally seen this eclipse of the ground of political (class) conflict and the accompanying shift in the means of state control of society (knowledge and mass culture) as representing the full accession of mass democracy, wherein the conventional dualism between elite and mass cultures was replaced by a single, homogenized, and 'democratized' culture.[120] Referring to Tocqueville's notion of the 'equalization of conditions' (*nivellement des conditions*) and K. Mannheim's notion of 'fundamental democratization' (*fundamentale Demokratisierung*), Matsushita argues that those who used to belong to the underclasses came to obtain an equal participation in society on the basis of their homogenized lives:

> The proletariat [i.e. the masses] who become economically *equal* individuals also become politically *equal* voting subjects, and simultaneously

become culturally *homogenized* participants. In other words, the increase of productivity results in: I. the proletarianization of the population; II. the homogenization of life-style due to technological development; and III. the substantiation of political equality in terms of mass democracy or mass nationalism.[121]

In this formulation, the rise of the mass form of democracy is the creation of a petite bourgeoisie whose sense of equality is affirmed largely by the consumption of petit-bourgeois culture, and whose depoliticized and pacified political energy is absorbed into the state power machinery mediated and disseminated by the mass media.[122] Here Matsushita concludes that 'the masses are the contradiction in democracy':

> While the masses are the subject of democratic polity (by having voting power), they are simultaneously subjugated as objects of political control, and the system and the masses repeat the vicious-circle. The 'masses' who were generated by the logic of the system were placed as the subjects of the system, whereas their political freedom is at the same time laden with the danger of being nullified from inside themselves due to the effects of mass control. Mass democracy as a means of controlling the 'masses' becomes non-functioning by virtue of the vicious-circle of the system and the masses, in which the subjects of control become its objects as well.[123]

In sum, the socialization of production and technology by corporate capitalism gives rise to a new mode of social hegemony, in which the economically and culturally homogenized masses constitute democracy, albeit in a paradoxically depoliticized form.

Generally speaking, the rise of mass society theory ought to be seen in context of the world-wide shift in philosophical orientation from analyses focusing upon the will and action of the individual as political agent to the more 'objective' and distant analyses, often infused to varying degrees by pragmatism and positivism, focusing on the systemic articulation of the social structure.[124] Despite the undeniable contributions of Matsushita's mass society theory, its systemic theoretical frame had virtually no room for examinations of the subject as a political agent, and thus tended to paint a deterministic and pessimistic picture of society governed by the law of capitalism. The Marxist historicist Shibata Shingo criticized Matsushita's depiction of the 'masses' as a 'powerless and formless crowd' as well as his total dismissal of class conflict as a failure to see that the emergence of mass society was itself 'the intensification of the contradictions between capital and labour at the stage of corporate capitalism,' at which stage contradictions were internationalized as those between 'colonizing and colonized countries.'[125] Shibata's criticisms have merit, and represented the main concerns of the Leftist intellectuals who resisted Matsushita's identification of technology as the ultimate agent of social transformation. At the same time, however, these critics could not come up with a satisfactory alternative theory to account for the structural changes in society nor with feasible strategies for countering its more diffused hierarchical power. Moreover, although we may criticize Matsushita's theory and its political implications on the grounds of its technology-derived pessimism and its weakening of human agency, one should also be aware that similar conclusions could be articulated in optimistic tones envisaging the current transformation as leading to 'a new utopian age' of greater choices and possibilities. Indeed, precisely this was argued by futurologist Koyama Ken'ichi in a 1967 work:

> To investigate as many possibilities as our knowledge would allow, choose one possibility among them and work with the present and the future toward that goal – this is what outlines the basic points of a new utopian idea in our time. This type of pragmatic thought (*mokutek-iron-teki shikō*) is something that should replace the deterministic thought of the nineteenth century, and it is such a future perspective that should replace the ideological 'illusionary future' [i.e. socialism, note by the author].[126]

This sense of optimism in the future, closely associated with economic development and the acquisition of new material wealth, allowed the intensification of systemic control to be viewed in a positive light. Taking full advantage of these ideas, LDP politicians, with their new conservative discourse, cultivated the socio-political, economic and cultural ground in which corporate capitalism could fully bloom.

And yet, Matsushita's theory of the masses demonstrates a symptomatic feature of the systems analysis that flourished in the Japanese intellectual discourse of the 1960s. In a nutshell, this could be described as an insufficient analysis of the contradictions of capital itself, especially its alienating and objectifying effects upon human subjects as conditions of its maturity. While Matsushita's theory assumes the advent of the mass society and mass culture as givens focuses its analysis on the description of their features, it remains disinterested in the inherent violence of the market system, the transformation of human subjects into anonymous and passive 'masses.' Drawing from the works of Marx, economic historian Hirata Kiyoaki argues that the market forces that once liberated individuals from feudalistic human relations eventually subjugated them to other dependent relations, this time thoroughly mediated by the objective laws of the market and its adjuncts, abstract civil codes and the disembodied truth internalized by the subject.[127] As the exchange economy matures, argues Hirata, a society of unique and concrete human relations is transformed into a society regulated by abstract laws and constituted by self-governing rational subjects, which is to say: a modern civil society.[128] In his view, human relations in a civil society are derivative of the productive relations of the society and the logic of the market in which the homogenization of qualitatively different goods is constantly reproduced, exchanged and consumed together with the values and perspective inherent in the logic of the market. Up to this point, Hirata's argument largely parallels Matsushita's characterization of the mass society; however, Hirata's analysis goes further to disclose the transformative feature of capitalist society in which the ontological relation between the market and people is reversed, that is, at some stage in its development, the market comes to create people rather than vice versa.

Hirata argues that the rise of this social system is the process by which bourgeois consciousness achieves its representation as autonomous from the material relations of society. Further, he argues that objectified and commodified relations of goods and humans in the sphere of exchange gave rise over time to the illusions of the governance of abstract law and the autonomous subject, as well as the latter's submission to the former, which is nothing less than an abstraction of the self.[129] In other words, the maturity of market relations and the repetition of exchange practices gave rise to 'completely "disillusioned" dependent human relations and abstract human labour as the true subject of history.'[130] The strength of this Marxian historian's view is, then, that of making clear the 'ideological' status of market society and the subject's displaced position in it, a state that is made increasingly invisible as the bourgeois social values are internalized by individuals. In Hirata's view, capitalism is not only the penetration of material forces and the transformation of a social structure, but also a metaphysical principle that recreates human subjects in its own design, a collaboration of 'the material' and 'the ideal' and the impossibility of separating the two. As this materially and ideologically driven structural transformation advances, and the above mentioned ontological inversion between the market and people continues, there arises a situation in which the popular social imaginary, or something to what Maruyama called the 'political ethos,' can no longer provide a generative ground for counter-political ideologies to mitigate the effects of the forces of capital. This last point demands some elaboration.

Not only did material prosperity mark a departure from the immediate postwar years, but the inner landscape of individuals also experienced a discontinuity in the late 1950s. Frustrated with the realist methodology that he felt had hampered him in depicting an invisible and seriously oppressive reality, Shimao Toshio, a novelist born before the war, lamented in 1958: 'how the fruits of postwar [realist] literature have helped express this disgusting place we are in!'[131] Shimao's irritation with realism was shared by others, including Sasaki Kiichi, a literary critic, who, echoing the declaration of the end of postwar era, declared the end of postwar literary realism in his 1962 article 'Sengo Bungaku wa gen'ei datta' ('Postwar Literature was an Illusion'). Sasaki argued that the intellectuals' commonly shared image of the postwar era, that is, the utopian dream and the image of a future just society achieved through democratic revolution, had completely floundered, not because of a lack of will and energy on the part of the people, but because of an inhuman mechanism of mass society operated beyond the will of the individual.[132] Going a step further than Sasaki, Okuno Takeo actively strove to create new literary methods suited to the new environment and needs. Okuno claimed that once the myth of Marxism had lost its power Japan was thrown into a state of uncertainty in which the future was no longer predictable. In modern society, he claimed, the world operates by accident, not by the subjective perception of the individual, and since the correlation between the inner world of the subject and the outside historical world was now lost, a deep cleavage between the two developed.[133] Like Sasaki, Okuno concluded that the foundation on which literary realism had been built was now completely dysfunctional and that the only way open was to abandon all established concepts and instead strive to create one's own vision of the future, with one's own ideas and judgement. With this notion of the indeterminacy of the contemporary age and the bankruptcy of established concepts, Okuno insisted that in order to understand current social conditions one had to rely on an extensive use of metaphors and symbols.

The same problem of the loss of language as a means of objectifying the world under the control of the subject, and the resultant troubled subject–object relation, were also observed by Etō Jun and Karatani Kōjin. Recalling the 1960s, they described their experience:

> Ten years ago, I used the words, such as individual, society, nature and art without much hesitation, and felt that they were alive. These words are still alive in the sentences I wrote at that time. However, today after ten years, I ask myself why the same words are no longer alive at all when I try to use them in the same way?[134]

> Indeed, in the last ten years there has been an unprecedented experience. Strangely, we do not really notice the fact that this is an unprecedented event. This is because we do not have the words to describe this experience, and, to say the same in reverse, there has been no other time in our history when words, which once used to function for long periods of time, have faded and become outdated so rapidly.[135]

This rapid fading of the efficacy of conventional categories was what made Japanese writers of the 1960s feel so powerless and desperate in face of the invisible, diffused and ever-systematized 'enemy,' and is probably the basis behind Ishihara's and Ōe's use of the metaphor of the 'wall,' to grasp their sense of confinement in their own interiors. Under conditions in which the subject is reduced to an object in a highly systematized society (e.g. labour as commodity), not only do the basic categories (such as 'individual,' 'society,' and 'nature') lose their meaning, but even the subject can no longer maintain its 'subjective position' of constituting the objective world because subjective interiority has itself become the product of market society. In the society of corporate capitalism, then, even the most intimate and essential realms of human life, such as the body and the family, appear rather foreign and perplexing, and this growing sense of the opacity of the self, the world, and meaning intensifies the level of anxiety both in the social climate and in intellectual discourse. Indeed, Japanese intellectual discourse of the 1960s was increasingly laden with a desire for reconstituting 'things lost,' as exemplified in calls for a return to conventional moral principles and their authorizing centre, such as the Confucian system in Etō and the emperor in Mishima.

In this historical context, then, the foremost danger for the Japanese society of the 1960s was no longer a revival of ultranationalism as such, nor the encroachment of oppressive state authority *per se*. Instead, if there was indeed a crisis taking place, it had to do with the intense changes in the social and subjective landscape, that had resulted from the penetration of the systemic power of corporate capital and ideology, on the one hand, and with the disturbances in the social imaginary and a resultant ambiguity in the individual's sense of identity, on the other. Throughout the 1960s, systems of control shifted from hard, tangible institutions to soft, intangible networks of knowledge in which one's enemies were to be found both inside and outside the self: the formerly objectifiable enemy was transformed into the more abstract systemic authority of which one was a part.[136] In this condition of political and discursive closure, the conventional political and ideological means of counter-hegemonic struggle lost their ground, and in the face of the encroachment of the rational, pragmatic, pacifist and individualist discourse of new conservatism, the only apparently remaining means of resistance were the reactionary and depoliticized expressions of anti-rationalist, anti-scientific and anti-establishment protest. These romantic rebellions were thus simultaneously various expressions of the eruption of an excluded pathos: a radical activism combined with a Marxist/populist theory of alienation in *Zenkyōtō*, the creation of an alternative philosophy in Umehara, the recovery of patriarchal authority in the family and the state in Etō, and the pursuit of the absolute spirit both in theory and practice in Mishima. These romantic ideas were all attempts to repair the broken linkage between the individual and the social whole and/or to fill the gap between rationality/mind and emotion/body; their effect was to replace the rational and autonomous subject upheld by the earlier generation of progressive leftism with a romantic and collective subject in the hope of endowing the latter with a renewed political agency in the conditions of mass society.

It is interesting to note in this context that both the *Zenkyōtō* movement and Mishima, although located at the opposite ends of the political spectrum, actually shared more similarities than differences, particularly in terms of their pursuit of a collective identity, albeit in quite different terms. The new left student movement relied on anti-technological, anti-elitist theory and practice, as the Tokyo University *Zenkyōtō* leader, Yamamoto Yoshitaka, articulated in his Marxist/populist language.

> The rising bourgeoisie thought that the liberation from religion would make mankind happy, and it was modern science which made them convinced that that was so. Although modern science has released an enormous amount of productive energy from nature, it made mankind subordinate to the commodity. Modern science and bourgeois society have developed hand-in-hand. And now, the emergence of national corporate capital has even made science a national policy.[137]

As I have argued, the *Zenkyōtō* movement was the child of progressive Leftism and as such retained an essential link between the hypothesized meaning of life and political action: to realize the former one had to undertake the latter. *Zenkyōtō* shared with Umehara and Ikeda Daisaku a (broadly speaking) religious dimension in their 'depoliticized political conceptions and practice' symbolized by the creation of *kaihō-ku*, the so-called liberated zones of the campus occupations, spaces in which the self could be extended beyond given reality.[138]

In addition to its general reactionary, anti-modern orientation, *Zenkyōtō*'s conceptions of time and space were clearly distinct from those generally accepted by the earlier postwar progressive paradigm. In a discussion with Mishima over the meaning of the liberated zones (*kaihō-ku*), one representative of *Zenkyōtō* advanced the following arguments:

Mishima: ... would it be correct to interpret the liberated zones as a space which emerges when one encounters the Thing [-in-itself]?
Zenkyōtō: Yes.
Mishima: That space, whether deformed or constructed, I do not know, maintains itself for a certain length of time ...
Zenkyōtō: Since [the space] does not have time, the conception of maintaining it is wrong-headed.
Mishima: Then, what caused the destruction of the liberated zones was not the Japanese defense forces (*kidōtai*) but the Thing.
Zenkyōtō: Most likely ...
Mishima: History is continuity. Time ...
Zenkyōtō: History is not continuity. But rather a space equivalent to an open possibility itself. Perhaps freedom itself. Nevertheless, mankind has acquired the habit of pulling back when they encounter freedom or the Other ...[139]

In the *Zenkyōtō* paradigm, space is understood as the moment of encountering the Other and history as a discrete moment irreducible to, or what escapes from, the linearly conceived time of modern progressivism. History outside of material and discursive relations, that is, only experienced by the subject in the moment, refuses to be subjugated to the synchronicity and homogeneity of any hegemonic system/discourse. This dematerialized conception of space and aestheticized history outside temporal progression bears some relation to French poststructuralist conceptions that became better known in Japan in the following decades. These utopian and metaphysical conceptions of time, space, and history, however, were perhaps necessarily confused with the material and historical space and reified in the liberated zones of Tokyo University.

Thus, just as was the case in the spring and summer of 1968 in the European context, the *Zenkyōtō* movement and its ideas contained aspects of both the modern and the anti-modern, progressive and regressive; its historical significance lay perhaps in its status as a turning point from the former to the latter. Indeed, liberal progressive intellectuals, including Maruyama Masao, came to be seen as siding with the establishment, against whose elitist oppressive power and abstract logocentrism the students' violence was directed. More significantly, however, Mishima and the *Zenkyōtō* movement were not as different from each other as their opposed political positions suggest. In the discussion with the *Zenkyōtō* representative Mishima claimed:

> This, I say this seriously. If you had only uttered the single word the emperor in confining yourself in the Yasuda lecture hall, I would have willingly joined with you and fought the same fight. . . . Because prewar imperial rule in the year 1 of the Shōwa era [1925] and what is called direct democracy today are hardly different as political concepts.[140]

What links the two positions goes much deeper than a shared romantic anti-modern orientation as such: it includes a shared impulse for transcendence and a radical desire for eliminating the impediments of institutional representation, thereby making the unattainable in the existing hegemonic discourse and material relations (supposedly) attainable. This inclination for an existential leap was put into practice by Mishima's suicide-performance as well as by the intra-membership murders within the ex-*Zenkyōtō* sects that resulted when, having become increasingly politically marginalized, the group turned on several of its own members, executing them as scapegoats. In these two cases the conventional political categories of left and right became meaningless; they were replaced by the newly emerged opposition between logos and pathos, often equated to the opposition between pro-establishment and anti-establishment.

In short, what characterizes the Japanese society of the 1960s was a seemingly diametrically opposed development between mainstream conservatism (e.g. political realism, economic functionalism, positivist structuralism, etc.) that went hand-in-hand with corporate capital's ongoing restructuring of society, and a counter-movement of radical leftism that operated within a broader discourse of 'romantic aestheticism' and alternative utopian visions. Taking advantage of the situation, the LDP conservatives consolidated their power machinery throughout the 1960s, while Leftist popular movements were largely unable to reflect the concerns of the greater society, and were thus increasingly radicalized and confined to the margins – i.e. the student rebellions – until they were ultimately led down the path of a bitter and rampant anarchism. These opposed movements, as has been argued, took shape in response to the structural transformation of Japanese society, and operated in a complementary manner as manifestations of the contradictions of corporate capitalism itself. Under these conditions, the notion of the rational-autonomous subject as the principal counter-hegemonic agent was overtaken by the popular notion of ideas and actions based on the collective-aesthetic subject. Moreover, in the Japan of the 1960s, intellectual thought in general could no longer carry the same weight, as the helmsman of progressive causes, as it did in previous decades; instead, the function of thought became increasingly descriptive of, and subordinate to, or even instrumentally to, increasingly powerful and autonomous material/structural forces. By the end of the 1960s, even the new left narratives based on a collective/aesthetic subject were subject to a general breakdown, signalling the end of both the postwar progressive narrative of the subject as political agent and the role of the intellectual as the leader of political change. Despite these failures, however, romantic narratives based on national and cultural identity, such as those advanced by Etō and Umehara, did not immediately acquire a popularity sufficient to affect the intellectual trajectory of the times; for that, they had to wait another decade.

Meanwhile, the Japanese economy, which had experienced uninterrupted and unprecedented growth during the decade began to stumble towards the end of the 1960s and the beginning of the 1970s, seriously shaking the confidence of economic leaders, the legitimacy of LDP politicians and the credibility of new conservatism. Although the rational–economist path was subject to serious questioning in the second half of the 1960s, as the negative effects of development, such as pollution and alienation, grew increasingly visible, what ultimately undermined its premises was a series of external shocks in the early 1970s. The unilateral American decision to delink its currency from the gold standard system and adopt a floating rate in August 1971, the so-called 'Nixon shock,' threw the Japanese economy into unprecedented confusion. In addition, the Japanese economy fell into a state of stagnation and high inflation (stagflation) in the face of the oil shock of October 1973, causing a series of consumer panics and a general trend towards energy conservation. By 1975 the oil shock's full effects were felt and the Japanese economy recorded zero growth in GNP for the first time in the postwar period.[141] Tanaka Kakuei, elected Prime Minister in 1972, took full advantage of this confusion to promote the financial interests of his political backers by first artificially escalating and extending the oil shortage and then later abetting the price fixing policies of some favoured trading companies (Marubeni was the most notable). These manoeuvres were merely part of a giant kickback machine that was to net him billions of yen.[142] During this period of turmoil between 1968 and the mid-1970s, the optimism founded on solid economic growth suffered a serious crisis of confidence in political, economic and ideological terms.

In this context of crisis, Japanese society and discourse continued to be subject to powerful material forces and increasingly opaque and fragmented discursive conditions. The following passages from Kōsaka Shūhei describes the general picture of Japanese society in the 1970s.

> Reality exists only in the network of a systematized relation; the fact that an individual is a product of this relation became obvious. Or, our era is in the midst of a series of changes and intensification of relations in which individuals are no longer capable of sustaining themselves. Was the individual/subject a mere dream dreamt by modernity after all? The atomization of the individual within the intensifying system of the network is the contradiction which cannot be resolved by civil society in itself. When reality is increasingly defined as nothing but a relation, becoming oneself means nothing but being left behind. The consciousness of people, then, wanders around aimless.[143]

> What happened after 1970 was a replacement of all the ideas that had been pursued in the 1960s with a desire to increase the speed of circulation. Only socially systematized desire tells us of the presence of our desire. We hardly know what our true desire is. The contemporary era is thus one of consumption and of fiction. Moreover, this society dissolves ideals, historicity and even death. Following Mishima's metaphor of death, in the 1970s we entered upon the age lacking exteriority, the age in which the image of language became inescapably vague.[144]

As I have argued throughout, the effect of the penetration of society by corporate capitalism, i.e. mass consumerism, the depoliticization of society, a loss of a sense of identity and a disintegration of the local cultural fabric, has perhaps been more serious in Japan than in many Western societies because historically Japan has had little success in developing counteracting protective measures, such as democratic institutions, grass roots movements and citizens or civil rights groups.[145] In the context of postwar Japan, radical structural transformation left society in a state of confusion in which it became increasingly difficult to establish individual identity, particularly among the young whose experience did not extend to the early postwar modern progressive period.

What possible ways were open to individuals struggling in this sea of nihilism? Given the near disintegration of the links – discourse and meaning – connecting individuals to the socio-cultural whole, how were those links to be reconstituted? There seem to have been only two logically conceivable outcomes to this state of affairs: either to recover meaning by means of some symbol of a collective cultural spirit – Etō's patriarchal state and Mishima's emperor – or to abandon identity/meaning altogether, allowing the sea of nihilism to continue to flood the inner landscape of the individual – the option 'chosen' by society at large.

5 Back to identity

'Postmodernity,' *nihonjinron*, and the desire of the other

Introduction

As we saw in Chapter 4, the 1960s marked what might be called the 'end of politics' in the aftermath of the breakdown of progressive political movements and triumphant economic success, accompanied by a rapid uprooting of individual and collective identity. In this process, I have argued, the effective links between individuals and society, intellectual productions and social movements, and formal politics and the social imaginary were practically lost by the early 1970s. This stagnant and insular state of discourse soon faced a radical intervention from the outside. That is, the Japanese political and business scene was challenged by a series of 'external shocks' in the mid-1970s, to such an extent that many felt that the country's economic survival was seriously jeopardized. However, the subsequent economic recovery from this crisis surprised many Japanese, as well as foreign observers, and catalysed the rise of a renewed sense of pride and optimism grounded in the successes of a 'Japanese-style economy' that began to lead international trends. Two related socio-cultural events, particularly significant for my purpose, followed closely thereafter. First, the loss of identity much lamented in the 1960s and early 1970s was no longer the case in the late 1970s; instead, this loss came to be seen as a state of freedom. Actively abandoning concerns over an intrinsic sense of self, this new cultural mind-set harnessed a nascent material snobbism and commodity fetishism, in which the subject's inner void was filled with commercialized signs signifying the individual's sense of their own personality. Second, the economic successes of the late 1970s gave rise to a new current of scholarship which initially attempted to explain Japan's economic strengths in terms of its cultural attributes, but soon came to be endlessly engaged in discussions of the unique characteristics of the Japanese culture and people – the discourse of *nihonjinron*. As I argue below, what held the discourse together was not a common theoretical concern, nor a commitment to the attainment of knowledge through reasoned debate, but rather pragmatic concerns and a moral and emotional imperative either to explain 'Japan' to outsiders or to seek the restitution of lost identity in national terms. As US–Japan economic relations deteriorated in the second half of the 1980s, the *nihonjinron* discourse began to nurture nationalist–exclusionist inclined arguments that made stringent demands for Japan's cultural autonomy in the world.

In the first section of Chapter 5 I critically examine the 1983 LDP government developmental guidelines entitled *Kindai o koete* (literally, 'beyond the modern age') which attempted to engineer a neo-conservative ideology for the new age of prosperity under the slogans of the 'age of culture' and the 'information society.' In this ideological invention, the government-business elite appealed to an ideally conceived Japanese identity as a source of inspiration for 'overcoming' the actual hardships the people were expected undergo in the transformation to a highly technologically and bureaucratically oriented society. The effect of this government-corporate designed transformation in the realms of the subject and the collective imaginary are dealt with in the second section. In the late 1970s and the 1980s, the intense commercialization of society dramatically altered various aspects of Japanese life, giving rise to what is commonly referred to as 'postmodern cultural conditions,' in which subjectivity and intersubjective meaning were increasingly defined by commodified signs and the desire of the other. In the third section, I examine the obverse of these commercial trends, the desire for identity expressed in *nihonjinron* (the discourse of Japanese uniqueness), a discourse that sought to reconstitute a culturally and collectively grounded identity. The emergence of this emotionally charged discourse played a major role in the radical transformation of the modality of Japanese knowledge, and in consequence Japanese intellectual discourse as a whole was beset by various problematic features, such as the dehistoricization and dematerialization of the notion of culture and a widespread vogue for quasi-scientific methods in social scientific enquiry, as well as an increasing loss of intellectual autonomy from political and commercial influences.

In the final section, I attempt to assess some aspects of the overall state of Japanese society in the 1980s that could be characterized by two seemingly contradictory tendencies: the fragmenting and decentring inclination commonly understood by the term 'postmodern,' and the inclination for condensation driven by a desire for identity and meaning as expressed in *nihonjinron*. In order to address the historical significance of these contradictory and simultaneous developments, I will trace some discussion on the 'origins' of the problem of Japanese identity and its unique inheritance from the past. I wish to stress, however, that what is often viewed as the unique cultural problem of Japanese identity as such is undeniably modern and universal in nature, that it arose in the process of Japan's reshaping itself into a new mould, in the historical context of its becoming of a part of the modern universal world. Borrowing a number of insights from various works of Karatani Kōjin, I seek to explore what underlies the intimate relation between 'postmodern conditions' and nationalist resurgence as manifestations of the troubled state of Japanese modernity.

The 'age of culture' and the 'information society' – 'Overcoming modernity' revisited

Faced with what he perceived as fundamental structural changes in the world and in the life-style of the individual, Prime Minister Ōhira Masayoshi presented in April 1979 his government's guiding principles for the national trajectory in the 1980s and beyond. In two volumes entitled *Beyond the Modern Age* (*Kindai o Koete*) published in 1983 (three years after Ōhira's death, and dedicated to him), a thematic and philosophical orientation is laid out in the form of an extensive display of scholarship by government-appointed research groups assigned to investigate a wide range of subjects including modernization, Japanese culture and psychology, the environment and technology, and the social order. The central emphasis that runs throughout the volumes is the possibility of culture as the remedy to the negative effects of postwar Japanese modernization and material development. The basic rationale for this claim is laid out in the opening of the book as follows:

> In the past thirty years since the end of World War II, our nation has been solely devoted to the goal of achieving economic affluence, and this was a fruit of over a hundred years of modernization since the Meiji era, an effort of learning from Western nations. What we enjoy today, for example, freedom and equality, progress and prosperity, is nothing but the result of unceasing efforts made by the Japanese people towards that goal. However, one cannot deny the claim that we have paid insufficient attention to the harmonious relations between man and nature, the balance between freedom and responsibility, a sense of satisfaction in life which is deeply rooted in our inner spirit. Today, these issues have become increasing concerns of our people. I understand this as a manifestation of the limitations of material civilization itself, which is based on urbanization caused by a rapid economic growth and rationalism. That is to say, *we have come to the age in which one must go beyond the modern, and we must shift from an economic-centered to a culture-centered age.*[1]

According to this declaration, the problems of the modern age, such as the exploitation of nature, an excess of freedom, and the lack of spirituality, are essentially caused by the rationalism and materialism inherent in Western civilization. Ōhira appears convinced that the time to re-evaluate Japanese cultural values, which he feels were undervalued in the period of postwar modernization, has arrived, and he seems almost to boast that the limitations of modern civilization will be overcome in the coming 'age of culture.'

As Harry Harootunian argues, the national developmental path of the Ōhira government was premised upon the assumption of a contextualist notion of Japanese culture based on communal social values that were thought to embody what it called a 'holonism' superior to Western modern rationality. Unlike the Western atomistic conception of humanity confronting nature and itself, so argue the authors of *Beyond the Modern Age*, the Japanese understanding of humankind is characterized by a consciousness of human's relations to one another, in much the same way that Watsuji in the 1930s ascribed the Japanese word *ningen* to a relational notion 'between men' and thus characterized Japanese society by the mutuality of its members (*aidagara*).[2] According to the authors of *Beyond the Modern Age*, this understanding locates itself in a harmonious balance among humans, and with nature, what they call a 'holonic' path; this path is one in which the unity of the whole (*hol*) would be allied to that of the parts (*on*) without reducing one to the other, and forms the central principle by which the challenges of the modern age will be overcome.[3] In contrast to the binary thought structure of the modern West (i.e. good/evil, humanity/nature, subject/object, mind/body), which the authors viewed as conducive to conflict and control, they characterize Japanese cultural orientation as having a three-legged structure, or what they call 'the logic of circles,' a logic that avoids determination of absolute winners or losers, maintains a greater openness to contextual factors, and has a greater potential for cooperation.[4] Basing their prescriptions on this logic, the authors argue that Japan should pursue neither a continuation of the modern 'hard path' nor a return to a premodern 'soft path'; instead, it should seek the mediation of the former by the latter. This middle way seeks to articulate the Japanese cultural concepts of *ningen-shugi* (humanism) and *aidagara-shugi* (relationalism), and would, they argue, successfully avoid the crude effects of both individualism and totalitarianism.

The holonic principle of integration and the logic of circles are applied to a wide array of policy issues including, for example, the environment, rural and community planning (including the household), international politics and security issues, Asia–Pacific developmental plans, and socio-economic planning. Throughout the volumes, the moral idealism that the authors see at the basis of Japanese cultural values predominates, particularly so in the discussions of specific policy areas, such as international security and economy, technology, and rural planning. The volume's discussion of these issues strikes one as general and unpragmatic with repeated citation of the key terminologies, such as 'soft' (gentler/milder), 'creativity,' 'integration' and 'decentralization,' while leaving more concrete issues such as planning processes and resource distribution untouched. What the text claims to achieve – a 'humanization of technology' in the 'age of culture' – thus curiously underplays the policy's highly strategic nature, and tacitly mollifies the brute consequences of such a technologically intensive developmental path. There is little doubt that the 'holonic path' towards an information society would logically result in an increasingly harsh commercialization of the private spheres of life and a further penetration of technological and bureaucratic control over society. In other words, the coming 'age of culture' was a political blueprint of the new national goal agreed upon by the government and the business elites, and a guidebook for Japanese people who would have to pay the high costs of remodelling themselves to suit the structural demands of the 'information society.'

It is particularly worth paying attention to the material context in which *Beyond the Modern Age* was produced, that is, the government political initiative and the institutional and financial supports for the project. The volumes were products of a government appointed, coordinated effort of nearly 200 prominent people in various fields and professions, including university professors and researchers in various fields of the social sciences, politicians and bureaucrats, private businesses, foreign diplomats, and writers and artists. With a wealth of resources and the involvement of the Ministry of Education, which could easily mobilize national universities and research institutes, the Ōhira government managed to persuade a bevy of intellectuals to cooperate, to influence the scope and orientation of academic contributions, and to inform and potentially coordinate the private sector within its general guidelines. In conjunction with the completion of the volumes, the government launched various follow-up studies, including the publication of thirty-seven booklets devoted to the study of 'soft-nomics,' that involved thirty-nine study teams with about 460 researchers.[5] In sum, Japanese social sciences in the 1980s were exposed to two powerful influences: active government intervention in the production of knowledge and, something I will come back to later, the rapid growth of the information industry targeting a fast growing educated middle class. These heavily government financed and orchestrated knowledge productions have been disseminated extensively, through educational institutions and the mass-media both in Japan and abroad.

Moreover, a determinate set of historical conditions prepared the ground for the government's bold assertion of going 'beyond the modern,' and we may say that this grand ideological blueprint was both a manifestation of and a remedy for the particular conditions of the mid- to late 1970s. First, to consider is the timing of the project. The declaration of the 'age of culture' and the call for the formulation of a new Japanese identity followed hard on the heels of the loss of a workable LDP political ideology once the period of high economic growth had begun to subside. It was during this period that the progressive conservative ideology of the 1960s – i.e. material wealth and a 'good middle-class life' – ceased to be as attractive as it once was, partly because this goal had been achieved by the growth of a large middle-income strata, and partly because Japanese GDP growth slowed from a previous rate of more than 10 per cent to around 5 per cent. These changes, combined with the increasingly manifest lack of, and the desire for, identity made an appeal to culture a preferred means for the new ideology. Moreover, in the same period, Japanese politics had experienced a severe legitimacy crisis when the public found out that Tanaka Kakuei, then Prime Minister, had been involved in corruption on a historically unprecedented scale. The Lockheed Scandal which broke in 1976 revealed that over $10 million had been funnelled from Lockheed Co. to LDP politicians and the Marubeni Trading Company in order to secure the sale of Lockheed Tristar jets to Japan Airlines.[6] The revelations of this scandal, following soon after by other revelations concerning the artificially created high inflation subsequent to the 'oil shock' and sundry electoral pork-barrelling, made the Japanese electorate resentful and distrustful of not only the LDP but of politics itself. The clear formulation of national goals as laid out in *Beyond the Modern Age* was the Ōhira cabinet's attempt to reestablish public trust by demonstrating their commitment to politics.

Equally significantly, the ideological blueprint of *Beyond the Modern Age* was strongly backed by neo-conservative politicians and intellectuals who had become dominant by that time. Unlike the populist rhetorical posture taken by the conservatives of the 1960s, who argued in favour of improving of the material life of the individual, the neo-conservatives of the 1980s instead appealed to collective goals for the nation, in terms of its culture and economy, in such a way to make politics irrelevant. Moreover, as perhaps best exemplified in the 1977 publication by Satō Seizaburō, Kumon Shunpei, and Murakami Yasusuke entitled *The Arrival of the Post-Conservative-versus-the Progressive Age* (*Datsu Hokaku Jidai no Tōrai*), neo-conservative arguments assumed that the radical socio-economic changes and the rapid expansion of the middle-class in the past decade marked a fundamental shift between, what they described as, 'postwar politics' and 'post-postwar politics.' In this work the authors argue that the burgeoning middle-income strata throughout the 1960s and 1970s made the conventional pattern of politics, based on the opposition between a conservatism grounded upon economic growth and a progressivism grounded upon the early postwar modernist ideals, obsolete.[7] In the new age of material enrichment, the authors emphasize, both conservative and progressive camps ought to reorient themselves towards common goals by cooperatively and productively relating to each other.[8] Instead of identifying and setting to work to tackle the very real challenges that resulted from the socio-economic changes of the past two decades, the authors completely dismiss the question of structurally embedded power relations by reducing politics to a battle between political parties. In eliminating politics from their agenda, they implicitly and tacitly lobby for the opening up of society to the flow of private capital and the logic of the market and to joint leadership between the government and corporate capital. Not surprisingly, all three authors graduated from Tokyo University (something of an academic factory for national elites) and soon after the publication, Satō and Kumon became powerful LDP ideologues.

These factors taken together help to demonstrate that the visions laid out in *Beyond the Modern Age* represent those of the large business corporations and the LDP government, and the assumed collaboration between the two in the coming age of information. These large business corporations, commonly called *keiretsu*, gradually grew to predominance in the postwar period, especially after the Korean War and under the LDP's rapid economic growth policies, by absorbing smaller enterprises and by structuring themselves in pyramid shaped, hierarchical structures with their vertically and horizontally integrated corporate bodies.[9] The six large corporate groups that emerged out of these strategic practices during the 1960s are Mitsui, Mitsubishi and Sumitomo (the prewar *zaibatsu* groups) and Fuyo, Sanwa and Daiichi kangin (the new comers), all of them centred on financial institutes as their core organs. As noted by foreign observers, each of these business groups tend to operate as one corporate body whose business practices are coordinated, while formally maintaining their independent corporate status. For example, they periodically hold unpublicized meetings of their core corporate representatives (*shachō kai*), in which decisions are taken on issues like the co-establishment of new companies, strategic mergers and acquisitions of other companies, the coordination of internal and external business relations, and important promotions.

Since the 1960s, each of these *keiretsu* conglomerates has constantly restructured its internal organizations, as well as its relation to the others, and by virtue of these oligopolistic business practices, it has often been able to outcompete Western firms in the acquisition of international market share. Rather predictably, these practices had come to the increasing attention of foreign economic observers by the early 1980s; a 1993 report by the United States Trade Representative Committee to the US Congress, for example, criticized Japanese economic structures, pointing out the unliberal nature of these large corporations' domination of the economy:

> The very large portion of Japanese production and marketing is controlled by sixteen business groups known as 'keiretsu.' Each of these groups forms an organic link including their banks, corporate producers, and trading company, maintaining mutually dependent relations. This side of the structure of the Japanese economy is functioning well to hinder the penetration of commodities and services from the US and other foreign countries.[10]

The timing of these criticisms is an important indicator of the moment when Japanese exports began to outperform those of other developed countries. Indeed, by the second half of the 1980s, Japanese political-economic practices came to be characterized in a variety of ways, including 'developmental state,' 'super-exploitative Fordism,' 'symbiotic relations between large and small firms,' and so on.[11] 'One of the more positive evaluations of the Japanese production system was presented, for example, by Martin Kenney and Richard Florida, who praised it as an effective form of post-Fordism.

> Post-Fordist industrial organization in Japan differs markedly from that of Fordism. In Japan, work teams, job rotation, learning-by-doing and flexibility have been used to replace the functional specialization, task fragmentation and rigid assembly-line production of US Fordism. This social organization of Japanese manufacturing was not the product of managerial fiat, but rather evolved from the outcomes of bitter postwar political struggles.[12]

The close relation between politics and economics noted by them is critical to understanding the *keiretsu* centred Japanese economy of the 1980s. The origins of the *keiretsu*, however, can be traced not only to the bitter postwar political struggles, but also to the creation of the *zaikai*, a semi-autonomous body of financial leaders with access to the highest levels of government, including the *keidanren*, or the Federation of Economic Organizations, which was established by the early postwar Yoshida cabinet as a device to mediate the political and the economic, a channel by which to convey the SCAP's political commands to the business sector.

It must be stressed, then, that the illiberal business practices of the *keiretsu*, which have annoyed American competitors, had their origins in the early postwar collaboration and intertwining of political causes between Japan and the US. This is one of the blind spots of the criticisms of 'modernism' made in *Beyond the Modern Age*, which consistently draws upon the new national pride engendered by Japan's quick economic recovery from the external shocks of the early 1970s. Viewing Japanese economic strengths within the frame contrasting Japan to the modern and Western, the swelling confidence generated by Western attention to the 'Japanese Miracle' only served to accelerate the ever more vocal Japanese criticisms of the modern. Instead of stepping out of the shadows of the Western gaze as it claims, the vision of the future depicted in *Beyond the Modern Age* merely reasserts the predominance of the West as a reference point for Japanese self-knowledge, the oppositional fame in which Japanese identity is conceived and affirmed.

Both the swelling confidence generated by Western attention to the 'Japanese miracle,' as well as the ever more vocal Japanese criticisms of the modern, should not lead us to believe that in the 1980s Japan had stepped out of the shadows of the Western gaze; rather, as I will argue in a later section, both phenomena merely demonstrate the unchanged importance of the West as *the* reference point, in relation to which Japanese identity is affirmed.

In short, the significance of the neo-conservative ideology so well exemplified in *Beyond the Modern Age* and its appeals to Japanese identity cannot be fully understood in isolation from the broader historical contexts of Japan in the later 1970s and the 1980s. The most important points to be stressed here are: (1) the formation of a close alliance between the government and large business corporations whose collaboration was assumed in the new national trajectory; (2) the changing nature of social control in the nascent cultural-information society and the increasing commercial and political interventions in the process of knowledge production; (3) the internationalization of Japan in the context of the globalization of economy and a resultant awakening of Japanese identity vis-à-vis an American other; and (4) the reactionary desire for identity in response to the intrusion of commercial and bureaucratic structuring forces into the realms of subjectivity and intersubjectivity. Since the first point was largely discussed above, the following section is concerned with the other three factors and their far reaching, but by no means self-evident, politico-cultural implications.

The triumph of 'postmodern surface' and the displaced self: hyperreal society, commodified identity and joyful wisdom

Replacing the real with simulacra – the corporate design of a hyperreal society

Rather unsurprisingly, there is a peculiar gap between the neo-conservative rhetoric of the information society, with its rosy picture of 'middle-class life,' and the actual experience of ordinary Japanese. On the one hand, the myth of the '100-million-strong-middle-class' seems to be corroborated by a recognized high standard of living in Japan, whose Gross Domestic Product per capita is the second highest in the world. On the other hand, however, for the majority of the Japanese, life is felt to be much harder than in many other Western societies. The social critic Yamamoto Hiraku gives an anecdotal description typical of Japanese middle-class life: the father is constantly working overtime, either voluntarily or partly coerced, to repay life-long housing loans while the mother strives to earn extra income in the low wage part-time job sector in order to pay for their children's education.[13] According to Yamamoto, the ordinary Japanese in this scenario are painfully aware that they cannot really attain in their life time what they have been told to expect from 'the good middle-class life.' Paradoxically, argues Yamamoto, it is for this very reason that the myth of the '100-million-strong-middle-class' has become so entrenched, since many of those caught up in this treadmill of supposed success wish upon their children a better chance in life; which is to say, a dream is needed to inspire the middle class to keep facing the harshness of their real lives.[14]

While the myth of 'the good middle-class life' keeps many fixed on dreams of luxury, more realizable, segmented dreams are made attainable in the form of various consumer goods. For example, most Tokyoites cannot realistically hope to own a house given the prohibitively high cost of real estate. Thus, so Yamamoto's anecdote recounts, the actual dream of middle-class life sold to those eager for it is a two-bedroom apartment that comes with a complete set of well selected furniture, a unit kitchen and a small space devoted to one's hobby. In this way, the 'individuality' of the consumer can be manifest in their choice of knick-knacks, decorations or aesthetic styles, without sacrificing the sense of belonging to the middle class which comes from residing in a homogeneous high-rise apartment.[15] Within this marketing scheme, not only is the segmented dream made readily affordable, but a sense of consumer choice makes possible the assertion of different 'personalities' in commodified terms. By means such as this, argues Yamamoto, the collective illusion of society is maintained, a '100-million-strong like-minded majority slightly differentiated from one another.' Choosing from a broad range of slightly differentiated commodities allows individuals to 'define' themselves, and by displaying the artefacts of their choice in the showroom of their home they confirm a sense of self. Given the dynamic of this economy, commodities – clothes, cars, furniture, etc. – are not sold and purchased for their specific utility (i.e. use value) but for the style and connotations associated with them, that is, largely for the purpose of affirming and displaying one's identity as a member of the middle class who shares his or her dreams with others. However, the satisfaction realized by consuming/possessing these commodities, a supposed 'fulfilment of identity,' does not often provide much fulfilment, for what it satisfies is not an internally originating desire but rather offers the pseudo-satisfaction of an externally given desire, the desire of the others, or a satisfaction of an artificially cultivated desire.[16]

And yet, the myth of a 100-million-strong middle class maintains an influential power over many individuals. Perhaps this is due to the disciplinary power of the discourse of the middle-class operating in the achieved condition of socio-cultural homogeneity, a triumphant success of corporate capitalism to have subjugated millions in part by means of image creation. In actuality, this homogeneity is substantiated neither by the political nor the economic status of the individuals, but is first and foremost *imagistic and cultural*; in political and economic terms the Japanese people are just as divided and differentiated from one another as elsewhere in the industrial world, while they are arguably more deprived of the means of collective negotiation and a sense of solidarity. One social scientist, Kurihara Akira, describes Japanese society as a society constituted by 'fragmented masses' who are politically reduced to replaceable parts of the whole while culturally burdened with the obligation of organizing their lives in ways that enable them to qualify as members of the middle class.[17] In other words, this culturally homogenized notion of the masses is a highly ideological, commercially-driven system of control in which each individual is first reduced to a nameless anonymity, thereby deprived of his/her specific identity, and then subjugated to externally imposed demands, the fulfilment of which allows them a sense of belonging to the ambiguous notion of the middle class.[18] In this new system of control by means of a nationally homogenized culture disseminated by the mass media – *taishū bunka* (mass culture) in Kurihara's term – has practically speaking superseded culture grounded in people's locally specific lives – *minshu bunka* (folk culture).[19] In this socio-economic and cultural context an externally defined identity is created for the populace by giant corporations and advertising campaigns, such that Japanese people's empirical selfhood has come to be subjugated to the ideal-type middle-class life depicted in the myth.

In this spectacle economy the urban landscape becomes the theatrical site for the performance of commercial display in which people themselves are artistic objects, or signs. Transforming themselves into nameless anonymities wrapped in fashionable goods and decked out with trendy hair-styles and accessories, individuals are 'different' enough from one another to communicate the subtleties of their sameness-in-difference while simultaneously affirming their collective identity.[20] The urban landscape is packed with artefacts that represent the images of a prosperous and glamorous modern high-tech life, the messages of which are disseminated by various entertainment venues, cafes and restaurants, fashion boutiques, cinemas, museums, and so on. Many Tokyoites punctuate their lives by participating in this somewhat 'unreal' theatrical space on the weekends, as a preparation for their return to the daily routine of real life on Monday; in doing so, they momentarily transform themselves into a part of the scenery of this urban space that has also been specifically designed and constructed by large business conglomerates, just like the good middle-class life.[21] The Shibuya–Harajuku–Aoyama district, for example, was in its present incarnation largely built by the Seibu group, one of the largest Japanese business conglomerates, and became a centre for youth fashion/culture from the 1970s onward by virtue of Seibu's successful strategy of focusing on the installation and presentation of commodities. Koen-dori (Park Avenue), running from Shibuya subway station to Yoyogi park – known until recently for the *Takenoko-zoku*, the near identically dressed teenage dancing groups whose clothes come from the Takenoko boutique – has became a strollers' paradise, with the highly successful Parco department store owned by Seibu as its pillar.[22] Parco, unlike previously popular large department stores, is a kind of 'value-added company' and merely rents space to boutiques filled with fashionable, fairly expensive, but not inaccessibly so, goods. This strategy has attracted hordes of fashion conscious young people eager to take part in and constitute the scene, and has resulted in what came to be known as the 'Parco-Seibu culture,' characterized by urban, 'avant-garde,' highly fashionable and cosmopolitan images.[23] The conglomerate owns a variety of other cultural and entertainment businesses including cinemas, restaurants, art galleries, sports centres, and so on, in the neighbourhood (as well as elsewhere throughout Tokyo) which together form the nucleus of a 'Parco culture' that has transformed the Shibuya district into stylistically coordinated space.

The commercial construction of urban space decorated with cultural/commercial artefacts, including the people themselves, comes, then, to 'realize' the myths of the middle-class society in a brutally commercialized form. Yamamoto explains this curious inversion of the 'illusion made into the real' in Japanese urban life of the late 1970s, by drawing on Jean Baudrillard's concept of the 'simulacra':

> Today abstraction is no longer that of the map, the double, the mirror, or the concept. Simulation is no longer that of a territory, a referential being, or a substance. It is the generation by models of a real without origin or reality: a hyperreal. The territory no longer precedes the map, nor does it survive it. It is nevertheless the map that precedes the territory – *precession of simulacra* – that engenders the territory, and if one must return to the fable, today it is the territory whose shreds slowly rot across the extent of the map.[24]

Yamamoto sees the Tokyo of the 1980s as an example of Baudrillard's 'hyperreal' metropolis produced and preceded by 'simulacra,' a city in which form (i.e. city plans) precedes its contents (i.e. people, society). Seibu, more recently known as the Saison group, has been inspired to become what they call a 'total life information business conglomerate' (*sōgō seikatsu jōhō kigyō gruupu*), dealing not only in retail trade, but also in finance, trade, transportation, and the development of leisure–entertainment facilities. Following Seibu's lead in the creation of 'simulacra' fashion districts, competitors like the Tokyu conglomerate, in urban sites, and smaller retail business groups like Daiei and Seiyu, in suburban sites, have attempted to duplicate miniaturized versions of Seibu's successes.[25] As the urban environment of Tokyoites has become increasingly subordinated to mass media generated images of middle-class life, so has the frontier of the hyperreal expanded outwards, displacing the preexisting forms of rural or semi-rural life by hyper-mediated images. Noteworthy is that, aware of the sophistication of consumer demands and greater competition, Seibu and other conglomerates do not expect an immediate return on their investments since they recognize that the more indirect benefit lies with controlling the diffusion of fashion information. The commercial tactic here is a long-term, capital and information intensive commercial investment focused on image creation; that is to say, if Seibu successfully and continually generates on a nationwide scale an image of trendy culture that many young people identify themselves with, it can expect a lifelong return from generations of constantly renewed youths dispensing their disposable income in its outlets.[26]

This drive to realize the 'hyperreal' and displace 'the real,' advanced by the power of information, advertising and the high-tech communication systems of monopoly capitalism, was one of the chief forces behind the booming domestic consumption rates in Japan in the 1980s. In this highly abstract, technocratic form of control, those who wield the levers of the development of communications technology and mass media exercise the most effective forms of power over society and reap the most profits. In fact, the largest investment projects in new media technologies in Japan have been monopolized by the government and giant business conglomerates. For example, the Ministry of Posts and Telecommunications' 'futuristic model city plan' nicknamed *teretopia*, the 'new media communication plan' developed by the Ministry of Transportation, and the 'INS – high information system' designed by NTT.[27] Despite their human-friendly sounding names, the degree of proposed intervention in personal life by these new media goes far beyond already achieved levels; their aim is to overcome physical distances and 'wasteful time' spent actually visiting the locations where services are conventionally offered – banks, shopping malls and offices – by developing a computerized home banking and shopping system.[28] Drawing attention to the traditional links between advanced information systems and the military, Kogawa Testuo, a critic of communication and technology, points out some of the adverse effects of this type of high-tech media and its control over society:

> Military rationalization is a typical example of a synchronic rationalism which has elevated itself to an instrumental rationality. Military electronic systems thoroughly standardize the naturally diachronic and unique event of communication, and new media attempt to extend this military rationalism into the sphere of civil society. For military media, the speed and accuracy of information is the chief value, and its technological innovation is solely dedicated to that purpose. Therefore in these systems, communication between people is as fast and as accurate as possible through standardization, eliminating all excessive, impeding elements.[29]

In this form of communication, the individual sender and receiver of information becomes something of an anomaly, a functional object who can be controlled by the creators of the system, or by the operative mode of the system itself.[30] Moreover, in order to obtain information in the fastest and simplest possible manner, the information itself has been detached from its original socio-human context which then becomes considered something excessive or irrelevant. Commercially constructed 'hyperreal' space, then, exploits profit by displacing diachronic, indeterminate and communally ordered socio-cultural space and by subordinating it to a synchronic technical rationalist mode of communication designed, owned, and regulated by a few who seek to extend its territory outward from the command centre to the periphery.

According to Kogawa, Japanese corporations began to target the cultural sphere – acquiring media outlets, organizing international conferences and entertainment events, and promoting artistic and academic activities – not only for the purpose of investment, but because, looking to the future, they began to be concerned for their own survival.[31] Kogawa describes this newly emerging state of capital as 'information capitalism,' a stage in which the information software industry is no longer the central area for profit extraction, for information itself has become a form of capital.[32] In this new paradigm the healthy competition among business firms assumed by classical-liberal analyses of capital is no longer the case since the economy has become dominated by large business conglomerates, or *keiretsu*, whose integrated structure encompasses financial institutions, communication systems, mass media, research institutions, and various cultural industries, such as fashion and entertainment businesses. This means that *keiretsu* control the entire process of this new mode of 'production' – planning, financing, marketing, advertising, and the dissemination of information – constituting and controlling a fixed feedback loop from investment to capital return. Moreover, Japanese government ministries are equal partners with the *keiretsu* in advancing the project of transforming 'the real' into 'hyperreal' in their near monopolization of information channels, by subjugating the population to their version of reality, by and controlling the dissemination of alternative views.[33] Coinciding with this 'private–public partnership' is the increasingly influential power of the *keiretsu* in political decision making, most notably since the 1970s and 1980s, to the extent that the conventional understanding of the segregation between public and private sectors has became merely nominal – a state of affairs that is often described by outsiders as a core constituent of the 'Japanese style economy.'[34]

The self as commodified sign in the economy of difference

Although consumers are subject to the commercial interests of big business, this does not mean that these mega-corporations can freely direct the public taste and inclination at will through the manipulation of images. Rather, the production of commercial information is subject to the immanent demands of society which takes part in determining what is to become fashionable. This reciprocal relation between the 'top-down' forces of capital and technology and the 'bottom-up' input of popular culture can be seen, for example, in the rise in the 1980s of a new, highly materialistic snobbism or elitism among the young Japanese, particularly college and university students. One of the landmarks that signalled the emergence

178 *Back to identity: 'postmodernity'*

of this new commercial culture was Tanaka Yasuo's fictional work *Nantonaku, kurisutaru* (*Somehow, Crystal*) (1980), a 'novel' based on a description of two weeks in the life of a female college student.[35] This 'novel,' written when the author was a student at Hitotsubashi, one of more traditionally established universities in Tokyo, does not have much of a story to tell and is not very interested in developing the central character or particular themes. Instead, it serves as a kind of cultural catalogue and 'how to' guidebook, filled with the names of fashionable boutiques, shoe and bag stores, trendy cafes, bars and restaurants, and perfect BGMs (Back-Ground-Musics) in which to spend one's idle time and so on, with some practical guidance in the elaborate notes of where to get these commodities and how to use them correctly in various situations. See, for example, the following passages (the asterisks in this and the following citation have replaced numbered footnotes in the originals):

> I glanced at Emiko's partner thinking that as she had a good two hours time to spare, she would be able to do so many things [with him]. Holding what looked like a Barracuda's* swing top* in one hand, the boy was wearing a shirt and a pair of pants with a Marlboro* logo on them and a Lanvins'* belt.[36]

> To buy cake, I would try on Le Conte* in Roppongi or El Dole* in Ginza. When I am with my girl friends from school, it would be most adequate to eat a large American-type cake* in Esto* of Roppongi or Capuccio* recently opened in Nogizaka*. When with Jun'ichi [her boy friend], I would sample a pie in a slightly more decent cake shop, Le Pose* at Takagi-cho*.[37]

As Norma Field argues, the vacuousness of the narrative captures something of the spiritual void, material affluence, and snobbism rampant among Tokyo's educated young people, whose personalities and lives have come to be filled by the consumption and display of commercial goods. However, this is not to say that this void or snobbism weighs heavily on these characters; the work is rather free from any kind of sentimental lament, and the material life of the heroine is described very matter-of-factly in a tone of neutral lightness. In fact, the novel reads like a curious celebration of affluence, of sophistication in taste, and of a sense of freedom from an identity that might anchor one to moral obligation or political responsibility. It has been suggested that this new material snobbism has freed young educated Japanese from the old academic snobbism of the 1950s and 1960s which demanded a familiarity (or at least a pretension of familiarity) with the works of Marx, Sartre and Dostoevsky for membership amongst the fashionable set; in this new snobbism, what counts is not the possession of knowledge but that of commodities demonstrating good aesthetic taste.[38] Following the book's publication, a group called the 'crystal tribe' (*kurisutaru-zoku*) – i.e.

young fashionable devotees of the lifestyle depicted in the novel – emerged and subsequently began to fill university and college campuses with the cool display of commodities in vogue, creating a nationwide trend.

This material snobbism, or consumerism, has in the Japanese society of the 1980s been taken to an extreme unimaginable in other parts of the developed world. This is partly because the 'crystal tribes' phenomenon 'coincided' with a new production and domestic consumption boom in Japan, partially induced by the government's attempts to reduce the export surplus that had been blamed for the US balance of trade deficit. Beyond that, however, this boom had a close affinity with the cultural and psychological orientations of what Lise Skov described as the 'boom-based society.'[39] Skov observed 'a rapid turnover of trends' in the Japanese consumer culture of the 1980s and early 1990s, in which '[a]dvertising designs, fashion colours, styles of consumer goods have been replaced regularly with new designs, colours and styles that are also quickly and intensively displayed in all possible sites for their display.'[40] According to Skov, this rapid succession of trends was fully exploited by the business world by constantly making whatever happens to be in style at the particular moment available in every thinkable form of consumable items – artefacts, fashion, arts, ideas and even political debates. Borrowing from Yoshimoto Mitsuhiro, Skov argues that:

> According to Yoshimoto (1989: 9), 'the boom artificially creates a new difference, which is expected through the process of massive commodification, and which ends when mass commodification makes it impossible for that particular difference to function as difference any longer. It is followed by another boom then, but this new boom based on a different kind of difference has to be over soon, too.' The temporal structure of the boom pushes trend-setters to choose among an indefinite variety of potential 'differences' to single out one 'difference.'[41]

According to this logic of the boom, the value of the object of the boom is ephemeral and rather independent of its content; it just demands a commercially profitable match between the trendsetters' choice of an object and consumers' willingness to follow. An interesting question one might ask on this account is whether such commercial exploitation of difference and the successive replacement of one trend by another is closely associated with a particular type of subjectivity willing and eager to accept the style of the moment, that is, a subjectivity willingly accepting externally defined values and living, the desire cultivated by commercial exchange as its own. In this instance, to describe a subject as 'accepting' the externally defined identity might be somewhat misleading in that it sounds like it assumes the presence of a self-defining subject who selects and controls the intrusion of outside forces. Rather, woven in its very texture into the intersubjective network of signs and images, the subject in question here might

180 *Back to identity: 'postmodernity'*

be more accurately conceived as the one constituted by the consumption of stylistically differentiated commodities, a constitution structurally analogous with the system of signification founded on *différance*, as Derrida conceived, the differential chain of signifiers.[42]

One of the distinctive features of Japanese consumerism in the 1980s is its peculiar bent for what might be called 'infantilism.' This trait is particularly evident in the celebration of childlike-ness, initially and largely (but not exclusively) by young Japanese women – the so-called 'culture of cute' – that came to be one of dominant popular culture traits in the 1980s. As Sharon Kinsella argues, the Japanese word for cute, *kawaii*, connotes by and large the positive attributes associated with children: 'sweet, adorable, innocent, pure, simple, genuine, vulnerable, weak and inexperienced social behavior and physical appearance.'[43] Not only are a wide range of cute commodities distinct sales hits – e.g. 'romantic' clothes, accessories, underwear, stationery and cute-character gift items (e.g., Hello Kitty and Tuxedo Sam by Sanrio) – but 'cute culture' has been extended to include the deliberate modification of one's behaviour, for example, the adoption of a 'cute writing style,' that is, the use of a round childish script, or even a 'cute speech' mimicking baby talk.[44] Beyond possessing cute objects, argues Kinsella, the trend has also entailed the fashioning of oneself into a cute object by deliberately acting childlike as an attractive way of being. As Kinsella writes:

> Being cute meant behaving childlike – which involved an act of self-mutation, posing with pigeon toes, pulling wide-eyed innocent expressions, dieting, acting stupid, and essentially denying the existence of the wealth of insights, feelings, and humor that maturity brings with it. In cute culture, young people become popular according to their apparent weakness, dependence and inability, rather than because of their strengths and capabilities.[45]

While 'becoming cute' was largely confined to teenage and young adult women, and most notably adapted by female pop singers, cute culture has also involved adult men who consume both cute objects (e.g. telephone cards with cute characters) and behold cute women as sexual or non-sexual objects. In the late 1980s, however, 'cute style became more androgynous and more asexually infantile,' and young men began to take part in 'becoming cute.'[46]

Once again, the linkage between the profound penetration of consumer culture and a relative lack of resistance on the part of the subject, this time in the mature subject, is at stake. What we see here is a rather unproblematic displacement of the self-assuming, that is, one pre-exists exposure to the inscriptional force of 'cute culture' – in the form of a voluntary self-mutation, and the replacement of the previous self with an idealized cute identity. Kinsella argues that cuties prefer to stay immature in order to be free of the social responsibilities that come with adulthood: '[b]y acting childish, Japanese youth try to avoid the conservatives' moral demand that they exercise self-discipline and responsibility and tolerate severe conditions whilst working hard in order to repay their obligation to society.'[47] In my view, however, this act of rejecting maturity is not so much of a conscious political protest, as it is an inability to be otherwise. What is important to note in the popularity of this sub-culture is the commercial exploitability of cute, that the desire for immaturity bears an affinity with an uncritical consumerism and material snobbism that is easily purchasable in diverse commodity forms.[48] Or rather, it could be argued that unlimited exposure to the highly information-driven market culture has disposed the subject to opt for consumption. Along this line of argument, Asada Akira has described the Japanese consumer society of the 1980s as 'infantile capitalism' – a notion borrowed from Lyotard's idea of *capitalisme énergumène*, 'temper-tantrum capitalism' – in which people rather innocently indulge in the sign-economy as if playing a part in a children's game.[49] Figuratively speaking, Asada argues that these 'children' are playing freely within a protected area under the supervision and permission of the 'adult' who guards the playground; that is to say, the controlling mechanism of Japanese society works through a seemingly spontaneous engagement (play) in the sign-economy, by means of a 'soft' ruling structure which constitutes the frame of the possible, and even of the subject's mode of being. The inference here is that while the desire for cute was already immanent in Japanese society, it has been mediated and cultivated by commercial forces as a means towards profit, by the 'adults' who want to keep their 'children' cute.

Arguably, an affluent commercial culture in a post-industrial society, such as the one in Japan, is conducive to a pluralization and liberalization of society that would allow individuals a greater potential for expressing their uniqueness. In the Japan of the 1980s, however, a strong countercurrent of normalization prevailed, and individual differentiation took place in large part to conform to what is generally accepted and appropriate.[50] This voluntary disciplining aspect can be most clearly seen in, for example, the popularity of the catalogue-type fashion magazines, entertainment and restaurant guides, such as *J.J.*, *Popeye*, *City Road* and *Pia*, which offer detailed 'guidance' on the pursuit of a satisfying social life: what to buy, where to go, what to display, what to read, who is suitable as a friend, how to impress your dates, and so on. These magazines are not necessarily read for their practical utility, but more often, they are read to catch up with 'what's new,' for the sake of informing oneself with current social trends. By informing people about these practical matters, the catalogue magazines serve the dual-purpose of advertising particular commodities and helping to regulate and categorize people according to the 'norm.' In his study of women's fashion magazines, John Clammer argues that the commodification of the body in Japan, i.e. the teaching of what is an appropriate body and how to manage it, is a relatively new, media induced phenomenon, and while similar to trends in North America, in Japan it is more extreme. The magazines dispensing this information are filled with tips on how-to 'engineer the shape, size, colour, and posture of the body through fashion, decoration, diet, "fitness" and even surgical alteration,' all, argues Clammer '[in order] to fit largely media-induced images of what the body "should" look like' into the minds of the consumers.[51] Clearly a Foucauldian disciplinary mechanism is at work here in this drive to construct an ideal body, and in the internalization by female (but to a lesser extent male) subjects of social imperatives regarding the body. Female bodies, these magazines tell us over and over, are consuming bodies, bodies which, in order to transform themselves, must purchase the necessary information and commodities. And, while they are themselves commodified signs, well disciplined and decorated, these bodies are at the same time objects of consumption and the specular gaze, as objects.[52]

The subject imbricated into this sign-economy is also him- or herself an object-sign whose subjectivity is constructed by the exchange of signs. Consumption no longer merely concerns the use value of the commodity but has became a function of an inarticulate desire generated by object-signs that freely permeate the subject. For example, the artificially cultivated sense of imperfection felt by the subject functions as one of the fundamental driving forces of this economy – in the above example, the disciplinary mechanism in effect upon the female body urges her to strive, exhorts her we might say, to reduce the gap between her own body and the idealized images of what her body could or should be. In this economy, the circulation of signs establishes a self-perpetuating system of exchange through the further generation of the desire for consumption; or to put it differently, it is the haunting sense of imperfection that drives the subject to desire and to consume in order to fill its perceived 'lack.' The logic with which this system operates, then, is one of commodity fetishism: the flood of exhortations upon the fabric of the self (which seem to reduce that fabric to a tissue of signs) generates in the subject a vacuum, giving rise to the subject's desire to fill the internal void brought about by the sense of a loss of its integrity. Within this dynamic, the desire and subjectivity become a direct target of commercial marketing strategies whose effect is to ever further objectify and transform the subject, imbricating it into the intensive chains of differing signs, and ultimately to subjugate the empirical body to the brute structuring forces of the market. In short, in the 1980s Japanese society and the Japanese people as a whole became objects of the logic of capital, themselves inseparably meshed within the signifying chains created and disseminated by the information industries, and thus, we may say, were continuously informed by the practice of exchange, by the constant negotiation between one's present state and the ideal images of the mass media.

Knowledge-as-play

If the self and society as a whole fell increasingly subject to the pressures of commercialization, the sphere of knowledge was no exception. Marilyn Ivy has shown how this nascent trend towards commercialization was intertwined with the rising popularity of postmodernism in the Japanese intellectual scene of the 1980s. Ivy contrasts an old mode of 'deep' person-to-person communication with a new type of communication assuming an anonymity that 'find[s] a feeling of security in the condition of dispersal itself.'[53] Reflecting a feeling of freedom from deep meaning and a sense of fastidiousness with styles, the new standard of what constitutes preferred knowledge, argues Ivy, is defined with respect to notions of enjoyment and appeal, in much the same way that commercial goods are.[54] In other words, this new mode of knowledge, a kind of 'knowledge-as-play,' has became the object of casual consumption, a mode befitting a society and a population that have grown comfortable with the omnipresence of commodified signs, what Ivy calls the '*CM-ka shakai*' (commercialized society). In this ambiance of playful knowledge some of Japan's most successful advertising copywriters have become pop-cultural heroes (e.g. Itoi Shigesato and Watanabe Kazuhiro), and are thought to be 'subversive artists' who challenge or undermine the hegemonic power of the corporate dominated, bureaucratized and rationalized culture.[55] Despite this optimism, however, the fact is that such optimism may well be precisely what corporate capital's advertising strategies aim at. As Ivy argues, the commercial effect of these copywriters' efforts only serves to affirm 'the same stubborn, self-referential impasse and the massive powers of recuperation of contemporary Japanese capitalism.'[56]

This trend for a pleasurable knowledge, however, was not limited to the world of commercial media productions, but evolved in other directions, including the new scholarly inclination known as 'new academism.' One example of this inclination was the new, avant-garde journal edited by Asada Akira, Yomoda Inuhiko and Itō Toshiharu, *GS: Tanoshii chishiki*, a commercially-backed intellectual publication intended to reach a broad range of educated Japanese (*GS: Gay Science*; the title refers to Nietzsche's 'joyful wisdom,' the tragi-comedic philosophy of 'complete nihilism,' of living a life of total immanence in love with one's own fate). This journal, together with *Herumesu* (*Hermes*), edited by Yamaguchi Masao, Nakamura Yūjiro, Isozaki Arata, Ōe Kenzaburo and others, has served as one of the principal media by which 'postmodernism' has been introduced to and popularized in Japan.[57] The manner in which 'postmodern knowledge' (the term in Japan largely designates French poststructuralism and those influenced by it) has been introduced into Japan is quite problematic, in part because of the radically different historical and intellectual contexts of its European origin and the Japanese destination. Asada Akira, in particular, has played a leading role in popularizing postmodernism in Japan, and

Asada's influence upon the young educated class has been something phenomenal. In 1983, Asada, then a young unknown writer, had a sensational debut with *Kōzō to chikara* (*Structure and Power*), an academic book that sold 80,000 copies in the first several weeks much to everyone's surprise.[58] The volume, introducing poststructuralism to elementary readers, was a lucid and accessible summary of some of the theories of Lacan, Battaille, Deleuze and Guattari. As a result, Asada captured a great deal of media attention and was soon taken up by various mass media as a spokesperson for the young and educated, a hero of the popular press and mass culture. Asada's rise to the position of a nationally celebrated young brain came to be referred as the *A-A genshō* (the 'Asada Akira phenomenon'), a watershed event in recent Japanese intellectual history signalling the arrival of a new mode of academism extensively influenced by postmodernism, however vaguely conceived.

Asada, a brilliant and flexible thinker considered one of the leading contemporary Japanese intellectuals, enjoys a high degree of competence in a number of areas, including Western philosophy, Japanese intellectual history, cultural theory, contemporary art and art history. However, in conjunction with the mass media campaigns for a 'new academism,' Asada seems to have pursued his 'joyful wisdom' in concert with the mass media's commercial interests. In his *Tōsōron* (*On Escape*, 1984), a collection of short articles originally published in the popular press, Asada writes with a causal lightness employing phrases he has made trendy such as 'schizophrenic culture,' and 'gay science.' The opening article of this collection, entitled 'Escaping Civilization' ('Tōsō suru bunmei'), he urges his readers to 'shift gears' and transform themselves from being guided by the paradigm of the 'paranoiac man' to that of the 'schizophrenic man,' so as to 'affirm the great transformation' of our time from civilization as that in which we live to civilization as that from which we escape.[59] This escape is described in terms of men running away from their wives and families, 'simply because that is much more fun.'[60] Elsewhere in the book, Asada suggests to his readers that they profitably employ a method of a casual, selective reading to quickly skim the contents of a work (*tsumamigui dokusho-jutsu*), rather than investing their precious time in a serious engagement. According to Asada, books are not something to be digested by deep reading but rather something to be instantly captured and communicated in the form of charts, since they are really nothing more than 'tool boxes' from which one extracts the most useful tool according to the need.[61] The boom of 'new academism' in effect served to radically elide the boundary between casual, easily accessible knowledge and its more serious incarnations, and has been accompanied by a vogue for intellectuals appearing in the popular media as icons of the educated class. More problematically, the popularity of 'new academism' has resulted in a situation where highly complex knowledge is recycled and simplified in Japanese academic discourses, or worse, often made into a form of entertainment, a fully commodified knowledge meeting the demands of a commercialized society (*CM-ka shakai*).[62]

The rising trend of postmodernism in Japan has not been the monopoly of younger scholars; many older intellectuals have been influential as well. Yoshimoto Takaaki perhaps best exemplifies the radical change in orientation on this account. In his 1984 work, *Theory of the Mass Image* (*Masu imeeji ron*), Yoshimoto described the rise of Japanese mass consumer society as an 'achievement' in the sense that the top-down impositions of the modernist elitist system, including the liberal progressive and Marxist theories that attempted to enlighten the masses, had completely lost their efficacy.[63] Yoshimoto argued that 'modernist' social theories were obsolete because they were incapable of grasping the contemporary Japanese society in which the structure of human desire was no longer determined by the practical utility of an object but rather by the consumption of certain images associated with it. In a mass consumer society, argues Yoshimoto, the masses have for the first time obtained a means of directly relating to the world, expressing themselves not by means of knowledge but by 'non-knowledge,' which is to say the senses and affects mediated by (and embodying) the collective unconscious (*muishiki*) of the masses that has become immanent in the 'postmodern' socio-cultural system.[64] In his analysis of commercial advertisements, Yoshimoto found that the commercial focus of the productions gradually recedes into the background as the products and their advertisements became more sophisticated. Thus, advertisements which once had the explicit purpose of selling a commodity have now begun to shift their focus to the depiction of images that the sellers wish to associate with the commodity. As this development evolves, commercial advertisements begin to pursue and to offer aesthetically satisfying images for their own sake, quite apart from direct commercial purposes; it is at this stage, argues Yoshimoto, that advertising images acquire an autonomy from the commercial control of their sponsors:

> When commercial image production has reached this stage, the advertisement perhaps obtains a chance to be autonomous from its control, paradoxically by pursuing the symbolic properties of its producers – capital and the system – to its limit. If this sounds too optimistic, I should say that it is the field of advertising, and not any other visual-arts genres, that most clearly and appropriately depicts the ways in which capital and the system will be in the future.[65]

Yoshimoto's argument here demonstrates a curious continuity and discontinuity with his previous works. His lifelong theme of incorporating images of the masses (*taishū no genzō*) into theory is consistently present, and as he sees it, consumer culture characterized by a free-play with signs is a kind of achievement of a 'democratic' cultural state in which the masses themselves are the main actors of the game since the sphere of their everyday lives has come to be centre stage – a goal Yoshimoto himself has long pursued. On the other hand, Yoshimoto's previous intention (in the 1950s and 1960s his works were framed within the broad stream of Marxist social theory) of overcoming the limitations of Marxism as a modern abstract theory, and in particular its historical and material determinism, were completely abandoned. In contrast to his previous designation of the concept of *taishū* (the masses) as the political agent defending and strengthening bottom-up social movements, in his *Theory of the Mass Image* and other works in the 1980s, Yoshimoto takes up a position as an abstract theorist, refraining from reflecting his own subject position. From a distance, he observes 'the system' determined by the total sum of image creations, and sees the manifestations of a collective unconscious devoid of agency. In arguing that the sophisticated production of images, the self-expression, in his terms, of a systemic unconscious, can subvert the values of the hegemonic culture constructed by elite corporate capital, Yoshimoto seems to nullify the effects of historically and institutionally embedded systems of power, including the nation-state and the *keiretsu*, and naively assumes that a change in the super-structure (cultural system) can transform the social hierarchy.[66] In some sense Yoshimoto's 'postmodern turn' can be seen as an erasure of materiality by theory (his use of the term 'the systemic unconscious' is key here), and in this sense, the romantic anti-modern, anti-rational inclination manifest in his work of the 1960s came to obtain in the 1980s its supreme expression: an autonomous theory delinked from the socio-political and historical. With this 'turn,' Yoshimoto was able to uncritically celebrate the consumer culture of the 'postmodern age,' in which he saw the presence of the subject in the collective unconsciousness arising out of the flood of phenomenal signs.

Constructing identity: the rise of *nihonjinron* discourse

Constructing homogenized space – cultural explanations of economic success

In the mid-1970s Japanese economic strengths came to be internationally recognized after Japan's successful recovery from the serious stagnation that plagued the economy in the years following the 1971 'Nixon Shock' and in the wake of the 1973 'Oil Crisis.' Hard hit by these external shocks, Japanese GDP in fiscal year 1974 saw negative growth; to the surprise of the entire world and the Japanese themselves, however, the nation quickly recovered, despite the climate of increasingly intense international competition, recording a GDP of around 5 per cent during the next few years. In spite of the continuing hostility of the international market to Japanese exports, large Japanese corporations successfully boosted their foreign sales, achieving a record trade surplus of $14 billion in 1987.[67] These successes were the context for much of the political-economic discussion of the decade, discussion seeking to account for the enigmatic rise in Japanese fortunes; sometime later, it became a commonplace to describe this phenomenon in terms of the rise of a 'Japanese style economy.' The rapid economic ascendance of Japan on the world economic stage received a great deal of Western attention, and was largely viewed as a challenge to the conventional economic paradigm, particularly by political-economy and international relations scholars and the elite segments of the US. Concurrently with these developments, the previously insular and inward-looking Japanese society began to rapidly 'internationalize,' at least in terms of people's self-consciousness. Japan's economic ascent both induced a reassessment of relations between Japan and the US, with each viewing the other, economically speaking, as a powerful external other to be reckoned with, and awakened a renewed sense of national identity in each country. From the Japanese perspective, the Japanese saw themselves reflected in an American mirror, and from that point on a new love–hate relationship between the two countries developed.

In the late 1970s, Western scholars first began to pay serious attention to Japanese style economic management as a possible model for the West. One of the first scholars to pursue this vein was Ezra Vogel in his *Japan as Number One* (1979), in which he described a Japan that could teach America some precious lessons. Vogel argued that Japan had succeeded in becoming the only fully industrialized non-Western country by 'consciously and rationally examining and restructuring all of its traditional institutions,' and inventing in the process a series of unique institutional arrangements, such as government-business partnerships and the paternalistic intra-company system, that successfully 'renovated' its unique cultural traits.[68] Gregory Clark, in a discussion with the popular opinion leader Takemura Kenichi, offered his own explanation of Japan's unique successes in terms of the country's traditional lack of a systematically constructed, universal organizational principles.[69] Referring to Japan's elaborate, contextually based, unwritten laws of human relations which are hard for outsiders to grasp, Clark metaphorically described Japanese society as the phylum 'Mollusca,' and offered some well-meant friendly advice to the Japanese on how to present their culture more successfully to the West. Books like these, the early result of a 'happy marriage' between Western fascination with radically different cultures and Japanese self-pride, that gave rise to the discourse of *nihonjinron*, a discourse that was to endlessly enumerate the unique characteristics of the Japanese culture and people. To be sure, there were precursors to *nihonjinron* that had attempted to explain Japanese cultural characteristics in a systemic manner. Among these pioneering works were late 1960s works of cultural anthropology like

Nakane Chie's *Human Relations in the Vertical Society* (*Tate-shakai no Ningen Kankei*, 1967), in which the author characterized the structuring principle of Japanese society as a vertical relation centred upon *ie* (the family), and Doi Takeo's *The Structure of Amae* (*Amae no kōzō*, 1971), in which Doi analysed *amae* – 'affectionate dependency' – as the defining socio-psychological feature of the Japanese.[70] These works undoubtedly provided the discursive context in which the later phenomenon of *nihonjinron* could develop; however, it was in the historical context of the late 1970s that these works became really known, experiencing a new wave of appreciation.

Western recognition of Japanese economic successes was extremely flattering to Japanese pride; outsiders' accounts of a 'unique Japan' often fascinated the Japanese, providing them with an opportunity to 'rediscover' themselves through the eyes of others. A flurry of Japanese publications soon followed Vogel's pioneering celebration of Japan's ability to adapt; forecasting Japan's eventual supersession of the West, most of these works offered up a theory of how to best explain the 'secrets' of Japanese success that were often assumed to lie in its unique cultural traditions. The systemic conception of an *ie*-type social organization as argued by Nakane was furthered by Murakami Yasusuke, Kumon Shunpei and Satō Seizaburo in their 1979 volume *The Ie-society as Civilization* (*Bunmei to shite no Ie Shakai*), now considered one of the most prominent works of the then booming cultural science trend. The authors attempt 'an analysis of the uniqueness of Japanese modernization' by drawing insights from various social sciences and humanities (i.e. sociology, economics, political studies, systems theory, and history).[71] The volume opens with the theoretical/methodological challenge of describing a plural, culturally particular, developmental path which would relativize the Western/modern notion of history and civilization, and the main part of the book elaborates the structural principles of Japanese social organization, namely the *ie*-society and its components, as well as its historical developmental processes. The concept of the *ie*-society is understood as the embodiment of relationalist thought and behavioural patterns, once again referring to Watsuji's popularized notion of *aidagara-shugi*, a contextualist conception of Japanese subjectivity and social relations. Following this line of thought, the authors describe the Japanese social order as being characterized by a functional division and a hierarchical order designed to pursue collective goals and purposes. The book closes with a diagnosis of some symptomatic problems in contemporary Japanese society and a blueprint for suggested remedies to restructure it based on the *ie* social concept. All in all, the volume clearly had a great deal in common with the vision and analysis of the Ōhira cabinet's blueprint, *Beyond the Modern Age*, especially in terms of its pragmatic *and* romantic culturalist orientation which attempts to find solutions to the problems of advanced capitalist society in the virtues of Japanese cultural attributes.[72]

Books like *The Ie-society as Civilization* raise a number of serious concerns.

What is at stake in such externally inspired, inward-looking 'scientific' enquiries into the uniqueness of Japanese culture is the creation of a particular 'Japan': a Japan reconstituted in the present out of images of Japanese tradition, in a comparative culturalist frame that erases internal differences and homogenizes 'Japan' vis-à-vis an assumed other, the West. This new culturalism differs from the previous romantic culturalism of the 1960s, principally by its 'scientific' orientation, in which the notions of culture and society are dehistoricized and dematerialized. Unlike the conventional culturalism that expressed a yearning for a return to the cultural/spiritual traditions of the Japanese past, culture in Murakami *et al.* was dealt with in a structural functionalist manner and reduced to a model encapsulating its essential mechanism – '*ie*-society' – abstracted by means of comparing and contrasting Japanese society with Western counterparts.[73] In effect, this 'scientific,' and static, culturalist approach imposes on culture an atemporal structuralist frame, thereby dehistoricizing Japanese social history, while simultaneously subordinating its culturally unique temporality to an abstract, universal perspective in which only Japan's difference from the West appears in the guise of 'cultural uniqueness.' Moreover, this dehistoricized notion of Japanese society and culture is then inserted in an equally ahistorical, timeless culturalist narrative that assumes a continuous evolutionary process in which a uniquely Japanese cultural essence develops from pre-history to the present. Thus, the *ie*-society of contemporary Japan is seen by Murakami *et al.* as a variant of an original cultural form directly descending from *uji* (clan) society, as if the essential category characterizing the Japanese socio-cultural structure had existed more or less unchanged throughout history.[74] This ahistorical, apolitical and anti-materialist vision of culture was the product of a present-centred imposition of a linear progressive narrative time upon the past, an imagined product of an inverted teleology, so-to-speak, according to which the present is 'analysed' with reference to an imagined archetypal cultural form. What emerges out of such intellectual obfuscations, reducing and distorting a heterogeneous and diachronic past into a caricature of its complexity, is a clear image of the cultural identity of the Japanese as distinct from the West, a reification of an abstractly conceived ideal Japanese culture.[75]

A similar dehistoricization and synchronization was also evident in a more conventional stream of culturalism produced in the 1980s. Umehara Takeshi, whose 1960s spiritually inclined culturalism was discussed in the last chapter, reoriented his theories in the 1980s towards the construction of a model aiming to explain the structure of Japanese identity to Westerners. This qualitative change in Umehara's *modus operandi* deserves attention, especially in light of the historical contexts that characterize the two periods and the way Umehara related to them: the loss of religious feeling and beauty that concerned him in the 1960s and the essence of Japanese culture in the 1980s. The spiritual quest for a transcendental

Nature and an overarching unity to the world that was clearly manifest in his earlier works is virtually non-existent in his 1980s works. On the other hand, however, his interest in Japanese culture and its religious and aesthetic ethos persists, albeit for the purpose of *explaining* (not understanding) that ethos and culture to those who view them from the outside. This intention is explicitly stated in the conclusion of his 1984 volume, *Thinking Contemporary Japan* (*Gendai nihon o kangaeru*; a series of discussions with other prominent intellectuals):

> For the West, Japan is still an enigma. It appears as a combination of mystery and rationality. . . . The things they want to know are: how have the Japanese succeeded in modernizing in such a short time, and in what direction will Japan head in the future. They think that Japan must have a deep spiritual tradition, in the same way that the Western nations have Christianity and Greek philosophy for a backbone, and this tradition is what must have made modernization successful . . . However, they do not understand the relation between Japanese traditional culture and modernization . . . Can we not create a theory that explains both Japanese modernization and the mysteries of the Japanese arts?[76]

Umehara can in no sense be deemed (self-, or otherwise) critical of fashioning a theory tailor-made for the presentation of Japan to foreign audiences and framed in the context of their needs. The result is a taxonomic depiction of Japanese culture in which the mediation of a Western perspective and categories are more explicit than in Murakami *et al*. In Umehara's model, Japanese society and culture are characterized as having an 'oval structure' (*nihon bunka no daen-teki kōzō*), a cultural space centred on two structuring poles. Appropriating Nietzsche's allegorical explanation of Greek culture as a combination of the opposing attributes of the Apollonian (roughly speaking: discipline, unity, light, intelligibility, being) and the Dionysian (grace, diversity, darkness, the ecstatic, becoming), Umehara analogously conceives Japanese culture in terms of a tension between the opposed categories of *Jōmon* and *Yayoi*, anthropological categories referring to two different pre-historical time periods. Umehara, however, extended these categories to designate life-styles (hunter-gatherers versus rice farmers), artistic styles (dynamic versus functional), spiritual and cultural orientations (pragmatic importers of foreign culture versus highly spiritual and moral), hierarchies of power (the former oppressed by the latter's establishment of the ancient Japanese state), racial/biological types (long-limbed, strong featured and hairy versus the contrary), and so on.[77]

What such homogeneous and synchronic modellings do is facilitate the constitution of an enclosed image of Japanese culture and society, once again freed from the material dimension and historical complexity. Not surprisingly, perhaps, Umehara's substantial labours in the study of

Japanese ethnic minorities, most notably the Ainu and the Okinawans, are presented in a similar manner in which the particularity of history, politics and cultural heterogeneity are erased. For example, in his conclusion to the 1984 volume, Umehara, eliding vast reaches of time and space, 'discovers' in present-day ethnic minorities the remnants of archetypal Japanese cultural lifestyles: as he remarks, 'if one turns to look at the religious beliefs of the Ainu and Okinawans, peoples whose lives were left untouched by Buddhist influence, the outlines of Japanese Shinto becomes clearly visible.'[78] Assuming that the imagined characteristics of prehistoric Japan's *Jōmon* era (10,000–300 BC), now lost in mainstream Japanese culture, 'have powerfully survived in Ainu religion ... unchanged since the age of *Jōmon*,' Umehara fills a lacuna in his historical narrative with a free interpretation of the *contemporary* cultural life of the Ainu and the Okinawans.[79] In short, the origin and essence of Japanese ethnicity, religion, and language as presented by the Umehara Japan Studies are the result of a series of symbolic and methodological violations in which the cultural *differences* of ethnic minorities are interpreted as forming the past of the present-day Japanese.

Umehara's work might be distinguished from more schematic versions of *nihonjinron* by its detailed research and his narrative dexterity with stitching facts and assumptions into an 'entertaining' story for general readers. Inspired to create a model that could explain the essence of Japanese culture, and incorporating Umehara's quest for identity into a study presented as an 'objective,' or social scientific, knowledge with elaborate 'empirical descriptions,' the Umehara Japan Studies group has advanced a radical blurring of the boundaries between subjective historical narrative and objective historical knowledge. Also of serious concern is the far reaching effects that Umehara Japan Studies has had upon Japanese social sciences at large, especially given the considerable institutional and financial supports they received from the International Research Centre for Japanese Studies, or *Nichibunken*, established in 1986 with a generous financial endowment from the Japanese government (see below).

The search for meaning – recovering symbolic authority by demonizing the other

Just as Umehara Japan Studies redirected its developmental trajectory in conjunction with the rise of *nihonjinron* discourse and the historical context surrounding it, so too did the more overtly political stream of thought of Etō Jun. Etō, who in his 1967 work *Maturation and Forfeiture: The Destruction of the Mother* saw modernization as a process of maturation to be attained only by renouncing the 'natural realm of sensuality' (see the last chapter), eventually came to endorse the recovery of a strong state. Once he discovered that maturation had not occurred in Japan as he had thought it would, and identifying the cause of that 'failure' in the loss of paternal authority

– the Symbolic or unifying principles of society that Etō equated with the Japanese nation-state – Etō's works in the late 1970s and early 1980s predictably took on increasingly nationalistic tones. More specifically, Etō's romantic yearning for things lost in the era of postwar modernization transformed into an anti-US sentiment, blaming the US postwar occupying regime for the weakened paternal authority of the Japanese nation-state and the subsequent cultural and spiritual decay.[80] Etō's insistence that Japan reclaim 'its' own history,' or what he calls 'what Japan was forced to forget,' resulting in his mind from the country's uncritical acceptance of the 'postwar myth' handed down to it by the US, was made in numerous works throughout this period, including *Another Postwar History* (*Mōhitotsu no Sengo-shi*, 1976), *Things Forgotten and Things One has Been Forced to Forget* (*Wasureta Koto to Wasuresarareta Koto*, 1979), *The 1946 Constitution and its Compulsion* (*1946 Kenpō Sono Kōsoku*, 1980), *The Record of Occupational History* (*Senryō-shi Roku*, 1982), and 'Occupational Army Censorship and Postwar Japan' (*Senryō-gun no Ken'etsu to Sengo Nihon*, 1984).[81] In these works, Etō made the same point over and over: the Japanese version of history had been erased by and replaced with an American narrative during the US occupation of Japan and in the context of the unconditional surrender.

Noteworthy here is that Etō's earlier 'romantic' and sentimental tone of yearning for 'things lost' was transformed in his later works into a resentment of US political power over Japan and into affirmations of state power politics and political realism. Over time, Etō's evaluation of postwar Japan becomes increasingly harsh; in his 1987 *The US–Japan War is Not Over* (*Nichibei Sensō wa Owatte Inai*), for example, Etō explicitly expresses his spiteful attitude towards postwar liberal democratic values and institutions. According to his analysis, the postwar Japanese espousal of the values of peace, anti-nuclear pacifism, democracy and basic human rights was imposed by US occupation policies, and as such constitutes the 'false freedom of domesticated animals.' In order for Japan to obtain true self-determination, he argues, it must actively participate in the creation of an international information system, the site, according to Etō, of the principal power struggles in a world in which the conventionally defined power of nuclear weapons is rapidly being superseded. Throughout all these works of the late 1970s and the 1980s, the US is identified as being ultimately responsible for Japan's postwar 'tragedy.'[82] Rather obviously, such an interpretation involves a present reconstruction of the past that only becomes possible when memories of the war have become remote.[83] Not only does this new narrative neglect the fact that in the period immediately following the war no Japanese intellectual felt it possible to defend prewar Japanese discourse, but it also nullifies efforts made by postwar intellectuals and citizens towards the democratization of the country. Moreover, what Etō describes as the loss of Japan's identity, its newfound 'fake,' 'vacuous' and 'superficial' character, are much more the results of radical socio-economic changes effected in the 1960s and 1970s, changes which are beyond his analytical scope and perhaps the unstated motivation of his critique. Presumably, it was the internal changes in Japanese society alienating and threatening Etō's personal integrity that lay behind his 'nationalist turn,' which he subsequently rationalized as the overpowering of Japan by the US. Indeed, Etō's arguments, supported by a multitude of other nationalists including Ishihara Shintarō and Watanabe Shōichi, began to win popularity in the early 1980s when inarticulate resentments in Japanese society found a new ground for articulation in the suddenly 'hot' sphere of international political-economic knowledge. By failing to include in his theoretical scheme the rapid social changes experienced in the 1970s and 1980s, Etō's calls for recovering the 'nation-as-father' were nothing more than nostalgic expressions of a desire to recreate in the present an idealized, imagined past.

This inclination towards nationalism was not, however, the monopoly of 'romantically' oriented intellectuals. Shimizu Ikutarō, a former liberal progressive leader in the early postwar era, is perhaps the best example of those who radically changed their previous positions. As the new technologically orientated, capital intensive economic development and bureaucratization of society began to destroy the ground of the popular political movements, and thus the potential for socially transformative theories, Shimizu radically readjusted his thinking about the role of the intellectual in society, from an advocate of liberal progressivism to a protagonist of national/cultural identity upholding the imperial court system (*tennōsei*). In his 800 page two volume work, *Contemporary Thought* (*Gendai Shisō*, 1966), Shimizu traced three crucial periods in modern Japanese history when socio-cultural conditions were deeply troubled by a wide-spread rise of nihilism: at the turn of the century, in the 1930s, and in the 1960s.[84] In post-1960s Japan, he argues, intellectuals can no longer pursue the progressive line they had previously pursued, they must instead combat the more pressing problem of nihilism. Thus, the questions that Shimizu the self-proclaimed pragmatist posed were: how to battle against increasingly abstract bureaucratic control and the resultant nullification of meaning in Japanese society.[85]

One such attempt to battle the demon of nihilism was his 1972 'Theory of the Imperial System' (*tennō-ron*), in which he points out the limits to rationalist/functionalist conceptions of the nation-state and their neglect of the 'problem of social unification' (*shakai-teki tōgō no mondai*). Recognizing the imperial order (*tennō*) as a collective belief system, a source of emotional unity and satisfaction for many Japanese, and a symbolic centre towards which the energy of the people is gathered, Shimizu argues that only the imperial system has the authority to guarantee the moral principles of the Japanese.[86] In his 1978 work, *Doubts about the Postwar Era* (*Sengo o utagau*), Shimizu advanced this moral-cultural demand for a symbolic centre a step further by infusing it with a harsh political resentment against the Western Allies. In a section of book discussing issues such as the dropping of the

Atomic bomb, the late Soviet entry into the Pacific War, the prewar strategic blockades of Japan by Western powers in Asia, and the Hull note which many felt left Japan with no other option than going to war, Shimizu describes Japan's movement towards and conduct during World War II as a logical consequence of the prevalent mode of international power politics – i.e. 'the law of the jungle' – a mode that for Shimizu is inseparably mingled with a racial hierarchy in which the Japanese as a non-Caucasian race could not escape from the spiteful attitudes of the Allies.[87] Shimizu went even further in his so-called 'nationalist manifesto' of 1980, *Japan, Be a Nation* (*Nihon yo Kokka Tare*). Here Shimizu's argument is no different than that of the aggressive political realists who call on the Japanese to regain their pride and autonomy from the US and to become a strong, independent sovereign nation-state. Underlying Shimizu's radical shift in position from an advocate of progressive popular movements in the 1950s to a protagonist of state-nationalism in the 1980s is his recognition of the desirability of reinforcing the weakened bond between the individual and state authority, and of reestablishing the national identity of the Japanese. In this shift on the part of Shimizu and a good number of Japanese intellectuals, the targeted enemy also changed, from state power politics and status quo hierarchies to the international power hierarchy, particularly that of the US. From this new perspective, Japanese internal political struggles took a back seat, while 'Japan' came to be seen as the single political, cultural and economic unit deserving of protection from outside forces.

Narcissistic enclosure and the loss of exteriority – the rise of historical revisionism

Such calls for state-nationalism were obviously not limited to the world of academia; prime minister Nakasone Yasuhiro himself issued his own 'nationalist manifesto' in the summer of 1985, thereby effectively legitimating the opening up of the question of the interpretation of World War II and postwar Japanese history. In his 1985 LDP summer seminar, he remarked:

> Before the war, there was the imperial vision of history. After the war rose the Pacific vision of history, that is, the history defined by the Tokyo War Crimes Trial, in which Japan was judged by the laws of the Allies in the name of civilization, peace, and humanity. On this matter, history will have ultimate judgment. However, since then, a self-tormenting ideological trend spread which argued that Japan alone was completely wrong, and this has survived to the present. There has been a tendency to think one only need talk about the negatives of Japan. I disagree. Whether it wins or loses a war, the state is the state. The state, and the people, should aim for glory, discarding shame. ... Now is the time to establish the identity of the Japanese.[88]

Nakasone's criticism of the Tokyo Trial, explicitly rejecting the legitimacy of a universalist vision of history and truth by relativizing it as one vision among many others, as well as his call for the recovery of Japanese national identity, was nothing new. Nakasone's novelty, however, was to put the idea into practice using the authority of his position as prime minister as collateral. In the same year, Nakasone attended a formal ceremony mourning the spirit of the Japanese war dead at Yasukuni shrine (the National Shrine for the War Dead), a ceremony which was in later years cancelled due to outrage from several Asian nations. The following year, responding to a proposal from Umehara and others, including Umesao Tadao, Kuwahara Takeo and Ueyama Shumpei, the Nakasone cabinet established a government funded research institute, *Nichibunken* (the International Research Centre for Japanese Studies). Umehara was installed there as a central figure, and actively pursued his Japan Studies agenda, going on to formulate a clutch of theories about Japanese cultural identity. This reciprocal and close relation between a research institute and the government, with the former creating and disseminating government ideology, was reminiscent of the services the Kyoto-School rendered to the prewar state; indeed, the *Nichibunken* group came to be known as the Neo-Kyoto-School.

Meanwhile, the initial 'happy marriage' between the curiosity of Western scholars and the affirmation of cultural pride of Japanese scholars was increasingly replaced by bitterness on both sides in the context of deteriorating US–Japan relations in the second half of the 1980s. As more critical works began to be published by American scholars on Japanese business practices and on their cultural roots, the 'political economy of Japan' increasingly turned into a political battleground for Japan-bashers, Japanese nationalists and *nihonjinron* theorists. In the climate of a prolonged worldwide recession and harsher economic competition, a new regionalization began to be manifest in world economic relations, and the opening salvos of a trade war between the US and Japan were heard when the resolution of the trade imbalance became one of the top priorities in US national policy. By the mid-1980s, the strength of the Japanese economy meant that the initial postwar economic relations between the US and Japan were replaced by a reversed dependent relation, as symbolized by the fact Japanese surplus capital was loaned to cover US fiscal debts. One of the measures applied to 'adjust' the trade imbalance was the Plaza Accord of 1985, in which the major industrial nations agreed to appreciate the value of the yen against the dollar from 260 to 180; subsequently for several years the value of the yen was to double again. As many observers reported, however, the principal effect of this measure was to induce a massive increase in Japanese direct foreign investment in Asia, the regional integration of Asian economies under Japanese leadership, and a change in trading patterns from US–Japan bilateral trade to a tripartite trading relation involving the US, Japan and Asia, changes that together helped reduce

196 *Back to identity: 'postmodernity'*

Japanese exports to the US but which did not solve the US trade deficit problem.[89]

Naturally, these years of the 'US–Japan trade war' gave rise to harsh criticisms of Japanese businesses and the 'Japan problem' from American authors, often in emotionally charged arguments. To take one among many similar examples, Theodore White's warning of the 'Japanese threat,' published in the *New York Times Magazine* in 1985, treated Japan as unknowable other who could be neither understood, trusted, nor communicated with. The intense anxiety and mistrust explicitly manifest in White's text was articulated in a more sophisticated and academic fashion in, for example, Karel van Wolferen's *The Enigma of Japanese Power* (1989) and Kenneth Pyle's *The Japanese Question* (1992), where the roots of the international political-economic 'inequality' were sought in terms of Japanese culture and socio-political structures. Both authors saw Japan as a cause of a number of the central problems in the contemporary world: Japan as a nation in which a modern, liberal democratic social system was unable to penetrate a 'premodern' native one (van Wolferen), or as a nation with an enormous imbalance between its economic and political powers and thus described as 'economic giant and political dwarf' – that rendered it incapable of taking political leadership in the international community (Pyle).

Predictably, the perception of Japan as a threat and a problem occasioned vigorous counter-arguments by Japanese scholars, all of which accelerated an increasing fusion between the cultural concerns of *nihonjinron* and nationalism in their discussion of the issues of political economy. A typical example of this was Ishihara Shintarō and Morita Akio's *'No' to Ieru Nihon* (*The Japan That Can Say 'No'*) (1989), in which the authors argue that Japanese economic strength is the result of a superior education system, production methods, and advanced high-technology. Counselling their readers to ignore the bashers' unfair accusations of Japan being a 'free-rider,' the book recorded sales of over a million copies in Japan, and two additional volumes on the same themes that Ishihara co-authored with other writers soon appeared. In the 1990 volume of what became a series, entitled *Soredemo 'No' to Ieru Nihon* (*The Japan That Can Still Say 'No'*), the initially defensive tone justifying Japanese economic expansion took a more offensive tack and extended its arguments to locating the roots of the current US–Japan tensions in the 'unjust causes' of World War II. One of the authors, Watanabe Shoichi, casually mentions the coming end of Western civilization and its dominance of the world. This argument was taken even further in the 1991 volume, co-authored with Etō Jun, *Danko 'No' to Ieru Nihon* (*The Japan That Can Firmly Say 'No'*), in which they call for a thorough re-evaluation of World War II and for a postwar history from 'Japan's own perspective.' During these same years, mainstream economic arguments also began to manifest more aggressive accents and competitive nationalistic overtones. Such books often argued in favour of strategic direct investment overseas, urging Japanese firms to replicate in their overseas production sites Japanese-style 'flexible manufacturing' and the intensive use of computed assisted design and production, as well as the creation of information networks, so that Japanese firms could strategically localize their production base.[90]

In this climate of increasing resentment against the US, historical revisionists, continuing their assault upon the universal vision of history, opened up a new front attacking Asian countries and peoples by advocating a radical reinterpretation of what used to be considered undeniable facts. One such example were the Japanese denials of the atrocities committed by the Imperial army at Nanking. The Nanking massacre (also known as 'the rape of Nanking') took place on December 13th, 1937, with an estimated 200,000 to 300,000 deaths.[91] Debate over the massacre captured the spotlight in 1982 in conjunction with a controversy triggered by a deliberate change in the wording of Japanese high school textbooks which now described the Japanese invasion of China as a (military) 'advance.' Naturally, Chinese and Korean governments and peoples responded with outrage, eventually forcing the Japanese government to issue a revised guideline on the historical accuracy of textbooks. However, this revision caused strong resentment among Japanese nationalists, including former army officers and right-wing scholars, who responded with a campaign advocating the 'fallacy thesis.'[92] The fallacy thesis is exemplified in the following passage by Tanaka Masaaki, a Rightist writer, who, in a 1987 book, claims that:

> In any case, the popular pseudo-theory which argues that the massacre of 200,000–300,000 in Nanking is nothing but a fallacy which distorts historical facts. Especially, to cite such a masochistic and anti-nationalist fallacy in the school texts, and thereby wrongly educate the future generations of national subjects is an intolerable violence against the history of our forefathers. Nothing would be more shameful to our race, more misleading to our nation. I would like to continue fighting, with my solid determination, for the elimination of this historical fallacy – and the [Tokyo War Trial] perspective which judges Japan guilty.[93]

Although the fallacy thesis had been around for some time, in the 1980s it was directly integrated into the general nationalist rhetoric calling for 'Japan's own story,' and, building upon earlier criticisms of the Tokyo War Trial, it managed to gain an established ground in *nihonjinron* discourse infused with nationalist sentiments.

During the same period, and along the same lines, the revisionists' assaults against Asia also appeared on the formal political domain by reinterpretation of the meaning of World War II, once again curiously directing its offensive against Asia rather than against Eurocentrism in universalist hegemony, just as earlier generations of revisionists had done. Problematic public comments by cabinet ministers regarding World War II – for many of them, the 'Great East Asian War' – became routine. For example, the following remarks were made by Fujio Masayuki, Minister of Education in the Nakasone cabinet in 1986, and Okuno Seisuke, Minister of National Land Agency in the Takeshita cabinet in 1988, respectively:

> The annexation of Korea was carried out with mutual consent, both *de facto* and *de jure*. Korea shares some of the responsibility; there is no guarantee that China and Russia would have stayed away from Korea, if Japan did not annex it.[94]

> I believe the war was to liberate Asians from the colonial control of the Caucasian race.... Indeed, many Southeast Asian people say that the independence of their nations came about through the Great-Asian war. Why, then, do the Japanese themselves have to deny this relation between the Great Asian war and the liberation of Asia.[95]

These remarks are permeated by a narcissistic desire for self-affirmation that seeks to portray the Japanese as victims and by a self-centred hegemonic perspective incapable of listening to the voices of the true victims of the speakers' violence. This resentful and solipsistic reinterpretation of World War II began largely in the late 1980s and rapidly gained popular currency in the decade of the 1990s, winning increasing support from the LDP rank and file. As one indication of this trend, membership of *kokkai giin domei* (the League of Concerned Parliamentarians) increased from its initial membership of 58 to 205 (two thirds of the LDP diet members) in less than four months.[96] This group was formally established in 1994 under Okuno Seisuke's leadership for the purpose of objecting to *fusen ketsugi*, the diet declaration affirming Japan's renunciation of all future wars and its recognition of war responsibility for the invasions in Asia. Even more disturbingly, variations of historical revisionism gained increasing tolerance, if not active support, from the ordinary Japanese in the 1990s, as I discuss in some detail in Chapter 6.

Significance of nihonjinron – *a summary*

The above findings collectively point to an intimate relation between the knowledge produced and the politico-historical context in which it is given shape. Curiously, it was in the field of international political economy that *nihonjinron* as a culturally oriented discourse was born and increasingly developed to serve as a nurturing ground for nationalistically inclined knowledge. It was this politically and ideologically charged cross-disciplinary arena that allowed *nihonjinron* discourse to be a dynamic scholarly forum capable of accommodating ideas from a wide array of scholarly positions and concerns. Simultaneously, this accommodation reflected the fact that the discourse had little consistency in terms of methodology, theoretical assumptions or thematics, so little in fact that the contradictory claims of liberal internationalism, scientific positivism, apolitical, ahistorical and holistic culturalism, neo-conservative state-nationalism and anti-universalist historical particularism have peacefully coexisted within it. In this catch-all discourse, the old romantic nationalist and culturalist themes of the 1960s were renovated with a new scientific methodology and within a new economically defined historical context. Umehara's and Etō's romantically inclined theory in the 1960s, for example, largely forgotten for more than a decade, reappeared in *nihonjinron* in the 1980s in a structural functionalist (Umehara) and a statist guise (Etō), perhaps in response to the 'internationalization' of Japan and the mediation of an acute consciousness of the West. In this sense the Japanese intellectuals' emotionally motivated reaction to Japan's powerful other – the US – awakened national identity among postwar Japanese intellectuals, and their newly emerged sense of solidarity vis-à-vis Americans made the coming together of their widely varied positions and orientations possible. Indeed, by virtue of this primary subtext of emotional unity, various scholarly streams with distinct and differing interests and themes, streams that formerly were quite separate from each other, ran together, often radically blurring conventionally established boundaries.

As *nihonjinron* emerged and developed into an influential discourse in the 1980s, the nature of Japanese intellectual discourse as a whole underwent a structural transformation into an insular, homogeneous discursive space focused on the question of identity. This new discourse of identity, however, was made possible only by constructing an imaginary past and violating non-Japanese others, as we saw in Murakami *et al.*'s nullification of history and Umehara's erasure of ethnic minorities in Japan. Similarly, since this insular, emotionally motivated discursive space simultaneously denotes the national-ethnic communal boundary of the Japanese nation-state, the inclination to reify 'Japanese culture' and 'nation' was immanent in its drive. The identification of the US as Japan's national enemy, already voiced by Etō and others in previous decades, became an increasingly popular view as economic relations between the two deteriorated in the second half of the 1980s. Once history was eliminated from the general scope and concern of the *nihonjinron* discourse, the political climate of mutual hostility was enough to nurture nationalist and historical revisionist assaults, pursued by Etō and Shimizu, among others, on the country's postwar commitment to internationalism under its peace constitution. Especially noteworthy here is that claims for the rightfulness of Japan's own history, and particularly over the causes of World War II, were once again made at the expense of violating the historical experiences of Asian peoples. Moreover, the inherently cultural-particularist foundations of this new discourse opened up an academic space in which political co-option of knowledge could be easily managed by means of massive government sponsorship in research projects, as exemplified in the Ōhira government's *Beyond the Modern Age* and in the collaboration between the Nakasone government and Umehara in the *Nichibunken*.

The expression of the desire for identity in the guise of a discourse constitutes a counter-current to the postmodern characterization of knowledge as casual and playful and the general socio-cultural trends seeking to exploit difference, including the commercially driven expansion of the sign-economy devoid of depth, identity and meaning. It has to be pointed out, however, that although *nihonjinron* discourse runs seemingly counter to these latter trends, it also has 'postmodern' components. By demolishing disciplinary boundaries and abandoning reasoned debate, *nihonjinron* discourse made itself much more accessible both to journalists and business writers and to the general reading public. Out of this rapprochement emerged what some have described as a 'business culture' led by a new elite, among whom are such figures as Ōmae Ken'ichi and Sakaiya Taichi. These last have written How-To books for successful businessmen, and have in the process become new opinion leaders, strongly backed by the colossal Japanese information industry, enjoying a substantial influence upon young business professionals and society at large.[97] Naturally, the Japanese elites are happy to hear what these opinion leaders have to say for it fits hand in glove with the government-promoted, corporate-sponsored future vision of the 'information society.' In short, the age-old distinction in Japan between high knowledge and low knowledge, between the intellectuals and the masses, and between education and entertainment, has been radically eroded by forces standing near the very centre of high culture. The relations between *nihonjinron* discourse and postmodern socio-cultural trends, however, are far more intimate, deeper and complex. What I hope to show in the following section is how their convoluted relations directly mirror the fundamental problematic of Japanese society of the 1980s.

'Postmodernism', the aesthetic subject and the paradox of Japanese identity – the rise of a contemporary emperor system?

Japanese society experienced a brightening of its mood in the late 1970s and the 1980s reflective of the newly acquired material wealth and a sense of pride in its economic achievements. The depressing atmosphere that dominated the early 1970s was replaced by an optimistic nihilism that welcomed the full advent of consumer culture and material snobbism as a new source of identity. By exploiting stylistic difference for commercial benefit and opening up the sphere of subjectivity to colonization by mass media imagery, this new economic mode harnessed the conditions in which the distinction between the artificial and the true, and surface and depth was radically blurred. At the same time, the opposite inclination, to reestablish the centre/identity in such a decentred discourse was equally manifest, as most explicitly exemplified in the new discourse of identity, *nihonjinron*. One can see, thus, that the 'battle for identity' that in the 1960s was expressed in the form of a struggle against the penetration of capital and technology into the empirical life spheres, had found a new expression in the 1980s. In the 1980s, the battle for identity was no longer formulated within the domestic political space; now the Japanese sense of self was 'internationalized': the country's successful economic performance on the global stage, and the growing attention bestowed on them by foreigners (especially Americans) made the Japanese think of themselves increasingly in terms of 'Japaneseness.' Moreover, in contrast to the 'romantic' battle lines of the 1960s, in which Leftist progressives defended themselves from the further erosion of identity, in the 1980s the identity pursued in *nihonjinron* was an abstract, idealized and homogenized, collective identity, seeking to assert Japan's national right on the international stage. Most significantly in this shift, the element of social resistance was completely lost, resulting in a situation where popular sentiment, formerly a motivating cause for progressive movements, came to be channelled in and articulated for the benefit of conservative politics. Moreover, the conservative calls for national identity endorsed by politicians and intellectuals in the discourse of *nihonjinron* collaborated perfectly, despite their seeming oppositions, with the general trajectory of corporate capitalism and 'postmodern' cultural trends. In order to fully understand the significance of these historical and intellectual developments, some discussion of the characteristics of 'Japanese identity' is necessary.

It could be argued that a new wave of commercialism, of commodity fetishism and materialist snobbery have been global trends wherever societies have successfully embraced a high-technology oriented information capitalism. However, it can be argued that a number of troublesome features belonging to the advanced stage of capitalist development – the organization of a commercially driven, rapidly changing differentiation and consumption of aesthetic styles, undergirded by a formalistic play with language barren of meaning and interiority – were manifest in Japanese social life in the 1980s to an extent unseen anywhere else in the industrial world. A number of foreign observers noted an affinity between these trends and aspects thought to be traditional to Japanese culture. The godfather of this affinity seeking was Alexandre Kojève who, in 1969, was astounded by Japanese society, describing it as 'post-historical civilization' where people live 'according to totally formalized values – that is, values completely empty of all human content in the historical sense.'[98] Characterizing the Japanese as 'post-historical Man' (and the Americans as 'post-historical animals'), Kojève argued that the interaction between the West and Japan would lead to a '"Japanization of Westerners."'[99] Some of this was picked up by Roland Barthes, who, discovering what he saw as the absence in Japanese society of a modern notion of subjectivity, described Japan as 'an empire of signs.' In Barthes' view, social interaction in Japan was guided and constituted by the stylized exchange of signs, without the subject taking an active part in ascribing meaning to the world they live in. Although there is perhaps more than a degree of 'Orientalism' in both of these analyses – they are insights obtained at the risk of 'imposing' on Japanese society outsiders' perspectives – their observations do, to my mind, nonetheless capture some core feature of the society with the freshness of the outsider's perspective.[100]

Western scholars, however, were not alone in pointing to the absence of subjectivity in Japan. As seen in Chapter 3, Maruyama Masao, in his *Thought and Behavior in Modern Japanese Politics*, argued that Japanese discursive space lacks a structuring principle or series of axioms by which foreign ideas could be tested and dialectically reflected upon vis-à-vis native ideas. Instead, he alleged, Japanese discursive space accepts foreign ideas without a filtering process, keeping them in a state of syntagmatic (horizontal/spatial) coexistence with all other ideas until they fall out of fashion.[101] Many have pointed out that this unfiltered acceptance is not a genuine acceptance, in the sense that it does not involve a critical understanding or engagement, and is unlikely to generate a fusion with existing native ideas nor a challenge to the modality of the native discourse in any constructive way. This lack of a paradigmatic axis in Japanese discourse may also bring to mind the prewar art historian Okakura Tenshin's description of Japan as the 'museum of Asia,' in which Asian ideas and artefacts are imported and warehoused with little trace of subjective intervention.[102] By virtue of this lack, Japan could be an ideal museum, an empty container that receives and stores things foreign in their original forms.[103] Similarly, speaking in the context of the lack of a dialectical engagement with external ideas in Japan, Takeuchi Yoshimi lamented the unprogressive and unconstructive climate of the Japanese intellectual tradition. Takeuchi attributed this deficit in the ability for dialectical engagement to a lack of self-defined identity (see Chapter 3). For Takeuchi, the rapid postwar economic growth was nothing but ironic, since it was made possible only by virtue of the absence of a subjectivity willing to and capable of resisting the penetration of capital and technology. Indeed, as argued above, it was externally imposed commercial forces that had come to define the 'identity' of the subject in Japan in the 1980s.

This relative lack of interiority, then, has made Japanese society appear to be, to many observers, the most 'advanced' among the industrialized nations, and particularly when it comes to discussion of things 'postmodern.' However, contemporary Japanese theorist Karatani Kōjin has rightly warned against such hasty equations of Japan and 'postmodernity.' Born out of a unique Euro-American context, argues Karatani, postmodernism has emerged as an attempted remedy, at least in intent, to modern Euro-American philosophical impasses, and as such is an attempt to revive epistemological confidence by taking a position consciously exterior to the interiority of the hegemonic Spirit.[104] In the Japanese historical context, the socio-discursive state of Japan in the 1980s cannot be postmodern in the same sense, since a self-defining modern subjectivity as such, the subject that objectifies the world in its transcendental gaze, has hardly ever been present in any clear form in Japanese history. Rather, argues Karatani, what appears to be postmodern in the socio-cultural state of Japan is more accurately grasped as a rehabilitation of certain nineteenth-century Japanese discourses, which Karatani describes as the 'paradise of fools,' referring to a sub-culture of the late Edo era. According to Karatani, the essence of nineteenth century Japan was most typically embodied in the behaviour exchanged between the sexes in the pleasure quarters of the late-Edo era, presumably the only place free from feudalistic class oppression, in which men and women pursued highly stylized aesthetic exchanges. The core principle of this sub-culture is understood by the notion of *iki*. As later formulated by prewar Japanese philosopher Kuki Shuzo, *iki* is the sensibility of keeping a certain distance from the woman one loves in order to avoid passion and folly, something that might be compared to nineteenth century European 'dandyism.' Karatani relates the core value of *iki* to what Heidegger called 'playing with the *Abgrund*,' or 'the abyssal depth,' the practice of the subject who deliberately negates all perspectives in favour of the sole purposeful pursuit of aesthetic sophistication.[105] One can see aspects similar to this aestheticism in the material snobbism and fetishism of the 'crystal tribes' mentioned previously, in the sense that the identity of the crystal tribes is kept vacant and undefined precisely for the purpose of leaving themselves open to all the possible identities they might want momentarily to embrace. It is this specific sense of the aesthetic subject, underlying the commercial successes of the rapidly changing succession of fashion booms and busts, that bears some affinity with the fragmented subject of the 'postmodern' age.

Karatani argues that the formalistic aestheticism prevalent in the Japanese nineteenth century was a result of previous intellectual trends, beginning in the late seventeenth century, that had persistently challenged *ri* (reason).[106] According to Karatani, 'the deconstruction of *ri* (reason) had already been accomplished' by the end of eighteenth century in the works of scholars like Itō Jinsai, Ogyū Sorai and Motoori Norinaga, who built upon a long standing tradition of criticism of *ri* contained in the *Shushigaku* – a neo-Confucian system of thought established in the twelfth century by the Chinese philosopher Chu Hsi, broadly speaking by conjoining Zen Buddhism and classical Chinese philosophy within its general frame of Confucianism. Itō Jinsai, claims Karatani, pointing to the limitations of singular perspective, logic and philosophy in the eighteenth century, 'discovered' textuality by recognizing a fundamental textual excess that cannot be reduced to any coherent system of thought.[107] This deconstructive awareness was furthered, according to Karatani, when Motoori Norinaga emphasized the importance of the *Kojiki* (an eighth-century text recounting the founding myth of the nation) over the government approved *Nihon Shoki*, which had conventionally earned more credit from the Japanese ruling classes, by criticizing the latter's Confucianist imposition of a single morality on its narrative, much as Nietzsche criticized Platonism and Christianity in his *Genealogy of Morals* for their 'nihilistic' negation of 'life' (plurality, becoming, contradiction, and pathos, in Nietzsche's terms) and for their invention of a 'true world' beyond existence.[108] Motoori insisted on the necessity of fundamentally altering our perspective from one governed by a particular reason and morality – what he called *kara-gokoro* (the 'Chinese mind') – to one free of such doxas, a perspective viewing the world outside hegemonic impositions and hidden ideologies by knowing the pathos of things (*mono no aware o shiru*) – what he called *yamato-gokoro* (the 'Japanese mind').[109] Motoori discovered this potential for going beyond the limitations of reason and morality in the realm of beauty/pathos and saw it not as a category opposed to reason, but rather as the foundation which gives rise to reason, and thus inclusive of any opposition between reason and non-reason.[110] What is noteworthy here is Motoori's naming this foundation *yamato-gokoro* ('Japanese mind'); rather predictably, and regardless of his own intention, Motoori's ideas were taken over and developed into a form of fanatical national Shintoism that served as an ideological underpinning of the Meiji restoration.[111]

The flourishing of aesthetic formalism in late-Edo was, to follow Karatani, a state resulting from the process of the nullification of universal reason ('Chinese mind') and a purification of native culture that had been attained by eliminating 'things foreign' (Chinese). That is to say, the process of nullifying reason became part and parcel of the process of establishing Japanese cultural essence (*yamato-gokoro*) and the identity of the Japanese. Karatani sees this same drive to realize cultural essence by means of nullifying reason at work in modern Japanese history as well, only with the difference that in the twentieth century the position of China as Japan's most powerful Other was replaced by the West.[112] Indeed, after the initial period of the Meiji restoration when the nation was motivated to modernize itself in order to defend itself from the Western powers, the subsequent romantic period was characterized by incessant attacks on the notions of the modern subject, reason, and progressive history, mingled with signs of a yearning for a return to the state of 'what Japan truly was.' This development reached its maturity, as discussed in Chapter 2, in the period of the 'cultural renaissance' (*bungei fukkoh ki*) that emerged out of the mid-1930s sense of spiritual void and wide-spread decadence. Thus we may see Nishida Kitaro's conception of the 'place of nothingness' (*mu no basho*) as a kind of parallel of Motoori's *yamato gokoro*, in that it attempts to formulate the foundation (or 'predicate') from which reason is derived, a place that would later be seen as the essence of Japanese identity. Yasuda Yojūrō's romantic irony, likewise, has much in common with the Edo notion of *iki*, the idea of playing with the 'abyssal depth,' a serious and distant 'play' that 'avoids passion and folly.' To repeat Karatani's point, the intellectual state reached in the 1930s was not the resistance of a 'premodern sensibility,' but a replication of nineteenth-century intellectual developments, 'a mode of thought which in some senses had already transcended "the modern".'

When this experience of the nineteenth-century Japanese native discourse is placed in the context of the modern universal world and the formation of the modern Japanese nation-state within it, one begins to notice a paradoxical mechanism inherent in Japanese national identity, an identity that establishes itself by negating the modern, a paradox that constitutes a haunting problem in modern Japanese history. Given the historical context in which the modern Japanese nation-state and its identity was formed, i.e. in reaction to the modern West as Japan's hegemonic Other, the process of negating traits of modern/Western philosophy (via a 'deconstruction' of reason) in the romantic period was at the same time a process constitutive of modern Japanese national identity accompanied by nationalistic sentiments calling for the recovery of Japan's 'true identity' supposedly erased by the process of modernization/Westernization. At the same time, however, Japanese cultural specificity as such could not find any other forms of representation than those open to it within the modality of the modern universalist perspective, and, therefore, 'Japan' came to be defined in terms of what stands out as peculiar when viewed in this universalist gaze. In other words, insofar as Japanese historical/cultural specificity operates within a modern universalist discourse that authorizes the universality of the modern world system itself, Japanese historical/cultural specificity is reduced to a 'difference-in-sameness' implicated within the general subjugation to the hegemonic power of the West. In order to go beyond this subordination and to establish a non-reductive identity of its own, therefore, some pre-war Japanese intellectuals thought Japan had to create hegemonic system of its own based on its superior value principles of the aesthetic. It was no accident, therefore, that the war against the Western Allies was conceived of as a reclamation of 'Japan's own identity'; Japan's wartime slogan, 'overcoming modernity,' was merely the verbal articulation of a project conceived to take Japan beyond modern time and space.

What was attempted in the war was, then, at least on this ideological level, a departure from the world defined in the modern way: it was an attempt to create an alternative system of representation superior to the modern, one in which Japanese cultural values, by employing the aesthetic imagination and by ascribing a higher value to beauty, could reorganize different temporal/spatial and human relations. Simultaneously, however, that alternative system erected itself solely upon the negation of the modern, since such negations furnished no ground for the transcendental structuring principles necessary to the constitution of the new system. Accordingly, the apolitical and anti-material nature of Japanese culturalism, in completely withdrawing from the social and the political, was paradoxically responsible for the political outcomes that followed. This critical lack left the door open for the imperatives embodied in monopoly capital and the nation-state, with its fully developed military capacity, to fill the void. At the opening of the war Yasuda's anti-essentialist, ironic aestheticism and the Kyoto School's foundationalist programme based on Nishida's notion of 'the place of nothingness' were conjoined to the state war ideology of 'overcoming modernity.' These same years witnessed the centralization of the decentred and de-essentialized discursive structure under the sign of the emperor as the ultimate authority for the alternative representative scheme signifying the essence of Japan. In short, in modern Japanese history the process of eliminating the foreign (most significantly reason) is not only a process constitutive of Japanese native identity, but it is also likely to be charged with anti-modern counter-hegemonic impulse.

Karatani sees a parallel development taking place in the Japanese discourse of the 1980s. In the postwar context, modern notions returned to prominence during the US occupation, but as we have seen were gradually eroded throughout the postwar era. The new version of 'overcoming modernity' was symbolically envisaged in works like *Beyond the Modern Age* at a time when society came to be increasingly characterized by two seemingly contradictory developments: an accelerating decentralization and fragmentation of the subject and reason and the advent of theories celebrating diffusion ('postmodernism'), on the one hand, and an inclination or desire towards centralization and homogenization in the form of a reclamation of national identity (*nihonjinron*), on the other. According to Karatani,

> Japan [in the 1980s] has become a highly developed information-consumption society, in which meaning is information and desire is the desire of the Other, because the 'subject' of the nineteenth-century West has never existed in Japan, nor has there been any resistance to the modern. In 1980s Japan (a Japan 'liberated' from its obsession with modernism), parody, pastiche and collage have become dominant trends. . . . There is an almost pathological play with language, with the reign of the superficial on the one hand and the regeneration of ultra-nationalistic ideology on the other. The overcoming of modernity is once again being touched upon, but in a different context.[113]

The development of a commercially driven sign-economy in the 1980s reached a point where everything became a matter of language or images, entirely reduced to their discursive properties (signs). At this point, dematerialized/dehistoricized networks of signs begin to constitute a hermeneutic surface in which an endless play of language and a narcissistic monologue can perpetuate themselves, completely disinterested in and delinked from representations of what is happening outside the closed system. Simultaneously, the nullification of the subject and meaning generate an 'excess' that seeks to find a ground for its articulation/materialization. In Japan of the 1980s, it was in *nihonjinron* that this 'excess' found its ground of articulation, expressing itself as a drive against the hegemonic perspective of the modern West (represented by the US). In this sense, the seemingly contradictory phenomena of the self-indulgent 'play with language' and the desire for subjectivity/meaning were both manifestations of a single historical event, namely, the troublesome maturing process of Japanese identity, taking form as a highly advanced 'postmodern' consumer society in which the absence of exteriority or the Other (i.e. that which stands outside of the hermeneutic surface) is increasingly felt.

If it was the emperor system that ultimately served as the symbol of Japanese essence in the years leading towards World War II, under which sign all contradictions were united in accord, can the emperor still function as a symbol of unity in contemporary Japan? Kurihara Akira, a contemporary social scientist, argues that current Japanese society has already constituted itself around a new form of the emperor system. According to Kurihara, the emperor has historically been a flexible concept, a socio-cultural system capable of transforming its content and form of representation according to the social conditions of the given epoch.[114] In the context of the 1980s, argues Kurihara, the emperor system has again transformed its temporal and spatial structure, this time into one in accord with the information-led consumer society characterized by extensive electronic webs for the intensive flow of information. In this system, the emperor is completely disembodied, no longer representing a living being but rather an abstract system designating emptiness as the essence of Japan. The efficacy of this system lies in its 'topological import as an "empty centre"' in which Japan is signified. As stated by Kurihara, this topological centre is represented by the imperial palace, and the new emperor system establishes itself by replacing a historically based space with an abstractly conceived one, constituting a circular expansion of the sphere of meaning all over Tokyo, and the nation itself, even into the rest of Asia.[115] Moreover, this new emperor system has the effect of and may be a mechanism for the nullification of historical time, in the sense that temporal distances can be easily overcome and the past and the future easily remade into properties of the present.[116] In the mediatized and bureaucratized Japanese society of the 1980s, argues Kurihara, the disembodied emperor as sign is infinitely and instantaneously multiplied without being known as such, since 'it alienates the very notion of alienation' in the minds of its subjects and, naturalizing the artificiality of the 'hyperreal,' it masks the fact that people are deprived of their subjectivity.[117]

Moreover, according to Kurihara, commercially driven material culture is accompanied in Japan by particular psychological and cultural effects, both in the individual subject and on the general atmosphere of the society: fetishism, egotistic materialism, narcissism, isolation and cynicism. Kurihara emphasizes that not only does commodity fetishism and snobbery prevail, but more problematically, by nullifying language's grasp of meaning this culture also advances a nihilistic play with difference to the point of extreme cynicism.[118] Free-floating signifiers delinked from their original meanings and/or historical referents now can arbitrarily attach themselves to almost any meaning/referent regardless of their original attachments, resulting in a situation where the assault on original meaning can go as far as to entail its opposite, just as in the Orwellian 'Newspeak'/'double think' slogans: 'war is peace and freedom is slavery.'[119] Moreover, since a subjectivity penetrated by and filled with the desire of others necessarily generates an 'excess' in the subject, the part of subjectivity that is displaced by the intrusion of external forces paradoxically generates a reactionary awakening of the desire for 'identity.' If the new emperor system is capable of absorbing this 'excess' in the subject into its empty centre, thereby rearticulating itself as a master signifier for the articulation of the 'ghost' of the displaced subject, then time and space will be completely dematerialized, and meaning annihilated. However, as I will discuss in Chapter 6, this negatively cultivated sense of lack, the vacuous feeling or excess that desires to be rearticulated, has not yet found its ground, at least in the 1990s, in the sign of the emperor new or otherwise; instead, the rearticulation was found in sub-national religious communities such as was exemplified by the *Aum Shinrikyō* cult group in the mid-1990s.

While the abandonment of deep, self-defined identity and the primacy of meaning in life allowed the Japanese cultural and economic scene of the early 1980s to prosper, this seemingly infinite game of exploiting difference became exhausted towards the end of the decade. As this happened, the cheerful nihilism and playful lightness of the earlier decade was gradually replaced by resentment and cynicism. This progression parallels the one observed in *nihonjinron* discourse; its initial optimism and narcissistic pride was later embittered with resentment, giving rise to more strident voices of cultural particularism and historical revisionism. Marking this mood of decay and embitterment, the 1980s closed with three major domestic and international landmark events: (1) the end of the Cold War and the emergence of the 'new world order'; (2) the death of Hirohito and the end the Shōwa era; and (3) the Heisei depression and the collapse of the 'bubble economy' in the early 1990s. Naturally, however, these endings were simultaneously the beginning of something new, whose structuring principle is yet to be defined in the continuing process of history in the making.

6 Japan in the 1990s and beyond

Identity crises in late modern conditions

Introduction

The landmark year of 1989 witnessed several clearly marked 'ends' and some less clearly marked 'beginnings,' both on the Japanese domestic and the international stages. Domestically, the six-decade-long Shōwa era (1926–89) that had seen the rise of the fascist regime and the war, as well as the postwar economic recovery and Japan's ascent to a post-industrial information society, ended with the death of emperor Hirohito. The end of Shōwa was accompanied by the financial deflation known as the 'burst of the bubble economy,' and was followed by the long and deep Heisei recession from which the economy has yet to recover. These domestic changes 'coincided' with a series of far reaching global structural transformations: the 1989 collapse of the Soviet Union marked the end of a period of relative international stability under the postwar bi-polar system, and the decade of the 1990s opened with the outbreak of the Persian Gulf War conducted under the US proposed 'New World Order.' In this changing international geopolitical climate, Japan's postwar commitment to liberal internationalism was deeply shaken, a disturbance that further exacerbated the growing appetite for nationalism. While these landmark events certainly introduced marked changes in the historical current, there were equally strong continuities with the previous decades. As seen in the last chapter, the radical erosion of empirical selfhood and the fragmentation of discourse in the 1980s had a 'double-function' of filling in the empty subject with commodified image-signs that in turn further displaced the subject. This trend towards the fragmentation and decentralization of the subject and discourse continued into the 1990s, while the optimism surrounding the reinvigoration and replenishment of identity by commercial signs waned. With the commercialization of subjectivity, society and knowledge expanding to its final frontiers – the family, sexuality and the body – reactionary responses to the increasingly severe challenges to identity began to take form in explosive acts of violence against society at large.

What one observes in the Japan of the 1990s, is a multifaceted breakdown of the political, economic and socio-cultural bases that had been the source of stability in previous decades. For instance, the 'unique' Japanese business practices and socio-cultural characteristics that were previously viewed as sources of pride and prosperity were now seen to be part of the problem. Moreover, the erosion of fundamentals, such as the sense of self and the body, conventionally held values and moral principles, and the family as an intimate private space, further intensified in the 1990s. As the everyday life of Japanese citizens was increasingly exposed to the influences of sophisticated technology and the incessant and seductive appeal of commercial images, supposedly displeasurable assaults on the empirical life sphere often came to be consumed as momentary pleasures. At the same time, this tendency evoked strong reactionary responses in a number of anxiety-ridden subjects who, failing to find peace in what appeared to them to be a senseless world, approached a breaking point of violent eruption. It was in this context that the desire to rehabilitate the broken social fabric found articulation in various historical revisionist voices calling for serious reflection on the postwar Japanese historical path and the meaning of being Japanese. In Chapter 6, I will discuss the acute manifestations of the crisis of contemporary Japan, seeing in them a mirror of the crisis of modernity at large. I pay particular attention to a series of events in the second-half of the 1990s that have symptomatically epitomized this sense of crisis: the violent acts of terrorism executed by the *Aum Shinrikyō* religious cult group and the growing popularity of historical revisionism that precipitated the emergence of a 'new nationalism.' Leading towards my conclusion, I identify the common structural problems underlying a host of troubling manifestations witnessed in various spheres of Japanese society in the 1990s.

Features of the crisis: the breakdown of the political economic structures and the challenge of the 'New World Order'

The death of the emperor and the sense of closure

When emperor Hirohito died on January 7th, 1989, the long and eventful Shōwa era finally ended. Men and women of all ages, vocations and political affiliations gathered together at the imperial palace, it was reported, in order to pay their respects in 'a moment of a deep sense of loss,' solemnly participating in a sacred ritual 'calling for a new spirit.'[1] Although there was an undeniable sense of closure throughout society, one should be sceptical of the nationalist claim that the majority of the Japanese were motivated to confirm 'their true self-image' as imperial subjects. Rather, it would be much more reasonable to say that this sense of closure was in large part derived from the way temporality is marked in the Japanese calendar system: in Japan periods of time are directly linked to the reigning emperor's name, such that Hirohito died in early Shōwa 64, and each decade of an era (e.g., the Shōwa 10s, 20s, etc.) is invested with the images associated with the key historical events that characterized that years in question.[2] By referring to this imperial periodization, historical narratives create a sense of spatial boundaries both inside and outside of the shared temporality.[3] Somewhat paradoxically, it was Hirohito's illness and the immanent and long awaited end of that era that revived the moribund image of the Shōwa era; which is to say, the impending closure of the historical epoch revived the era itself, in such a way that numerous academic and popular projects were initiated to narrate the history of the past from this privileged present point of view of the era's end. These efforts and the consequent extended affirmations of closure evoked a sense of nostalgia – if such efforts themselves were not already its product – that persisted well into the 1990s, during which time they increasingly became enmeshed with the resentments, feelings of powerlessness, and the cynicism that was to mark the second half of the decade.

I argued in Chapter 5 that in contemporary Japan the emperor has tended to function as a demythologized symbol, transformed from his once-sacred status in the prewar era to the late-Shōwa notion of the emperor as a popular figure. Given that the emperor has for some time represented something of a mere formality, a nationally recognized sign, we can see that images of Hirohito's life, and particularly his death, were wildly exploited both by the Japanese mass media, for their high commercial value, and by many individuals who made great use of their symbolic value to enhance their own power in various local discourses. Public and private corporations, as well as many individuals, competed in completely formal displays of respect by voluntarily practising 'self-restraint' during the emperor's illness, postponing and/or cancelling various events.[4] All the major national newspapers and the daily television news reports recounted often embarrassingly detailed account of his illness and his deteriorating condition, replete with 'biological facts' of scientific accuracy, such as his daily body temperature, blood pressure level and the amount of blood he had lost. Although the death of Hirohito reaffirmed the purely symbolic status of the imperial court in contemporary Japanese society, the populace's spontaneous acts of public mourning also raised concerns about the possibility that such a symbol could be employed to evoke a sense of national unity and mobilize a uniform society-wide response, albeit in a completely depoliticized manner. During the 1990s, this formalized and supposedly apolitical symbolic power of the Imperial Court has had ambiguous implications with respect to Japanese nationalism. For some, this symbol has represented the spiritual unity of the nation, while for others it has become the symbol of postwar Japanese peace and prosperity, even a democratic civil society. Whatever content the symbol represents, with Hirohito's death a sense of closure was more or less shared by the entire society. Indeed, we ought to say that the crux of the symbolic power of the emperor lay precisely in its ambiguity and thus its ability to accommodate a variety of feelings, its high value utility as the ultimate symbol of the nation.

The philosopher and critic Takeda Seiji has emphasized that the emperor system (*tennō-sei*), unlike the office of President or Prime Minister in Western societies, cannot solely be explained as a symbolic centre in a semiotic sense, nor either in purely political-institutional or sociological terms.[5] Instead, argues Takeda, for many Japanese the emperor occupies both the endpoint of the empirical and affectionate relationships that extend outwards from the individual to the family, relatives, friends, local communities, and eventually to the nation, as well as functioning as a transcendental absolute being (*chōetsu-sha*) gathering together general society-wide existential anxieties.[6] Remarking on this notion of the emperor's dual function, Takeda explains that the symbolic power of the emperor tends ultimately to absorb a diversity of historical narratives and streams of ideas:

> In Japanese society, there is always an empty space between the verbal expression of ideas and the sense of reality (the feeling of void). The reason for this, as I have argued above, is that all ideas as such have historically been regarded as external and foreign, [what might be described as] the Chinese spirit (*Kara-gokoro*), at odds with the native discourse. Given this external assignment, the foundation for universality in Japanese discourse has been thought to reside outside the system, and has impaired the ability of ideas to develop a passageway bridging the gap between words and reality. This empty space between words and ideas (in which the centre is an empty one) has been derived from the unique historical experience and social configuration of the Japanese, the unique 'anxiety,' as it were, of the Japanese understanding of reality.
>
> Therefore, either on the level of 'narrative' or on that of 'thought,' this empty space tends to be filled in by the forms of communal sensitivity that negate such 'anxiety.' Needless to say, what symbolizes these forms of Japanese sensitivity on the level of 'narrative' has always been the emperor, and on the level of 'thought,' they are symbolized by types of transcendental 'reason' coming from the outside, bearing the power of universality.[7]

Takeda's own position in these passages is unclear, and one wonders whether the argument is his own or if he is merely describing as an outsider a problematic tendency among the Japanese. Operating with this ambiguity and identifying in the insurmountable distance between words and reality the source of an anxiety unique to the Japanese, Takeda cannot escape the charge that he is constructing an insulated, imagined community called 'Japan.' From this position, Takeda attributes the source of the power of the Japanese emperor system to the nation's problematic encounter with modernity and its ambivalent modern identity. According to Takeda, when Japanese intellectuals become aware of this gap between ideas and reality they usually adopt one of the following strategies: they tend to base their notion of transcendental reason on their existential anxieties, or they tend to understand and affirm all historical changes by rationalizing them by means of imported ideas.[8] He believes that as long as Japanese intellectuals continued to pursue one of those two strategies, rather than devoting their efforts to creating a universal foundation for truth and morality in Japanese discourse itself, then the empty symbol of the emperor will remain powerful in Japanese society.

Problematic as it may be, Takeda's argument nevertheless sheds some light on troubling features of Japan's national identity that are encapsulated in the emperor symbolism that he sees as constituting a national/communal myth. As I discuss later, the conceptual slippage here described between ideas and the sense of reality, namely, the inclination to reify communal space, seems to be at the crux of the 1990s resurgence of communally oriented Japanese nationalism. Indeed, the spiritual and political value of the emperor may have actually been increasing in the context of the declining authority of the Japanese state, the troubled economy, the increased sense of anxiety in the subject, and the nation's ambivalent position in the changing tide of the 1990s international order. In what appeared to be a multifaceted nationwide crisis during this decade, the desire for a remedy, as I argue below, tended to manifest itself in calls for the erection of symbolic authority as the last resort of national unity. In this internally motivated inclination to overcome fragmentation and structural breakdown, the individual subject is identified with the homogenized communal identity of the 'Japanese,' which in turn simultaneously constitutes the national boundary segregating the inside from outside.

The burst of the 'bubble economy' and the Heisei depression

Not only did the 1990s open with this mood of mourning, but it saw two additional closures triggered by political and economic difficulties, which together reinforced the sense of the end of an era. The prolonged Heisei recession and the financial downturn, the so-called 'burst of the bubble economy,' clearly marked an end to postwar economic growth and the nearly four decades of the LDP's monopoly on power, the so-called 55-*nen taisei*, the 1955 system. It is important here to note the intimate relation between the breakdown of the bi-polar international geopolitical order and that of the elite Japanese political and economic system that had flourished under the US–Japan security framework. As argued in previous chapters, the zenith of Japanese economic power in the 1980s was achieved under the umbrella of the LDP/business elite coalition that had successfully established an oligopolistic political and economic structure during the rapid growth of the 1960s and which had been consolidated in the international competitive climate of the 1980s, in both decades accompanied by versions of a conservative ideology. In the context of an increasingly internationalized economic environment and the intensification of political tensions derived from economic competition with the US (and, to a lesser degree Europe), Japanese capital came to be increasingly invested in East and Southeast Asia in the second half of the 1980s, generating a series of regionally integrated productive relations. By the early 1990s, however, the competitive power of Japanese firms waned as the leading sector of the international economy shifted from the production of high value-added industrial goods, such as automobiles and computer hardware, to information technology software, and technology networks. These developments and the resultant economic breakdown cannot be understood outside the context of the structural problems embedded in the world economy.

Robert Brenner has recently scrutinized the structural problems of the world economy, particularly the problem of over-production in the post 1970s global economy and the subsequent shift in investment patterns from productive to speculative economies. Brenner maintains that the causes of the Japanese bubble and its subsequent collapse have much to do with the changes effected in the financial sector by the 1985 Plaza Accord, the principal repercussion of which for Japan was a radical revaluation of the yen–dollar exchange rate.[9] Between 1985 and 1988 the value of the yen virtually doubled vis-à-vis the dollar. As there was no corresponding decrease in the costs of Japanese production, Japanese producers confronted a situation in which the higher yen and increasingly protected foreign markets meant that demand for their goods was rapidly shrinking. According to Brenner, the Japanese government's response to this crisis was fourfold: (1) it attempted to increase domestic consumption to compensate for the drop in exports; (2) it fostered a runaway speculation and inflation in Japanese real estate and equities (Tokyo land and stock market prices doubled between 1986 and 1989); (3) it encouraged the reinvestment of this 'flush money' in manufacturing plant modernization and research and development in order to take Japanese industry to the next level of high-tech sophistication, productivity, and international competitiveness; and (4) it encouraged direct foreign investment (which tripled in the years 1985–89; in addition, sales of Japanese US-manufactured automobiles grew at an annual rate of 5 per cent in this period) to take advantage of tariff barriers and the cheaper East and Southeast Asian labour market.

The primary consequences of the post-1985 economic policies were a tighter integration of the Asian and Japanese economies, and the creation of a tripartite regionally-based economic relation between the US, Japan and Asia. In this new regionally integrated economy, Asian producers managed to acquire a percentage of the US market corresponding to the percentage of that market lost to Japanese producers, as well as to increase their share of the Japanese market, while Japan's high-tech exports to East and Southeast Asia rose. However, as Brenner sees it, the overall result of the Japanese government's fourfold measures to halt the decrease in Japanese competitiveness was less than sterling, with 'Japanese manufacturers [finding] themselves unable to use the growth of exports to transcend the structural problems inherent in their particular form of export-oriented development.' He argues:

> The increase in costs entailed by the massive revaluation of the yen was simply too great to offset by means of increasing manufacturing efficiency, entering new, technology-intensive manufacturing lines where competition was less intense, and refashioning their overseas commercial production networks. In the end, Japanese producers could neither avoid a sharp fall in the rate of growth of manufacturing exports nor achieve a significant recovery of manufacturing profitability.[10]

In short, as a result of the Plaza Accord and the subsequent failures to adjust to the international productive and wage structures, Japan lost its competitive edge vis-à-vis the US.[11] Further, the strategy employed notably by the US in this decade, of shifting production to non-manufacturing sectors where wages were relatively low, or could be lowered, was not viable in Japan because of socio-cultural constraints, such as lifetime employment policies which do not allow for a competitive wage scheme, and the limitations of fully utilizing the English language. The only option left to the Japanese was that of initiating a massive corporate investment in stocks and portfolios. By creating unsubstantiated economic growth that by-passes the 'real' economic activity of production, distribution, and the exchange of goods and services, however, such investments widen the gap between the nominal (market) value and the 'real' value of equities. Devoid of the complex chains of human and material interaction, such an unsubstantiated 'virtual economy' is bound to collapse at some point. In fact, not only was the huge surplus engineered by the expansion of the speculative economy incapable of effecting the structural transformation of the economy, it magnified the volatility of the Japanese economy as a whole, exposing the populace to great economic risk.

Reflecting the economic constraints felt in the early 1990s, criticisms of the once unshakably solid, elite Japanese power oligarchy began to emerge from liberal economists like Ōmae Ken'ichi, a successful businessman who for a long time had lived and studied abroad. According to Ōmae, the world economy in the 1990s has been characterized by the recovery of the Anglo-Saxon economies, particularly those of the US, England, New Zealand, and Ireland, with Canada and Australia being less successful exceptions.[12] He argues that these Anglo-Saxon economies followed a course of economic deregulation and domestic restructuring, most clearly exemplified by the Thatcher and Reagan administrations, in which the brunt of negative effects were suffered in the 1980s with high unemployment and a low rate of expansion. However, thanks to the application of these tough neo-liberal policies they emerged, Ōmae claims, as the strongest economies in the 1990s, with few 'obstacles' to the free-flow of goods and services, and soon began to enjoy the positive results of their economic discipline.[13] Conversely, he argues that the Japan of the 1980s was so complacent with its prosperity that it did not take the need for such restructuring seriously, and that, in addition to the belated recognition of these necessities, Japanese politicians and bureaucrats of the 1990s have been incapable of and unwilling to demonstrate leadership in the internal restructuring necessary to integrate Japan into the globalized economy. As an example of such failures, Ōmae points to Japan's continuing archaic English language pedagogical system, its failure to embrace a pragmatic and functional approach to teaching English as a means of global communication. He points out that many Asian non-English speaking countries, such as Taiwan and even Korea and Indonesia, are far more advanced in this respect than Japan, and that Singapore, which made English its national language in the early 1980s, has practically replaced Japan as the new central commercial hub in Asia.[14] According to Ōmae's liberal economist viewpoint, Japan's conservative socio-economic and political structure, and particularly its resistance to change, have been the greatest causes of the relative decline of the Japanese economy.

Indeed, one great merit of Ōmae's critique is its disclosure of the role that 'structurally embedded conservatism' has played in exacerbating the Japanese financial crisis, itself unprecedented in postwar Japanese history. As mentioned in the last chapter, Japanese corporate capitalism of the 1980s was buoyed by a series of highly inflated speculative economic practices, including real-estate and portfolio investments that were accompanied by a set of manipulative policy instruments and the control of information by the elite power group. In Japan, as has been argued, the largest portion of stocks are corporately rather than individually owned, and the longstanding mutual support system among the companies within the same *keiretsu* (large business conglomerates) artificially inflates the value of corporate stocks in order to generate a greater return of equity for the business group.[15] To support this system, the company heads of a *keiretsu* hold closed meetings without disclosing their decisions to individual stockholders, a practice that has been targeted by the US representatives in the Strategic Impediment Initiative talks (*Nichibei Kōzō Kyōgi*) as unfair.[16] Moreover, Japanese private banks have been under the strong influence of the Ministry of Finance (*Ōkurashō*), and were strongly 'recommended' by the Ministry to purchase large sums of US government bonds in order to prop up the US budgetary deficit in the late 1980s. Given that it is an accepted convention for private Japanese banks to place retired Finance Ministry bureaucrats in high-ranking management positions (a practice known as *amakudari*, 'descent from heaven'), private financial institutions in Japan are not as autonomous from the government as banks are elsewhere in the developed world. In other words, as Ōmae correctly points out, the Japanese financial system is characterized by many illiberal practices sanctioned by manipulative government and private sector policies that discriminate against the interests of individual investors.

When the financial bubble began to burst, the traditional methods for dealing with the crisis employed by both the Japanese and the US governments were either unavailable or not forthcoming. In September 1989, the Japanese government began to raise interest rates in an effort to slow the precipitous expansion of the bubble (over the course of the following twelve months they rose from 2.5 to 6 per cent). In mid-1990 a US cyclical downturn came into effect and the newly-elected president refused to do what generations of his predecessors had done in similar circumstances – deficit finance his way out of the recession. It was about this time that the Japanese bubble burst, and Japan experienced the worst recession in its postwar history, with an average annual growth rate of only 0.8 per cent between 1991 and 1995. This recession was exacerbated by the fact that during the expansion of the bubble a high percentage of Japanese investment had been deficit financed; when the bubble burst, huge quantities of Japanese capital invested in American bonds, securities and asset purchases were liquidated and repatriated, further driving up the value of the yen, with its value against the dollar rising 54 per cent in the period 1990–5. Due to the over-investment and the over-accumulation of manufacturing capacity during the expansion of the bubble, as well as corporate Japan's reluctance to engage in massive layoffs and the growing over extension of the big banks, domestic demand levelled off, and the fourfold policy of the mid- to late 1980s was no longer effective or even possible. The economic statistics were devastating: between 1990 and 1995 relative unit labour costs rose faster than the effective exchange rate; between 1988 and 1995 the profitability rate of non-financial corporations fell 37 per cent, and in the manufacturing sector, for which there is no data, it was surely worse. Moreover, because the currencies of the Asian economies (where Japan had placed the bulk of its direct foreign investment) were pegged to the US dollar, every rise in the yen made investment in Asia that much more appealing, and it seemed as though Asian direct foreign investment was the only way out of the Japanese quandary. Thus Japanese annual direct foreign investment in Asian manufacturing grew a whopping 280 per cent in the same period, 1991–5. Not only did these measures not halt the precipitous slide in the Nikkei stock exchange index, they had the effect of spreading the financial bubble syndrome to Asian economies, economies less diversified than the Japanese and thus less able to stave off the inevitable collapse.[17]

Fearful of a further plunge in values, the Japanese government was reluctant to acknowledge the seriousness of the recession, and instead its

Economic White Paper of 1992 advocated supporting 'the continuing expansionary trend,' even after near zero growth in late 1991.[18] Belatedly applied remedial measures attempting to stimulate domestic consumption – an expansionary monetary policy (lowering interest rates) and the concentration of public expenditures in the early fiscal year – failed miserably.[19] Instead of adopting a policy of fundamental financial restructuring and clearing up deflated loans, which would have involved the large scale bankruptcy of the worst performing banks, the Ministry of Finance kept up its massive investment in domestic construction projects by further borrowing from the domestic banks. In doing so, the Japanese government and the banks silently shifted the burden of the debt from the banks (as financial institutions) to the population (as investors in the banks) in a series of buyouts and tax hikes.[20] Moreover, the results of these fiscal stimuli were further undercut by new rises in the value of the yen. As Brenner points out, with the Mexican peso crisis in the Spring of 1995, 'a flight from the dollar pushed the yen's exchange rate to the unprecedented height of 80/$, threatening the economy with collapse.'[21] It took the concerted intervention of the G3 governments in the summer of 1995 to reverse the decade-long decline of the dollar, and by late 1996 the yen had fallen to about half of its former peak against the US currency.[22] It seemed, for the time being, that the crisis had been forestalled.

This financially driven economic crisis in the first half of the 1990s had a number of important outcomes on the domestic political front, the first of which was the severely weakened power base and legitimacy of the LDP. Indeed, the LDP experienced a defeat in the fall 1993 Lower House elections, for the first time in thirty-eight years, virtually marking the end of 'the 1955 system,' the decades of LDP domination based on the US–Japan security treaty and the elite alliance among politicians, bureaucrats, and financial giants that formed the inner circle of the conservative power base. The immediate cause of the defeat was a challenge posed to the core party factions by the younger generation of mostly LDP politicians who demanded administrative reforms and an end to corruption.[23] Out of this spirit of political reform was born the progressive conservative parties, the Shin Nihon Party led by Hosokawa Morihiro, the Sakigake Party formed by disaffected LDP diet members, and the opportunistic search for an alternative political base that was seen in the creation of the Shinshin Party among ex-LDP members and other moderately conservative parties. With the formation of the coalition government under the leadership of Hosokawa Morihiro, the public's hopes for a more accountable and representative form of governance were given a voice. Despite popular expectations for change and some affirmative signs, however, the political reforms initiated by the Sakigake Party and other progressively minded politicians were frustrated by a reassertion of power by the alliance of the remaining LDP politicians and bureaucrats, themselves usurping the superficially adopted rhetoric of reform.[24] In the 1996 election the LDP regained its majority and the existing elite power structure largely recovered the ground it had lost, while the spirit of democratic reform was largely transformed into the deregulation of the economy and the downsizing of the central bureaucracy along neo-liberal economic lines.[25] While the nation suffered from various difficulties and challenges in the 1990s, the failure to adopt meaningful reforms and the continuing weak leadership have simply prolonged the initial crisis, and have created widespread public disillusionment and apathy about politics as a whole.

The eclipse of liberal internationalism and troubled US–Japan/Japan–Asia relations

Internationally, the year 1989 saw the beginning of the end of the half-century long US–Soviet bipolar system and the beginning of structural transformations in the search for a new order. The fall of the Berlin wall and the collapse of the Soviet Union led many to adopt the neo-conservative euphemism of the 'end of history,' and to believe that the triumph of democracy and the coming age of freedom and prosperity of the now singular capitalist world was at hand. In reality, the intensive integration of capital and technology networks across national boundaries was limited to the most advanced economies, while large parts of the global economy lay outside these networks. In political terms, the doublespeak of global democracy was clearly shattered with the advent of the Persian Gulf War. Indeed, the nature of the war allowed one a glimpse into the darker side of this new order, symbolically represented in the near theatrical performance of high-tech 'smart-weapons' carrying out their missions and supposedly hitting their targets with a calculated precision, and the well managed media coverage televising these highly successful 'missions' with 'aesthetically pleasing' night-time views of Baghdad under aerial bombardment. During this war, the world also witnessed the smooth diplomatic manoeuvring by which George Bush's vision of the 'new world order' was quickly and successfully transformed into the UN multilateral expeditionary force that took up position on the frontiers of Iraq, violator of the sovereign right of Kuwait. This mission won the broad, albeit passive, support of the international community for the cause of international justice, and allowed a crisis-laden US domestic polity to regain passionate public support. The Gulf War was a test case for the US, and the world at large, to define the new norms for international politics in the coming century.

The Persian Gulf War also had an enormous impact upon the Japanese, suddenly making them aware of the system of power politics, and can be said to have induced a turning point in Japanese intellectual and popular discourse in which the previously unquestioned commitment to universal international principles was subject to serious doubts. As an economically powerful and loyal ally of the US, Japan was urged to participate in the financing of the war, and this caused a number of questions that had been long forgotten in the postwar era to be resurfaced. The nation's over 13 billion (US$) contribution to the UN multilateral forces meant a new tax had to be imposed on the population, while the reception of the international community to this contribution was rather lukewarm, when it was commented on at all.[26] Domestically, this financial contribution, together with logistical support behind the front-lines, opened up a constitutional debate, particularly with respect to Article Nine of the Constitution, prohibiting any form of participation in any war, at any level.[27] Parallel to this constitutional debate were increasing resentments of US international policies, and together these events forced open the question of Japan's postwar relations with the US, Japan's war responsibility to Asian nations, and the overall meaning of World War II. Due to the combination of Japan's unique constitutional restrictions and a renewed upsurge of historical revisionism, Japanese intellectual discourse witnessed a radical politicization and polarization in the months leading up to, during, and after the war. In short, the Gulf War and Japan's involvement in it triggered a re-evaluation of the past and present position of Japan in the world, as well as anxieties over the future status of the country in the changing international context, particularly with respect to the parameters of US–Japan security arrangements in the post-Cold War era.

This whole complex of events gave rise to a deep dilemma and moral paralysis among the present generation of Japanese intellectuals who were, for the first time in decades, confronted by the brute fact of international power politics. While many found that neither the US nor Iraq could be justifiably supported, they were shocked to discover that a multilateral international institution like the UN was not outside of, or at least not powerful enough to remain outside of, such political pressures. Itō Seikou, a novelist of the younger generation, expressed his embarrassment and unpreparedness when faced with the moral vacuum of the world and himself in a real historical context beyond the security of the 'postmodern' theories he had endorsed, claiming that:

> Both the participants and the bystanders to the war lack any reason, principle or standpoint, and this situation clearly reveals nothing but the fact that the world itself has no reason and principle. This is why I fell into an aphasia, for words cannot exist without reason (meaning). As one of those who had grown up in the era of so-called postmodernism, I thought I understood this absence of reason and principle in the world as a matter of fact. [But I did not.] ... I was suspended in the midair of darkness without reason or principle. However, [when called upon to respond] I see now that I had been firmly tied to a lifeline at that time.[28]

Itō came to understand the lack of moral foundation, reason, and meaning in real terms when the postwar liberal international ideal was challenged by a brute power politic barely disguised behind the rhetoric of peace and order. Taking Itō's recognition as representative of a shared sense of difficulty, we can say that the Gulf War made many Japanese intellectuals aware of the direct impact on the life and well-being of people in the world of the international hegemonic power hierarchy, and, more importantly, of the role that the nation-state and its standing in this hierarchy played in the life of its citizens, who ultimately were dependent upon it. In other words, with the advent of the Gulf War, the relationship between international hegemony, the nation-state, and citizens within the state, a relationship which was formerly relatively invisible in postwar Japan, became apparent to many Japanese.[29]

To break this inertia, a group of highly successful and relatively young writers and critics (*bungakusha*), including Karatani Kōjin, Kawamura Minato, Nakagami Kenji, Shimada Masahiko and Tanaka Yasuo, published a collective statement objecting to Japan's participation in the war. A symposium subsequently held in Tokyo on February 9th, 1991 was attended by about fifty writers, and a collective statement against the war was issued, signed and publicized in the New York Times. The statement was divided into two separate parts so that participants could choose to sign only one or both. They read:

> Item One: I oppose the participation of the Japanese state in the Gulf War.
>
> Item Two: Article Nine of the postwar Japanese Constitution proclaims Japan's intent to 'renounce war.' This renunciation has been maintained by the spontaneous will of the Japanese people, and not by the imposition of any other country. It is based upon the regret felt by the Japanese people for fighting WWII as 'the final war,' and especially for wrongs inflicted upon neighboring Asian nations. In addition, we believe that Article Nine embodies the hopes and aspirations of all those in the West who themselves experienced two world wars. In this transitional age, we believe that because of the principle embodied in Article Nine our present Constitution is the most universal and radical Constitution in existence. We strongly object to Japan's direct or indirect participation in the Gulf War. We believe that Japan should make every possible effort to further the international 'renunciation of war.'
>
> We oppose Japan's participation in the Gulf War and all possible future wars.[30]

As could be expected, various criticisms of the statement immediately followed, one of which was made by the critic Kasai Kiyoshi. Kasai's critique was issued from the position of 'postmodernism proper,' warning of the risk of repeating the same old modernist mistake. While agreeing with Itō Seikou's recognition that the groundlessness of the world was made apparent in the Gulf War, Kasai censures the signatories for nonetheless issuing the statement and thereby making an 'unfounded decision.' For him, these unfounded decisions tend to erect an absolute reason, meaning or morality as their bulwark, and thus necessarily end up subordinating human life and history to ideology.[31] Although this pursuit of the absolute was once conceived as a 'solution' to the problems of modernity, it now, claims Kasai, seems like an illusory escape from the unbearableness of a meaningless world. Kasai argues that the danger and untenability of such unfounded radicalism came to be widely recognized in the scholarship of the 1970s, and was demonstrated in the history of Japan and other nations. It was in this context that Kasai saw postmodernism emerge:

> The postmodernism of the 1980s arose as a passive resistance, so-to-speak, to the ideological perversion [or ethically motivated leap] of making unfounded choices and decisions that the meaninglessness and philosophical void of the twentieth century tend to produce. I believe that at least the best part of postmodernism has conceptualized the resistance to such ungrounded choices and decisions. Even if one cannot deny the fact that Japanese postmodernism had been absorbed into an ideology which simply rationalized the existing conditions of capitalist high consumer society, one is no longer allowed to recede to the terrain where unfounded choices and decisions are justified.[32]

Assuming that one can no longer justifiably fall back on any absolute authority, since returning to it is an illusion of a 'safe-haven' and would lead to nothing but a repetition of past catastrophes, Kasai argues that this same problematic was revisited in, and intensified by, the advent of the Gulf War. As a result of being confronted for the first time by the concrete historical limitations of their strategies, many of those who used to refer to themselves as 'postmodernists' were in the forefront of the calls for 'action.'

> During the time when postmodernism was indulging in its empty prosperity, the appropriate criticism to be made against it was not to affirm the metaphysical construction of narratives in opposition to its meaninglessness. Because the absence of meaning was already assumed as a condition for thought at that time, the truly difficult problem was [the seductive power of] the absence of meaning which calls for unfounded choices and decisions to erect 'Reason.' [The supporters of the anti-war statement] perhaps felt that the postmodern affirmation of meaninglessness could have no impact as a criticism, in the face of a 'Reason' arising out of the ideologically inverting mechanism that takes control of history and results in unlimited terrorism.[33]

Kasai continues by arguing that in the contemporary world we are locked in a situation where 'one no longer has the freedom of even choosing and deciding without meaning,' and thus talking about peace is as frivolous as not talking about it.³⁴ Accordingly, he reaches the conclusion that one can no longer discourse in terms of 'meta-statements' or universal principles. This, he claims, is the burden we must all bear: the burden of living with aphasia in a world of banality:

> There is no privileged position, solution, or 'decision' that allows one to immediately recover from aphasia. If one thinks there is, one is embracing an illusion. The enormous psychological pressures that make one want to grab hold of an illusion are, even when one is aware of them, simply painful ... [What is necessary is] to bear the burden of banality that is absolutely imposed upon one, to choose that banality with one's own will, and to find the words, one by one, that are worth uttering in the pain of aphasia.³⁵

In short, the Gulf War forced Japanese intellectuals into a 'double-bind' between the untenability of erecting in good faith a principle of reason, and the awareness of the loss of the efficacy of postmodernism as a passive resistance in the unbearable urgency to act. Remaining faithful to his conclusion, Kasai criticizes those 'ex-postmodernists' who, with the advent of the Gulf War, 'rediscovered' a positive value in the postwar Japanese Constitution, and himself refrains from supporting the statement, from making an 'unfounded choice' that would rationalize peace and the Japanese Constitution as absolutes and universals.

A number of critical doubts ought to be cast on the 'position' Kasai has taken. First, although we may agree that the anti-war statement was a result of each supporter's 'unfounded decision,' the issuing of the universalist statement does not necessarily entail the erection of the 'Reason' feared by Kasai. The statement is presented not in the form of a positive value principle, as the US justified its attack on Iraq in the name of 'the effort to establish international peace and order,' but rather in the form of a negation, 'the renunciation of the war.' Since the statement does present itself in absolute and universal terms, it can only halt action and not be the cause of it. Second, if issuing a statement grounded in universal principles could induce potential violence, Kasai's 'positionless position' seems to have its own oppressive effect insofar as it passively accepts the violation of universal values. One senses a note of defeatism in his strict prohibition of action and his passive acceptance of the banality of the meaningless world. If there is no universal ideal to be upheld and no agent in history, how can one possibly conceive the making of history? These questions, however, cannot discredit Kasai's argument, for what is problematic (i.e. the state of the world we live in) is beyond his analysis, and his argument is consistent with his sense of intellectual faith. Yet, by standing outside of history and analysing it from that vantage, his argument perpetuates the present sense of historical impasse. Prior to any intellectual critique, this is a *political objection* to his argument.

In this new global context, not only did US–Japan relations became troublesome, but Japan–Asia relations also became equally, if not more, strained. As the geopolitical order under US hegemony entered into a transitional phase in the post-Cold War era, and as intra-Asian economic interactions increased dramatically in the same period, the region began to seek a new institutional framework and a new common vision of the future, and this inevitably led, in Japan, to a rigorous interrogation of the past.[36] This interrogation included open discussions of the issues of apologies and of reparations for Japan's conduct in World War II, and coming to terms with past wrongdoings by directly answering the grievances of many Asians. Generally speaking, the Japanese mass media and the public have become more willing to discuss quite openly sensitive issues of this nature, issues that were previously thought to be 'taboo,' such as the Nanking massacre, the forced prostitution of Asian women by the Japanese military, (*jūgun ianfu*, 'comfort women'), and the human experiments of the infamous Unit 731, the Japanese Army's top secret bacteriological warfare and research organization.[37] Thanks to the Japan Socialist Party leader Doi Takako's years of lobbying for Japan to follow Germany, a draft statement renouncing World War II (*fusen ketsugi*) was discussed in the Diet in May 1990. However, as the Persian Gulf crisis heated up, the draft statement began to come under strong criticism from various conservative politicians, and the questions of the Japanese Constitution, US–Japan postwar relations, and Japan's role in the international community were discussed with unprecedented intensity. The political context complicated the issue, basically dividing the conservative camp into two opposing groups: those eager to endorse the statement for pragmatic reasons as a policy instrument furthering Asian–Japanese political and economic integration, and those who insisted on its rejection. Although general agreement was reached on acknowledging Japan's war responsibilities in one way or another, the spirit of the apology was largely compromised (about one-third of all Diet members opposed the statement) and the ideological dispute was reduced to a matter of semantics.[38] With the announcement of an official apology by Prime Minister Hosokawa in 1993, Japan affirmed its war responsibility to Asia, at least in formal terms.[39]

Soon after this event, however, various voices of discontent were raised by opposing politicians contesting 'one-sided' condemnations of Japan's war conduct. Ishihara Shintarō, for one, emphasized that the apology should only be directed towards Asians, and not to the Western Allies and Russians who, he believed, equally preyed on Asia. Much like Takeuchi Yoshimi in earlier decades, Ishihara adopted a dual attitude towards World War II, seeing it as an aggressive war of invasion against Asia and a defensive war against the Western imperial powers.[40] Okuno Seisuke, the leader of the Diet-members League (*kokkai giin dōmei*) established in December 1994, went a step further by highlighting the racial aspects of the war, emphasizing that Japan had 'contributed' to the enhancement of Asian independence in the postwar era. Okuno and his League's view was reminiscent of that of the prewar Pan-Asianists who conceived the war as a form of counter-hegemonic resistance, under Japanese leadership, to Western colonialism. In this view, Okuno *et al.* painted the world in a single-power political colour, in which nation-states have no choice but to compete against each other for supremacy, while at the same time they assumed the superiority of the Japanese nation-state within 'Asia,' according to the linear progressive vision of history in which nations advance towards greater and greater 'civilization.' While advancing this dual-war argument, the focus of Okuno *et al.* was clearly on Japan as victim, expressing their resentment of US power politics, and once again at the expense of silencing Asian voices.[41]

While difficult to accurately assess, the general opinion of the Japanese public seems to lie somewhere between Hosokawa's position of willing apology and that of the reactionary opposition. As reports reached Japan of the aggressive display of US nationalism at the Smithsonian Museum exhibit for the fiftieth anniversary of the end of the World War II, where the nuclear bomber the Enola Gay was on display, the term *kenbei* (US hating) began to increasingly circulate in the popular lexicon. Also in the 1990s, popular sentiment grew more critical of Asian countries, as indicated by a government statistic showing that over 50 per cent of the Japanese felt no sympathy for the plight of the Chinese and over 60 per cent felt none for the Koreans.[42] In terms of the perception of World War II and its historical significance, the Japanese public showed mixed feelings, again divided between two opposed camps. According to a NHK public opinion poll, 51.4 per cent of those questioned agreed with the view that one period of modern Japanese history 'was the history of Japan's invasion of neighbouring Asian countries,' while 44.8 per cent also thought that it was 'inevitable' in the given historical context and necessary 'to Japan's survival.' A similar ambiguity was evident in the figure of 45.5 per cent answering positively to the question, 'Did the Pacific war result in the earlier independence of Asian countries from Western colonialism?' On the question of war responsibility, 36.3 per cent saw the ordinary Japanese as 'victims,' more than the number who believed the Japanese were 'aggressors' (29.5 per cent), while 17.6 per cent viewed both the Japanese and Asians as victims of state violence.[43] These responses seem to suggest that the war is (still) viewed with mixed emotions and that Japanese perceptions of the boundaries between aggressors and victims, and subjective responsibility and historical inevitability are very unclear, even though a disjunction between the actions of the Japanese state and the will of the Japanese people is rather uncritically assumed. With the fiftieth anniversary of the end of World War II, the debate in the Japanese media between opinion leaders and intellectuals on the significance of the war and postwar Japanese history became increasingly polarized into two opposing camps, while most of the populace remained ambivalent.

Erosion of social hegemony and the identity crisis

Virtual self and commodified bodies

On a socio-cultural and discursive level, the internal and external shocks of the 1990s broke the widespread state of self-complacency that had plagued the 1980s and seriously discredited the hegemonic values and codes symbolized by the patriarchal corporate economy and its culture. As the decline of the values that had long reigned in postwar Japan proceeded, Japanese society in the 1990s began to manifest some aspects of a civil society, namely pluralization and segmentation, although these were not necessarily accompanied by citizens' freedom or a widespread sense of social responsibility. Some emergent sub-cultural groups – including the young generation described as the *shinjinrui* ('new humankind'), the narcissistic male devotees of virtual media called the *otaku*, and the defiant young girls referred to as the *kogyaru* (little-gals) – openly challenged the hegemonic culture with different values and previously unthinkable behaviours. These sub-cultural groups typically adopted survival strategies incorporating the high-tech media and commercialized images of the self in the construction of their identities. On the other hand, those who could not live with these 'artificially constructed identities' felt left behind, often seeking remedies in the 'recovery' of a lost identity and meaning freed from the threat of the flood of ever increasing meaningless signs and challenges to the hegemonic codes. In short, the split characteristics of modernity which had become manifest in the 1980s – the commercially driven fragmentation of the self and meaning and the reactionary impulse for a recovery of identity and the centralization of meaning – were further intensified in the 1990s.

As the phenomenal development of mass consumer society steamed ahead, popular culture in the 1990s came to play a leading role in shaping the imagination of Japanese youths and adults, ever more closely integrated into their everyday lives. In this context, comic books and animations became more than ever influential forms of media. According to a study by Frederik Schodt, 2.3 billion comic books (*manga*) were produced (1.9 billion purchased) in 1995, with an enormous diversity of target ages, genders, vocations and tastes. The total sales of comic books in the same year amounted to US $6–7 billion, the equivalent of US $50 per person, and constituted about 40 per cent of the total of all book and magazines sales.[44] The frequency of violent and pornographic images in these comics has raised deep concerns among grassroots activists, feminists, educators, and mothers' groups, and in 1991 a nationwide 'movement to banish harmful *manga*' arose, resulting in tougher regulations and some arrests of publishers and retailers.[45] On the whole, however, the vaguely worded Article 175 of the obscenity laws was nothing but an appeal for public consensus, falling far short of regulating the mass circulation of degrading expressions of pornographic and violent images. A subsequent reactionary movement to protect the producers' 'freedom of expression' gained public support from the standpoint that expressions of sex are seen as a form of resistance against the central power of the state, although this is at the expense of subjugating women to violent images.[46]

One of the targeted 'harmful *manga*' was the genre of 'ultra-cute (*chō-kawaii*) girl's *manga* written by and for men,' which emerged towards the end of the 1980s and was designed for teenagers, depicting 'the most provocative stories possible' overtly exploiting the images of 'prepubescent girls as sex objects.'[47] These comic books typically featured 'a girl heroine with large eyes and a body that is both voluptuous and child-like' who was often a tough fighter for justice or, less commonly, a helpless cutie-pie.[48] In either case, the sex appeal of the heroine was front and centre, and such sexualized representations, frequently combined with violent and pornographic imagery, made this genre exemplary of *rorikon manga* (a term derived from the Japanese for 'Lolita complex'). This popular genre of 'sexy little girls' merged in some sense with the long-established discourse of the 'cute girls' of the 1980s, which many young Japanese women had endorsed, but in the general cultural context of the 1990s, it became more exclusively the fantasy object of young males. Referring to this shift in cultural landscape, Sharon Kinsella argued that the popularity of *rorikon manga* 'reflects simultaneously an awareness of the increasing power and centrality of young women in society, and also a reactive desire to see these young women disarmed, infantized and subordinated.'[49] In other words, these sexualized cute-girl figures serve as idealized substitutes for what does not exist, and also as sites of fantasy for those wishing to avoid facing the difficulties and imperfections of the real world and real women. One might even say that the virtual relations between these ideal girl characters and their enthusiastic fans were for some preferred over relations with real women; and indeed, if the high-tech visual technologies continue to advance in sophistication by leaps and bounds fully virtual companionship may not be a too far-fetched, or too distant in reality.

Expanding on developments witnessed in the previous decade, industries related to the computer entertainment business – animations, TV-games and other computer software – are proceeding full-speed ahead in their exploitation of the virtual medium, especially in the youth cultural market. The intersection of the fascination with virtual media and the above described pornographic discourse gave rise to a type of youth known as the *otaku*, literally a polite and distant form of the second person address ('you'). As Schodt writes, in the early 1990s the word *otaku* acquired the connotation of a 'socially inept young male' who maniacally indulges in computer-related hobbies in an anti-social or even criminal manner, particularly after the horrifying Tsutomu Miyazaki incident (1988–9) was publicized, in which the *otaku* youth Miyazaki kidnapped, raped and murdered several pre-teenage girls. The discovery of nearly 6,000 horror and pornographic videos in Miyazaki's personal collection suggested that his motivation was to fulfil an elaborate sexual fantasy exclusively associated with very young girls, as well as his desire to cross the boundary between fantasy and the real world.[50] While their numbers are limited, the phenomenon of the *otaku* is a real social problem that points to the emergence of a new breed of sexually frustrated young males obsessed with the somewhat perverse hobby of seeking refuge in the virtual rather than in the actual world. In Schodt's opinion the *otaku* can

> no longer effectively relate to real world people (especially women) and thus find an escape in pornographic *manga* and animation and masturbatory fantasies, and harbour dangerous sexual proclivities and fetishes; in short, [*otaku* designates] people who might be mentally ill and perhaps even a threat to society.[51]

This masturbatory attitude of confining oneself in a world of one's own creation might be seen as a retreat to the safe haven of fantasy and a narcissistic indulgence, without having to confront living women and thus precluding any potential source of embarrassment. As in Miyazaki's case, it is not surprising that some might come to feel this imaginary world is more real than the world and themselves, and indeed, the sub-cultural category of the *otaku* found its legitimate place in society later in the decade. This is in part related to the global success of the Japanese animation industry, but more significantly because of the rapidly changing social context of the second half of the 1990s, characterized by the ongoing intrusion of the virtual into the everyday. One critic has argued that, the family having lost its bonds of natural affection (the 'virtual family') and society having lost its shared values and morality (the 'virtual society'), everyone in contemporary Japan lives to a degree in an artificial reality; since the inversion of artificial and real images is all too commonplace and the inversion of fantasy and real human relations pioneered by the *otaku* is thus no longer a problem.[52]

Indeed, the 1990s has witnessed the increasing valuation of cultural goods that capitalize on the idea of 'virtuality,' goods that are often more valued than 'real' goods. For example, *tamagochi*, the LED electronic screen 'virtual pets' that demand to be fed and cared for, became the marketing sensation of the decade and annoyed countless school teachers whose classes were constantly interrupted by the beeping sound of their students' hungry virtual companions. Another virtual marketing success of the 1990s is the 'virtual idol,' Date Kyōko, the brainchild of the Hori production company, is one of the best known idol producers in the Japanese pop-music industry. Date Kyōko's virtual music concerts, CDs and videos, and Internet chat-line attracted large numbers of young male fans. In both these phenomena, the fact that the object of one's affection lacks a real or historical referent does not matter; rather, the pleasure of the products stems from the consumption of images one knows full well are virtual. This marketing of virtuality, however, goes beyond the realm of possessing images of desired objects to the repossession of the self. In recent years, school boys and girls have begun collecting a series of miniature stickers of their own photographs, usually taken with friends and inserted into their choice of frame, an enormously popular form of 'play' called *purikura* (a short form of *purinto kurabu*, 'print club').[53] Although some create thick photo albums to show and exchange with others, the core pleasure of this form of play is acting out imagined and possible identities in the 'context' of the framed narrative and possessing a purely imagined self that has little to do with who one actually is.[54] By operationalizing the notion of virtuality, and by allowing the players to act out their virtual identities, *purikura* satisfies its players' narcissistic and fetishistic desire for possessing their virtual selves and the accompanying stories in a visible and materialized form as photographs. Virtual goods like *purikura* are harbingers of the emergence of a form of pleasurable indulgence in a self-referential sign-economy, in which the players are motivated by a sense of nostalgia to 'repossess' pets, idols and above all the self in a virtual form, the real versions of which are beyond one's ability to possess.[55]

Together with the popularization of virtuality, a radical shift in ideal gender types, especially among youths, is a significant feature of the social changes in the 1990s, in which the conventional power relation between the sexes has been seriously challenged. For one thing, the commodification of what used to be considered 'sacred' in Japan – the family and women's sexuality – has in many ways contributed to the liberation of women, who in the 1990s enjoy more options in life. While the working conditions and status of women saw little real improvement, despite the enactment of the equal employment opportunity law, their status was in some measure set back in the 1990s due to the general economic decline and the tightening of the job market. On the level of consciousness and lifestyle, however, there have been significant changes among the younger generations of women who began to challenge long-uncontested gender roles and family relations. For one thing, many women simply began to reject marriage and childbearing, no longer considering the role of wife and mother as an attractive option.[56] For another, as sexuality became increasingly commercialized, the conventional belief in the family and women's bodies as the last remaining bastions of morality, supposedly 'sacred' private realms free from commercial enterprise, have undergone substantial changes. The 'myths of the mother,' that is, the idealized images of motherhood which have long been a staple of the incestuous sexual fantasies of Japanese men (as innumerable novels and films have documented) were, perhaps for the first time in postwar history, seriously shaken. In response to these challenges, some young Japanese men began to modify their ideal images of manhood, and this has been well reflected in the characteristics of the new young male idols and musicians whose selling points have now become sensitivity, gentleness and good looks, attributes in the past largely tied to the female ideal. Another common trait among this new type of young men is ambiguity both in terms of gender and ethnicity, creating a generation of young men who are eager to experiment with 'things feminine' and 'things foreign' as constitutive parts of their identities. Obviously, these trends have not been welcomed by the majority of the older generations of men, who tend to view the younger generation as morally corrupt, and many of whom are seriously concerned about what they see as the loss of masculinity (or the 'feminization of men') and what they perceive as the crisis of sexual identity among the Japanese youth who are unwilling to carry the 'burden' of tradition.

The identity of middle-aged Japanese males, on the other hand, experienced a series of challenges on various fronts throughout the 1990s. Japanese men typically do not occupy the central place in the household and increasingly so in the 1990s, when they came often to be described as 'oversized garbage' (*sodaigomi*) by their families. Moreover, the sputtering engine of a decades-long successful corporate capitalism has also induced a loss of confidence and an identity crisis among white collar Japanese males. From the late 1970s onwards many Japanese workers found emotional satisfaction and a sense of pride in their employment, in hard work, and in an often total devotion to their employers that entailed a significant sacrifice of their personal lives. For this they were rewarded both in social and emotional terms as contributing team players of a successful company and a prosperous nation, and as a result work meant much more than a mere source of income. Based on the paternalistic company–worker relation that included lifetime employment, seniority promotion and a corporate welfare system, Japanese corporations of the 1970s and 1980s managed to operate within a shared illusion of family-like 'corporate culture' which in many senses provided employees with a 'corporate identity.'[57] However, by the early 1990s newspaper reports of *karōshi*, the phenomenon of early death from overwork, started becoming more and more common, especially among the middle-aged, lower-ranked managerial class, brought on by the intensification of the workload and responsibilities that stretched these employees to their physical limits. When by the mid-1990s the business corporations lost interest in maintaining the paternalistic code, they began to embrace new employment policies, favouring younger, multi-skilled, flexible employees and promotion based solely on competence.[58] As these policies began to materialize, the suicide rate of those facing dismissal, or already dismissed, from their companies took a sharp upswing, becoming one of the major social problems of the day. During the course of the 1990s it seems as if middle-aged and older Japanese men typically lost the feeling of being at 'home' with themselves, both in the public's eyes and in the family space.

If young males are boldly experimenting with their identities in crossing the conventional boundaries, young females are doing the same by actively turning themselves into commodified signs. At the intersection of the willingness of young women to commodify their sexuality and the sexual fantasy of Japanese men for young girls, there flourished a wide range of sex businesses targeting young 'ordinary girls.' In close collaboration with the mass media, the Japanese sex industries have since the early 1980s been unrestrainedly exploiting images of 'innocence,' erasing the boundary between professional and non-sexual workers as well as age restrictions. Nationwide, high-school girls have become the most preferred sexual objects, and fetishized images of teenage girls have become ubiquitous in the mass media.[59] The commodified image of young girls has its own designator, the *kogyaru* (little-gals), and a generation of schoolgirls has arisen eager to replicate its signatory images by adorning themselves with loose white knee socks, a very short skirt and brown-dyed hair. In this commodified climate there emerged around 1993 an extraordinary business called *burusera*, sex-shops specializing in teenage-girls' used underwear, which quickly multiplied.[60] About the same time, dating services (*deeto-kurabu*) offering young girls, mostly under eighteen, emerged, and their fast-growing popularity gave birth to a social phenomenon called the 'compensated date' (*enjo kōsai*), a date typically between a teenage girl and a middle-aged man (called by the girl '*papa*'/daddy) that could include sexual relations. 'Compensated dates' became a fashionable way of spending idle time for girls and a popular service for men. The negotiation is made between the parties at widely known 'pick-up' spots where men are prepared to spend between US $200 to $1,000, depending on the type of 'service.'[61] Some European reporters have interpreted the phenomenon as 'a possible future state of our societies,' while a reporter from *Der Spiegel* explained the phenomenon as an indicator of the breakdown of ethics in a country where morality, dependent upon social norms rather than upon religious belief, has been unable to counteract the logic of the market, i.e. profit maximization.[62]

Within this context, the phenomenon of *enjo kōsai*, and especially the combination of defiant young girls (*kogyaru*) and the troubled generation of middle-aged men (*oyaji*) deserves renewed attention. While the behaviour of teenage girls has received much media attention and moral criticism, the role played by the middle-aged male consumers has hardly been noted, and, somewhat predictably, the loudest critics of the commercialization of women's sexuality and the family have been members of the same group who are the premier consumers of the girls' services. The standard accusation raised against this consensual form of exchange has focused on the girls' materialist desire for money to purchase brand-name goods (Chanel suits or Prada bags), while the *oyaji*'s pleasure of possessing and consuming fashionable girls as fetish objects has been much less condemned. However, this exchange has more than a material dimension, insofar as it involves a degree of social fulfilment for both parties, albeit in different ways. For the girls, these non-material needs include the desire for access to the world outside the school yard and the family embrace, and the desire for experiences teaching them things about the 'real world' otherwise not taught, with a tint of rebellion against parents, teachers and society at large.[63] On the part of the *oyaji*, the dates seem to compensate for their low valuation in a sign-economy in which the young and beautiful are valued the most; in this sense, the consumption of girls' services seems to momentarily fulfil what they feel, consciously or not, they themselves are lacking. To the extent that the girls market themselves by becoming pure and empty signs to be filled in by the *oyaji's* ideal, the girls erase the traits of their 'true' personalities to become an anonymous social type, the *kogyaru*, allowing them to momentarily free themselves from their everyday context and the governance of self-consciousness and social morality.[64] By virtue of identifying themselves with the anonymous social type of the *kogyaru*, the girls act out an imagined identity as defiant, attractive sexual icons (and in doing so appear to adopt the role of the cute-girl characters in the *otaku's* favourite comic books), all the while thinking that their 'true selves' remain unaffected. In short, this consensual exchange seems to be a product of a combination of factors characteristic of the 1990s: the flood of information through which the new image-based economy operates, a new sense of self mediated by virtual media and commercial signs, the narcissism and fetishism associated with such a media economy, and the changing landscape of gender power relations.

The romanticism of erasing the self and the emergence of a sublime superego

The popularity and ubiquity of virtual media and sub-cultural phenomena seem to suggest that the Japanese society of the 1990s has become increasingly cognizant of the world's artificiality, the loss of identity, and the changing status of the body. Miyadai Shinji, a popular critic of contemporary cultural events, argues that the commodification and consumption of one's own body has become itself a pleasurable activity and views *enjo kōsai* as the cultural marker of this shift.[65] According to Miyadai, this shift has resulted from the prolonged, intense production and circulation of commodified images that began in the previous decade and which transformed the body onto a new horizon of existence and meaning. Miyadai repeatedly emphasizes that the search for a 'deep self' beneath one's socially and commercially mapped surface is meaningless. Today, he claims, the body is no longer the 'last fortress of the self' but has become rather an 'environment,' a set of given conditions that one can modify in the same manner that one modifies one's habitat, and thus is no more than a vehicle for 'changing one's feelings' about oneself. By abandoning such 'inner depths,' one is accordingly able to feel better about oneself by simply altering, for example, one's body shape or appearance by piercing, dying, or tattooing:

> By modifying one's own body, just by making a hole, one can be free from self-consciousness. In other words, the body is not the last trustworthy foundation of the self, but rather the last controllable environment, the modifiable exterior. That is why there is no problem with the body being consumed by others.[66]

In this new relation of the body to the self, not only is one no longer bothered by injury or violations of the interior self, but bodily inscriptions, which used to be seen as causes for displeasure, can now be seen as the means of affirming the self. In Miyadai's conception, the body as such, supposedly resistant to inscriptional forces from outside, has become virtually non-existent; the pleasure of consuming the self is mediated by others' consumption of it, which in turn is itself consumed by the self. One wonders if the advent of this new feedback loop is indeed pleasurable, and if a change in the structure of our perceptions is taking place that is transforming the displacement of the self into a source of pleasure.

Miyadai's view of the self-body relation is directly linked to his sense of the survival strategies possible in the 1990s, strategies that have been deeply entrenched by the generational legacy of Japanese political culture, and in particular by the evaporation of the popular political ethos of the 1960s. Miyadai and his colleagues were born between the late 1950s and the early 1960s, forming part of the generation coming after the student movements of the late 1960s, the first generation after the climatic changes of the early 1970s, when activism motivated by larger hopes and causes became untenable. Following this collapse, Japanese society witnessed the opening up of a politico-spiritual void followed by a flood of commercial signs that filled out the vacuum. In a discussion with three popular culture commentators, Nakamori Akio claims that the Japan of the 1990s has been experiencing a 'revolution' entirely different from what that term signified in the 1960s, a revolution which has made the very idea of revolution impossible.[67] One of Nakamori's interlocutors, Fujii Yoshiki, recounts with irritation how he came to realize that the world continues to exist despite all his apocalyptic fantasies of a catastrophic end, and how that realization made him think 'the lack of hope itself is a hope,' a strategy for living in an age in which the notion of the end itself has ended.[68] Miyadai, the third interlocutor in this discussion, less desperate or anxious than Fujii, describes as his ultimate 'romanticism' his desire to erase his self, in order to enlarge his 'function' to the maximum:

> I want to see what will happen when I pursue [the 'revolution'] to its ultimate forward limit. Why? Because my memory of past occasions when I abandoned one set of illusions only to jump onto another still pains me. If I can pursue this [erasure of the self] to its ultimate limit, perhaps I can succeed in shrinking my very being. I think this desire of mine is generational – it amounts to a form of self-destruction. When

I concentrate on making myself into a function, I can minimize my 'self' while maximizing my function. This is where my romanticism lies. In other words, I want to erase myself.[69]

According to Miyadai, we ought to abandon the desire to discover meaning and should instead learn how to enjoy momentary pleasures with the same lightness of being that he sees animating those young girls who painlessly sell their bodies. Miyadai's well-publicized slogan, '*owarinaki nichijō o ikiro*' ('be prepared to live an endless routine life'), is designed to fashion what he calls '*seikimatsu no sahō*' ('etiquette for the end of the century'), in which the meaning of life is nothing more than a technique of living, and in which the self's relation to consciousness – Miyadai's 'function' – is merely that of a decaying body which will, regardless of the content of life, inevitably come to an end.[70]

In such a climate of ever potent commercial and technological assaults upon the empirical self, Japan in the 1990s appears to be plagued by the loss of an end, death or the absolute, the loss of a structuring frame for cognition and a system of meaning authorized by a sense of the finite. In this terminal condition, Miyadai's 'romanticism' is little more than a passive, aestheticized form of 'resistance' that seeks to survive by adjusting its mode of thinking, modifying the structure of the senses, and ultimately by erasing the self altogether. In this sense, his elaborate self-consuming technique is a form of slow suicide, and moreover, despite his intentions, one that annulling depth, meaning, and identity, could paradoxically open up a space for an equally intensified phantasmatic desire for catharsis. Indeed, one incident in the second half of the decade seems to exemplify a reification of this vague sense of anxiety, resentment and the inarticulate floating 'excess' permeating society, seeking a war of revenge for the burden of the 'unbearable lightness of being'. In June 1997, a 14-year-old schoolboy from an ordinary middle-class family was arrested for a series of attempted murders of young children, two of which were successful, deeply shocking the entire nation. The murders were planned in advance, cruelly, calmly and effectively executed, and the whole process and its effects were carefully observed and recorded in detail in the murderer's diary. The detached and 'artistically' mutilated head of one 12-year-old victim was left in front of the school gate for display, and stuck in the victim's mouth was an agitated letter from the killer declaring that he was starting a 'game' with the 'foolish police' as a 'revenge against the school system' that made him a 'transparent being'.[71] Later, in his response to the police/court examiner, the 14-year-old offender explained his motivation for the murder, corroborated by his diary, as a 'sacred experiment to test the fragility of humanity' in the name of the god of his creation, called *Bamoidooki*.[72] The boy revealed his fascination with killing and his pleasure in doing it, escalating from insects and small animals like birds and cats to eventually humans.

Public shock stemmed as much from the fact that the 14-year-old had successfully fooled what he called the 'adult world,' i.e. the police, the mass media and the school system, as from the sensational murders themselves. Indeed, the 'game' was almost won by the young offender, whose behaviour deeply puzzled and frustrated many members of Japanese society since they were unable to determine a 'true cause' for the crimes. Failing to comprehend his motives, most of the subsequent discussions focused on remedies for such anti-social behaviour, such as the control of horror videos and animations, educational reform and amendments to the youth offender laws, tending to treat the crime as an isolated incident perpetrated by an 'abnormal' boy, although some commentators probed into deeper problems in society as a whole. This murder without a 'true cause' highlights some of the salient hardships faced by contemporary Japanese youths that, unlike others, the murderer had failed to come to terms with in a socially acceptable manner: namely, the difficulties of constituting the self and workable linkages between the self and the world, the poverty of the immediate experience of the living body, and the increasing dominance of an enlarged self-consciousness that no longer has a clear sense of the borders between inside and outside.

It was the poetic eloquence and maturity of the writing in this 14-year-old's diary that impressed many professional writers and further troubled educators, while such positive evaluations outraged many as amoral. In the prose-poem written after his third and fourth attacks entitled 'a thirteen-year sentence,' presumably referring to his life since birth, the boy expressed his feeling of being imprisoned in a space where he was subordinated to the control of a higher-being:

> In any world . . . the same thing repeats itself.
> What cannot be stopped cannot be stopped, and what cannot be
>   killed cannot be killed.
> In some cases, it can be living inside oneself . . .
> The 'Monster.'
> In the assumed heaven of the 'brain universe,'
> Inside an isolated inner cell, the cell of an infinite darkness and
>   depth, filled with a rotting odour . . .
> Standing amongst the spirits of the dead and staring at the
>   void,
> 'What' was captured there in the eyes of the monster?
> I cannot even imagine.
>
> It tells me from within my heart of attacks from the outside,
>   stirring a sense of crisis in me.
> It controls me as a skilled puppeteer makes its puppet dance to a
>   musical tune.
> It makes me feel the 'madness of an absolute degree zero,'

> as if what used to have been myself is now turned into the Evil.
> I can barely manage to oppose, but can never resist it.
> And I am being cornered into the 'inside myself' . . .
>
> Those who fight against the Monster must be careful not to become in that process monsters themselves.
> When you gaze into an abyss, the abyss is also gazing at you.
> 'Mid-way in my travel into my life,
> I happened to notice I was lost in a deep dark forest,
> losing sight of the path leading straight forward.'[73]

As the critic Ōsawa Masachi has noted, one can read here an acute sense of doubt about the self-evident fact of life, and the less evident fact of death, a doubt which has clearly and deeply troubled and fascinated the boy.[74] This state of anxiety perhaps represents a split between consciousness and an empirical selfhood, a state in which the former attempts to dominate the latter, often beyond the subject's control. This monstrous consciousness emerges from the void of human existence and a vision of the abyss that holds an empty subject enraptured, an empty subject whose consciousness is fixed to the enigma of the human condition and who desperately seeks to 'resolve' it.

It might be claimed, to borrow from Ōsawa's insight, that what the 14-year-old attempted was to envisage the sacred world of the 'Real' supposedly existing beyond the screen of meaning, by stripping the humanly ascribed meaning from the assumed world of objects.[75] Pursuing this line of thought, we might surmise that the offender's anxiety about the artificiality of the world became so compelling, and the urge to destroy it in order to reveal the 'Real' pushed him so hard that he decided to carry out his 'sacred experiment' to disclose the truth of what most puzzled him: the 'materiality' of the body and its relation to the human subject. By razing this illusory system of mediation and splitting meaning from objects, the boy seems to have attempted to view the world from a point of view outside the realm of human constructions, a world of sheer 'material,' seen from the eyes of the 'monster.' Or rather, obsessed with the enigma of the human condition, perhaps he was already living in such an otherwise-world, a subject enraptured by an internal void and desperately driven by a monstrous consciousness demanding a 'solution' to the enigma. In this sense, the troubled ontological terrain he inhabited constituted the reverse of what his fearful desires expressed; namely, a world of an endless spatial expanse filled with an inconsequential, floating tide of meaningless phenomena out of which the monstrous consciousness cultivated in him a desire for the abyss.

Whether the boy's experience as I have interpreted it is in some sense symptomatic of the more widespread feeling of malaise, is impossible to tell. However, from the other evidence presented we can infer that the deepest problem of the Japan of the 1990s may lie in the loss of an end, death or the absolute, and the resultant loss of a structuring frame for human cognition and the system of meaning authorized by a sense of the finite. Without such a notion of the finite, the world loses its shape, life loses its meaning, and the subject loses its identity, and all that appears to remain is a seemingly omnipotent, all encompassing consciousness. In such a shapeless, meaningless, identity-less existence, the material basis of consciousness – things empirical, including the human body – has to all appearances been jeopardized, and the subject is thus haunted by the return of an imaginary version of the 'material' it seeks to supersede. Something similar to the haunting vision of the world held by the 14-year-old murderer was also advanced in a more ambivalent and inconsistent way by the religious cult *Aum Shinrikyō* which rushed headlong towards self-destruction, as if programmed by an intense and cathartic desire for apocalypse. While these violent expressions of a crisis-laden subjectivity seemingly constitute the polar opposite of Miyadai's 'romanticism of self erasure,' they also represent another survival technique for living one's life in an all but meaningless world.

Two responses to the crisis : the *Aum Shinrikyō* cult and historical revisionism

1995: The Great Hanshin earthquake and the Aum Shinrikyō *cult*

Foreshadowed by a series of tremors that swept over the country in the early 1990s, the Great Hanshin earthquake of January 1995 laid waste to the city of Kobe, killing over 6,000 people, leaving over 300,000 homeless, and causing damage worth 10 to 20 trillion yen.[76] The earthquake registered 7.2 on the Richter scale, hitting a city considered a no-risk zone with a surprise slip-fault type of quake (characterized by a vertical shock and more destructive than the tectonic type of earthquake with its horizontal shock), causing major damage to the city's basic infrastructure.[77] Major transportation systems, including the bullet train (Sanyō *shinkansen*), the underground railway, and the Hanshin expressway were disabled, and communications and the water supply were destroyed, cutting victims off from badly needed relief supplies. The newly-developed bay-front area, land utilized for the 1981 'Portopia Expo,' was also devastated, and the two recently built manmade islands of Port and Rokko were turned into a mush of rubble sinking into the sea.[78] The collapse of the bay-front area was particularly shocking for the people of Kobe since, with its glittering futuristic buildings and a development plan supported by nearly all segments of the city, it had symbolized the city's economic success.[79] This destruction of the city's symbol of prosperity shattered shared dreams, and the shock spread nationwide, making many acutely aware of the vulnerability of the Japanese urban space. Televised images of the worst hit part of the city, depicting the population reduced to bare subsistence or less, stories of the loss of families and friends, as well as homes and other lifetime assets, cast a shadow of doubt upon the glamorous images of hyper-modern technological life. Partly because of timing, 1995 being the 50th anniversary of the end of the war and the nuclear atrocities, many commentators suggested the devastation recalled the images of Hiroshima and Nagasaki following the atomic bombings.[80]

In addition to the natural causes, there were several human factors that made the disaster substantially worse. The slow and ineffective government response to the quake made the lack of a systematic plan and emergency preparations, at all levels of government, all too evident. The city's major hospital, the emergency facilities of the prefectural police, and the city heliport were all located on the submerged island, and there was no alternative water supply line.[81] In addition, the disaster was exacerbated by Japanese construction companies' long standing neglect of construction safety-standards. The Ministry of Construction, in cahoots with the companies, had turned a blind eye to these violations and never seriously acted on warnings issued by private institutions and civilians calling for a reassessment of the city's safety standards.[82] Moreover, the majority of foreign emergency relief was turned down by the federal government in its desire to prioritize 'national autonomy,' to the disadvantage of the victims: the use of a US aircraft carrier as a refugee camp was rejected, and offers of help from foreign doctors were declined because they lacked the necessary registration papers. Stepping in where and when the government would not, civilians and even organized crime groups (*yakuza*) supplied daily necessities to victims in the city of Nishinomiya, the worst hit and poorest area, mostly inhabited by working-class Japanese, Koreans and Chinese, illegal foreign workers and Japanese outcasts (*burakumin*). The image of the catastrophe, naturally caused and humanly enlarged, symbolized for many the dark side of technologically advanced urban life as well as a loss of trust in the government resulting from a feeling that the authorities were more interested in controlling people than in saving their lives.

Before the country had time to get over the shock of the earthquake and its aftermath, another horrifying incident occurred. In March 1995, a series of indiscriminate attacks in the Tokyo subway system involving the deadly chemical agent sarin killed and injured more than 5,000 people. When the motivations of the perpetrator of the attacks, the religious cult group *Aum Shinrikyō* (Supreme Truth of *Aum*, established 1984), were revealed as the initiation of what the cult called 'Armageddon,' the initial shock of the attempted mass murder was quickly replaced by a deep chill, shattering the long-held myth of Japanese internal security. According to the cult's apocalyptic narrative, the attack was the opening salvo in the cult's attempt to take control of Tokyo, the first phase of its self-declared rescue 'mission' to purify world-wide spiritual decay and to inaugurate a new era under the leadership of a cadre of 'psychically-gifted' human beings. The cult's guru taught that the outbreak of Armageddon would come between 1999 and 2003, and would involve the entire world in a nuclear war, out of which only a handful of 'enlightened ones,' the disciples of *Aum*, would survive as leaders of a new human race endowed with great psychic powers. The stark contrast between the seriousness of the crimes and the banality, or even indifferent playfulness, of their intent in this sci-fi animation-like scenario was particularly striking.[83] Moreover, the cult's leaders were among the nation's brightest minds, with science degrees from high-profile universities, which made many wonder how and why society had failed these elite-to-be. With its talented manpower, the once small religious cult had organized itself, amassed the human, financial and material resources necessary for its designs, and carried out a horrifying campaign of terror with a breezy lightheartedness. Japanese society was deeply chilled and fascinated by the enigma of why and how these events had come to be, and a torrent of news reports and discussions saturated the mass media during the following days and nights. The sensational coverage lasted for several months after the event, and the cult's fantastic vision of apocalypse was eagerly if morbidly consumed by many.

This sense of fictiveness was one of the central elements of the *Aum* ideology. The cult made full use of images, symbols and narratives borrowed from popular religions, animations, comic books and TV games, combining them into a series of inspiring and appealing image-narratives of its own that aided the group in attracting to its ranks a surprising number of students and young adults between the ages of 20 and 35 years old. The 'doctrine' of the cult was based on a New Age blend of Tibetan Buddhism, yoga, and occult mysticism, combined with modern medicine, a Hindu pantheon of gods, and notions of Christian apocalypse: in short, an eclectic mishmash of religious icons and spiritual ideas.[84] The cult's apocalyptic narrative owes much of its imagery to popular animation stories and comic books such as 'Space Battleship Yamato,' 'The Genma War,' and the 'Akira' stories that became immensely popular in the late 1970s and early 1980s. 'Space Battleship Yamato' (*'Uchusenkan Yamato'*), for example, recounts how the crew of the Yamato, whose names and faces are Japanese, attempt the heroic rescue mission of saving mankind from certain extinction from a race of aliens, whose names and faces are Western.[85] Building on these popular narratives and images, *Aum* published comic-books of its own, recounting, for example, how Asahara Shoko, the cult's leader, achieved enlightenment, how individual followers came to join *Aum* and live happily ever after, all graphically illustrated by images of Armageddon and rescue missions. One ex-*Aum* follower has been reported as saying that *Aum* was 'the last rescue vessel on which the fate of the earth depended,' as if *Aum* followers were the doubles of the animation characters.[86] It has also been suggested that the organizing idea behind the 'cult-kingdom' stemmed from a popular video game. The promotion system within the cult, for example, in which one received a holy name and gained status by means of donations and training until eventually becoming an enlightened soldier eligible to take part in the 'salvation mission,' is nearly identical to the pattern of role playing games like 'Dungeons and Dragons.'[87] The variations of choice and procedures of play in these games also mirror in many ways contemporary Japanese society, in which life is codified and reduced to a number of predetermined patterns from which members choose among the given range of educational institutions and corporate employers. In short, the occult fantasy of this new religion, the spiritual fulfilment it promised, the dramatic images and appealing animated characters of its narratives, and the working principles of video games were all fused together to offer the students the pseudo-experience of living in a fantasy world in which enlightenment is the prize for following a strict religious teaching of overcoming one's desire.

Not only was the cult creative in its borrowings from popular culture and virtual media, it also had a solid material and institutional foundation backing it up, including numerous sources of income, and a well thought out systemic structure. The cult's financial wheels were greased by the minimum donation of $700 demanded of students seeking to join the commune (*shukke*), and by the various cult-run ordinary businesses outside the compound, including computer stores and restaurants.[88] By taking advantage of the followers' naive passion for the psychic powers the cult promised, 'religious goods' were rented and sold to students at enormous prices. A popular electrode-laden 'head-gear,' supposedly capable of enhancing one's ability to learn by synchronizing one's brain waves with those of the guru, was rented out for $7,000 a month, or sold for ten times that price.[89] The guru's body parts also were sold as fetishized religious commodities: clippings of the guru's beard cost $375 per half-inch and his used bath water, called the 'Miracle Pond,' cost about $800 a quart.[90] Life inside the cult was hierarchically differentiated according to one's religious rank. The inner core of the group was constituted by the guru and his 'Ministries'; these latter were staffed by some of the brightest science and technology graduates from the nation's highest ranking universities, and it was their task to manage the financial, military, religious and political arms of the cult. The overwhelming majority of cult members were largely oblivious of this inner core and endured a strictly regimented religious life with less than modest food, little sleep and poor sanitary conditions. Within the cult compound, religious 'shrines' and the living quarters of the students coexisted side-by-side with science laboratories and 'disciplining' wards for delinquent members. Disciples who attempted to run away and/or leak information to the media about the cult's doings were kidnapped and tortured in various horrifying ways including being subject to technological experiments and the disposal of their bodies in the cult's industrial microwave oven. Using the various legal and financial privileges granted to religious organizations under Japanese law as a protective shield, *Aum*'s underground laboratories developed some of most deadly chemical and biological weapons known to man, including sarin (invented by the Nazis), VX (more deadly per volume and more stable than sarin), mustard gas, and Q-fever (a highly contagious form of typhus), as well as stock-piling Soviet-made military helicopters and AK-47 assault rifles, and conducting research into other weapons of mass destruction such as lasers and nuclear bombs.[91]

The role science played in the cult goes far beyond the practical uses of technology: its core beliefs were constituted around a hybrid of scientific rationality and occult religion. As one critic argued, occultism shares with science the rational desire to explain every facet of human existence by means of cause and effect, but differs from science in its willingness to go beyond the limits that science deems verifiable into the realm of the imaginary.[92] In other words, running through the cult elite's cool indifference to human experimentation and its students' obsessive attempts to overcome earthly desire by means of daily religious exercises was a kind of hyper-rationality, an intense desire to transform the imperfect state of the self into a higher, ideal mould. From this ideal transcendental perspective, things empirical – human bodies, emotions and pains – were seen as objects subject to legitimate control by the higher truth, and *Aum*'s transcendental rationalism was symbolically represented by the cult's omnipotent superego, the guru's super-natural power, or the truth of *Aum*. This Spiritual rationalism was a dynamic factor of the cult discourse, a transcendental gaze that functioned as the enabling vehicle bringing *Aum*'s fantastic vision of apocalypse to fruition. From this perspective, the subject/disciple was considered a mere instrument for the self-fulfilling project of realizing *Aum*'s 'sacred mission' as prescribed in its apocalyptic prophecies, in which history was considered to be a process that revealed a series of doomsday predictions: for example, 'the sinking of Japan' in 1996, the outbreak of nuclear war between 1999 and 2003, catastrophes which the dissemination of *Aum*'s teachings, producing more 'awakened ones,' would supposedly remedy. The transcendental gaze of *Aum* matured in tandem with the cult's development of the weapons technology necessary to the realization of the cult's vision. Naturally, however, its obsession with Armageddon and increasingly involuted discourse made the cult a victim of its own paranoia, and hindered it from making any objective and reasoned judgements about events in the world beyond the confines of the *Aum* compound. For example, according to the official cult line, the Great Hanshin earthquake of January 1995 was caused by an 'electromagnetic power or some other device infusing energy into the ground,' a kind of 'earthquake machine' the cult believed was operated by the US military.[93] The guru urged the Japanese to take up arms in a war of 'Armageddon' against both the US and the Japanese states, a war that had already begun.

Enslaved by its own fears and the rapid eclipse of any sense of the outside world, *Aum Shinrikyō* at this point had no other path to follow than that of hurtling towards its imagined catastrophe.

If the cult's idealization of occult superhuman power, its war narrative, and its systemic principles represent the militaristic side of the cult, the gentler, salvational side could be seen in its retreat into a spiritual life subordinated to the guru's authority. Typically, the students who joined *Aum*, especially the female ones, were later to explain their motivations for joining the cult in terms of satisfying an emotional lack, and of giving themselves a second chance to 'mature' in a protected space away from the 'real world' in which they felt they had failed. Also common among *Aum* students was the attraction of living a communal life with those who shared the same beliefs, often as a substitution for their broken family life. One 27-year-old female ex-student, who consistently won top grades in school, later described her state of being during her time with the cult as though she were 'floating 10 cm above the ground.'[94] Diagnosing her flirtation with the cult, she claimed:

> [*Aum* was] where I could train myself in a protected space, expressing and understanding myself as I am, and creating relations with others. It was a place I could develop my premature self. In *Aum* I did what I could not do in my family . . . Just as I entered *Aum* by necessity, so too *Aum* was born by necessity.[95]

By virtue of offering the vision of a safe 'home,' *Aum* presented itself as a refuge for those lost souls who had escaped from the corrupt, malicious, and alienating world outside. Elsewhere the same student remarked:

> I sometimes feel at a loss, not knowing what to do with my feelings of anxiety and emptiness, something that nobody could possibly understand when I try to explain it; something even I do not understand the reason for. *Aum* accepted me as I was. There was nowhere else other than *Aum* that would have accepted me, I thought.[96]

This young woman's yearning for a graspable link to life was converted into religious submission, channelled into the inward-looking daily task of attaining enlightenment. In giving oneself over to this inner world of 'love' and 'purity,' by submitting to the higher virtue of the cult, one felt freed from the burden of dealing with the brutal world outside, the world where one had to endure the pain of conflict with others, failure, anger and bitterness. Joining the narcissistically enclosed cult-world was, then, something like a retreat back to the 'mother's womb,' to a place where one would remain forever pure and innocent, freed from any sense of lack, suffering or the responsibilities of the adult world. In short, successfully absorbing its followers' inarticulate desires, *Aum* gave them expression by presenting itself as a refuge to return 'home' to, while at the same time providing them with a sense that they had a 'self' capable of returning to that home.[97]

In addition to offering its followers the promise of internal peace by effacing the self, *Aum* also offered them a glimpse of a vision of an alternative, higher self, the supposedly higher being within, attainable by means of violently denying the world of others and by transcending one's earthly self through the technologically mediated techniques of occult spiritualism. The conservative critic Nishio Kanji has argued that the *Aum* phenomenon manifest a series of closely linked features symptomatic of contemporary Japanese social unease: deepening nihilism, weakening identity, and a growing ambiguity in values, morality and meaning, a combination of factors often experienced as an acute sense of 'boredom,' but which, says Nishio, is really caused by an excess of 'freedom.'[98] This 'boredom,' he argues, is not situational but existential, rooted in the modern condition, and, once experienced, is utterly unbearable: 'haunting freedom' is a function of 'the weakening of the binding power of the discourse that mediates the historical world and makes sense of it for its subjects.'[99] According to Nishio, this existential anxiety ultimately stems from what he calls the loss of a place 'to hide the subjectivity' society once enjoyed; hence, he concludes, 'once something threatening happens, people are unable to contain themselves and feel compelled to reveal everything without limit.'[100] Generally speaking, if one attempts to affirm a sense of self in such a climate of intense nihilism, there are two principle routes open to one: voluntarily confining oneself in an artificially enclosed imaginary space (what I called the feminine side of *Aum*, a flight from society also seen in the *otaku* phenomenon), and/or waging war against the outside world until such time as one runs smack up against an invisible wall that knocks one down (i.e. Armageddon, the masculine side of *Aum*), a wall that thereby confirms the limits of the self, the boundary between one's self and the outside, and the fact that the body is alive because it is in pain.[101] In a society where one's anguished screams go unheard, unjudged or unpunished, perhaps these are the only alternatives, either to confirm one's identity by submitting to a fantasy or by wildly violating others. Nishio argues that contemporary life in Japan, and particularly for its young people, lacks a defining frame in which identity might be healthily constructed, and is so awash in infinite freedoms, ambiguities, and a lack of moral guidelines that these young people are haunted by the desire to fill their lives with meaning. He concludes that many of the *Aum* followers' sense of self-identity was on the verge of collapse, and that *Aum* merely 'rescued' them from their immanent self-destruction by having them submit their egos to the omnipotent superego represented by the guru.

In short, the *Aum* incident mirrors the immanent problems of contemporary Japan: a fragmented, disembodied, and claustrophobic subjectivity, whose desperate attempts to recover a lost integrity have reached a point of violent explosion. In the eyes of its followers, *Aum Shinrikyō* promised two things contemporary Japanese society could not: a collective imaginary where life was filled with meaning, and a vision of an ideal worth living, and indeed, dying for. In a society where the ever intensifying penetration of the structuring forces of technology and rationalism into the remotest corners of life has jeopardized the subject's access to the empirical realm of life outside consciousness, the subject is left, in Nishio's terms, with no 'place to hide.' In such a situation, and this may be a constant among the various cults populating the developed world, the subject's sense of connection to his or her own body and the 'real'/historical world is increasingly jeopardized, while at the same time the desire to regain the lost sense of the world and the self is exponentially magnified. The *Aum* incident revealed a dimension of contemporary Japanese society where a substantial number of 'subjectivity-stressed subjects' are willing to dissolve their selfhood in the supreme superego of the guru or leader, a phenomenon also seemingly at work in cults in other parts of the world. In the Japan of the late 1990s, the spectre of an inarticulate, free-floating desire for identity seeking a concrete foundation upon which to fix ideal meaning appears to be intensely present. Put differently, modern Japan suffers from a seriously troubled state of intersubjective meaning in which the 'superstructure' is no longer capable of bonding the Japanese subject to a vision of collective unity. By promising its followers an identity and goals and an appealing collective imaginary where life was filled with meaning, the cult was able to establish a sub-nation within Japanese society. The cult 'saved' its followers from the evil pain of 'haunting freedom' by only subjugating them to another malignancy, namely, the hybrid fantasy of occult science and technological power according to which every detail of empirical life would be recreated in the mould of *Aum*'s own self-terminating, destructive discourse. Despite its counter-hegemonic critique of the 'hyper-modern' aspects of contemporary Japanese society, however, *Aum*'s reactionary revolt could not have constituted itself without resorting to making instrumental use of the structuring forces and pragmatic benefits of the scientific rationalism against which it reacted; and the violence inherent in this rationalism took the worst form of expression possible: a large-scale terrorist attack, guided by a super-ego made absolute, upon civilian society.

Historical revisionism and the advent of 'new nationalism'

If the *Aum Shinrikyō* phenomenon was a youthful and explosive response to the deep-rooted crisis of the Japanese subject and society in the 1990s, a less dramatic response could be seen in various challenges to the core attributes of modern knowledge, the universal and progressive view of history, the centrality of reason and objectivity, and the notion that the rights of the rational and autonomous individual subject superseded those of the collective (national) subject. These challenges to modern enlightenment ideas have been particularly apparent in the historical revisionism claiming that the dominant view of the war and postwar Japanese history is false and 'masochistic.' In this section, I will examine two of the most influential revisionist arguments presented by Fujioka Nobukatsu and Katō Norihiro, briefly discussing and analysing their consequences. In his more complex and sophisticated argument, Katō effectively challenges the grounds of postwar Japanese liberalism by establishing a linkage between the nation, memory and the subject in such a way as to allow the constitution of a historically grounded Japanese subject. Despite their focus on national questions, however, these revisionist arguments were, I think, fundamentally responses to the perceived problems of Japanese society in the 1990s, albeit this link is either understated or unstated. What revisionists seek in the knowledge they create is, consciously or not, the reconstitution of a national community in order to 'repair' the diffusion of the intersubjective meaning of the Japanese nation, a repair that would, they believe, restore the damaged link between the subject and society as a whole. In this sense, despite the very different expressions they have taken, the revisionists are motivated and inspired by the same problematic that plagued those who saw *Aum* as the answer. Noteworthy here is a not so noticeable link between the emergence and popularity of revisionist ideas and the breakdown of politico-economic structures in the current stage of capitalism, a breakdown, affecting socio-cultural conditions and the state of subjectivity, that makes revisionist ideas appealing to some individuals.

Building upon the conservative politicians' reactionary responses to US power politics in the Persian Gulf war, a systematic campaign to disseminate the historical revisionist point of view emerged in 1996, led by a group of academics and opinion leaders. The most visible of these was the Liberal View of History Group (*jiyū-shugi shikan kenkyū-kai*) – a puzzling name given its aims of challenging postwar Japanese liberal internationalism – established by Fujioka Nobukatsu, a Tokyo university professor of Education, together with Nishio Kanji, a professor of German philosophy and history, and Hata Ikuhiko, a military historian.[102] The group strongly objected to the government's apologies for Japanese war atrocities in Asia and the compensation of ex-'comfort women,' contesting what they described as the 'excessively negative view of [our] own history' in school textbooks. The same members also formed the Japanese Institute for Orthodox History Education early in 1997, with the specific aim of educating the younger generation in a more 'affirmative view' of the Japanese state and Japanese history, a view they believed would help students recover from their negative habits of 'self-flagellation' (*jigayku*) and 'Japan-hating.'[103] Like some *nihonjinron* scholars in previous decades, Fujioka argued that the currently dominant view of history in Japan is a product of the Tokyo War Crimes Trials and represents the victor's perspective imposed upon the Japanese by the postwar democratic institutions controlled by the US occupation forces.[104] Fujioka and his colleagues call for a recovery of Japanese 'national pride,' without which, they believe, Japan as a nation is not likely to be 'respected in the world,' nor able to compete against other nations in the future. This revisionist mission is basically motivated by resentment of Japan's low geo-political profile and a sense of injustice about the harsh criticisms that the Japanese state has been exposed to on all fronts, not only from 'Asia' and 'the West' but also from its own people.[105]

The revisionists' desire for self-affirmation and their calls for a Japan-centred view of history is narcissistic, less than rational, and unjustifiably focuses on the opposition of two historical perspectives represented by the US and Japan ('the Tokyo Trials view of history' and 'Japan's own view of history'). Particularly noteworthy here is that Asia has no place in this thinking, and the voices of Asians, and Asian women in particular, are effaced from the narrative. For example, Japanese soldiers who maltreated Dutch women in internment camps during the war were charged with B and C class criminal offences by the Tokyo War Crimes Trials, while those Japanese soldiers who did the same to Asian women, including Japanese women, were not charged.[106] In addition, the continued US (self-)exemption from moral responsibility in the dropping of the nuclear bombs on Hiroshima and Nagasaki – seen today by a significant community of mostly non-US historians as an unnecessary and excessive means of 'persuading' Japan to end the war – clearly compromises US adherence to codes of international human rights. In this conjunction, the aggressive displays of US national pride during the fiftieth anniversary of the end of World War II celebrations, and in particular the controversial Smithsonian exhibition of the nuclear bomber the Enola Gay, inflamed Japanese public opinion.[107] While these basic components of the revisionist argument are not new and have been employed by conventional nationalists for decades, their resurgence in the 1990s, however, could make a critical difference in light of the increasingly opaque international order and doubts over the future status of Japan's relations to the US and Asia. Contradictions surrounding the moral foundation of international law, supposedly universal and non-partisan, surfaced especially with the advent of the Persian Gulf War, in which the US-led multilateral forces bombed Iraq in the name of the defence of the sovereign right of Kuwait, while the unstated economic and political goals were all too obvious. In all this, Fujioka and his supporters made the most of Japanese resentments of US hegemonic power, demonstrating wherever possible how the US continues to humiliate the Japanese.

Up to this point, Fujioka and his colleagues' revisionism was rather similar to the conventional nationalism of previous decades. Their motivations, however, were not quite the same since the concerns of most of the older revisionists, like Ueyama Shumpei, were solely derived from events in the realm of international politics. In contrast to this, Fujioka *et al.*'s revisionism should be seen along the lines of Hayashi Fusao and Etō Jun's resentment-driven reconstitution of a historical narrative allowing for the creation of an alternative image of Japanese identity. In addition, the fact that the new revisionists have targeted the younger generation rather than educated adults is perhaps a reflection of their deep concerns with the future of a Japan seemingly on the verge of collapse. Referring to the *Aum* incident, Nishio Kanji, a founding member of the revisionist group, argues that the only way to remedy the misdirection he sees as prevalent among Japanese youth, the loss of meaning and shared values in society that plagues them, is for the state to reestablish its national authority.[108] Much like Etō Jun in his *Seijuku to Sōshitsu* (1967), Nishio and his compatriots collapse moral and emotional appeals into often distorted arguments characterized by a selective use of self-confirming evidence. These revisionists' concerns are also shared by conservative politicians and intellectuals often annoyed by the current socio-cultural state of Japan, particularly its youth culture, in which scant deference to conventional values is paid and Western-style fashions and behaviour are omnipresent. Opening his scholarly volume, *The Ideology of Contemporary Japan* (1998), with a fifty-page diagnosis of the 1997 Kobe murder incident discussed above, Saeki Keishi, a Kyoto University professor of Social Thought, calls for the recovery of national authority as a remedy for the troubled state of a Japanese society that has lost, he claims, the minimum moral code of 'thou shall not kill.'[109] Like Fujioka and others, Saeki ultimately seeks to reestablish a 'lost' linkage between the national subject and the individual and to restore a morality that is, albeit not always consciously, formulated in terms of reinforcing 'Japan' as a nation-state.

Nishio's and Saeki's arguments have encouraged some to argue that the motivation behind contemporary historical revisionism stems from a perceived threat to Japanese national and masculine identity caused by the weakening of the conventional gender and generational roles and the rifts in ethnic segregation (at least on a superficial level) caused by the increase of migrant labour. This sense of threat and the reactionary impulse to renovate the social order are articulated in terms of a national and paternal authority that discloses the location of the subject in revisionist discourse. Arguing along these lines, the social critic Saitō Minako contends that the Liberal View of History group is little more than a 'masturbatory historicism of middle-aged men' (*oyaji ibu shikan*) designed to massage the egos of the fatigued *oyaji* generations.[110] Moreover, in their efforts to recreate a hegemonic national identity, Kang Sang-jung, a Korean–Japanese intellectual, argues that Fujioka and his colleagues' revisionist ideas have fostered an inclination for an enclosed, monological and internally consistent discursive space that singularizes plural identities and histories and eliminates the heterogeneous space of dialogue.[111] We may, accordingly, see historical revisionist *kenbei* (US-hating) sentiments as at least in part derived from the resentment typically felt by conservative Japanese men who seek to project domestically generated rancor onto the images of things foreign (largely American) as 'external' obstacles to the self-affirmation of their identities. At the same time, however, the true cause of anti-American resentments which have made historical revisionism so popular in the 1990s must be sought, I believe, and beyond such projections onto a surrogate enemy, in the merger of two distinctly derived but simultaneously emergent resentments.

While Fujioka *et al.* have attempted to transpose their resentment by employing the same categories and conceptual frame used by the conventional nationalists and revisionists, thus limiting their appeal to those who have already adopted a nationalist bent, the 'revisionism' of Katō Norihiro, on the other hand, creatively formulated, less politically biased and much more emotionally appealing, has been rather more successful in garnering a broader audience. Katō, a writer schooled in the Leftist student movements of the 1960s, advanced a more ambiguous argument than any of the other revisionists in his highly popular and controversial 1995 work 'Haisengo ron' ('Japan After Defeat'). The book version of this article, published in 1997 under the same title, and accompanied by two other articles, attracted enormous attention, receiving the highest number of votes for 'the year's best book,' as well as the second highest number for 'the year's worst book' at the annual unofficial rating of the year's books.[112] Katō begins by observing two sharply polarized camps dividing postwar Japanese intellectual discourse: those who have tried to reform Article Nine of the Constitution in conformity with the *de facto* power practices of international politics ('nationalists'), and those who insist on the transformation of political practices to conform with Article Nine of the Constitution ('liberals').[113] Borrowing a distinction from the psychoanalyst Kishida Shu, Katō describes these divisions as the manifestations of a schizophrenic split in postwar Japanese identity, into a Dr. Jekyll and a Mr. Hyde, so-to-speak.[114] Katō argues that what is missing on both sides of this divide is an acknowledgement of what he calls the 'warp' deeply embedded in postwar Japanese discursive space stemming from the way the postwar Constitution was 'received' by the Japanese. Katō took issue with the above mentioned 1991 anti-war statement published in the *New York Times*, a statement grounded in the Constitution's renunciation of war. Condemning the statement as dismissive of various problems embedded in modern Japanese history, Katō objected to its highly rhetorical depiction of the Constitution's humanistic ideals as being the result of the efforts of the Japanese themselves. For Katō, this is an erasure of the past and a distortion of the facts, for, as he is quick to point out, the Constitution was imposed upon the Japanese by the US forces of occupation.

Unlike conventional nationalists, however, Katō does not seem to argue for a recovery of Japanese national identity, at least not in a straightforward manner, and he distances himself from other historical revisionists' attempts to reform the Constitution as part of an effort to make Japan a 'normal,' militarily capable nation. Katō instead emphasizes the importance of recognizing the historical facts surrounding the origin and meaning of the Constitution, facts subsequently distorted and concealed, as a precondition for the free and rational assent to a Constitution that would then be truly meaningful for the Japanese. He also acknowledges Japanese war responsibility to Asian nations and peoples and recognizes that World War II was distressing display of Japanese aggression. At the same time, however, Katō's position is profoundly ambiguous in terms of his political stance. As Tessa Morris-Suzuki argues, Katō's text 'operates pre-eminently at the psychological level,' 'translat[ing] the political and the epistemological into psychology' by 'drawing on philosophy and literary theory to create an understanding of the meaning of defeat for the human personality.'[115] Writing from this position of ambiguity, Katō directs his sharpest criticisms towards the liberal notion of the universal abstract subject, a subject he believes is unable to take up the task of grounding morality in a concrete historical place. He claims that liberal and poststructuralist universal notions of the individual subject fail to recognize that the Japanese *collective* subject is the only subject capable of being responsible for crimes against other Asian nations, and that without this national limitation one cannot think in concrete terms about the issues of morality, responsibility and history, for all are closely caught up in the modern notion of nationally bound spaces.[116] For Katō, what is most essential to the appropriate understanding of history is the presence of such historically grounded subjects who recognize and accept the specific conditions given to them at a specific time and in a specific place and thus think and act from within those constraints. Katō contends that one cannot seriously challenge the logic of Japanese community from a position of nowhere; rather, if one really hopes to criticize Japanese communalism, one must seek a critical position within it.[117] In this sense, his argument is a critique of the anti-essentialist challenges to 'nationalism' that, he believes, stand outside history and thus reflect a simplistic and one-sided view of the history which can only and must necessarily take place in a particular space. While Katō's use of schizophrenia as a metaphor to describe the postwar political and intellectual polarization between Japanese liberals and nationalists seems to call for the recovery of a unified subject in the minds of his readers, this is something that, at least in the first instance, he refutes.

To add even more ambiguity, Katō sees his revisionism as an attempt to 'deconstruct' the belief, so dear to *nihonjinron* scholars, in the uniqueness of the Japanese. In his discussion with Kang Sang-jung, Katō argues for the necessity of 'deconstructing' the deep-rooted 'corporeality of the Japanese,' their firm and unchanged belief in their 'uniqueness,' a belief reinforced, he says, by the evidence of the senses, and thus one that cannot be challenged by rational and objective criticism.[118] Pointing out that a new generation of 'hybrid-conservatives' emerged in the 1980s, who, while flexible in adapting new ideas and styles, firmly believed in the notion of an innate Japaneseness, Katō emphasizes the need for a theory capable of penetrating the structure of belief itself.[119] Seemingly contradicting his espousal of overcoming the reigning schizophrenia, Katō claims that his real aim is to dissolve the logic of community (*kyodosei*), the position uncritical of concrete and immediate historical experience, and to do this he borrows Hannah Arendt's notion of the mediation and surveillance of the public (*kokyōsei*) by universal morality. In short, it can be said that Katō's position attempts to establish is a middle-ground between nationalism and anti-nationalism, and/or essentialism and anti-essentialism, by bringing in the notion of the historically accountable subject as agent, and thereby opening up a public sphere within the national community (i.e. 'civil society'), rather than dismissing the question of the communal altogether. His critical attitude and moral passion to come to terms with history may be part of his appeal for those resentful minds tormented by 'the painful record of self-negation and hypocrisy derived from the masochistic view of [Japanese postwar] history.'[120] In this sense, Katō's text offers 'a kind of national psychotherapy whose appeal lies in its power to trace all the diffuse and disturbing anxieties of the present back to a single unresolved "childhood trauma".'[121] However, excluded and erased from this 're-view of history,' and in this Katō's 'remedy' parallels those of the various streams of *nihonjinron*, are the heterogeneous and diachronic lived experiences of the past that are overwritten by the presently reconstructed and imposed vision. Given the intense ambiguities and complexities inherent in both intellectual and popular contemporary Japanese discourses, Katō's convoluted and often contradictory argument will likely be simplified, and, if precedents hold true, in that simplification the path opens up for his arguments to be fused into conventional nationalist discourse and the revisionism of Fujioka *et al*. On the whole, Katō's work is symptomatic of Japanese intellectual discourse in the 1990s, and is marked by ahistorical, dematerialized, and synchronic inclinations characteristic of a troubled cognition conducive to condensation and fixation.

Works like Katō's 'Haisengo ron,' while enjoying a wide-ranging appeal with the general public, suggest that a new version of nationalism is in evidence, as distinguished from the more conventionally understood variety of previous decades. Unlike conventional forms of nationalism closely linked with the ideology of state power politics, this new type of 'nationalism' is a highly ambiguous and hybrid amalgam of different versions of revisionism, whose ideological messages and political positions are often at odds. While Fujioka's and Katō's arguments differ, for example, in their positions vis-à-vis a strong Japanese state, they are united in their criticism of liberal internationalism for its 'distortion of history' and in their national consciousness of being the people's representatives. For Katō in particular, what counts is not the 'state' but the 'nation' part of the nation-state, its people and its communal space, what he describes as the organically unitary, shared linguistic and cultural values and norms and views of history (national historical narrative) that guarantee a common past and future for its members. Intrinsic to this populist notion, then, is the affirmation of the boundary distinguishing insiders from outsiders, an affirmation that evokes a sense of the imagined, secure space called 'Japan' within the anarchic, exterior world where nation-states compete for power. The 'new nationalism' attempts to rehabilitate the broken communal fabric based on shared intersubjective meanings, and thereby seeks to recover the hegemonic social order that is perceived by these nationalists as being on the verge of collapse. It is revealing in this light that Katō takes the phenomenon of the 'compensated date' (*enjo kōsai*), and more generally the loosening of female sexuality, very seriously, although he does not make an explicit link between these phenomena and revisionism.[122]

Ironically, however, the strategy employed by the new nationalists is dependent upon the very commercial forces that they see as disrupting intersubjective meanings (discourse); for, the communal space now is so fully mediated by a commercially driven commodity sign economy, that it cannot but mediate their proposed reconstitution of communal space. What accelerated the emergence and the popularity of new nationalism was the wide-spread ambiguity of meaning in the discourse of the 1990s; new nationalism took root by both further cultivating this ambiguity and at the same time cultivating an axiety in the subject that is rechannelled into the new nationalist narrative structure. Produced and consumed within the extended chains of the sign-economy and, swimming in a sea of surplus meaning, this new type of nationalism seems also to provide a consumable pleasure; however, because it no longer conveys meaning through logically coherent argument, it seems more destined to engender a greater desire for meaning than a satisfaction of pleasure. For example, Fujioka calls this revisionist perspective the 'Liberal View of History,' and the title of his book, *The History Not Taught in the Textbooks*, appropriates an anti-revisionist phraseology, both strategies taking tacit advantage of the ambiguity and anxieties already prevalent in mid-1990s Japanese discourse.[123] As Aaron Gerow points out in his analysis of the presentation and narrative structure of Fujioka's text, the author's use of equivocal catchwords tacitly elides the historically given temporal and spatial boundaries between the past and the present, author and reader, the individual and the social collective, and history and its representations. These violations are fashioned to evoke a sentimental pleasure in the minds of Japanese readers, and can be said to successfully reconstitute a national subjectivity. In the case of Katō, a similar technique is employed with a writing style that radically cuts across the boundary between creative literary writing and the 'objective' (social scientific) presentation of ideas, tempting his readers towards the reconstitution of national subjectivity in a text written in an emotionally and morally appealing manner.[124] As discussed above, Katō's ambiguous political position seemingly rejects both ends of the ideological spectrum and points to the potential for a third path, a middle-ground that would eventually discredit the universal ethics of liberal internationalism in favour of national/cultural contingency.

In short, the ultimate source of the popularity enjoyed by revisionism and new nationalism stems not from the content of the texts per se, but from the historical context within which they circulate. This nationalism feeds on the inarticulate excess cultivated and accumulated in highly commercialized discourse, the crisis of identity and social hegemony, as well as the more 'visibly' recognizable historical events they directly problematize, such as US–Japan–Asian relations. In this sense, the new nationalism, with revisionism as its vehicle, is a symptomatic manifestation of greater historical problems which encompass all spheres of human life, including the breakdown of the subject and discursive meaning, the eclipse of the transcendental perspective, and the resultant collapse of the structuring frame of objective thought and temporality. Beyond this symptomatic character, however, revisionism also proposes to offer a 'remedy' for the troubled sense of self felt by many Japanese. It attracts resentful souls who seek to ground themselves in concrete history and generate an insular communal place, at the expense of fixing the subject, meaning and history to idealized, singular and homogeneous modes. This return to concrete history and the national subject is an old song heard before, a ghost from the past that once again expresses the twisted self-denial of the Japanese state in favour of the people.[125] The popularity enjoyed by Fujioka's and Katō's texts could have been quite easily dismissed in the earlier postwar decades, as the works of Ueyama Shumpei and Hayashi Fusao were in the 1950s and 1960s, when the structural frame of the subject and discourse had a clear centre and integrity. However, the socio-political implications of these new revisionist texts are much more resonant and their consequences possibly more far-reaching in the twenty-first century, when the notion of history is increasingly blurred by autobiographical memoirs and anecdotal accounts of many possible 'narratives.' In such instances, the past becomes subject to present reconstitution as a means of gathering together temporally scattered fragments of memory, and this ahistorical reconstitution tacitly tends to eliminate the Other, both in the form of transcendental ethics and different identities.[126]

'Representational crises' and the returning spectre of 'Japan'

Adopting the categories put forward by Fredric Jameson, we can subsume the various economic, political and socio-cultural shocks that befell Japan in the 1990s under the common notion of a 'representational crisis.' This crisis concerns an allegorical failure, the increasingly visible gap between representation and its historical referent, between the form and its content, between the image and its substance, and between the self and the body. In the sphere of economics, for example, the divergence between market values (i.e. the surplus bubble) and 'real' values (i.e. use value) reached its limit with the 'burst of the bubble,' disrupting the economic system as a whole. On the political terrain, Japan as a nation has become uncertain of what it should represent, while the Japanese population has largely lost confidence in the ability and the will of political parties to represent their interests. Together, these phenomena have exacerbated the rift between the 'nation' (people) and the 'state' (government). Perhaps, the most extreme allegorical gap – if it can still be described as a 'gap' when the notion of a correspondence between content and form has all but lost its meaning – has been seen in the sphere of popular image production where a virtually infinite number of images can be produced without historical referents. While each of these spheres has been embroiled in its own crisis, the temporal coincidence of these interlocked forms of representational crises is no mere accident, but rather reflects the greater structural breakdown that Jameson and others have called the crisis of late capitalism.

The contradictions of the deepening crisis of capitalism in the 1990s are most acutely manifest in two phenomena: in the growing prevalence of unsustainable financial speculation and in the fact that shrinking commercial opportunities now mean business growth depends upon the artificial creation of consumer demand by means of generating a sense of displacement and cultivating a desire to be otherwise in the subject. At this stage, the problematic in the sphere of economics can no longer be conceived separately from the realms of culture and subjectivity; rather, what is called for is to address the lateral links in society which encompass both material and non-material spheres. As discussed above, this crisis-laden state of capitalism has had far-reaching consequences in all spheres of Japanese social life, from the erosion of the elite power system to the proliferation of seemingly odd youth sub-cultural practices in the search for identity. Capitalism here does not denote a narrowly conceived economic system, but a system that demands particular modes of social organization in accord with the existing modes of production: the corresponding social relations of production, specific legal and political frameworks, a social infrastructure, and a set of values and codes of behaviour. These structural underpinnings together give rise to a particular mode of social organization, or hegemony, at a given historical time. In the present, the difficulty of constituting a viable social hegemony in contemporary Japan has called up the spectre of 'Japan,' in which all aesthetic desires to transcend the imperfections of the self and the historical world are gathered together in an ideal vision, supposedly capable of rehabilitating the fragmented self and social imaginary. Noteworthy here is that the various crises at the root of these developments are not unique to Japan but are, in an age lacking a clear structuring frame, seemingly being experienced on a global scale (although more exacerbated in the less developed countries): they are part of the general structural breakdown whose symptoms are manifest in the various geo-political, economic and 'cultural' domains.

Searching for new commercially exploitable domains in the realm of the imaginary, 1990s capitalism has exposed the Japanese people to an intense and seemingly limitless expansion of virtual images, an exposure which has assaulted and fragmented subjectivity and has at the same time cultivated a desire for consumption and identity. To be sure, these commercial challenges to the bases of everyday life, and the reactionary responses to them, are not new to the 1990s onwards but a continuing trend from previous decades. In Chapter 5, I identified in the 1980s two seemingly contradictory but complementary cultural and discursive inclinations, namely, a fragmentary tendency towards the decentring of society and the subject, driven by commercial forces, and the counter-tendency seeking to recreate an identity and meaning felt to be in jeopardy, strongly manifest in *nihonjinron* discourse. In the socio-cultural conditions of contemporary Japan, however, it seems we are at the point of reaching yet another level, a point where the structure of our perception and sensation may be themselves subject to transformation. One survival strategy against such ontological challenges is that proposed by Miyadai: to alter the relation between consciousness and the body, to treat the body as an environment to be modified, and to erase the self, techniques all, perhaps, for lessening the pain of displacement by rationalizing such displeasure as an objective in itself. However, in addition to advocating the nihilistic celebration of endless routine, momentary pleasures, and the cynicism of self-erasure, Miyadai conceives his completely depoliticized ironic stance as a form of revolution. This inversion of the pleasure–displeasure principle accompanied by the ascription of value to irony and nihilism reminds one of Benjamin's well-known remark on the ultimate state of the self-estrangement of humanity: 'Its self-alienation has reached such a degree that it can experience its own destruction as an aesthetic pleasure of the first order.'[127] Seen from a slightly different angle, the extent to which such rhetorical moves incarnate the logic and the culture of the market must be questioned, insofar as in them an absolute ironic consciousness is authorized in its attempts to transform human subjects in the shape of its own design.

Just as the fragmentary tendency has come to manifest its ultimate form as an absolute ironic consciousness, an opposite inclination for condensation and centralization of identity and meaning have given rise to the return of various spectres at the individual, sub-national and national levels. Japanese society in the 1990s witnessed a number of violent explosions of the suppressed self in revolt against society, on the individual (the Kobe murderer), the sub-national (the *Aum Shinrikyō* cult), and the national levels (historical revisionists), by those desperate to restore the broken linkage between the self and the world. *Aum Shinrikyō*'s apocalyptic attacks and the Kobe boy's lonesome revolt against the symbolic order are manifestations of the failure of the self to repair this broken link with the world outside, while the new nationalist calls for identity and the reimposition of symbolic hegemony are capturing substantial support from society at large. Despite the radically different means by which their goals were pursued, all of these incidents were responses, and attempts to find answers, to a troubled state of subjectivity permeated by a flood of meaningless signs and a resultant vague but profound sense of anxiety and resentment. The inarticulate 'excess' cultivated at each level gave rise to a desire for an absolute supposedly capable of transcending either the this-worldly triviality of human existence or the chaos of social disorder. While such returning spectres tempt us with images of the fullness of life which are themselves the 'concrete grounds' of their articulations – i.e. 'materiality/the body,' 'spiritual community,' and 'Japanese nation' – the underlying aesthetically motivated desires are products of the troubled consciousness that articulates and projects the perceived loss and source of pain onto a fetishized object. In this sense, these quests for identity and meaning are not the antithesis of absolute ironic consciousness; rather, it would be more accurate to see them as products of aesthetic consciousness which are at the same time inspired to overcome the two ends of the duality – form and content, meaning and being, mind and body. In this move towards the union of what are irreducible opposites, the absolute ironic consciousness sublimates imagined and projected 'things' by eliminating all things empirical.

This return of an omnipotent consciousness can also be detected in Katō's advocacy of the historically grounded subject as the only subject accountable to the moral and historical responsibility of the Japanese nation. However, one should be suspicious of Katō's usage of the term 'history' here. As Harry Harootunian has pointed out, the claustrophobic inclination in present historical consciousness tends to confuse history with memory, and is 'symptomatic of our conservative age dreaming only of the conservation of the present state.'[128] He argues that revisionists like Fujioka and Katō, narrating an imagined history that has never been experienced, are driven by a passion to recall 'the otherwise history' which would allow them, or so they think, to 'realize' their fetishized desire for Japanese identity.[129] Like the *nihonjinron* of the previous decade, by imposing on the past-as-it-was-experienced a presently imagined past, this otherwise-history works a kind of inverted teleology and this, argues Harootunian, is directly linked to the nostalgia for the '[wartime] colonialism [in Asia] that the Japanese were forced to abandon' due to their defeat in the war: for them, what was abandoned not stands as an obstacle to the full realization of the identity of the Japanese.[130] In a similar vein, Victor Koschmann, borrowing from Ogoshi Aiko, argues that Katō's notion of history falls into a Hegelian frame that aims to 'rehistoricize postwar consciousness' by replacing the lived experience of history with a 'self-consciousness of one's historical existence.'[131]

> In [Katō's] view, history should rather manifest itself in the memory of communities such as the state and ethnic nation (*minzoku*), and thus he assumes that he can be involved in history only as a citizen of the state or as a member of the nation ... It is clear that Katō's

argument is based on the modern, Hegelian view of history that finds the meaning of subjectivity in self-consciousness of one's historical existence.[132]

These observations point to the emergence of another spectre, this time of History as the fetishized desire of a consciousness that seeks a concrete ground in which to embody the idea of nation and its imagined history, a consciousness that subordinates lived historical experience to the hegemonic, present-centred, and narcissistic omnipresent gaze.

Perhaps the text that best exemplifies the often invisible yet intimate relation between ironic consciousness and the underlying desire for transcendence is Fukuda Kazuya's 1993 *Nippon no Kakyō*. In this work, clearly demonstrating the symptoms of historical revisionism discussed above (the sense of anxiety, the attempt at discursive unification, and a conceptual slippage), Fukuda reclaims Yasuda Yojūrō and the Japan Romantic School's ironic romanticism for critique by endowing 'Japan' with an excess of meaning, and calls for a coming to terms with the profound abyss of human existence, what Fukuda calls 'the nothingness of "Japan."' For Fukuda, this task lies at the core of all the attempts to rejuvenate the ethos of Japanese literature and the 'critical literary consciousness,' attempts which have amounted to naught in the 'fallacy' of postwar Japanese history:

> Now that the self-deceiving fallacy has been maintained since the end of World War II, critical literary consciousness has reached an important intersection. Perhaps there are only two options possible. [The first is] to continue accepting 'realistic' and collective utterances as 'literature' by maintaining the same self-restrictions. Or, once again to face up to the nothingness of 'Japan.'
>
> Once again to germinate the language to fill the chalice (*sakazuki*) called 'Japan,' by facing up to that nothingness from which the desire for 'condensation' arises, and from which both the distasteful and the luminous are given birth.[133]

What is referred to here as 'Japan' is a purely imaginative and abstract symbolic space bearing little resemblance to the existing island nation, a space freed from the realist epistemic function of representing historical referents. By naming this imagined metaphorical space 'Japan,' Fukuda indulges in an inclination we have witnessed many times before in modern Japanese intellectual history, the proclivity to interpret the ontological instability inherent in modern subjectivity as something unique to the Japanese cultural and linguistic orientation: the repudiation of representation and the materiality of language. At the core of this inclination lies the notion that the Japanese native narrative is laden with a 'cultural desire' to encapsulate life in language, a desire symbolically manifest in the Japanese term *kotodama* (literally 'word-spirit'), as well as the idea that the native narrative tends to resist every intrusion of a synchronic representational scheme which would violate the authenticity of native space. This line of argument closely echoes Takeda's notion of the significance of the emperor (which I discussed at the beginning of this chapter) as a form of communal sensitivity that simultaneously fills in, and negates the anxiety arising from, the empty space between the verbal expression of ideas and the sense of reality.

Unlike many others who uncritically adopt this nativist interpretation into their rhetoric, Fukuda is fully aware that the condition of modern subjectivity makes such a 'unity of language and meaning' impossible. Moreover, Fukuda's notion of 'Japan' is nothing like that of the romantic nationalists, and here I include Katō, who seek to 'recover' a lost identity/history of the Japanese. Instead, Fukuda accepts and embraces, at least in his theoretical posture, this lack of content as the essence of modern Japan itself, Japan as void, so that this identity of nothingness is for him the true 'home' one ultimately returns to.[134] However, this theoretical anti-essentialism is not thoroughly sustained, and shows signs of a violent irruption of desire, as the above passage exemplifies ('Or, once again to face up to the nothingness of "Japan"'). Indeed, Fukuda's transcendental aestheticism recalls the troubled intellectual terrain of Japan in the 1930s, when the material dimension of history was removed behind the import of the metaphysical and when political struggles on the historical stage were replaced by the struggle with consciousness. Seen in this light, what should concern us is not the 'Japan' that Fukuda would have us imagine, but the eclipse of flexibility in the subject who cannot bear the burden of groundlessness without placing the cause of its unease in the external, on the one hand, and the troubling contemporary historical conditions that have caused the subject to be so preoccupied with defending its selfhood from the intrusion of meaningless, subject-fragmenting images, on the other.[135]

In this light, one ought to be also concerned with the recent tendency for history to become increasingly obscured and confused with autobiographical memoir and anecdotal accounts of many possible 'narratives,' a blurring in which the past has been made subject to present reconstitutions in the recollection of a fragmented memory.[136] In a decade when the crossing of temporal and epistemological boundaries has been made all too easy, there is a great danger that the images produced and consumed by various revisionists could be freely conjoined and rearranged by each subject and indeed, by the discourse at large.[137] As this happens, mutually contradictory arguments and the distinct problematics within them – i.e. Fujioka's narcissistic Japan-centrism, Katō's populist moralism, Fukuda's transcendental aestheticism, and conservative politicians' anti-US power politics – become consolidated and amalgamated, giving rise to the phenomenon I am calling 'new nationalism.' In an age when high-tech computer-guided arsenals can carry out campaigns of mass destruction with little reverberation or repercussion for the perpetrators of a war, the greatest source of contemporary danger does not lie in nationalism *per se*, but rather in things that are much more familiar to us, namely, the ongoing socio-economic, cultural, intellectual and political practices that reduce 'the *nation* to a narration of commodified images and *nationalism* to consumption of these images,' practices that nurture and promote an omnipotent gaze that objectifies all empirical beings.[138]

In short, contemporary Japan finds itself locked in the double-bind of late modernity, torn between two contrary 'aesthetic solutions' to its dilemma: the nihilistic and ironic positioning of simulated identities, and the attempted recovery of 'true' identity and meaning by means of an existential leap into the realm of imagination. These two seemingly contrary positions are two sides of the same coin, since both entail a paradoxical self-defence premised upon an inversion of the pain of self-destruction into a seemingly unshakable self-certainty. Moreover, I say 'two seemingly contrary positions' because the former anti-essentialist stance is pregnant with the possibility of the latter: the transcendental perspective emerges out of the repetition of an ironic practice that ultimately frees consciousness from things empirical; and the eruption of suppressed reactionary sentiment is the precursor to the rise of a sublime superego. The challenge of our times would be, then, to sustain ourselves in the narrow space between these two forms of aesthetic departure from concrete historical problems.

7 Japanese nationalism in the late modern world

In place of a conclusion

In a recent discussion with Komori Yōichi, the Chinese intellectual Sun Ge expresses her doubts about the efficacy of contemporary Japanese criticisms of the Japanese emperor system.[1] She argues that while critiques of Japanese nationalism have by and large completely dissolved its intrinsic foundations on the level of rational knowledge, they do not appear to have had any effect whatsoever on the 'society of the emperor system' (*tennōsei shakai*), the ideology grounded in the socio-historical base of Japanese society and the everyday lives of the Japanese. Referring to the critiques of nationalism advanced in previous generations, Sun takes present-day Japanese scholarly discourse to task for focusing on criticism as an end in itself rather than making any meaningful contribution to changing the current state of affairs. According to Sun, the present Japanese discourse is especially lacking in its ability to take into account what she calls 'the realm of the sense of the skin [*hifu kankaku*],' the only route, she argues, by which criticism can penetrate the ideological centre of the system.[2] While Takeuchi's postwar efforts to advance people's rights by creating a channel for articulating popular sentiment into a democratic politics (what he called nationalism) is singled out for praise, as an attempt to reroute popular sentiment away from the state nationalist cause, Sun thinks the majority of Japanese postwar intellectuals have failed miserably on this score. This, as far as it goes, is a criticism that every Japanese intellectual should take very seriously. At the same time, however, it has been my contention that while the problem of nationalism necessarily entails the question of practice, it must also be located in the context of strategic difficulties of integrating popular voices into the public political domain in our increasingly complex, pluralistic, and information-based societies. Only by doing this will we be able to see the current state of Japanese society, what Sun describes as 'the society of the emperor system,' in a historical context, one that is intimately related to the structural transformations of postwar Japanese society.

There are a number of parallels between Sun's critique and my own: what she describes as an extra-rational knowledge 'of the skin,' I call 'the aesthetic,' claiming that the aesthetic discursive terrain, a characteristic feature of late modernity, is the realm where a depoliticized and ahistorical ideology prevails. However, gesturing to the necessary awareness of this extra-rational factor does not mean that rationalist criticisms of nationalism in contemporary Japanese intellectual discourse are missing the point, but rather that they are, by themselves, insufficient, especially in the post-Cold War era when the illusion of national myths has been so bluntly exposed and has become such a cause of disturbance. As I have argued, the kind of nationalism we have been witnessing since the 1990s is not merely a simple reassertion of nationalist sentiments, but is rather directly linked to the structural breakdown of national hegemonies and the malfunctioning of the discursive terrain, the fact that it no longer sustains the political feedback-loop between state governance and the social imaginary. This means that the Japanese identity claims of the 1990s onwards are not a sudden outbreak of nationalism but have a structural and discursive genealogy: they arose as early as the late 1950s, when the realms of subjectivity and intersubjectivity began to be permeated by commercially and technologically driven forces, and when, in the 1980s, attempting to reconstitute the lost integrity of the self and society by reifying the notion of the 'national body,' popular sentiment began to articulate new forms of individual and national identity constituted on the basis of artificially recreated notions of Japaneseness.

These artificially constituted identities have arisen in the context of the late capitalist culture-economy, and are also thus fuelled by resentment of a highly bureaucratized and fragmented society and of the prevailing abstract–rational mode of knowledge. Given these underlying factors, conventional adversarial critiques are not all that effective in combating these new kinds of nationalism, and even run the risk of inviting additional reactionary responses. Fuelled by anti-rationalist feelings, many of the recent manifestations of Japanese identity shelter under the sign of the emperor, not so much in support of an ideological national symbol, but because such ambiguous sentiments have lost their traditional political-cultural site for meaningful articulation. Popular sentiment may seem to be in a somewhat benign and apolitical discursive state, far removed from the rise of aggressive militarism seen in the past. However, it is precisely such an aestheticized, dehistoricized and apolitical state of discourse that, in combination with the growing security concerns of the current international context, invites the merger of various nationalistic expressions in the Japan of the 1990s. The public inclination in contemporary Japan for 'mood' and 'feelings' over reasoned argument is one result of the socio-economic and cultural transformations taking place in the current stage of capitalism. It must be emphasized, however, that this inclination is not unique to Japan: it is a characteristic shared by most of the contemporary world, in which the global hegemonic structure has become increasingly less defined in structure and more and more opaque in its boundaries. Under these rapidly changing geo-political conditions, moreover, global capital and technology are freely recreating the world in their universalist vision, while people's desire for existential certainty tends to be linked to the status of national, sub-national, or trans-national identities. All in all, the complexity of causes and implications of the current 'problem of a resurgent Japanese nationalism' cannot be adequately understood without widening our scope to locate the problematic in the context of the universal problematic of the late modern world.

Readers may well ask why this is the case. If, as I have contended, the problem of nationalism is a complex and multivalent one, it is because it is imbricated in the manifold of political, cultural and economic relations out of which the fabric of modern social and political life is woven. Following the Gramscian notion of hegemony, I have argued that if we are to truly comprehend modern life and its transformations we must come to grips with the structural transformations taking place *in and between* ideas, institutions, and production, and we must do that with an awareness of their dynamic, historical and international terms of reference. Taking only a part of this constellation into view affords only a partial perspective. Some poststructuralist informed critiques of nationalism, for example, while yielding genuine insights, tend to see the problem in static terms, focusing on the discursive formation of the nation-state and its problems; but the problem of nationalism cannot be reduced to the cultural or discursive. Similarly, conventional socio-historical analysis, while telling us much about the structural underpinnings of social transformation, tends to leave to the side the realm of subjectivity and the ways in which social life is organized, and as a result the problem of nationalism gets lost in the trees. By way of conclusion, I want to look at both these forms of analysis, suggesting ways they may be broadened and woven into the others, and to suggest that the problem of nationalism is by no means isolated to Japan: the ebbing of the universal ideal and the concurrent closure of historical consciousness are in fact global phenomena. If my analysis has any merit, it is because it is founded on a dynamic, historical and international perspective on developments that are an intrinsic part of the global transformations reshaping the world we all inhabit. Let me take these issues in turn.

The critique of nationalism and its difficulties

Following in the footsteps of such pioneering works as Benedict Anderson's *Imagined Communities* (1983), E. J. Hobsbawm and Terence Ranger's volume *The Invention of Tradition* (1983), and Ernest Gellner's *Nations and Nationalism* (1983), a wealth of new scholarship informed by poststructuralist insights emerged into the mainstream of the study of nation and nationalism, challenging conventional disciplinary boundaries and presumed conceptual categories. While these works made a very significant contribution to the existing scholarship and had a critical impact on our understanding of the 'ideological uses of the past,' such arguments are today somewhat superfluous, especially given that the ontological groundlessness of the nation has been now so bluntly revealed, a situation that has in turn nonetheless inspired recreations of the nation precisely by inventing and reinventing traditions and national memories as the founding mythologies of new nations. Naturally, however, the invention of myths alone does not create a nation; to create a nation one must successfully enmesh such myths with the pre-existing discourses guiding people's everyday practices. In other words, the constitution of a nation demands much more than knowledge production: it necessitates the willing participation of the national subject who accepts and practices the state's hegemonic myths as an integral part of their everyday lives. By placing too much focus on the creation of national myths divorced from the political and material dimensions, critiques of nationalism tend to obscure the import of everyday practice on the one hand, and the dynamic and historical international context and the problems which arise from the structure of the modernly configured world, on the other.

This is not to say I endorse simple historicist accounts viewing the nation-state as an unproblematic cultural space, as generations of Japanese nationalists have sought, each in their own ways, to do. As they treat it, the nation is either traced back, unmediated by modern inscriptions, to antiquity or transfixed in a timeless space of essence. Rather, my aim has been to establish a theoretical stance that is more accountable to our understanding of the nation by building upon the contributions made by the pioneering works of the 1980s. The difficulties of discussing the problem of nationalism, however, often lead one into a series of categorically opposed positions – 'historicism versus deconstruction,' 'Marxist social theory versus poststructuralist discursive analysis,' or 'political economy versus literary studies' – and not enough constructive effort has been invested in creating dialogues between these positions or in critically examining the assumptions involved in each assertion. As these antagonistic oppositions have continued to persist for quite some time now, the *modus operandi* of scholarly practice has tended to favour the reproduction of previously successful arguments, thus contributing to a general decline of intellectual rigour that by and large supports the political conservatism of our times. Let me consider one example of the difficulty of establishing bridges over these opposing positions.

Referring to the work of Hobsbawm and Ranger, Stephen Vlastos, the editor of a recently published collection of articles, *Mirror of Modernity: Invented Traditions of Modern Japan* (1998), writes in his introduction:

> The broad movement across the humanities to deconstruct culture had just been launched, and Hobsbawm's ironic representation of tradition as invention made an important fact unmistakably clear: tradition is not the sum of actual past practices that have perdured into the present; rather, tradition is a modern trope, a prescriptive representa-

tion of socially desirable (or sometimes undesirable) institutions and ideas thought to have been handed down from generation to generation.[3]

Vlastos' critical focus seeks not to explore how, why, or under what historical conditions such a 'prescriptive representation of socially desirable institutions and ideas' came to be invented, but rather simply to reveal the inventedness of tradition. Dipesh Chakrabarty, in his contribution to the volume, problematizes a contradiction that inheres in the phrase 'invented traditions,' for traditions, he points out, are always modified and reinvented everywhere, and it is, thus, hardly meaningful to describe 'formally instituted cultural practices ... enjoying a rapid rise to the status of something time-honoured ... [as] invented traditions.'[4] He further argues that the 'invention of tradition' framework is 'theoretically innocent with regard to its own implications in modern systems of thought' because it projects a modern critical perspective upon another culture, describing it in terms of modern categories.[5] Although there is little room for doubt that the discourse of the nation-state and its institutional apparatus have substantially contributed to the production and dissemination of hegemonic norms guiding and disciplining national subjects, Vlastos does not take into account why the national form of organizing space 'attain[ed] the singular importance that ... [it did] in a given historical context.'[6] Indeed, the sovereign nation-state is still the only internationally recognized form of representation for the collective polity in the modern world, and one does not need to be reminded of the potential violences that would follow from the loss of reliable national representation (on both the domestic and international fronts).

Chakrabarty, for his part, does highlight the role played by agents in national hegemonic systems; material and non-rational factors in particular – i.e. political economic institutions and the bodily aspects of cultural life such as the senses and emotions – as seen as essential components needing to be incorporated into the study of nationalism:

> Ideas acquire materiality through the history of bodily practices. They work not simply because they persuade through their logic; they are also capable, through a long and heterogeneous history of the cultural training of the senses, of making connections with our glands and muscles and neuronal networks. This is the work of memory, if we do not reduce the meaning of that word to the simple and conscious mental act of remembering.[7]

This formulation is not without its own problems, however. Chakrabarty overstates, I think, the desirability of culture and 'materiality,' which in his account appear to be refractory to rational enquiry and thus open to employment as effective categories for the uncritical affirmation of national hegemonic power. What especially interests me in this regard is the tendency of counter-criticisms to the anti-essentialist critique of nation and culture to fall into the trap of essentialization, as if the unrepresentability of 'materiality' necessarily makes such unwitting formulations inevitable. The alternative approach I have outlined in these chapters aims to avoid falling prey to either of these two dangers – Vlastos' 'invention' and Chakrabarty's 'materiality' – by, on the one hand, situating the formative process of national hegemony in relation to the dynamic structuring process of historical forces, both domestic and international, and on the other, by problematizing the ontological status of 'materiality,' often linked to 'the body' and 'the senses'. In doing so, I have attempted to view the nation-state within the dynamic historical process of capitalism and modernity and the dynamic of international geo-politics.

As a collective human organization, the nation necessitates a common set of functional rules articulated in the form of narrative. In this sense, a nation is, as Timothy Brennan has put it, 'precisely what Foucault has called a "discursive formation" – not simply an allegory or imaginative vision, but a gestative political structure.'[8] For the modern nation-state to establish hegemony, a successful integration of its invented narrative into the pre-existing discourses is essential, at least to the degree that people do not see too clearly the invented-ness of the narrative. What is at stake here is the status of the nationalized cultural space, and especially the way in which the national narrative (often appearing to outsiders as an 'allegorical imaginative vision') is transformed into concrete lived experience for (most of) those who reside within that space. By conceiving the nation as a symbolically structured field of intersubjective meanings, embodied to a significant degree in individual citizens and institutions, one obtains a perspective on the problem that encompasses the realm which rationalist critiques of nationalism have difficulty penetrating: the aesthetic.[9] Since individuals are born into a socio-cultural system that ontologically precedes them, they are predisposed to certain patterns of meaning and behaviour operative in the existing symbolic system; their sensory experiences, emotional attachments, and sense of moral duty, all of which occupy an important place in the social life of humanity and society, are built upon such cultural bases.[10]

State hegemonic power, thus, rests on its ability to weave the identity of its subjects into the reigning system of symbolic meanings, which the subjects in their everyday practices then embody. Further, the survival of the nation-state and the well-being of its subjects are dependent upon, and reinforced by, the existing symbolic system. Naturally, the form and intensity of such connections between the state and the subject varies from place to place; arguably, the linkage is much less significant in the advanced industrial societies of the West, where 'culture' appears less of an immediate issue and the state's power to regenerate 'hegemonic consensus' is constituted more by the legal and institutional apparatus. The question of degrees not withstanding, however, the fact remains that the hegemonic reproduction of the nation is dependent upon its subjects being provided with such socio-cultural foundations for shared memories of the past, a sense of communal moral obligation, a coherent vision of the world and collectively articulated hopes. If in the current global context the nation-state is indeed being dismantled, then the danger looms nigh that highly disruptive forces contained within the bounds of the modern nation-state will be unleashed, forces which at present are more or less circumscribed by the established symbolic links constituting, albeit hierarchically, the order and stability between a nation and its subjects. Since the normal functioning of the nation-state is a necessary condition for the stability of the individual subjects whose everyday lives are integrated into hegemonic politico-cultural institutions, contesting hegemony runs a number of risks, for 'to battle the temporal constructions of power is to battle the self and to damage the readily available means of achieving comfort and assurance.'[11]

This is the context in which Japanese nationalist discourse has flourished over the past decade, seeking ways of giving expression to the unrepresentable but immanently figured space called 'Japan.' However, in order to truly understand the advent of these calls for 'Japan,' one must take stock of not only the changing conditions in which discursive and symbolic meaning is fashioned and how individuals are linked to the national hegemony, but the ways in which national hegemony alters its shape according to the mode of economy in operation at a specific historical time. If, as I have argued, reactionary responses to the intensification of the logic of capital are absorbed into nationalistic expressions *via* aesthetic cognition, then a further crucial constituent of the problematic of 'nationalism' is the underlying structural mechanism that simultaneously transforms both the subjective and objective spheres of human life.

Nationalism in the context of the problematic of modernity

Based upon Japanese economist Uno Kozo's original interpretation of Marxian economy, Robert Albritton, in part by adapting the contributions of his teacher-colleague Thomas Sekine, has developed an analysis of the 'unique ontology of capital' as a self-expanding and self-valorizing value.[12] While the unadulterated logic of capital would, in this analysis, be constitutive of a purely capitalist society, capital's logic is in fact compromised to various degrees in existing societies by those aspects of social experience and practice beyond the reach of what capital can successfully objectify and thus reproduce in social life. According to Albritton, 'in order to establish a workable mode of capital accumulation,' capital 'must "compromise" with existing institutions,' and thus particular, historically specific institutions and modes of social organization are constituted. Sekine and Albritton have described a number of 'stages' marking the most characteristic manifestations of the logic of capital in each distinct period of capital accumulation.[13] Further, these stages – mercantilism, liberalism, imperialism, and consumerism, which developed from the early eighteenth century onward in the course of capitalism's 'self-reifying' process – not only reflect the state of capital accumulation but are also endowed with distinct characteristics and identifiable structures that encompass all spheres of social life. Albritton's reading of Marx's analysis of capital as a dynamic structuring force 'suggest[s] that the social relations that characterize capitalism are of a very peculiar sort – they possess the attributes that Hegel accorded to *Geist*.'[14] This is a useful notion as it allows us to address the interdependence of economic, cultural, and political factors in our analysis of the problematic of nationalism.

A number of authors have pointed to the allegorical co-relation between the self-expansionary and intensifying movement of capitalism and a similar inclination in enlightenment reason to strive towards transcendental truth and absolute identity. Taking up Lukács' formulation of this relation in his 1923 work *History and Class Consciousness*, Adorno later argued that

> The reification of logic as the self-alienation of thought is equivalent to and modeled on the reification of what thinking relates to, namely the unity of objects which are coagulated into the thought at work in them, and so to identity ... It [abstract logic] takes its cue from the form of commodities whose identity consists in the 'equivalence' of exchange values.[15]

In Adorno's analysis, capitalism and enlightenment rationalism are conceived as following the same structural transformative process of abstraction and reification in which the initial disembodiment of ideas and objects is then endowed with a material substance of its own. Adorno, and the Frankfurt School in general, maintained that the synchronic, intelligible sphere of modern market society established the ground for the transcendental ideas and the rationalist consciousness that aspire to subsume the diachronic and heterogeneous empirical world in their all-encompassing gaze.[16]

The society in question here is one where 'the law of equivalence' reigns. The law of equivalence is the implicit agreement assumed in capitalist society in order to foster the free exchange of commodities by converting the value of utility (use value) into the universally quantified value of the market (exchange value). In this system, people in their daily activities unproblematically convert qualitatively distinct, particular goods into standardized market values; in doing so, they enact what might be called a 'fetishistic inversion,' a displacement of the use value inherent in concrete objects into exchange value, which then 'appears as a real Substance' by having been 'successively incarnated ... in a series of concrete objects.'[17]

In this process, money – itself having no use-value and thus supposedly beyond the dynamic of desire – becomes the ultimate object of desire, despite, or rather because of, its practical worthlessness (zero use-value). Unconstrained by its materiality (since its value is not subject to physical corruption), and de-linked from its 'initial obligation' to serve as a medium for exchange with other goods, money becomes an autonomous value.[18] As the market economy proliferates and develops into a complex system, money becomes increasingly autonomous from producers and social demands, transforming into an entity that represents the power of instantaneous transferability to any other commodity. In this ascent of money from a simple means of exchange to *the* embodiment of universal value, society is transformed into a market society in which the intensive circulation of commodities generates a culture of 'fetishism,' the desire for possessing and consuming commodities as embodiments of symbolic power.

Produced in the context of modern capitalist development, one can argue that the consciousness of the modern subject is structurally conditioned by such reified subject–object relations and a dualistic identity (the gap between use and exchange, the real and the virtual), and that it tends to operate according to the same principle of identity/equivalence. And indeed, evidence suggests that this is the case: atomized individuals in modern civil society are typically linked to each other as citizens by their common subjection to a set of abstract laws and institutionally coded behaviours in which they treat each other as equal autonomous beings.[19] Alienated from nature and their fellow humans by virtue of having internalized the governing logic of society based on enlightenment rationalism and the *modus operandi* of the capitalist economy, atomized rational subjects mutually affirm their political and economic autonomy and individual rights as citizens in the public sphere. However, as it developed the society of the marketplace simultaneously generated its own other half, the realm of the private, endowed with the task of accommodating all those things excluded from the public domain, such as emotions and beliefs. This dualistic form of social organization is the founding basis for liberal democracy and the institutional forms of the modern sovereign nation-state system.

In such a society, one can intuitively sense both the attraction of aesthetic cognition, which garners significance as 'the very secret prototype of human subjectivity,' and the role it might play in politics by providing 'a vision of human energies as radical ends in themselves.'[20] Those empirical, moral and imaginative aspects of human life made unintelligible by the existing mode of public representation find their expression in aesthetic categories and aesthetic modes of knowledge tending to favour the reassertion of utopian hopes for the recovery of a 'lost identity.' Located between the faculties of intuition and understanding, the peculiarly ambiguous status of aesthetic cognition makes possible an imagined reunification of the categories that Kant had segregated into separate spheres – the cognitive, the practical, and the affective.[21] Moreover, this same ambiguity allows the aesthetic to encompass not only 'a liberatory concern with concrete particularity,' but also 'a specious form of universalism' that offers us a utopian vision otherwise disabled by modern instrumental reason and its synchronic structuring forces.[22] By virtue of its ability to accommodate both ends of enlightenment dualism, then, aesthetic cognition offers a refuge from various dehumanizing conceptions and a political and or ideological site upon which counter-hegemonic resistance to modern rationalism can be articulated and mobilized.

As we have seen in Japanese postwar experience, as the dynamic progression of modernity advances and the reactionary aesthetic currents of anti-universalist, anti-rationalist sentiments become increasingly immanent in society, the modern nation-state typically finds itself faced by a particularly modern, or late modern, difficulty: effective channels for the incorporation of popular will and the collective imaginary in ways conducive to the reproduction of national hegemony are increasingly foreclosed. What results from this difficulty is a political version of the 'representational crisis,' in which the dual functions of the nation-state – as the principal unit of the modern political system on the international stage (the state) and as the representative of the will of the sovereign subjects (the nation), upon whom its legitimacy ultimately rests – stand at odds with each other. In postwar Japanese experience, this crisis became apparent in the 1960s and advanced unabated through the 1970s and 1980s; by the 1990s it had reached a point where the abstract and idealized national discourse no longer functioned as a feedback channel linking the state and society. Concurrent with the burgeoning political crisis of the nation-state, contradictions in the sphere of culture-economy (the gap between use and exchange, the real and the virtual) have become increasingly apparent; troubled by its own representational crisis derived from the contradictions of the capitalist economy, the sphere of culture-economy is now in the process of rapidly losing its effectiveness as an operative channel for the reproduction of national hegemony. Postwar Japanese capitalism, in step with global trends, reached a critical turning point in the early 1970s when a new mode of production, 'flexible accumulation,' came to replace the previous expansionary mode of production. As the productive ability of modern economies began to exceed society's ability to consume, additional consumption was generated by cultivating demand, and it is from this point in history that the realm of the imaginary increasingly became the immediate object of capitalist exploitation. This new economic mode fostered the emergence of artistic styles and expressions characterized by the rapid expansion of syntagmatic equivalences freed from the one-to-one correspondence of realist representation, as well as the dislocation of sign-images from their historical referents.

Just as the circulation of commodities in the economy was historically intensified by displacing their empirical ground according to the law of equivalences, so the intensified circulation of sign-images in the discursive domain of late modernity delinks language from its established meanings and corresponding historical referents or objects. As this economy matured and intensified in the 1980s and 1990s, 'postmodern' cultural trends proliferated, infinitely expanding unsubstantiated, self-referential image-signs, themselves becoming commodities of exchange in a way that further undermined the representational function of the sign-economy. Subjectivity was not immune to this erosion of symbolic–discursive conditions: it too has become increasingly disembodied and fragmented, and subject-object relations are becoming increasingly opaque. The same process can be described in terms of the constant restructuring of the subject's relation to the self and the body that has resulted from the penetration of commercial and technological forces into the empirical life sphere, a restructuring that generates an increasingly intolerable anxiety and pain. In the 1980s, reactionary responses to these developments, as I have argued, made increasing use of aesthetic cognition and categories for the assertion of a unique Japanese cultural identity. By the 1990s, historical consciousness had become so attenuated that the erasure of the boundary line between historical facts and subjective interpretations was a subject of open discussion.

In short, the advanced state of late modern capitalist society manifests numerous signs of its troubled condition: the stability of national hegemony is being seriously disrupted by the legitimacy crisis of the nation-state, discursive representations are experiencing a state of general failure, and an unproductive (speculative) mode of capitalism has become a principal engine of economic growth. Within this manifold hegemonic crisis, two contradictory aesthetic inclinations can be identified: a proliferation of 'postmodern cultural conditions,' or an obsession with stylistic differences and artistic forms, and a concurrent 'return' of the displaced 'things empirical,' asserting themselves in a desire for transcendental meaning, truth and identity. We know that in 1930s and 1940s Japan, these aesthetic inclinations gave rise to a fascism in which the emperor was reified as the essence of the national body. In the first decade of the new millennium, the situation appears in many respects remarkably similar. Komori Yoichi has characterized the contemporary Japanese discursive ethos as a 'forward-looking [*mae ni mukau*] *and* reactionary national movement' attempting to reconstitute the national narrative by rearranging historical facts and rewriting history.[23] Satō Manabu, in dialogue with Komori, argues that the general Japanese cultural orientation in the years following the emergence of the religious cult group *Aum shinrikyō*, in conjunction with the loss of confidence in economy following the 'burst of the bubble' in the early 1990s, is filled with a 'longing' to believe that historical conditions can be transformed merely by changing the way one looks at them.[24] Satō warns of the rise of a solipsistic mind-set that seeks to eliminate all that does not agree with its predetermined assumptions. The result of such a disposition, he argues, is the kind of naked ego-centrism exemplified, for example, in the assertions of the 'liberal view of history' group who, operating on the assumption that historical facts are dependent upon the memory of living subjects, seek to subvert historical consciousness and reality. Distressing as they are, it must be emphasized that these developments are not unique to contemporary Japanese discourse, but rather are manifest, with some variations, worldwide. It is to these I now turn my focus.

Imaginary closure and eclipse of the utopian ideal?: the world in late modernity

Since 1989 a number of fundamental transformations in the dynamic of the world order have been underway that in part repeat our experiences of the past and in part chart new territories of experience. Heralds of the bright future promised by 'globalization,' trendy catch-phrases like 'borderless world' and 'information highway' have become ubiquitous, as if the intensification of technological and communications networks automatically assures greater human understanding and sympathy. The euphoria surrounding such promises grossly overstates the ability and the desire of the global market to diffuse wealth and enhance communications by means of commercial interactions; it seems to assume that obstacles such as structurally embedded power relations and tragic memories of the past can be transcended with little concerted human effort. Viewed from another angle, however, the contemporary world is also plagued by increasing fragmentation, bitter conflicts, and a multitude of exclusivist movements whose aspirations are often expressed in terms of cultural and ethnic identity at either the national, sub-national, or trans-national levels. While the most extreme cases are the genocidal assaults on ethnic minorities in places like ex-Yugoslavia and Rwanda, milder forms are not nearly so rare and it would be difficult to cite a multi-ethnic/cultural nation that has not been faced with one or more groups asserting the exclusivity and superiority of their particular identities. In short, the contemporary world is marked by the contradictory trends of universalization and fragmentation – the former largely in economic terms, the latter in cultural terms. As I have argued by referring to the Japanese case, one cannot fully understand the recent resurgence of national, sub-national, and trans-national identity claims without considering the ongoing erosion of the conventional politico-institutional framework at both the national and the international levels of hegemony. Behind the ubiquitous calls for a heightened security and the claims of affiliation to 'things most intimate' lies an attenuation of national hegemonic structures and codes that 'invites' alternative powers into the arena where political, institutional and cultural principals are contested.

These contradictory trends of universalization and fragmentation are symptoms of the troubled state of late modernity in which objectifying forces have come to so permeate the realms of subjectivity and intersubjectivity that the foundation of national hegemony is in jeopardy; and a hegemony in disarray invites a variety of reactionary responses attempting to impose abstractly formulated notions of a national hegemonic ideal. As I have argued with respect to Japan, contemporary attempts at hegemonic consolidation often result in a further attenuation of the built-in flexibility in national hegemony sustained by the spontaneity of people's everyday practices. However, these problematic trends, including narcissistic closure and xenophobic national identity assertions, are not peculiar to Japan, but are rather a tendency whose manifestations are global. For a good twenty-five or thirty years the concept of universalism has been subject to a number of vigorous critiques throughout the world, and while in Japan these critiques have been part of, or led to, a series of national identity claims, in the West they have often accompanied vindications of exclusionary identity politics. The common feature of the response to hegemonic breakdown is thus not nationalism per se, but rather what I call a 'closed historical consciousness' whose forms vary according to local circumstances and historical conditions – racial supremacy movements, religious fundamentalisms, jingoistic political parties and those forms of new religions advocating a withdrawal from society. In the realm of international studies (in English speaking discourse) 'closed historical consciousness' takes a number of forms, two of which I would like to address: the epistemological issue of the detachment of the writing subject from the object of observation, and the open affirmation of the particularity of Western culture combined with an attack on the universal basis of international moral codes.

Edward Said's landmark work *Orientalism* (1978) has had an enormous impact in the history of international studies, opening up a new intellectual horizon of alternative perspectives, and has invited both constructive and reactionary criticisms. Among the many criticisms, I am particularly concerned with those raising epistemological questions surrounding the universal representation of the Western Self and the exclusion or relegation of the non-Western subject as the other. For example, in a 1983 work, Dennis Porter, criticized Said on two counts: for eliding the distinction between what Porter called 'pure' and 'political' knowledge, and, by criticizing others' representations of the Orient as flawed, for implying that a 'true' and knowable Orient could only be misrepresented by Orientalism. Questioning the status of this implied 'real' Orient, Porter argued 'Orientalism in one form or another is not only what we have but *all we can ever have*.'[25] In Porter's view, Said's argument cannot be 'justified on the basis of a radical discourse theory which presupposes the impossibility of stepping outside of a given discursive formation by an act of will or consciousness.'[26] It is unfortunate that Said's raising the question of the inscriptional violence of universal representation, and the consequent disfiguration of Asian subjects, have been reduced by Porter to a purely epistemological question, and that Said's ideas on the unintelligibility of the other and the relativity of the knowable, another poststructuralist insight, have seemingly caused Porter to turn against Said's arguments.

In a similar vein, Said's 'Orientalism' has been criticized by those arguing that the identity constructions operating between the Western Self and the non-Western other are mutual. David Pollack, for example, in his *Writing Against Culture: Ideology and Narrative in the Japanese Novel* (1992), argues that Said's position, what he calls the 'victim's monological view,' fails to be 'truly dialogical.'[27] Referring to his own experience in Japan, Pollack claims that Said did not take into account the fact that when 'we "Orientalize" Japan, we too . . . are being "Orientalized" from the other side,' 'being made exactly the same sort of debased object.'[28] In Pollack's logic, since the construction of the self and the other is a mutual affair, to problematize only the displacement that the other is subject to is one-sided and 'monological.' This short-circuited misconstruction of the self–other relation forgoes consideration of the context in which such identities are constructed, both the structurally embedded power relations and the hegemonic power inscriptions that such image making involves, one of the seminal points of Said's argument. Approaching this mutually constructive relation solely on the level of consciousness, Pollack formulates his critique of Said in terms of a mirror metaphor:

> What Said seems to take to be a matter of simple racism, then, turns out to be more like a hall of mirrors in which we stare at others, some more like ourselves and some less, all of whom are staring back at us. Recall Kipling's uncomfortable perplexity over the ambiguous Oriental 'look': as brutally or anxiously as we glower at them in this hall of mirrors, our gaze is returned from every angle to brutalize and express anxiety about us in turn.[29]

In this 'hall of mirrors,' 'Orientalism' is detached from its historical context and development, allowing Pollack to dismiss the role that hegemonic power formations play and thus reducing Said's account to an unfairly justified 'reaction.' By reducing history to a reciprocal reflective process of consciousness, Pollack is able to argue that 'Japan and we are actually in complicity, locked in the embrace of mutual self-definition,' and that 'at the moment we "Orientalize" Japan, we, exactly as Kipling discovered, are being "Orientalized" from the other side.'[30] As Brett de Bary has pointed out, Pollack uses three distinct notions of the self that he employs on different occasions for different purposes: the experience of oneself as an individual, a racially assumed differentiation between 'us' and 'them,' and individuals categorized as members of a nation.[31] One result of this sleight of hand is to nullify the workings of power and violence in hegemony, and to make it seem as if both parties are equally responsible for their mutual rejection: 'One wonders whether he [Said] is finally willing to extend to both sides of the Israeli–Palestinian conflict' the necessity of 'see[ing] others not as ontologically given but as historically constituted.'[32] Such narcissistic self-affirmations at the expense of the other are made possible by dehistoricizing of the self–other relation and are intimately tied to the current vogue for the indeterminacy and ironic detachment of the self from objects, historical events, and other cultures.

In both Porter's and Pollack's cases, such dehistoricizations, or a reduction of historical relations to cognitive ones, allow them to adopt a stance of ironic, detached relativity. Once relativity and detachment have been effected, positive affirmations of one's own cultural identity, especially in the historical context of the post-Cold War era, often seem to follow. In his *The Clash of Civilizations and the Remaking of World Order*, Samuel Huntington, for example, loudly calls for the re-establishment of Western hegemony in this new historical era in which 'the patterns of cohesion, disintegration, and conflict' are determined by 'civilizational identities.'[33] Arguing that the universal project of modernization has not necessarily Westernized the entire world, Huntington observes that the West is in relative decline vis-à-vis 'the Rest': 'Asian civilizations are expanding their economic, military, and political strength; Islam is exploding demographically with destabilizing consequences,' and non-Western civilizations in general 'are reaffirming the value of their own cultures.'[34] He contends that a 'civilization-based world order is emerging' – in which, since the question of identity is 'the most basic question humans can face,' the affirmation of one's own cultural values is increasingly important – and that '[t]he West's universalist pretensions [are] increasingly bring[ing] it into conflict with other civilizations, most seriously with Islam and China.'[35]

After assembling the various empirical and extra-empirical data for his analysis, Huntington reaches the following conclusion:

> The survival of the West depends on Americans reaffirming their Western identity and Westerners accepting their civilization as unique not universal and uniting to renew and preserve it against challenges from non-Western societies. Avoidance of a global war of civilizations depends on world leaders accepting and cooperating to maintain the multicivilizational character of global politics.[36]

It is rather surprising to see the word 'multicivilizational' tacked on here when the proposition being advanced so bluntly concerns the 'survival of the West.' It is also interesting that the categories of Westerners and Americans are used inter-changeably, seemingly to bolster Huntington's calls for the reaffirmation of Western (or European) identity in US domestic politics and for the necessity of strong leadership in both the domestic and international arenas. However, what is most striking, at least to me, is his suggestion that the founding ground of postwar international institutions – universal values based upon, and established during the course of, modern historical experience – be abandoned. Elsewhere Huntington dismisses the 'Western belief in the universality of Western culture' as altogether 'false,' 'immoral' and 'dangerous,' and warns against Western interventionism in intercivilizational affairs because 'it could lead to defeat of the West.'[37] How Huntington imagines international institutions like the UN, the World Bank and the IMF would function without being backed by the universalist principles, values, and ideals that have been slowly and painfully established in the process of modern history is not at all clear. There is in his analysis a curious application of cultural relativism to the discrediting of the universal values and justice that have taken two hundred years of modern history to mature.

Since the fall of the Berlin wall and the resultant but momentary euphoria of a supposed victory of democracy over communist totalitarianism, the international climate appears to have been far from conducive to greater tolerance and understanding between different peoples and nations. On the contrary, growing political indeterminacy and the declining profitability of non-speculative economic ventures have fostered a climate of indifference and intolerance, both on the national and international political fronts. Growing intolerance has been manifest, for example, in the rhetoric of 'equal' competition that affirms the doctrine of the survival of the fittest, regardless of the differentiated positions of each actor in international or national power hierarchies. Related to this intolerance is a refusal to acknowledge the sufferings of others, a retreat into the spheres of the individual or the family, and a growing propensity to focus on private interests and pleasures. Seen in this light, what characterizes our age is not so much the global ascendance of the democratic idea as a decline in the universal goal of striving for utopian ideals. Indeed, perhaps we should characterize the present as the post-postwar era, the period in which the greatest fruits of the post-war world, the universal utopian ideal that arose out of the experience of the two world wars and the institutions built upon them, are in decline. Huntington's thesis appears to typify the sense of withdrawal that has arisen from the recognition that world politics today are dangerously fragmented; and, at the same time, it attempts to quickly overcome this fear by resorting to an aggressive affirmation of identity that Huntington characterizes as being the essence of the 'Western.' This latter characteristic seems to be in accord with the current politico-cultural and economic conditions in which the political commitment to liberal internationalism is in jeopardy, while economic liberalism, in the name of globalization, is seemingly realizing its full potential.

As a way of closing this book, let me share some general thoughts on what, given what I have learned in my study of Japanese nationalism, can be done. My first and foremost suggestion is that there is an urgent need to reestablish or re-invigorate workable channels for dialogue across nations and peoples in order to counter-act the burgeoning tendencies towards imaginary closure, narcissism and indifference. The contemporary world is increasingly charged with nationalist identity claims, disregarding their national, religious or sub-national forms, and as a result a general sense of unease has spread throughout the international community accompanied by a heightened concern about security. As I see it, what is now at stake both in Japan and in the world at large is an eclipse of the utopian vision, the very best component of the liberal internationalism established in the early postwar era in the wake of the tragic experience of World War II. The idealism of the postwar international institutional regime has been subject to serious erosion, and the growing sense of insecurity has been generating the pre-conditions for an accelerated militarization of the world. This general tendency is also the case in East Asia, where the assertion of China's growing political and economic presence over the past decade has been altering the regional balance of power, and the desperate socio-economic situation in North Korea have both created a multitude of new anxieties in their neighbouring nations. The nations of East Asia, together with the world at large, are faced with the urgent task of establishing trustworthy channels for dialogue, in order to enhance mutual confidence in peaceful coexistence and to further efforts towards the achievement of common goals. Rather obviously, such channels for dialogue cannot be established without a willingness to share the burden of supporting the common good, nor without a concerted effort on the part of committed actors. Global technological and communications networks may indeed be in the process of constituting a 'single world,' but this appears to be in the present situation only possible by neglecting the interests and concerns of the weaker players. We must ask ourselves what kind of 'common' future is being designed when so many voices are left out of the negotiations.

I have emphasized that national identity claims have arisen in the particular historical context in which society and individuals are in a desperate struggle to come to terms with the ever intensifying objectifying forces of the market and advanced technology. I have also argued that contemporary Japanese society is suffering from the malfunctioning of national hegemony, is in the process of losing a functional mechanism for the channelling of popular voices into the formal political terrain, and has fallen into an unproductive economic mode in which the profits of speculation are alienating and obscuring the real economy grounded in production. This economic modality has also overtaken the global economy at large, resulting in the declining profitability of non-speculative ventures, the narrowing of market opportunities to limited sectors, and falling levels of disposable income. One must remember, however, that the logic of capital is not sustainable, that its autonomous self-propelling movement converting society into its own object is ultimately leading to a system-wide crisis that will have catastrophic results for and bring untold suffering to many. In order to forestall further desperate 'revolts of the senses' articulated in counter-hegemonic aesthetic-political movements, more creative efforts for the global redistribution of income must be made. In the long run they would benefit us all.

Notes

1 Approaching the questions of Japanese identity and nationalism

1 Mishima, Y. quoted in Bungei Shunjū (ed.) *Sengo 50-nen: Nihonjin no hatsugen*, vol. 1, Tokyo, Bungei Shunjū, 1995, pp. 363–4.
2 The phrase is indicative of the universalist bias that seeks to contain the problematic of the modern world on the national level.
3 Eagleton, T., *The Ideology of the Aesthetic*, Oxford, Blackwell, 1990, p. 3.
4 The term 'social imaginary' connotes the images, future visions and hopes held, expressed and shared by the members of a given society. It constitutes the intangible institution linking the state and society.
5 Mishima, Y. quoted in Kōsaka, S., *Hizai no umi*, Tokyo, Kawade Shobō Shinsha, 1988, p. 155.
6 Eagleton, *Ideology of the Aesthetic*, p. 13.
7 Building upon Antonio Gramsci's studies of interwar Italian society, Robert Cox has conceived the nation-state as a hegemonic system in which the state and society are linked in an organic manner at a given historical moment to constitute a structural unity. In this formulation, three mutually influencing forces – material capabilities, ideas, and institutions – come together in hegemony to constitute a historical structure: '[i]nstitutions are particular amalgams of ideas and material power which in turn influence the development of ideas and material capabilities.' See R. Cox, 'Gramsci, Hegemony and International Relations,' in S. Gill (ed.) *Gramsci, Historical Materialism and International Relations*, Cambridge, Cambridge University Press, 1993, p. 219.

Elsewhere Cox describes these tripartite relations: 'ideas and material conditions are always bound together, mutually influencing one another, and not reducible one to the other. Ideas have to be understood in relation to material circumstances. Material circumstances include both the social relations and the physical means of production. Superstructures of ideology and political organization shape the development of both aspects of production and are shaped by them.' R. Cox, 'Social Forces, States and World Order,' in R. O. Keohane (ed.) *Neorealism and its Critics*, New York, Columbia University Press, 1986, p. 56.
8 Mishima, quoted in Kōsaka, *Hizai no umi*, p. 155.
9 A number of the articles collected in M. Miyoshi and H. D. Harootunian (eds) *Postmodernism and Japan*, Durham, Duke University Press, 1989, make reference to this point.
10 Jameson, F., 'Cognitive Mapping,' in C. Nelson and L. Grossberg (eds) *Marxism and the Interpretation of Culture*, Urbana and Chicago, University of Illinois Press, 1988, p. 350. The basic idea argued here is based on arguments developed in

Jameson's *The Political Unconscious: Narrative as a Socially Symbolic Act*, Ithaca, Cornell University Press, 1981.

11 Doi, M. *et al.* (eds) *Sekaishi*, Tokyo, Sanseidō, 1986, pp. 368–9. The invasion of Beijing by an English–French coalition army during the second Opium war, and the Civil War in the US were both key contributors to Japan's successful avoidance of wholesale colonization.

12 Ibid. The contenders to the Edo *bakufu* were largely lower class samurais, many from the Satuma and Chōshu regions of Kyūshū, led by Saigō Takamori and supported by powerful merchants. To finance the war, the *bakufu* borrowed $6,000,000 from France to purchase battleships and other military necessities, in turn granting the French special access and rights to key economic sectors, such as silk and railways, which remained unfulfilled due to the *bafuku*'s defeat in the conflict. The restorationists on the other hand gained some support from the English.

13 Cf. Miyoshi, M., *As We Saw Them: The First Japanese Embassy to the United States*, Berkeley, University of California Press, 1979.

14 See, for example, Connolly, W. E., 'Identity and Difference in Global Politics,' in J. Der Derian and M. Shapiro (eds), *International/Intertextual Relations*, Lexington, MA, Lexington Books, 1989.

15 Karatani, K., 'Bijutsukan to shite no Nihon: Okakura Tenshin to Fenorosa,' *Hihyō kūkan*, 1994, vol. II–1, p. 68.

16 Ibid., pp. 68–9.

17 Cf. Clarke, J. J., *Oriental Enlightenment: The Encounter Between Asian and Western Thought*, London, Routledge, 1997, pp. 102–3.

18 Karatani, K., 'Bijutsukan to shite no Nihon,' p. 68.

19 Sakai, N., 'Modernity and its Critique: The Problem of Universalism and Particularism,' in M. Miyoshi and H. D. Harootunian (eds) *Postmodernism and Japan*, Durham: Duke University, 1989, p. 105.

20 Karatani, K., *Origins of Modern Japanese Literature*, B. de Bary (trans.), Durham, Duke University Press, 1993, p. 43.

21 This point is more elaborately argued in my article 'Fleeing the West, Making Asia Home: Transpositions of Otherness in Japanese Pan-Asianism, 1905–1930,' *Alternatives*, 1997, vol. 22.

22 My discussion in this paragraph owes much to R. B. J. Walker's notions of 'sovereignty from the inside' and 'sovereignty from the outside.' See his *Inside/Outside: International Relations as Political Theory*, Cambridge, Cambridge University Press, 1993, pp. 169–74.

23 Quoted in Pyle, K., 'Japan, the World and the Twenty-first Century,' in M. Yasusuke and P. T. Hugh (eds) *Political Economy of Japan* 2, Stanford, Stanford University Press, 1989, p. 482.

24 Quoted in Morio, S., *Kyōiku chokugo*, Tokyo, Mizuho Shobō, 1986, appendix.

25 Gluck, C., *Japan's Modern Myths: Ideology in the Late Meiji Period*, Princeton, Princeton University Press, 1985, p. 5.

26 W. T. de Bary, D. Keene and R. Tsunoda (eds) *Sources of Japanese Tradition*, New York, Columbia University Press, 1958, p. 787.

27 Ibid., p. 786.

28 Cf. Karatani, K., Kawamura, M., Murai, O. and Yamaguchi, M., 'Shokuminchi-shugi to kindai Nihon,' *Hihyō kūkan*, 1992, vol. 7.

2 'Overcoming modernity': towards an aesthetic politics of identity

1 Miyoshi, Y. and Takemori, T. (eds) *Kindai Bungaku* 5, Tokyo, Yūkaikaku, 1977, p. 12.
2 In his 1916 article, considered to have given a definition to Taishō democracy, Yoshino saw the relation between the state and the people in the following terms: 'the basic objective of the exercise of the state sovereignty is politically in its people.' Ibid.
3 Miyoshi, Y. (ed.) *Kindai bungakushi hikkei*, Tokyo, Gakutō Sha, 1987, pp. 22–3.
4 Miyoshi, Y. (ed.) *Kindai nihon bungakushi*, Tokyo, Yūkaikaku, 1975, p. 42.
5 Ibid.
6 Hasumi, S., 'Taishō-teki Gensetsu to Hihyō' ['Taishō-esque Language and Criticism'], in Karatani, K. (ed.) *Kindai Nihon no hihyō, Meiji Taishō-hen*, Tokyo, Fukutake Shoten, 1992, p. 137–8.
7 Karatani, K., *Origins of Modern Japanese Literature*, B. de Bary, trans., Durham, Duke University Press, 1993.
8 Hasumi, S., 'Taishō-teki,' p. 26.
9 Ibid., p. 138.
10 Ibid., p. 139.
11 Ibid., p. 138–9.
12 Ibid., p. 139.
13 Ibid., p. 135.
14 Ibid., p. 140
15 Ibid.
16 These participants included: Arishima Takeo, Hirabayashi Hatsunosuke, Aono Suekichi, Ishikawa Sanshirō, Shiratori Shōgo, Hasegawa Nyōzekan, Henri Barbusse, and others. For the origin of *Tane maku hito*, its relation to *Clarté*, and its significance in the subsequent development of Japanese proletarian literature, see I. Anzai and S. Yi (eds) *Kurarute undō to Tane maku hito*, Tokyo, Ochanomizu Shobō, 2000.
17 In his 1922 'Sengen hitotsu,' Arishima Takeo recognized the historical significance of the shift from intellectual-led popular movements to the labourers' self-organized struggle. However, as a result he was to personally suffer from his status as an intellectual, a part of the elite establishment to be overturned by the lower classes. Tormented by the loss of ethical foundation and purpose in his writing, possibly combined with other factors, Arishima committed suicide in the following year. His death raised various questions about art and politics, as well as the then deepening nihilism. See Nishigaki, T., 'Sengen hitotsu no ichi' in Miyoshi and Takemori (eds) *Kindai Bungaku*, vol. 5.
18 P. Duus (ed.) *The Cambridge History of Japan*, vol. 6, New York, Cambridge University Press, 1988, p. 535.
19 Hanes, J., 'Urban Planning as National Progress,' p. 1, paper presented at the conference 'Competing Modernities in Twentieth-Century Japan, Series Part II: Empires, Cultures, Identities 1930–1960,' University of California at San Diego, February 12th–16th, 1998.
20 Funato, Y. in Wada, S. and Funato, Y. (ed.) *Nihon no Kindai Bungaku*, Tokyo, Dōhōsha, 1982, pp. 85–6.
21 Funato, ibid., p. 86.
22 Chiba, S., 'Zenei geijutsu tono sōgū,' in Miyoshi and Takemori (eds) *Kindai Bungaku*, p. 41. Like proletarian literature, *shin-kankaku-ha* also emerged to challenge to streams derived from *shizen-shugi*. While proletarian literature challenged the conformity of universal humanism, *shin-kankaku-ha* challenged the subjective

and non-analytical descriptive method of *shi-shosetsu*, although there are authors who in their early stages had an affinity with both approaches. Nevertheless, as proletarian literature transformed into Marxist literature, the difference in their political stances undeniably set them apart, and the members of *shin-kankaku-ha* became increasingly self-consciousness of their status as 'bourgeois writers' against the tide of the times.

23 Odagiri, H., *Gendai bungakushi*, vol. 2, Tokyo, Shūei Sha, 1975, p. 346.
24 Ibid.
25 Kamiya, T., 'Shin-kankaku-ha no hōhō,' in Miyoshi and Takemori (eds) *Kindai Bungaku*, p. 51. By equating form with content, and nullifying distinctions, Yokomitsu's further disturbance of an already jeopardized state of meaning in language is difficult to defend. His original intention of depicting the misery of a fragmented humanity, and developing a new literary method for that purpose, seems to have been reversed at this point. Indeed, Yokomitsu's work soon came to show signs of being overly artificial with little social and human content. In 1927, *Bungei jidai* ceased publication.
26 Quoted in A. Tansman, 'Images of Loss and Longing in 1930s Japan,' p. 27, paper presented at the conference 'Competing Modernities in Twentieth-Century Japan, Series Part II: Empires, Cultures, Identities 1930–1960,' University of California at San Diego, February 12th–16th, 1998.
27 Kamiya, T., 'Shin kankaku-ha no hōhō,' p. 53.
28 Quoted in Tansman, 'Images of Loss,' p. 5.
29 Miyoshi, Y., 'Akutagawa Ryūnosuke no shi,' in Miyoshi and Takemori (eds) *Kindai Bungaku* 5, p. 61.
30 Ibid., p. 62–3, 70. These statements were made by Ōyama Ikuo, Inoue Yoshio and Hagiwara Sakutarō, respectively.
31 Ōkubo, N., 'Shōwa bungaku-shi no kōzō,' in Miyoshi and Takemori (eds) *Kindai Bungaku* 6, Tokyo, Yūkaikaku, 1977, p. 10. The quoted words are by Tosaka Jun.
32 Tansman, A., 'Images of Loss,' p. 5.
33 Miyoshi, Y., 'Akutagawa Ryūnosuke no shi,' p. 61.
34 Funato, in Wada S. (ed.) *Nihon no kindai Bungaku*, p. 88.
35 Ibid.
36 Akase, M., 'Shōwa jūnen zengo,' in Wada (ed.) *Nihon no kindai Bungaku*, p. 108.
37 Karatani, in Karatani, T. (ed.) *Kindai Nihon no hihyō – Shōwa-hen*, Tokyo, Fukatake Shoten, 1991, p. 126.
38 Akase, 'Tenkō Bungaku,' in S. Wada (ed.) *Nihon no kindai Bungaku*, Tokyo, Dōkō Sha, 1982, p. 98.
39 Ibid.
40 These literary magazines are, for example, the *Literary World* (*Bungakukai*), the *Japan Romantic School* (*Nihon Rōman-ha*), *Action* (*Kōdō*) and *Literary Art* (*Bungei*).
41 Karatani, in Karatani, *et al.* (eds) *Kindai Nihon no hihyō*, p. 126.
42 Ibid., p. 127–8.
43 Harootunian, H. D. and Najita, T., 'Japanese Revolt against the West,' in Peter Duus (ed.) *The Cambridge History of Japan*, vol. 6, New York, Cambridge University Press, 1988, p. 755.
44 Doak, K., *Dreams of Difference: The Japan Romantic School and the Crisis of Modernity*, Berkeley, University of California Press, 1904, p. 79.
45 Ibid. See Doak's discussion in his Chapter 4 for a detailed account of Kamei.
46 Ibid., p. 108.
47 Watsuji, T., *Fūdo: ningengaku-teki kōsatsu*, Tokyo, Iwanami Shoten, 1979, p. 3.
48 Ibid., p. 3–4.
49 Ibid., pp. 19–20; my translation, modified by borrowing some phrases from Geoffrey Bownas' translation of the passage in Watsuji, *Climate and Culture: A Philosophical Study* New York, Greenwood Press, 1961, p. 10.

50 Watsuji, *Ningen no gaku toshite no rinri-gaku*, Tokyo, Iwanami Shoten, 1934, pp. 10–12.
51 Ibid., p. 8.
52 Tosaka, J., 'Nihon rinri-gaku to ningen-gaku,' in Yasuo Y. (ed.) *Watsuji Tetsurō*, Tokyo, San'ichi Shobō, 1973, p. 212.
53 Abe, M., 'Introduction' to Nishida K., *An Inquiry into the Good*, M. Abe and C. Ives (eds), New Haven, Yale University Press, 1990.
54 Karatani, 'Fashizumu no mondai: de Man, Heidegger, Nishida Kitarō,' *Kotoba to higeki*, Tokyo, Daisan Bunmei Sha, 1989, p. 280.
55 Karatani, 'Senzen no shisō,' *hihyō kūkan*, II–1, 1994.
56 Ibid.
57 Cf. Simomura T., *Nishida Kitarō: hito to shisō*, Tokyo, Tōkai Daigaku Shuppankai, 1977, pp. 215–19.
58 Karatani, 'Posuto-modan ni okeru "Shutai" no mondai,' *Kotoba to higeki*, p. 291.
59 Ueyama, S., 'Nishida Kitarō no Tetsugaku Shisō,' *Hihon no shisō: dochaku to ohka no keifu*, Tokyo, Saimaru Shuppan, 1971, pp. 91–2; emphasis added.
60 It is highly debatable whether, and to what extent Nishida's philosophy in the mid-1930s was an active constituent of the discursive state of the time. While it is true that the discursive context and modality of the times was reductive in its employment of Nishida's concept of absolutely contradictory self-identity, the concept itself – as an image of harmonious 'synthesis' in which all contradictions are transcended – was also latent with a totalizing tendency. According to Karatani, Nishida's misunderstanding of Descartes is largely responsible for his ambiguous philosophical position, particularly on the question of subjectivity.
61 Matsumoto, K., 'Posuto-modan kara Nishida tetsugaku e,' *Shōwa saigo no hi*, Tokyo, Riburepōto, 1989, pp. 284–5.
62 Ibid.
63 Hagiwara S., 'Nihon eno Kaiki,' *Hagiwara Sakutarō zenshū*, vol. 4, Tokyo, Shinchō Sha, 1960, p. 478.
64 Yasuda Y., 'Bunmei Kaika no Ronri no Shūen ni tsuite,' *Yasuda Yojūrō senshū*, vol. 1, Tokyo, Kōdan Sha, 1971, p. 424.
65 Ibid.
66 Hagiwara Sakutarō's disaffection with the modern, for example, took the form of a sense of homelessness and eternal wondering whereas Jinbo Kōtarō thought that historical time might be displaced by a new time grounded in the spatial relationships of poetry. Jinbo's aim was furthered by Tanaka Katsumi who sought the potential for transcendental beauty in a redefinition of Asia as an alternative temporality. Kamei Katsuichiro pursued the problem of the split self, and suggested that all traits of the modern be rejected and a return to Japan, the place of ethnic and cultural unity, be effected. Hayashi Fusao, building upon Kamei's return to Japan, hoped for a cultural rebirth and a recovery from the imaginative impasse of the Japanese emperor system. See Doak, *Dreams of Difference*, pp. xli–xliii.
67 Tansman, 'Images of Loss,' p. 6.
68 Karatani, 'Edo no Chūshaku-gaku no Genzai,' *Kotoba to higeki*, pp. 123–5. See also his '"Ri" no Hihan,' ibid., pp. 143–5.
69 Ibid.
70 Doak, *Dreams of Difference*, p. 7.
71 Karatani, *Kindai Nihon no hihyō*, pp. 145–6. The following passage by Yasuda also exemplifies this perspective: 'Ours is a time of irony; it is a day when all who are great and glorious must think of irony as their own home. It is a day that compels us to remember that. And while we long for what is natural as our form of expression, as our true attitude, we can grasp only what is artificial.

282 *Notes*

Yet it must be said that our new age makes us aware of this artificial attitude and conscious of its enforcement.' In Doak, *Dreams of Difference*, p. 6.
72 Ibid., p. 19.
73 Ibid., pp. 6–7.
74 Ibid.
75 Yasuda, 'Bunmei Kaika no Ronri,' p. 424.
76 Ibid.
77 Matsumoto, K., 'Kindai no chōkoku Oboegaki,' *Rekishi no seishin*, Tokyo, Kashiwa Shobō, 1982, p. 32.
78 Hashikawa, B., *Nihon Rōman-ha Hihan josetsu*, Tokyo, Mirai Sha, 1964, p. 42.
79 Matsumoto, *Sengo no seishin*, Tokyo, Sakuhin Sha, 1985, p. 21.
80 Yasuda, 'Ajia no Haikyo,' p. 418.
81 Matsumoto, *Sengo no seishin*, pp. 23–4.
82 Hashikawa, B., *Nihon Rōman-ha Hihan josetsu*, p. 26.
83 Ibid., p. 33.
84 Ibid., p. 42.
85 Ibid., p. 43.
86 Ibid., p. 95.
87 Kawakami *et al.*, *Kindai no chōkoku*, Tokyo, Fuzanbō, 1979, pp. 171–2; emphasis added.
88 Takeuchi Y., *Kindai no chōkoku*, Tokyo, Fuzanbō, 1979, p. 74.
89 Ibid., pp. 76–7, and p. 85.
90 Ibid.
91 Matsumoto, 'Jizoku suru seishin,' in Takeuchi, *Kindai no chōkoku*, p. 284.
92 Matsumoto, 'Kaidai,' in Kawakami and Takeuchi *Kindai no chōkoku*, p. iv.
93 Kawakami *et al.*, *Kindai no chōkoku*, p. 166.
94 Takeuchi, *Kindai no chōkoku*, p. 66. The following supplementary information will be useful here. The Kyoto School's view was represented by Nishitani Keiji and Suzuki Shigetaka, whose positions were more or less shared by non-participant members such as Kōsaka Masaaki, Kōyama Iwao, and contributed to the formation and dissemination of the official war doctrine. *Bungakukai*'s modern rationalist position was fairly represented by Nakamura Mitsuo and by some of those outside the circle such as Shimomura Toratarō (Philosophy), Moroi Saburō (Music) and Kikuchi Masashi (Science), although to different degrees. Other members of *Bungakukai*, including Kawakami Testutarō, Kobayashi Hideo, Kamei Katsuichirō, Hayashi Fusao and Miyoshi Tastuji, were increasingly influenced by the Japan Romantic School's position, and their views show an ambiguous mixture of the two incompatible positions. The Japan Romantic School, a newly formed romantic literary circle, was most properly represented by Yasuda Yojūrō who did not participate in the symposium for some unspecified reason.
95 For example, Kamei Katsuichirō, a romantically inclined member of *bungakukai*, argued that modern Japanese history since the Meiji *bunmei kaika* (literally, 'opening up of civilization,' or adoption of the modern) was nothing but a gradual degradation of the Japanese spirit (*seishin*), its effects being described as 'poison circulating in our body' (in Takeuchi, *Kindai no chōkoku*, p. 201). Going a step further, Hayashi conceived the current crisis as resulting from the intrusion of Western pragmatic culture, and thus urged his compatriots to 'recover the true Japanese essence' by 'going back to the root' (in Takeuchi, *Kindai no chōkoku*, pp. 239–40, pp. 110–11). Protesting this antagonism of Japanese tradition and 'the modern' equated with the Western, and the simple-minded advocacy of returning to the past, Nakamura and Kikuchi pointed out that Japan was already 'modern' at least to some degree, and that the problematic of the modern as universal was not unique to Japan. In terms of how to 'over-

come' the crisis, Nishitani, Yoshimitsu, Hayashi and others sought remedies in the rearticulation of Japanese traditional spirit, while Kobayashi made it clear that the problem of 'the modern' could only be overcome by the modern itself. For example, Kamei Katsuichirō, a romantically inclined member of *bungakukai*, argued that modern Japanese history since the Meiji *bunmei kaika* (literally, 'opening up of civilization,' or adoption of the modern) was nothing but a gradual degradation of the Japanese spirit (*seishin*), its effects being described as 'poison circulating in our body' (in Takeuchi, *Kindai no chōkoku*, p. 201). Going a step further, Hayashi conceived the current crisis as resulting from the intrusion of Western pragmatic culture, and thus urged his compatriots to 'recover the true Japanese essence' by 'going back to the root' (in Takeuchi, *Kindai no chōkoku*, pp. 239–40, pp. 110–11). Protesting this antagonism of Japanese tradition and 'the modern' equated with the Western, and the simple-minded advocacy of returning to the past, Nakamura and Kikuchi pointed out that Japan was already 'modern' at least to some degree, and that the problematic of the modern as universal was not unique to Japan. In terms of how to 'overcome' the crisis, Nishitani, Yoshimitsu, Hayashi and others sought remedies in the rearticulation of Japanese traditional spirit, while Kobayashi made it clear that the problem of 'the modern' could only be overcome by the modern itself.

96 Kawakami *et al.*, *Kindai no chōkoku*, p. 29.
97 Ibid., p. 32.
98 Ibid., p. 248.
99 Ibid., p. 231.
100 Najita, 'Japanese Revolt against the West,' p. 761.
101 Karatani, in Karatani *et al.* (eds) *Kindai Nihon no hihyō*, p. 152.
102 Ibid. Although influenced by the Japan Romantic School, Kobayashi did not entirely abandon reason (unlike many of his contemporaries), as the following statement clearly demonstrates. '... thinking from my own perspective, overcoming modernity is not an attempt to bring in something else because the modern is wrong. The modern person can only overcome it with the modern. We do not have materials to work with other than what we have today. I am convinced that we must find a key to overcome the modern with those materials.' In Kawakami *et al.*, *Kindai no chōkoku*, p. 254.
103 Najita, 'Japanese Revolt against the West,' p. 755.
104 Kawakami *et al.*, *Kindai no chōkoku*, p. 239.
105 Ibid., pp. 200–1.
106 Ibid., pp. 202–4; emphasis added.
107 Minamoto, R., 'The Symposium of Overcoming Modernity,' J. Heisig, trans., in J. W. Heisig and J. Maraldo (eds) *Rude Awakenings: the Kyoto School, and the Question of Nationalism*, Honolulu, University of Hawaii Press, 1994, p. 213. Original in Kawakami *et al.*, *Kindai no chōkoku*, pp. 16–17.
108 Ibid., p. 214. Original in Kawakami *et al.*, *Kindai no chōkoku*, p. 17.
109 Takeuchi, *Kindai no chōkoku*, p. 70.
110 Ibid., p. 110.
111 Ibid.
112 Doak, *Dreams of Difference*, pp. xxxiv–xxxv.
113 Harootunian, H. D., 'Disciplining Native Knowledge and Producing Place: Yanagita Kunio, Origuchi Shinobu, Tanaka Yasuma,' in T. Rimer (ed.) *Culture and Identity: Japanese Intellectuals During the Interwar Years*, Princeton, Princeton University Press, 1990.
114 On the transformation of the ideal rural vision into reality via the agrarian movements of the 1920s and 1930s, see for example, A. Waswo's 'The transformation of rural society, 1900–1950,' in P. Duus (ed.) *The Cambridge History of*

Japan, vol. 6, The Twentieth Century, New York, Cambridge University Press, 1988.
115 Tanaka, S., *Japan's Orient: Rending Pasts into History*, Berkeley, University of California Press, 1993.
116 I have argued this point at length in my 'Fleeing the West, Making Asia Home: Transpositions of Otherness in Japanese Pan-Asianism, 1905–1930,' *Alternatives*, 1997, vol. 22.
117 This point made by Asada A. in the discussion, Karatani *et al.*, 'Senzen no shisō,' p. 41 and p. 32.
118 Cited in Hashikawa, *Nihon Rōman-ha hihan josetsu*, p. 41. Original in 'Bunshi no shosin ni tsuite,' 1939.
119 Ibid., pp. 41–2; emphasis added. Original in 'Shinchō,' 1938.
120 Ibid., p. 40.
121 Ibid., pp. 99–100.
122 Ibid., p. 144.
123 Cited in M. Jay, 'What Does it Mean to Aestheticize Politics?,' *Force Fields: Between Intellectual History and Cultural Critique*, London, Routledge, 1993, p. 75.

3 Uneasy with the modern: the postwar revival of the modern and the return of dissent

1 Koschmann, V., *Revolution and Subjectivity in Postwar Japan*, Chicago, University of Chicago Press, 1996, p. 15.
2 Ibid., p. 14.
3 General Douglas MacArthur, 'Message to the Japanese People on the First Anniversary of the Constitution,' in Supreme Commander for the Allied Powers, *The Political Reorientation of Japan, September 1945–September 1948, Report of the Governmental Section of SCAP*. 2 vols, Washington, US GPO, 1948, p. 788.
4 Ibid.
5 Ibid., pp. 788–9.
6 Ibid., pp. 363
7 Haruhiro Fukui, 'Postwar politics, 1945–1973,' in P. Duus (ed.) *The Cambridge History of Japan, Vol. 6, The Twentieth Century*, New York, Cambridge University Press, 1988, p. 167.
8 SCAP, *The Political Reorientation of Japan*, p. 364.
9 It would be useful here to note that a number of American cities voiced reservations about SCAP initiated reforms and propaganda campaigns in occupied Japan. For example, the journalist I. F. Stone (who inclined politically towards the left), seriously questioned SCAP's policy of attempting to effect institutional reforms without completely transforming the old government and bureaucracy. Another critic, the former US bureaucrat John Maki, argued that the reforms were undermined by the 'identity of interest [created] between the Occupation [forces] and the [Japanese] government.' Cited in M. Schaller, *The American Occupation of Japan: The Origins of the Cold War in Asia*, New York, Oxford University Press, 1985, p. 46.
10 Barshay, A., 'Postwar Social and Political Thoughts, 1945–90,' in B. Wakabayashi (ed.) *Modern Japanese Thought*, Cambridge, Cambridge University Press, 1998, pp. 283–4.
11 There have been generations of these nationalistically inclined theorists, emphatically indignant at the oppression Japan was subject to during the US occupation. The best known today are Etō Jun and Katō Norihiro.
12 Honda, S., 'Kaisetsu,' *Ara Masato Chosakushū*, vol. 1. Tokyo, Sanichi Shobō, 1983, pp. 326–7.

13 Koschmann, *Revolution and Subjectivity*, p. 43.
14 Ibid., pp. 43–4.
15 Cited in ibid., p. 44; his translation except for the last sentence, which is mine. Original in 'Geijutsu rekishi ningen,' *Kindai Bungaku* 1, 1946, p. 7.
16 Ibid., p. 43.
17 Ibid., p. 41.
18 Honda, S., quoted in Kajiki, G., '*Kindai Bungaku* – eikō to hisan,' in Dentō to Gendai Sha (ed.) *Sengo Shisō no genzai*, Tokyo, Dentō to Gendai Sha, 1981, pp. 34–5.
19 Honda, 'Kaisetsu,' p. 325.
20 Koschmann, *Revolution and Subjectivity*, p. 54.
21 Ibid., p. 52.
22 Ibid., pp. 52–3.
23 Ibid., pp. 51–3.
24 Ibid., p. 53.
25 Ibid.
26 Ibid., p. 57.
27 Ibid., p. 63. In his 1946 work Ara wrote: 'Human beings are egoistic, ugly, despicable, and human conduct is submerged in nothingness – Let us feel this keenly, and all else will follow!'; and 'Instead of those humanist gladiators who expected no reward for their selfless service, it is rather the greedy, ambitious disciples of egoism who are the purest followers of humanism.' In ibid., p. 57. As Koschmann argues, Ara's work is filled with 'ironic twists linking naiveté with cynicism, illusions with disillusionment, youth with maturity, humanism with egoism, heaven with hell,' and such extensive use of radical irony allowed him to nullify the meaning. Ibid., p. 55.
28 Ara used a similar argument in his 'Nakano Shigeharu-ron' ['On Nakano Shigeharu'] to discredit the moral basis of 'humanism' that *Shin Nihon Bungaku* had generally restored: 'Rather than disinterested humanism, shouldn't we be attempting to mobilize self-interested egoism? Shouldn't the petty bourgeoisie be connected to the revolution through the urge to provide for themselves rather than for the people and, indeed, the urge to feel that they themselves are people?' Quoted in Koschmann, *Revolution and Subjectivity*, p. 67.
29 Ibid., p. 79.
30 According to Alan Wolfe, the *Burai-ha*, unlike other literary movements such as the naturalists and the sensualists, did not have a coherent and clear 'philosophy toward life nor advocated a doctrine of literature or art'; rather, they were a group of writers who shared a similar' life-style involving dissipation, debauchery, and irrelevance.' As Wolfe argues, 'It is thus more appropriate to see *Burai-ha* as a coalescence of life and literary styles appearing to certain critics and sectors of public opinion as the embodiment of a mood of gloom and despair beneath the facade of buoyant optimism and progress that had so quickly taken hold after the war and defeat.' Wolfe, *Suicidal Narrative in Modern Japan: The case of Dazai Osamu*, Princeton, Princeton University Press, 1990, pp. 86–7.
31 Okuno, T., 'Kaisetsu,' in Dazai, O., *Shayō/Ningen shikkaku*, Tokyo, Shinchō Sha, 1979, p. 382.
32 Faced with the unprecedented challenge, the Yoshida government responded by forming a new cabinet with Yoshida's 'best students' in its key posts – Ikeda Hayato as Minister of Finance, Satō Eisaku as Minister of Transportation, and Okazaki Katsuo as Minister of Foreign Affairs. This cabinet formed the core establishment of the mainstream conservative politics of the following decades.
33 Dazai, 'Kunoo no nenkan,' cited in Okuno, 'Kaisetsu,' p. 380.
34 Ibid., pp. 380–1.

35 Honda, 'Kaisetsu,' pp. 332–5.
36 Ibid., p. 343.
37 Koschmann, *Revolution and Subjectivity*, p. 84.
38 Hashikawa Bunzō, for example, discusses the shock he and others first experienced when they first encountered the 'penetratingly logical thinking' of this work of Maruyama's. See the discussion: 'Sensō to dōjidai: sengo no seishin ni kaserareta mono,' (with participation by Usami Eiji, Sone Motokichi, Maruyama Masao, Yanaihara Isaku, Sō Sakon, Hashikawa Bunzō, Yasukawa Sadao), in *Maruyama Masao Zadan 2*, Tokyo, Iwanami Shoten, 1998, pp. 212–13.
39 Maruyama, 'Fukuzawa ni okeru Chitsujo to Ningen,' in Hidaka R. (ed.) *Kindai shugi*, Tokyo, Chikuma Shobō, 1964, p. 56.
40 Maruyama, 'Chōkokka shugi no ronri to shinri,' in Hidaka, R. (ed.) *Kindai shugi*, p. 269. Maruyama argues that this was in place during the Edo era with the division of powers between the spiritual authority of the emperor and the political authority of the Tokugawa *shōgunate* (albeit the former did not have any control over the latter's exercise of power), both of which, with the advent of the Meiji restoration, came to be subsumed under the modern Japanese state.
41 Ibid., pp. 272–3.
42 Ibid., p. 270.
43 Ibid., pp. 272–3; emphasis in the original.
44 Ibid., pp. 278–9.
45 Ibid.
46 Maruyama, 'Fukuzawa ni okeru jitsugaku no tenkai,' *Maruyama Masao Shū* vol. 3, Tokyo, Iwanami Shoten, 1995, p. 115.
47 Ibid., p. 116.
48 Ibid., p. 121; emphasis in the original.
49 Koschmann, *Revolution and Subjectivity*, p. 180.
50 Maruyama, 'Fukuzawa ni okeru,' pp. 123–4.
51 Ibid., p. 125.
52 Ibid.; emphasis in the original.
53 I put quotation marks around the words 'optimistic belief' because this adherence to scientific rationalism might have arisen, especially in Fukuzawa's case, from an awareness that Japan had little choice to be otherwise in the tense political climate of the early Meiji years.
54 Maruyama, 'Fukuzawa ni okeru,' p. 127.
55 Koschmann, *Revolution and Subjectivity*, p. 181.
56 Ibid., p. 191.
57 Ibid., p. 179.
58 Ibid., p. 178.
59 See, for example, the volume *Maruyama Masao o Yomu*, edited by the Jōkyō Shuppan editorial collective (Tokyo: Jōkyō Shuppan, 1998), in which Maruyama's lack of criticism of the colonial gaze upon Asia is pointed out by Endō Katsuhiko and others.
60 Matsumoto, K., 'Maruyama Masao, Ōtsuka Hisao to Kindai Shugi,' in Dentō to Gendai Henshu-bu (ed.) *Sengo shisō no genzai*, Tokyo, Dentō to Gendai Sha, 1981, p. 57.
61 Maruyama, 'appendix' to *Gendai seiji no shisō to kōdō*, Tokyo, Mirai Sha, 1964, p. 574.
62 Koschmann, V., 'Intellectuals and Politics,' in A. Gordon (ed.) *Postwar Japan as History*, Berkeley, University of California Press, 1993, p. 397.
63 Fukuda, T., 'Sinpo-shugi no jikogiman,' *Heiwa no rinen – Fukuda Tsuneari Hyōron Shu* 6, Tokyo, Sinchō Sha, 1966, pp. 122-3.
64 Kuno, O. et al., *Sengo Nihon no shisō*, Tokyo, Keisō Shobō, 1959, p. 81.

65 Yamada, K., *Sengo shisō shi*, Tokyo, Aoki Shoten, 1989, p. 13.
66 Cited in Yamada, ibid.
67 Tsuda, S., 'Rekishi no gaku ni okeru Hito no kaifuku,' *Tsuda Sōkichi zenshū*, vol. 20, Tokyo, Iwanami Shoten, 1965, p. 131.
68 Ibid.; emphasis added.
69 Ibid., p. 157.
70 Ibid., pp. 158–9.
71 Nippon Hōsō Kyōkai (ed.) *Nihon no sengo*, vol. 1, Tokyo, Nippon Hōsō Shuppan Kyōkai, 1977, pp. 272–3.
72 Ibid., pp. 252–81. This study, based on historical documents, takes the form of a dramatization of events and gives one a good sense of both the climate of the times and the politics that was played out between the labour leaders, the politicians and SCAP.
73 For a detailed account of police investigations and judicial procedures, see Hirotsu Kazuo, 'Sinjitsu wa uttaeru,' *Chūō Kōron*, October 1953.
74 Koschmann, 'Intellectuals and Politics,' p. 401.
75 Odagiri, Hideo, 'Ningen no shinrai ni tsuite,' cited in Yamada, *Sengo shisō shi*, p. 83.
76 Yamada, *Sengo shisō shi*, p. 76.
77 Maruyama, 'Aru Jiyushugi-sha eno Tegami,' *Maruyama Masao Shū*, vol. 4, Tokyo, Iwanami Shoten, 1995, pp. 327–32. The first publication of the article was in *Sekai*, September 1950.
78 Koschmann, 'Intellectuals and Politics,' p. 401.
79 These publications are 'The declaration of concerned Japanese scientists on war and peace' ('Sensō to heiwa ni kansuru nihon no kagakusha no seimei') in March 1949, 'The declaration of concerned Japanese scientists on peace treaty issues' ('Kōwa mondai ni tsuite no seimei') in March 1950 and 'The declaration on peace after the third debate' ('Mitabi heiwa ni tsuite') in October 1951. All appeared in *Sekai*, and enjoyed a tremendous influence among Leftists.
80 Yamada, *Sengo shisō shi*, p. 73.
81 Ibid., p. 80.
82 Ibid., p. 101. The Treaty's Article Five reads: 'We recognize that a military challenge against either Japanese or US territories is a threat to the peace and security of each nation ... and thus declare our intention to act in response against such a common threat.'
83 Ibid., p. 102.
84 Ibid., pp. 102–3.
85 Maruyama, 'Gendai ni okeru Taido Kettei,' *Sekai*, July 1960, p. 453; emphasis in the original.
86 Shimizu, I., 'Imakoso kokkai e,' quoted in Takeuchi S., *Sengo shisō e no shikaku*, Tokyo, Chikuma Shobō, 1972, p. 189.
87 Takeuchi, Y., 'Minshu ka Dokusai ka,' quoted in Yamada, *Sengo shisō shi*, p. 110.
88 Koschmann, 'Intellectuals and Politics,' p. 406.
89 Ibid.
90 Yoshida, M., *Sengo Shisōron*, Tokyo, Aoki Shoten, 1984, p. 31. According to the author, these critics included Shibata Shingo, Kawamura Nozomu, Handa Hideo and Fukuda Shizuo.
91 Ibid.
92 Matsumoto, 'Maruyama Masao, Ōtsuka Hisao to Kindai Shugi,' pp. 55–7.
93 Maruyama, *Gendai Seiji no shisō to kōdō*, Tokyo, Mirai Sha, 1964, p. 585.
94 Matsumoto, 'Maruyama Masao,' p. 54.

95 Maruyama, 'Rekishi Ishiki no "Kosō",' *Nihon no Shisō 6: Rekishi shisō shū*, Tokyo, Chikuma Shobō, 1972, p. 29.
96 Ibid., p. 41.
97 Ibid., pp. 32–3.
98 Drawing from Takeuchi Yoshimi, Matsumoto argues that 'the enlightenment position cannot be more than an external stimulus, and whether that will generate a new history is solely dependent upon whether internal self-negation is attempted or not.' Matsumoto, 'Maruyama Masao,' p. 53.
99 Yoshimoto, *Geijutsu-teki teikō to zasetsu*, Tokyo, Mirai Sha, 1963, p. 140.
100 Karatini, K. (ed.) *Kindai Nihon no hihyō, Shōwa-hen* 1, Tokyo, Fukutake Shoten, 1, Tokyo, Fukutake Shoten, 1990, p. 29.
101 Yoshimoto, 'Machiu-sho shiron,' *Yoshimoto Takaaki zen chosaku shū*, vol. 4, Tokyo, Keisō Shobō, 1969, p. 106.
102 Yoshida, *Zoku Yoshimoto Takaaki ron*, Tokyo, Parōru Sha, 1991, p. 17.
103 Yoshimoto, 'Maruyama Masao Ron,' in J. Etō and T. Yoshimoto (eds) *Warera no Bungaku*, Tokyo, Kōdan Sha, 1962, p. 343.
104 Ibid., p. 344.
105 Ibid.
106 Ibid., p. 345.
107 Yoshimoto, 'Nihon no Nashionarizumu,' in Yoshimoto (ed.) *Nashionarizumu*, Tokyo, Chikuma Shobō, 1964, pp. 12–33.
108 Yoshimoto, *Geijutsu-teki Teikō*, p. 140.
109 Yoshimoto, 'Nihon no Nashionarizumu,' pp. 8–9.
110 Ibid., pp. 10–11.
111 Taniguchi, T., *Yoshimoto Takaaki no hōe e*, Tokyo, Seikyū Sha, 1987, p. 56.
112 Quoted in ibid., p. 56; original in 'Zenei-teki Komyunikeishion ni tsuite.'
113 Takeuchi, *Kindai no chōkoku*, Tokyo, Chikuma Shobō, 1983, p. 425.
114 Takeuchi, 'Kindai-shugi to minzoku no mondai,' *Nihon ideorogii: Takeuchi Yoshimi Hyōron Shū* vol. 2, Tokyo, Chikuma Shobō, 1966, p. 267.
115 Ibid.
116 Ibid.
117 Takeuchi, 'Chūgoku no kindai to nihon no kindai,' in Ueyama, S. (ed.) *Nihon no nashionarizumu*, Tokyo, Tokuma Shobō, 1966, p. 258.
118 Ibid.
119 Takeuchi, 'Kindai towa Nanika,' *Kindai no chōkoku*, Tokyo, Chikuma Shobō, 1983, pp. 9–10.
120 Takeuchi, 'Chūgoku no kindai,' p. 269.
121 Takeuchi, 'Kindai-shugi,' pp. 274–6.
122 Matsumoto, 'Maruyama Masao,' p. 53.
123 Takeuchi, 'Kindai-shugi,' p. 278.
124 Ibid., pp. 278–9.
125 See N. Sakai's 'Modernity and Its Critique: The Problem of Universalism and Particularism,' in M. Miyoshi and H. D. Harootunian (eds) *Postmodernism and Japan*, Durham, Duke University Press, 1989, especially pp. 118–21.
126 Muraishi K., 'Takeuchi Yoshimi ni okeru Kindai no chōkoku,' *Nihon kaiki: seiō kindai to Nihon no sōkoku*, Tokyo, Dentō to Kindai Sha, 1975, p. 120.
127 Takeuchi, 'Kindai towa nani ka,' p. 42.
128 Ibid., p. 20.
129 Ibid., p. 18.
130 Matsumoto, 'Jizoku suru Seishin,' *Kindai no chōkoku*, Tokyo, Chikuma Shobō, 1983, p. 289.
131 Ibid., p. 274.

4 The age of rapid economic growth and romantic resurgence

1 Yoshimura, K., *Ikeda seiken 1575 Days*, Tokyo, Gyōsei Mondai Kenkyū Jo, 1985, p. 35.
2 Quoted in Hayashi, F., *Ikeda Hayato*, Tokyo, Sankei Shinbun Sha, 1968, p. 451.
3 Itō, M., *Ikeda Hayato: sono sei to shi*, Tokyo, Shiseidō, 1996, p. 87.
4 Yamada, K., *Sengo shisō shi*, Tokyo, Aoki Shoten, 1989, pp. 130–1.
5 For example, Kōsaka Masataka, one of these new realists, confronted the pacifist arguments of Katō Shuichi and Sakamoto Yoshikazu by claiming they had failed to take into account the contribution that the US military presence in Japan could make, both to the deterrence of nuclear war and future Japanese economic prosperity. Yamada, *Sengo shisō shi*, pp. 136–7.
6 Itō, *Ikeda Hayato*, p. 89.
7 For details, see Matsushita, K., *Sengo seiji no Rekishi to shisō*, Tokyo, Chikuma Shobō, 1994, p. 156.
8 Matsushita, *Sengo seiji no rekishi to shisō*, p. 157.
9 Hayashi, *Ikeda Hayato*, p. 453.
10 Quoted in ibid., p. 495.
11 The primary author of this draft is Kōsaka Masaaki, a well-known conservative intellectual. The draft was developed clearly along the lines of prewar moral codes as laid out in state-sponsored ideological tracts like *Kokutai no hongi* (*Fundamentals of Our National Polity*, 1937) and *Shinmin no michi* (*Way of the Subject*, 1941).
12 Yamada, K., *Sengo shisō shi*, pp. 148–9.
13 Ibid. However, we should not forget the negative side to this success story, the pollution, consumerism and education-hype that began to be clearly manifest already in the mid-1960s, fallouts that led to the coining of new words and phrases such as 'economic animal,' 'management society' (*kanri shakai*) and 'education mother' (*kyōiku mama*).
14 Takabatake *et al.*, *Tōron: Sengo Nihon no seiji shisō*, Tokyo, San'ichi Shobō, 1977, p. 82.
15 Yoshimura, *Ikeda seiken 1575 Days*, p. 396.
16 Ibid.
17 Takabatake *et al.*, *Tōron: Sengo Nihon*, p. 82. The speakers here are Takabatake Michitoshi, Hidaka Rokurō and Hashikawa Bunzō.
18 Ibid., p. 84.
19 Ibid., p. 96.
20 Oda, M. and Tsurumi, S., *Hansen to Henkaku*, Gakugei Shobō, 1968, p. 1
21 Oda, *Beheiren*, San'ichi Shobō, 1969, pp. 12–13.
22 Ibid., p. 3.
23 Ibid., pp. 3–4.
24 Kuno, O. and Takabatake, T., 'Gendai Nihon-ron no keifu,' *Gendai Nihon ron*, Tokyo, Chikuma Shobō, 1974, p. 37.
25 Oda, *Beheiren*, pp. 4–5.
26 Takabatake *et al.*, *Tōron: Sengo Nihon*, p. 86.
27 Ibid., p. 84.
28 Yamada, *Sengo shisō shi*, p. 182.
29 McCormack, G., 'The Student Left in Japan,' *New Left Review*, 1971, vol. 65, p. 48. For a sense of the previous factional spirit among the *Zengakuren* (the All-Japan Federation of Student Self-Governing Bodies), see especially pp. 7–9.
30 This point is made by Takabatake Michitoshi in his discussion with Kuno Osamu in 'Gendai Nihon-ron no Keifu,' *Gendai Nihon Ron*, Tokyo, Chikuma Shobō, 1974, p. 27.

31 Takagi M., *Zengakuren to Zenkyōtō*, Tokyo, Kōdan Sha, 1985, pp. 114–18.
32 Ibid., pp. 118–20.
33 McCormack, 'The Student Left in Japan,' pp. 47–8.
34 Yamamoto Y., *Chisei no hanran*. Tokyo: Zen'eisha, 1969, p. 188.
35 Ibid.
36 Koschmann, V., 'Intellectuals and Politics,' in A. Gordon (ed.) *Postwar Japan as History*, Berkeley, University of California Press, 1993, p. 416.
37 It should be noted, however, that Yoshimoto himself was largely absent from this activist decade, concentrating on his theoretical works.
38 This point is made by Takabatake Michitoshi in his discussion with Kuno Osamu in 'Gendai nihonron no keifu,' *Gendai Nihon ron*, Tokyo, Chikuma Shobō, 1974, p. 42.
39 This point is made by Shibata Sho and Kiwada Takeshi in T. Chikushi (ed.) *Zenkyōtō – Sore wa Nan data no ka*, Tokyo, Gendai no Riron Sha, 1984, p. 148 and p. 154.
40 This point is made by Asada, A., Sawa, T. and Shindō, M., 'Discussion: posutomodan to neomodan,' *Sekai*, April 1990, p. 77.
41 Quoted in Hashikawa, B., *Nihon Rōman-ha Hihan Josetsu*, Tokyo, Mirai sha, 1965, p. 337. Original is in Ishihara's 'Sashikorose!'
42 Quoted in ibid., p. 336. Original is in Oe's 'Genjitsu no teitai to Bungaku.'
43 Etō, J., 'Kaisetsu,' *Ishihara Shintarō shū*, Shin nihon Bungaku zenshū 5, Tokyo, Shūei sha, 1962, pp. 433–4.
44 Ibid.
45 Quoted in Isoda, K., *Sengoshi no kūkan*, Tokyo, Shinchō Sha, 1983, p. 542. Original is in Ishihara's *Shokei no Heya*.
46 Quoted in Etō, 'Kaisetsu,' pp. 434–5.
47 Ibid., pp. 433–4.
48 Quoted in ibid., p. 434.
49 Ibid., p. 443.
50 Ibid., p. 442.
51 Furubayashi, T. and Satō, M., *Sengo no Bungaku*, Tokyo, Yūkaikaku, 1978, p. 108.
52 Oe K., 'Warera no sei no sekai,' *Shuppatsuten*, Tokyo, Iwanami Shoten, 1980, p. 145.
53 Ibid., pp. 147–8.
54 Quoted in Isoda, K., *Sengoshi no kūkan*, p. 107. Original in Ōe's *Sebuntiin*.
55 Isoda, 'Kaisetsu,' *Nihon no Bungaku: Ishihara Shintarō, Kaikō Takeshi, Ōe Kenzaburō*, Tokyo, Chūō kōron sha, 1968, p. 347.
56 Quoted in Nagata, H., *Ōe Kenzaburō*, Tokyo, Kōdan Sha, 1971, p. 427.
57 Quoted in Isoda, *Sengoshi no kūkan*, p. 131.
58 Isoda, 'Kaisetsu,' p. 347.
59 Ibid.
60 Hashikawa, *Nihon Rōman-ha*, p. 321.
61 Himeoka, T., 'Onna no sengo 50-nen,' *Sengo 50-nen o doo miru ka*, vol. 2, Tokyo, Jinbun shoin, 1998, p. 94.
62 Furubayashi and Satō, *Sengo no Bungaku*, p. 151.
63 Etō, J., *Seijuku to soshitsu: 'haha' no hōkai*, Tokyo, Kawade Shobō Shinsha, 1975, p. 83.
64 Ibid., pp. 33–4.
65 Quoted in Sakurai, T., *Shisō toshite no 60-nendai*, Tokyo, Kōdan Sha, 1988, p. 168.
66 Sakurai, *Shisō toshite*, pp. 108–9.
67 Ibid., p. 109.

68 Etō, *Seijuku to Sōshitsu*, p. 91.
69 Quoted in Kawamoto, J., *Dōjidai no Bungaku*, Tokyo, Toju Sha, 1979, p. 174.
70 Ueyama, S., 'Dai tōa sensō no shisōshi-teki imi,' in Yoshimoto, T. (ed.) *Kokka no shisō, Sengo nihon shisō taikei 5*, Tokyo, Chikuma Shobō, 1969, pp. 317–18.
71 Ibid., p. 320.
72 Ibid., p. 322.
73 Ibid., p. 324.
74 Ibid., pp. 319–20.
75 Ueyama, 'Rekishi-kan no mosaku,' *Shisō no kagaku* 1, 1959, pp. 28–9.
76 Ueyama, *Juyō to sōzō no kiseki*, Tokyo, Kadokawa Shoten, 1991, pp. 15–17.
77 Takeuchi, Y., 'Futatsu no ajia shikan,' *Takeuchi Yoshimi zenshū*, vol. 5, Tokyo, Chikuma Shobō, 1981, pp. 87–8. It should be noted that Takeuchi refrained from criticizing Umesao because of the clear sense of the limited scope of his work; his criticism is directed at Takeyama alone.
78 This position is most clearly seen in Ueyama's 1959 article 'Rekishi-kan no mosaku,' *Shisō no kagaku*, 1, 1959, in which he compares and contrasts Umesao's ecological view of history with Marxian historical materialism. Ueyama is more favourable to the former than the latter, but does try to strike a balance.
79 Ueyama, 'Rekishi-kan no mosaku,' p. 37.
80 Hayashi, F., *Daitōa sensō kōtei ron*, Tokyo, Kabushiki Gaisha Rōman, 1974, p. 17.
81 Ibid., pp. 170–2.
82 Ibid., pp. 309–12.
83 Ibid., p. 15.
84 Ibid.
85 Umehara T., '*Anya Kōro* ni okeru Warai ni tsuite – Nihonjin no Warai' ['On Laughter in *Anya Kōro* – Laughter for the Japanese'], *Yami no Patosu*, Tokyo, Shūeisha, 1960.
86 This point is most explicitly made in his 1967 work 'Jitsuzon-shugi no jitsuzon-teki hihan' ['Existential Critique of Existentialism'], although similar arguments began to appear in his earlier works, such as 'Testugaku no fukkō' ['Revitalization of Philosophy'] (1960), and the article mentioned in the previous note on *Anya kōro*.
87 Uozumi, Y., 'Kaidai,' *Tetsugaku no fukkoh*, Tokyo, Shūeisha, 1983, p. 546.
88 In his 1954 work, 'Kamigami ga shinda ato ni,' for example, Umehara criticized the wartime Kyoto school's attempt to enforce their beliefs by fully utilizing/abusing the faculty of reason; in his 1956 article, 'Sarutoru no sōzō-ryoku ni tsuite,' he criticized the general tendency in early postwar philosophy to undervalue the necessity of scientific reason and objectivity in favour of ontological questions.
89 Umehara, T., *Bi to shūkyō no hakken*, Tokyo, Chikuma Shobō, 1967, p. 20.
90 Ibid., p. 62.
91 Ibid., p. 63.
92 Ibid.
93 Takabatake, M., *Tōron: Sengo Nihon no seiji shisō*, Tokyo, San'ichi Shobō, 1977, *passim*.
94 Ikeda, D., *Ikeda Kaicho zenshū*, vol. 1, Tokyo, Sōka Gakkai, 1967, pp. 4–5.
95 Ibid., pp. 176–7.
96 For the impact of the war on Mishima, his humble survival and the meaning of postwar Japan, see, for example, Hashikawa Bunzō's 'Yousetsu-sha no kinyoku – mishima yukio ni tsuite,' included in his *Nihon Rōman-ha hihan josetsu*.
97 Hashikawa, 'Chūkan-sha no me,' *hihyō to kenkyū: Mishima Yukio*, Tokyo, Hōga Shoten, 1974, p. 140. Hashikawa notes that Mishima's initial reaction to Japan's

defeat in the war was not as emotionally charged as the sudden death of his sister soon after the end of the war.
98 Kōsaka, S., *Hizai no Umi: Mishima Yukio to sengoshakai no nihirizumu*, Tokyo, Kawade Shobō Shinsha, 1988, p. 53.
99 Mishima, Y. and Hayashi, F., *Taidan: Nihonjin ron*, Tokyo, Banchō Shobō, 1966, p. 78.
100 Kōsaka, *Hizai no Umi*, p. 55.
101 Quoted in ibid., p. 155.
102 Mishima and Hayashi, *Taidan: Nihonjin Ron*, p. 15.
103 Ibid., p. 230
104 Hashikawa, 'Chūkan-sha no me,' p. 144.
105 Cited in Bungei Shūnjū Editorial's *Sengo 50-nen: Nihonjin no Hatsugen*, vol. 1, Tokyo, Bungei Shūnjū, 1995, pp. 363–4.
106 Itani, R., *Hisen no Shisō*, Tokyo, Kinokuniya Shoten, 1967, p. 131.
107 The broad picture of the times given in this paragraph is based on Mikami Osamu's argument in 'Sengo nashionarizumu no taishū-teki kitei,' *Sengo shisō no genzai*, Tokyo, Dentō to Gendai Sha, 1981.
108 Matsushita's intellectual debts are to the theorists of a generation previous to those cited above, theorists such as E. Fromm (*Escape from Freedom*, 1941), K. Mannheim (*Mensch und Gesellschaft im Zeiltalter im des Umbaus*, 1953), D. Rieseman (*The Lonely Crowd*, 1953), and W. Mills (*The Power Elite*, 1956). His work deserves recognition both for quickly absorbing, if not anticipating, the scholarly development of his Western counterparts.
109 Matsushita, K., 'Taishū shakai ron no konnichi-teki kadai,' *Shisō*, October 1960, p. 1.
110 Matsushita, 'Taishū kokka no seiritsu to sono mondaisei,' *Shisō*, November 1956, p. 32.
111 This point is made in reference to Max Beer's work on the experience of industrialization in the early twentieth-century England, *History of British Socialism* (1919).
112 Matsushita, 'Taishū kokka,' p. 35. My translation has borrowed, in the last sentence, from P. F. Drucker's translation in his *The New Society: The Anatomy of the Industrial Order*, 1951.
113 Ibid., p. 32.
114 Ibid., p. 32 and p. 35.
115 Ibid., p. 32 and pp. 36–7.
116 Ibid., p. 36.
117 Honma, N., 'Taishū shakai ni okeru bunka no mondai,' *Shisō no kagaku* 21, September 1960, p. 22.
118 Matsushita, 'Taishū kokka,' p. 36. Referring to the Japanese society of the 1960s, Fujita Shōzo, another mass society theorist, characterizes this quality as pleasure-naturalism (*yokubō shizen shugi*), and links it with the *tennō-sei* mentality that resists rational autonomous subjectivity.
119 Matsushita, 'Taishū kokka,' p. 33.
120 One of the representative works in this vein is Katō Hidetoshi's *Chūkan bunka*, Tokyo, Heibon Sha, 1957. 'Chūkan bunka' designates 'middle culture,' a mass culture in which the cultural goods and ideas formerly the monopoly of the middle-class are made available in popularized forms. This book is noteworthy for being jargon-free, addressed to this 'middle strata' of society, and marked by a tone of argument more affirmative and optimistic about the phenomenon than Matsushita's more 'objective' and detached account.
121 Matsushita, 'Taishū kokka,' p. 44.
122 Ibid., p. 45.

123 Ibid., p. 47.
124 Yamamoto, H., *Gendai Nihon no yuifutsu ron*, Tokyo, Shinsen Sha, 1981, p. 155.
125 Cited in Gotō, M., 'Taishū shakai ronsō,' in Tokyo Yuifutsuron Kenkyūkai (ed.) *Sengo shisō no saikentō*, Tokyo, Shiraishi Shoten, 1986, p. 93.
126 Yamamoto, H., *Gendai nihon*, p. 155.
127 Hirata, K., 'Kahei haaku to rekishi ninshiki,' *Shisō*, nos. 553, 554 and 556, 1970.
128 Ibid., pp. 46–7.
129 Ibid., p. 47.
130 Ibid., pp. 47–8.
131 Furubayashi, T. and Satō, M., *Sengo no Bungaku*, Tokyo, Yūkaikaku, 1978, p. 163.
132 Ibid.
133 Ibid., p. 165.
134 Quoted in Kawamoto, J., 'Seijuku no Sōshitsu,' *Dōjidai no Bungaku*, Tokyo, Tōju Sha, 1979, p. 163.
135 Quoted in ibid., p. 164.
136 Kōsaka, *Hizai no Umi*, p. 28.
137 Yamamoto, Y., *Chisei no Hanran*, p. 336.
138 Kōsaka, *Hizai no Umi*, p. 143.
139 Mishima, Y. and Zenkyōtō, *Tōron: Mishima Yukio vs. Zenkyōtō*, Tokyo, Shinchō Sha, 1969, pp. 43–6.
140 Ibid., p. 64.
141 All statistical and chronological information cited in this paragraph is from Itō M. *et al.*, *Sengo shisō no chōryu*, Tokyo, Shin Hyōron, 1978.
142 Yamada, *Sengo shisō shi*, p. 203.
143 Kōsaka, *Hizai no Umi*, p. 202.
144 Ibid., p. 204.
145 Yamada, *Sengo shisō shi*, p. 13.

5 Back to identity: 'postmodernity', *nihonjinron*, and the desire of the other

1 Nagatomi, Y., *Kindai o koete*, vol. 1, Tokyo, Ōkura Zaimu Kyōkai, 1983, p. 2; emphasis added.
2 The analysis of the text in this and subsequent paragraphs is based on H. D. Harootunian's article, 'Visible Discourse/Invisible,' in M. Miyoshi and H. D. Harootunian (eds) *Postmodernism and Japan*, Durham, Duke University Press, 1989.
3 Ibid., p. 85. The concept of the 'holon' was proposed by Arthur Koestler 'to designate those Janus-faced entities on the intermediate levels of any hierarchy, which can be described either as wholes or as parts, depending on the way you look at them from "below" or from "above" ... "holon", from the Greek *holos* = whole, with the suffix *on*, which, as in proton or neutron, suggests a particle or part.' Koestler, *Janus: A Summing Up*, London, Picador, 1978, p. 33.
4 Harootunian, 'Visible Discourse/Invisible,' p. 80.
5 Murakami, Y. *et al.*, *21-seiki sisutemu no tenbō*, Tokyo, Ōkura-shō Insatsu kyoku, 1987, pp. 2–3. According to the authors, thirty-nine study teams with about 460 researchers were involved in the study of 'soft-nomics.'
6 Ishikawa, M., *Sengo seijishi*, Tokyo, Iwanami Shoten, 1995, p. 136.
7 Yamada, K., *Sengo shisō shi*, Tokyo, Aoki Shoten, 1989, pp. 204–7.
8 Ibid.
9 Okumura, H., *Shin: Nihon no rokudai kigyō shūdan*, Tokyo Daiamondo Sha, 1983, pp. 46–7.

10 Ibid., p. 9. Original in *Economist*, January 4th, 1983.
11 Ibid. These phrases represent key concepts used to describe the Japanese economy by Chalmers Johnson, K. Dohse and David Friedman respectively.
12 Kenney, M. and Florida, R., 'Japan's Role in A Post-Fordist Age,' *Futures*, April 1989, p. 142.
13 Yamamoto, H., '70-nendai no shisō no henbō to shakai jōkyō,' in S. Kōsaka, S. Takeda and H. Yamamoto (eds) *Gendai Shisō Nyūmon II*, Tokyo, JICC, 1990, p. 37.
14 Ibid.
15 Yamamoto, '70-nendai,' p. 39.
16 Ibid.
17 Yamamoto borrows Kurihara Akira's concept, '*bunshū*' (the fragmented masses), from Kurihara's *Kanri Shakai to Minshū Risei*, Tokyo, Shinyō Sha, 1982.
18 Yamamoto, '70-nendai,' pp. 38–9.
19 Kogawa, T., 'New trends in Japanese popular culture,' in G. McCormack and Y. Sugimoto (eds) *The Japanese Trajectory: Modernization and Beyond*, Cambridge, Cambridge University Press, 1988, p. 54.
20 Yamamoto, '70-nendai,' p. 42.
21 Ibid. According to the study by Seibu's own research team (Saison Research Group Forum, *Seibu Saison renpō*, Tokyo, Nihon sofuto banku, 1988), in 1988 Seibu, also known as the Saison group, owned ten core business corporations, ninety-eight related companies, four research institutes, and employed 78,000 people with an annual income of 34 billion yen.
22 Havens, T., *Architecture of Affluence: The Tsutsumi Family and the Seibu-Saison Enterprises in Twentieth-Century Japan*, Cambridge, MA, Harvard University Press, 1994, pp. 102–3. The volume excellently demonstrates how the Seibu group has reached the zenith of the Japanese fashion industry.
23 Ibid., p. 104.
24 Baudrillard, J., *Simulacra and Simulation*, S. F. Glaser trans., Ann Arbor, University of Michigan Press, 1994, p. 1; emphasis in the original.
25 Yamamoto, '70-nendai,' p. 42.
26 According to Kogawa Tetsuo, this urban-centred development took two contradictory forms: as a part of the newly cultivated frontier replicating urban centres, and as a national homeland representing tradition as the other of the urbanites' hegemonic perspective. This was most clearly exemplified in the Japanese National Railways' nationwide campaign slogans 'Discover Japan' in the 1970s, and 'Exotic Japan' in the 1980s. See his 'New trends,' p. 59.
27 Yamamoto, '70-nendai,' p. 43.
28 Ibid.
29 Quoted in Yamamoto, '70-nendai,' p. 40.
30 Ibid., p. 41.
31 Ibid., p. 51.
32 Ibid.
33 Kogawa Tetsuo provides an explanation for this top-down structure of Japanese media, strictly controlled by government regulations. See his 'New trends,' pp. 62–3.
34 Ibid.
35 See N. Field, 'Somehow: The Postmodern as Atmosphere,' in Miyoshi and Harootunian (eds) *Postmodernism and Japan*, for an in-depth analysis of the narrative structure of Tanaka's book and its significance with respect to 'postmodernism.'
36 Tanaka, Y., *Nantonaku, kurisutaru*, Tokyo, Kawade Shobō Shin-sha, 1981, p. 25.
37 Ibid., p. 31.

38 Inoue, S., 'Jyōhō to seikatusu-ishiki no henka,' in Masaichi N. (ed.) *Jyōhō to Nihonjin* Tokyo, Kyōbun Dō, 1992, pp. 131–2.
39 Skov, L., 'Environmentalism Seen Through Japanese Women's Magazines,' in L. Skov and B. Moeran (eds) *Women, Media, Consumption in Japan*, Honolulu, University Of Hawaii Press, 1995, pp. 175–6.
40 Ibid.
41 Yoshimoto, M., cited in Skov, 'Environmentalism Seen Through Japanese Women's Magazines,' p. 176.
42 Karatani, K., *Kotoba to higeki*, Tokyo, Daisan Bunmei Sha, 1989, p. 9. The quotation is from Mark C. Taylor, 'Introduction: System . . . Structure . . . Difference . . . Other,' in M. C. Taylor (ed.) *Deconstruction in Context: Literature and Philosophy*, Chicago, University of Chicago Press, 1986, p. 33. Taylor writes that 'Deconstruction is, among other things, a critical rereading of all Western philosophy in which Derrida tries to dismantle (the) tradition, *as if* from within, by tracing philosophy's other.' Ibid., pp. 32–33.
43 Kinsella, S., 'Cuties in Japan,' in Skov and Moeran (eds) *Women, Media, Consumption*, p. 220.
44 Ibid., pp. 222–8.
45 Ibid., p. 237.
46 Ibid., p. 239; p. 244.
47 Ibid., p. 251. As the author notes, the characterization of contemporary Japan by this attitude of postponing coming to terms with adulthood and social responsibility is called by Okonogi Keigo '*moratoriam jidai*,' the age of moratorium.
48 That is to say, 'maturity' would induce a more critical attitude towards materialism and consumerism and thereby problematize the commercial interests of the large corporations.
49 Asada, A., 'Infantile Capitalism and Japan's Postmodernism: A Fairy Tale,' in Miyoshi and Harootunian (eds) *Postmodernism and Japan*, p. 275.
50 Clammer, J., 'Consuming Bodies: Constructing and Representing the Female Body in Contemporary Japanese Print Media,' in Skov and Moeran (eds) *Women, Media, Consumption*, p. 215.
51 Ibid., pp. 214–16.
52 Ibid.
53 Ivy, M., 'Critical Texts, Mass Artifacts: The Consumption of Knowledge in Postmodern Japan,' in Miyoshi and Harootunian (eds) *Postmodernism and Japan*, p. 34.
54 Ibid.
55 Ibid., p. 38.
56 Ibid.
57 Kogawa, 'New trends,' p. 140.
58 Ivy, 'Critical Texts,' p. 26.
59 Asada, 'Tōsō suru bunmei,' *Tōsō ron: sukizo kizzu no bōken*, Tokyo, Chikuma Shobō, 1984, p. 4.
60 Ibid.
61 Ibid., p. 223.
62 Kogawa, 'New Trends,' p. 140.
63 Takeda, S., 'Yoshimoto Takaaki no genzai,' in Kōsaka, Takeda and Yamamoto (eds) *Gendai Shisō*, pp. 27–8.
64 Ibid., p. 28.
65 Ibid., pp. 28–9.
66 Yamamoto, '70-nendai,' p. 53.
67 Itō, M. *et al.*, *Sengo shisō no chōryū*, Tokyo, Shin Hyōron, 1978, p. 243. The US dollar–Japanese yen exchange rate radically changed from $1 = 360 yen in

August 1971, to $1 = 200 yen by July 1978. T. Sawa, M. Shindō and M. Sugiyama, *80-nendai Ron*, Tokyo, Shinyō Sha, 1987, p. 19.
68 Vogel, E., *Japan As Number One: Lessons for America*, Tokyo, Charles E. Tuttle, 1979, p. 5.
69 Clark, G., *Yuniikuna nihonjin: G. Kuraaku, kikite Takemura Ken'ichi*, Tokyo, Kōdan Sha, 1979, pp. 10–13.
70 According to Nakane, what makes Japanese society distinctively coherent and homogeneous relative to other societies is this *ie*-based social structure in which people are hierarchically placed. In Doi's theory, it is the notion of *amae*, most often used to describe the mother–child relation, that makes Japanese society less individualistic and rationalist.
71 Murakami, Y., Kumon, S., and Satō, S., *Bunmei toshite no ie-shakai*, Tokyo, Chūō Kōron Sha, 1979, p. ii.
72 See Harootunian, 'Visible/Invisible,' especially pp. 82–4.
73 Ibid., p. 83.
74 Ibid., p. 82.
75 Ibid., pp. 81–5.
76 Umehara, T., 'Waga Seishin no Henreki IV,' *Gendai Nihon o kangaeru*, Tokyo, Shūei Sha, 1984, pp. 579–9.
77 Ibid., pp. 679–80.
78 Ibid., p. 652.
79 Ibid., p. 653.
80 Mikami, O., *Mishima, Kakuei, Etō Jun: Hoshu Shisō no Kōzu*, Tokyo, Saryū Sha, 1984, p. 8.
81 Ibid.
82 Matsumoto, K., '"Sengo"-waku no Kanoo to Genkai,' *Shinpen Etō Jun Bungaku Shūsei*, vol. 3, Tokyo, Kawade Shobō Shinsha, 1985, pp. 3–4.
83 Sugiyama, M., 'Sin-Kokkashugi to Sengo-shisō: Gendai Ideorogii Hihan,' *Sekai*, January 1986, p. 80.
84 Tsuzuki, T., *Sengo Nihon no chishiki-jin: Maruyama Masao to sono jidai*, Tokyo, Seori Shobō, 1995, pp. 415–16.
85 Shimizu, I., *Ningen o Kangaeru*, Tokyo, Bungei Shunjū, 1970, pp. 423–5.
86 Tsuzuki, *Sengo Nihon*, pp. 419–20.
87 Shimizu, I., *Sengo o Utagau*, Tokyo, Kodansha, 1980, pp. 134–9.
88 Cited in Sugiyama, 'Sin-Kokkashugi to Sengo-shisō,' p. 69.
89 See Richard Cronin, for one, on this change in the trade dynamic of the Asia Pacific region in the post-Plaza Accord era. R. Cronin, *Japan, the United States, and Prospects for the Asia–Pacific Century: Three Scenarios for the Future*, New York, St. Martin's Press, 1992, pp. 8–26.
90 For example, see Ozawa Terutomo's article 'Japan in a New Phase of Multinationalism and Industrial Upgrading: Functional Integration of Trade, Growth and Foreign Direct Investment,' *Journal of World Trade*, 1991, vol. 25 (1), in which he lays out his suggestions on how to best strategize survival in the current competitive international economic climate.
91 Hora, T., *Nankin daigyakusatsu no shōmei*, Tokyo, Asahi Shinbun Sha, 1986, p. 3
92 These arguments denying the historical fact of the Nanking Massacre can be found in Suzuki Akira's '*Nankin Daigyakusatsu' no Maboroshi* (*The Illusion of the 'Nanking Massacre'*), Tokyo, Bungei Shunjū, 1973, and Yamamoto Shichihei's, *Watakushi no naka no Nihongun* (*The Japanese Army in Myself*), Tokyo, Bungei Shunjū, 1976. A group of scholars, including Hora Tomio, Honda Katsuichi, and Fujiwara Akira, responded with counter-arguments refuting the 'fallacy thesis.' For a general idea of how the debate between the two groups progressed, see Hora Tomio's *Ketteiban: Nankin daigyakusatsu*, Tokyo, Tokuma Shobō, 1982.

93 Tanaka, M., *Nankin Jiken no Sōkatsu: Gyakusatsu Hitei Jyūgo no Ronkyo*, Tokyo, Kenkō Sha, 1987, p. 343.
94 Wakamiya, Y., 'Sengo Seiji ni okeru "Ajia Ishiki,"' *Chūō Kōron*, February 1995, p. 46.
95 Cyamoto, S., 'Kusanone no han-"Fusen Ketsugi"-ha,' *Sekai*, May 1995, p. 187.
96 Ibid., p. 190.
97 Sugiyama, M., Sawa, T. and Shindō, M., *Hachijyū-nendai Ron*, Tokyo, Shinyō Sha, 1987, p. 178. These leaders are essentially neo-liberals who advocate a smaller, more efficient, decentralized government and increasing private leadership; their guiding logic falls largely under the mantra of the survival of the fittest rationale.
98 Wolfe, A., 'Suicide and the Japanese Postmodern: A Postnarrative Paradigm?', in Miyoshi and Harootunian (eds) *Postmodernism and Japan*, p. 221.
99 Ibid., pp. 220–1.
100 As Karatani Kōjin argues ('One Spirit, Two Nineteenth Centuries,' in Miyoshi and Harootunian (eds) *Postmodernism and Japan*, p. 265), Barthes was keenly aware of the problem; for him, Japan designated not a geographical place historically existent but an imagined place outside of European subjectivity.
101 Karatani, 'Foucault to Nihon,' *Huumoa toshite no Yuiifutsu-ron*, Tokyo, Chikuma Shobō, 1993, p. 112.
102 Ibid.
103 Ibid., p. 113.
104 Karatani, 'One Spirit,' p. 260. See also his 'Postomodan niokeru Shutai no Mondai,' *Kotoba to higeki*, Tokyo, Daisan Bunmei Sha, 1989. This is what Derrida means by deconstruction, at least in his *Of Grammatology* (1968), the simultaneous affirmation and undermining of reason.
105 Ibid., p. 266. For a more in-depth discussion on the notion of *iki* as formulated by Kuki, and its significance, see Leslie Pincus' *Authenticating Culture in Imperial Japan: Kuki Shūzō and the Rise of National Aesthetics*, Berkeley, University of California Press, 1996.
106 Karatani, '"Ri" no Hihan,' *Kotoba to higeki*, pp. 137–8. It bears pointing out that according to Karatani's historically and philologically informed analysis, the Japanese word for 'reason' encompasses a much broader field than what can be translated by logos, reason, or rationality, such that when the Chinese character designating *ri* is used in combination with another adjunct character signifying various concepts – sense/way, principle, truth, logic, philosophy, rationality, reason, etc. – any subsequent criticisms of reason encompass all of these connotations.
107 Ibid., pp. 140–2.
108 Ibid., p. 144.
109 Karatani, 'Edo no Chūshaku-gaku to Genzai,' *Kotoba to higeki*, pp. 114–15.
110 Ibid.
111 Karatani, 'One Spirit,' p. 270.
112 Ibid.
113 Ibid., p. 271.
114 Kurihara, A., 'Kuukyo na chūshin no Jōen,' *Seiji no fookuroa*, Tokyo, Shinyō Sha, 1988, p. 147.
115 Ibid., pp. 148–9.
116 Ibid.
117 Ibid.
118 Ibid.
119 Ibid. and Orwell, G., *Nineteen Eighty-four*, Harmondsworth, Penguin, 1990, pp. 28–9, 51, 312–26.

6 Japan in the 1990s and beyond: identity crises in late modern conditions

1 Kurihara, A., Sugiyama, M. and Yoshimi, S. (eds) *Kiroku: Tennō no shi*, Tokyo, Chikuma Shobō, 1992, pp. 373–81.
2 Karatani, K., '1970-nen = Shōwa 45-nen,' *Shūen o meggutte*, Tokyo, Kōdan Sha, 1995, pp. 8–13.
3 It should be pointed out, however, that the images of the Shōwa era itself began to fade before its end, sometime in the Shōwa 40s (the mid-1960s), when temporal reference to the Shōwa reign began to be replaced by the designators of the Western calendar. See Karatani, ibid.
4 Kurihara *et al.* (eds) *Kiroku: Tennō no shi*, pp. 373–81.
5 Takeda, S., 'Tennō to iu Kin'i,' *Gendai hihyō no enkinhō*, Tokyo, Kōdan Sha, 1998, p. 244.
6 Ibid., p. 245.
7 Ibid., p. 243.
8 Ibid., p. 242.
9 Brenner, R., 'Uneven Development and the Long Downturn: The Advanced Capitalist Economies from Boom to Stagnation, 1950–1998.' *New Left Review*, 1998, vol. 229. All quotations and statistics in this section from Brenner's Chapter 4, Section III, Part 2: 'Japan in the 1980s and 1990s: From Bubble to Bust and Beyond,' pp. 213–26.
10 Ibid., p. 219.
11 A number of key statistical indicators show that Japanese exports as a percentage of world trade declined from 10.3 per cent in 1985 to 8.5 per cent in 1990; according to the OECD, Japan was only able to pass on through price increases 75 per cent of the increased costs incurred by the higher yen; and the Japanese manufacturing rate of profitability remained stagnant, on a level with 1985 and 1978 peaks.
12 Ōmae, K., *Kinyū kiki kara no saisei*, Tokyo, Presidento Sha, 1995, pp. 16–29.
13 Ibid., pp. 17–9.
14 Ibid., pp. 28–9.
15 Okumura, H., 'Hojin-shugi no tasogare,' *Sekai*, March 1994, pp. 49–50.
16 Ibid.
17 McCormack, G., 'From Number One to Number Nothing: Japan's *Fin de Siècle* Blues,' *Japanese Studies*, 1998, vol. 18, no.1, p. 4.
18 Sawa, T., *Heisei fukyō no seiji keizai gaku*, Tokyo, Chūō Kōron Sha, 1994, pp. 40–1.
19 Ibid.
20 Ōmae, *Kinyū kiki kara no saisei*, pp. 152–8.
21 Brenner, 'Uneven Development and the Long Downturn,' p. 225.
22 McCormack, 'From Number One to Number Nothing,' p. 4.
23 The immediate causes which led to the LDP's loss of accountability with the public were public disclosures of deep-seated corruption among LDP politicians, particularly after the publication of the large-scale tax evasion by Kanemaru Shin, the head of the largest LDP faction, and the failure, by the then prime minister Miyazawa Kiichi, despite his alleged promises, of electoral reforms aiming to make parliamentary representation fairer.
24 Nakano, K., 'The Politics of Administrative Reform in Japan, 1993–1998,' *Asian Survey*, 1998, vol. XXXVIII, no. 3, p. 292.
25 Yamamura, K., 'The Japanese Political Economy after the 'bubble': *Plus Ça Change?*,' *Journal of Japanese Studies*, 1997, vol. 23, no. 2, p. 294.
26 The first set of financial contributions to the UN multilateral forces were made in August 1990 to the tune of US$1 billion, followed by an additional $3 billion

in September, $1 billion for the UN forces and $2 billion in support of the neighbouring nations of the region. In January of the following year, the Japanese government contributed an additional US $9 billion to the US-led UN multilateral forces.
27 Article Nine of the Japanese Constitution reads as follows:

Article Nine.
(1) Aspiring sincerely to an international peace based on justice and order, the Japanese people forever renounce war as a sovereign right of the nation and the threat or use of force as a means of settling international disputes.
(2) In order to accomplish the aim of the preceding paragraph, land, sea, and air forces, as well as other war potential, will never be maintained. The right of belligerency of the state will not be recognized.

28 Kasai, K., 'Wangan sensō to mukonkyo na 'heiwa',' *Gendai shisō*, 1991, vol. 19, p. 5.
29 Comment made by Kang Sang-jung in a discussion with Narita Ryūichi, Komori Yōichi, Kang Sang-jung and Satō Manabu, in Narita, R. *et al.*, 'Taiwa no kairo o tozashita rekishikan o dō kokufuku suru ka,' *Sekai*, May 1995, p. 197.
30 In Kawamura, M., *Sengo hihyō ron*, Tokyo, Kōdansha, 1998, pp. 234–5.
31 Kasai, 'Wangan sensō,' pp. 72–9. Kasai argues that the temptations for and the danger of making 'unfounded decisions' is rooted in the conditions of the twentieth-century subject, who, by definition, is deprived of a self-evident reason and meanings. He argues that the void of meaningless that first became apparent after World War I prepared the ground for radical 'departures' from the historical impasse, as exemplified in the Heideggerian 'leap' in the 1930s and the Sartrean existential 'choice' for an empty subject in the 1950s. For Kasai, the former generated Nazism, and the latter, totalitarianism.
32 Ibid., p. 74.
33 Ibid.
34 Ibid.
35 Ibid., p. 79.
36 Hein, L. and Selden, M., 'Learning Citizenship from the Past: Textbook Nationalism, Global Context, and Social Change,' *Bulletin of Concerned Asian Scholars*, 1988, vol. 30, no. 2, p. 5.
37 Ibid., p. 7. Located outside Harbin, Manchuria, from 1935 to 1945, Unit 731 exposed mostly Chinese, but also some Korean, American, Russian, British, Australian, and New Zealand captives to bubonic and pneumonic plague, typhoid, syphilis and other diseases in an effort to obtain data for the development of biological weapons. Evidence of Unit 731 was suppressed after the war by the Japanese and American governments, and the perpetrators of these crimes against humanity were allowed to escape prosecution in exchange for cooperating with American biological warfare researchers. See Tamura Yoshio, 'Unit 731,' in H. T. Cook and T. F. Cook, *Japan at War: An Oral History*, New York, New Press, 1992, pp. 158–67.
38 Ishizaka, K., ''Fusen ketsugi' towa nani ka,' *Sekai*, September 1994, pp. 183–5.
39 Irie, Y., 'The History of the Textbook Controversy,' *Japan Echo*, August 1997, pp. 34–7. According to Irie, the Japanese government's apology stated: 'Undeniably this was an act that, with the full involvement of the military authorities of the day, severely injured the honor and dignity of many women. The government of Japan would like to take this opportunity once again to extend its sincere apologies and express its remorse to all those, irrespective

of place of origin, who suffered immeasurable pain and irreparable physical and psychological wounds as comfort women.' The statement also added: 'We hereby reiterate our firm determination never to repeat the same mistake by forever engraving such issues in our memories through the study and teaching of history.'

40 Yoshida, Y., 'Rekishi ishiki wa henka shita ka,' *Sekai*, September 1994, p. 30. According to Gotō Kenichi, Hashimoto Ryūtarō, then Minister of Transportation and later Prime Minister, and Ozawa Ichirō, the leader of the newly born Shinsei Party, expressed more or less the same understanding to Ishihara. See his '"Daitōa sensō" kaihō-shikan no kyomō-sei,' *Sekai*, September 1994, p. 172.

41 McCormack, 'The Japanese Movement to 'Correct' History,' *Bulletin of Concerned Asian Scholars*, 1988, vol. 30, no. 2, p. 17. As McCormack notes, under this conception various events were organized by the League, including the 1995 'Celebration of Asian Togetherness' which sought to 'praise Japan for its contribution to the independence of Asian countries.'

42 Narita *et al.*, 'Taiwa no kairo,' p. 193.

43 Yoshida, 'Rekishi ishiki wa henka shita ka,' p. 27.

44 F. Schodt, *Dreamland Japan: Writing on Modern Manga*, Berkeley, Stone Bridge Press, 1996, pp. 19–20.

45 Ibid., pp. 55–6.

46 Ibid., pp. 57–8.

47 Ibid., p. 54.

48 Kinsella, S., 'Japanese Subculture in the 1990s: Otaku and the Amateur Manga Movement,' *Journal of Japanese Studies*, 1998, vol. 24, no. 2, p. 305.

49 Ibid., p. 306.

50 Schodt, *Dreamland Japan*, p. 45.

51 Ibid., p. 46.

52 Miyadai, S., Fujii, Y. and Nakamori, A., *Shinseiki no riaru*, Tokyo, Asuka Shinsha, 1997, pp. 163–4.

53 Okuda, Y., 'Purikura no tonari ni uttsute iru no wa dare ka?,' *Hayari no bunka chōkenkyu*, Kyoto, Seigen Sha, 1998, pp. 54–8.

54 Okuda's idea of *purikura* as an alternative mode of photography is helpful. According to her brief but insightful discussion, the self recorded in *purikura* is mediated by a teleological gaze which dematerializes and dehistoricizes real time, space and the self.

55 Cf. J. Treat, 'Yoshimoto Banana Writes Home: The *Shōjo* in Japanese Popular Culture,' in J. Treat (ed.) *Contemporary Japan and Popular Culture*, Richmond, UK, Curzon Press, 1996, p. 303. Referring to Raymond Williams' notion of 'mobile privatization,' Treat characterizes contemporary Japanese society as enjoying 'a high standard of living and a wide range of consumer choices . . . allied with an inward-looking privacy.' According to Treat, these are the pre-conditions in which a modern sense of nostalgia prevails, and in which nostalgia is attributed to 'a lost faith in the possibility of social change, prompting a retreat to the private enclave of the family and the consumption of certain retro styles.'

56 According to the November 14th, 1994 issue of *Time* magazine, Japanese women's average age for first marriage is about 26-years-old, one of the oldest in the world, while the average rate of child-bearing among Japanese women of reproductive age is 1.46, one of the lowest in the world.

57 Okumura, 'Hōjin-shugi no tasogare,' pp. 48–9.

58 Ibid.

59 See, for example, Treat's 'Yoshimoto Banana Writes Home,' in which he describes how the Japanese media constitute the image of 'girls' as others.

60 In these stores, the used underwear of high-school girls, with the ex-owner's photo in school uniform attached, sells for about US $10, mostly to men in their 20s–50s.
61 Miyadai S., *Seikimatsu no sahō: owarinaki nichijō o ikiru chie*, Tokyo, Media Fakutorii, 1997, p. 19.
62 Ibid., pp. 181–2.
63 Ibid., pp. 142–4.
64 Yonahara, K., 'Mirareru shintai to sei' ['Body and Sexuality'], *Hayari no Bunka Chō kenkyu*, Kyoto, Seigen sha, 1998, pp. 196–9.
65 Miyadai Shinji in discussion with Suzuki Takayuki, 'Shōhi sareru jiko,' *Hayari no Bunka*, p. 27.
66 Ibid.
67 Miyadai *et al.*, *Shinseiki no riaru*, Tokyo, Asuka Shinsha, 1997, p. 228.
68 Ibid., pp. 227–9.
69 Ibid., pp. 228–9.
70 These slogans were unearthed in Miyadai's extensive research into the social anthropology of popular culture and his detailed field work study of high-school girl culture. While defending the girls from the moral condemnation of older male critics, Miyadai's uncritical affirmation of girl culture as the symbol of the end of the millennium is obviously simplistic. It can be argued that his conceptual formulation is permeated by a voyeurism related to the challenge posed by girl culture to his masculine identity, and his denial of these two dynamics, taking the form of a self-erasure.
71 *Kyōjutsu chōsho* [police investigation reports.] cited in Tachibana, T., 'Seijō to ijō no aida,' *Bungei shunjū*, March 1998, p. 134 and pp. 139–41.
72 Ibid., pp. 153–4.
73 Tachibana, 'Seijō to ijō no aida,' p. 103; my translation. I have incorporated a few lines from the translation published in *The Japan Times, Weekly International Edition* (October 27th–November 2nd, 1997) into my translation. The ellipses between stanzas are mine; all other ellipses are the author's. The last three lines are from Dante's *Inferno*.
74 Osawa M., 'Bamoidooki-shin no kao,' *Gunzō*, October 1997, p. 226.
75 Ibid., pp. 232–6.
76 McCormack, 'From Number One to Number Nothing,' pp. 9–10.
77 Ibid., p. 8.
78 Ibid., pp. 7–8.
79 Ibid.
80 *Time* magazine of January 30th, 1995 cites the comment of a Kobe survivor, who also experienced the war as a child, expressing a fusion of the memories of the two catastrophes.
81 McCormack, 'From Number One to Number Nothing,' p. 9.
82 Ibid., p. 11.
83 Nishio, K., 'Aum Shinrikyō to gendai bunmei,' *Shinchō*, August 1995, pp. 248–50.
84 Kaplan, D. and Marshall, A., *The Cult at the End of the World: The Incredible Story of Aum*, London, Hutchinson, 1996, p. 15.
85 Kaplan and Marshall, *The Cult at the End of the World*, pp. 56–7.
86 Quoted in Yoshimi S., *Sekai*, July 1995, p. 56.
87 Ibid.
88 Ibid., p. 19.
89 Ibid., p. 33.
90 Ibid., p. 18.
91 Ibid., pp. 213–14.

92 Yoshimi, 'Wareware jishin no naka no Aum,' p. 50.
93 Ibid., p. 224.
94 Nishiyama, A., 'Kaeru basho ga nai,' *Sekai*, March 1997, p. 112.
95 Ibid., pp. 133–4.
96 Ibid., p. 111.
97 It is interesting to note the ambivalent role the cult played in relation to the nostalgic subject. As typified by the words of the 27-year-old woman I cite, the nostalgic aspects of the cult are obvious. Simultaneously, however, *Aum* students can also be seen as anti-nostalgic in that their individual decisions to join the cult and 'materialize' their wills seem to be an attempt to break through the everyday and to forgo the indulgence in nostalgia, even though such attempts did end up arriving at yet another system of the everyday.
98 Nishio, 'Aum Shinrikyō to gendai bunmei,' pp. 253–4.
99 Ibid.
100 Ibid., p. 237.
101 Ibid., pp. 253–4.
102 According to Gavan McCormack, the group's puzzling name was a tactic employed by Fujioka to present the facade that they differed from conventional conservatives; the group name was a banner under which they thought their views would gain more credence. McCormack, 'The Japanese Movement to "Correct" History,' p. 17–18. Also, in terms of their intent, Fujioka and his group's view of history is supposed to 'liberate' the Japanese from the dominant postwar view of history that is, for them, nothing but an imposition of the American and Allied forces' vision upon the Japanese.
103 Hein and Selden, 'Learning Citizenship from the Past,' p. 9.
104 Ibid., pp. 9–10.
105 Ibid.
106 Ibid., p. 10.
107 In the same vein, it should be noted that there was an Indian judge named Radhabinod Pal who insisted on the innocence of the Japanese war leaders at the Tokyo War Crimes Tribunal. Pal wrote a 1,275-page statement of judgment, longer than the total of all other documents submitted in the trial, in defence of the accused Japanese. This episode is well-known and well-circulated in nationalist circles as a third-person proof of the biases embodied in the framework of the tribunal.
108 Nishio, 'Aum Shinrikyō to gendai bunmei.'
109 See Saeki, K., *Gendai Nihon no ideorogii: groobarizumi to kokka ishiki*, Tokyo, Kōdan Sha, 1998, Chapter 1.
110 Cited in Miyadai, *Seikimatsu no sahō*, p. 269.
111 Katō, N. and Kang, S., 'Haisengo ron to aidentitii,' *Nashionarizumu o yomu*, Tokyo, Jōkyō Shuppan Sha, 1998.
112 Katō, N., 'Coping with Japan's Postwar Schizophrenia,' *Asahi Evening News*, January 1st, 1998, p. 1.
113 Katō, 'Haisengo ron,' *Haisengo ron*, Tokyo, Kōdan Sha, 1997, pp. 50–3.
114 Ibid., pp. 47–9.
115 T. Morris-Suzuki, 'Unquiet Graves: Katō Norihiro and the Politics of Mourning,' *Japanese Studies*, 1998, vol. 18, no. 1, p. 24.
116 Katō, 'Haisengo ron,' pp. 46–8.
117 Ibid.
118 Katō and Kang, 'Haisengo ron to aidentitii,' pp. 217–18.
119 Ibid.
120 H. D. Harootunian, 'Jizoku suru kioku/Bōkyaku sareru rekishi,' *hihyō kūkan* II-24, 2000, p. 90.

121 Morris-Suzuki, 'Unquiet Graves,' p. 28.
122 During my visit to Japan in the summer of 1998, I had a chance to attend Katō's third year undergraduate course which was more or less focused on the subject of the '*enjo kōsai*' ('compensated date').
123 Gerow, A., 'Consuming Asia, Consuming Japan: The New Neonationalist Revisionism in Japan,' *Bulletin of Concerned Asian Scholars*, 1998, vol. 30, no. 2, p. 30.
124 For an example of this multiple violation of temporal and spatial boundaries and the merger of writing styles, something akin to a pastiche of creative and more scholarly 'objective' writing, see Katō's 1991 work, 'Kore wa hihyō dewa nai' ['This is Not a Criticism'], *Gunzō*, May 1991. Written as Katō's immediate response to the above discussed statement issued against Japan's involvement in the Gulf War, Katō seems to have wanted to indicate an expression of the inexpressible by means of stylistic oddities.
125 See V. Koschmann's 'National Subjectivity and the Uses of Atonement in the Age of Recession,' *South Atlantic Quarterly*, vol. 99, no. 4.
126 This problematic of the fusion of memory and history in recent Japanese intellectual discourse is discussed by Tessa Morris-Suzuki in her 'Remembered Worlds: Rethinking Historical Space in a Global Age,' *Geography Research Forum*, vol. 19, 1999.
127 Benjamin, W., 'The Work of Art in the Age of Mechanical Reproduction,' *Illuminations*, H. Zorn trans., New York, Schocken, 1969, p. 242.
128 Harootunian, 'Jizoku suru kioku/Bōkyaku sareru rekishi,' p. 92.
129 Ibid., p. 85, p. 92.
130 Ibid., p. 92.
131 Koschmann, 'National Subjectivity and the Uses of Atonement,' p. 9.
132 Cited in ibid. Original in Ōgoshi Aiko, 'Mōhitotsu no 'katarikuchi no mondai': dono yō ni rekishi jijitsu to deau ka?,' *Sōbun*, April 1997, p. 22.
133 Fukuda, K., *Nippon no Kakyō*, Tokyo, Shinchō Sha, 1993, p. 150.
134 Ibid. On this point, see his discussion of Hagiwara Sakutarō on pp. 136–44.
135 Interestingly, and disturbingly, while exploring the point where literary criticism intersects with nationalism and agitatedly calling upon the aesthetically motivated desire in the minds of his fellow nationals, Fukuda is also an articulate spokesperson for the *Realpolitik* of the international system. As Katō's reference to him indicates (a 'hybrid conservative'), Fukuda displays a remarkable intellectual versatility that allows him to freely cut across various scholarly fields and problematics while combining a literary sensitivity with informed political analysis.
136 Aaron Gerow's detailed analysis shows how Fujioka's text reconstructs Japanese history by recollecting fragments of images and 'facts' which are then contextualized in an overarching 'narrative of suffering' that imparts to his readers the masochistic pleasure of victimization and melodrama. See his 'Consuming Asia, Consuming Japan,' pp. 30–6.
137 Paul Ricoeur advanced a concept of 'narrative identity,' initially at the end of the third volume of his *Time and Narrative*, Chicago, University of Chicago Press, 1983, and later in an article in *Philosophy Today*, Spring 1991, pp. 73–81. In these works, he describes how identity, or the narrative of the self, is constituted by a 'fusion between history and fiction' and claims that the personalized form of narrative is also applicable to national identity construction. This breakdown of objective temporality seems to be closely related to the *purikura* phenomena, the photographic recording of personal narratives, discussed earlier, in which 'narrative identity' is produced in a crudely commercialized and fetishized manner.
138 Gerow, 'Consuming Asia, Consuming Japan,' p. 36.

7 Japanese nationalism in the late modern world: in place of a conclusion

1 Sun, G. and Komori, Y., 'Kindai tennōsei tabuu no koozu,' *Sekai*, October 2000.
2 Ibid., p. 66.
3 Vlastos, S., 'Tradition: Past Present Culture and Modern Japanese Tradition,' in Vlastos (ed.) *Mirror of Modernity: Invented Traditions of Modern Japan*, Berkeley, University of California Press, 1998, p. 3.
4 Chakrabarty, D., 'Afterword: Revisiting the Tradition/Modernity Binary,' in Vlastos (ed.) *Mirror of Modernity*, p. 286.
5 Ibid., p. 287.
6 Gupta, A., 'The Song of the Nonaligned World: Transnational Identities and the Reinscription of Space in Late Capitalism,' *Cultural Anthropology*, February 1982, vol. 7, no. 1, p. 74.
7 Chakrabarty, 'Afterword,' p. 295.
8 Brennan, T., 'The National Longing for Form,' in B. Ashcroft, G. Griffiths and H. Tiffin (eds) *The Post-Colonial Studies Reader*, London, Routledge, 1995, p. 170.
9 See P. Bourdieu, *Outline of a Theory of Practice*, R. Nice trans., Cambridge, Cambridge University Press, 1977.
10 Lakoff, G., *Women, Fire and Other Dangerous Things: What Categories Reveal About the Mind*, Chicago, University of Chicago Press, 1987.
11 Combs-Schilling, M. E., *Sacred Performances: Islam, Sexuality, and Sacrifice*, New York, Columbia University Press, 1989, p. 25.
12 See, for example, T. Sekine, *An Outline of the Dialectic of Capital*, 2 vols, London, Macmillan, 1997; R. Albritton, *A Japanese Reconstruction of Marxist Theory*, London, Macmillan, 1986; R. Albritton, *A Japanese Approach to Stages of Capitalist Development*, London, Macmillan, 1991; R. Albritton, *Dialectics and Deconstruction in Political Economy*, New York, Macmillan, 1999.
13 Albritton, *Dialectics and Deconstruction*, p. 7.
14 Ibid., p. 10.
15 Adorno, T., *Against Epistemology: A Metacritique – Studies in Husserl and the Phenomenological Antinomies*, W. Domingo trans., Oxford, Basil Blackwell, 1982, pp. 69–70.
16 Nakamasa, M., '"Dooitsusei" no kigen o megutte,' *Jōkyō*, May 1998, p. 91.
17 Zizek, S., *The Sublime Object of Ideology*, London, Verso, 1989, p. 31.
18 Ibid., pp. 95–7. Noteworthy here is that capital for Zizek is not a central authority where value is concentrated, but rather an empty point, a purely symbolic authority that Zizek calls, after Lacan, '*le point de capiton*,' literally, the 'quilting point' representing the void in the marketplace by means of which exchange is made functional. Zizek sees an analogous fetishistic inversion in the realm of the Symbolic; with analogy to Lacan's notion of surplus-enjoyment, the surplus generated by signifying practices gives rise to, and is gathered towards, what is perceived as the ultimate object of desire – what Lacan calls the '*objet petit a*' – the pure signifier, the essence of the desired object beyond its instantiations.
19 Nakamasa, '"Dooitsusei" no kigen o megutte,' pp. 92–3.
20 Eagleton, T., *The Ideology of the Aesthetic*, Oxford, Blackwell, 1990, p. 9.
21 Ibid.; see, for example, pp. 20–1, p. 75, pp. 81–4, and pp. 85–6.
22 Ibid., p. 9.
23 Satō, M., Komori, Y., Kang, S. and Narita, R., 'Taiwa no kairo o tozashita rekishi-kan o doo kokufuku suru ka?' ['How to Overcome the Historical Consciousness which Cuts Itself Off from the Passage of Communication'], *Sekai*, May 1997, p. 188.
24 Ibid., p. 186.

25 Porter, D., 'Orientalism and its Problems, in P. Williams and L. Chrisman (eds) *Colonial Discourse and Post-Colonial Theory*, New York, Columbia University Press, 1994, p. 150; emphasis added.
26 Ibid.
27 Pollack, D., *Writing Against Culture: Ideology and Narrative in the Japanese Novel*, Ithaca, Cornell University Press, 1992, footnote 22, p. 23.
28 Ibid., pp. 20–1.
29 Ibid., p. 21.
30 Ibid.
31 de Bary, B., 'Nihon bassingu no jidai ni okeru Nihon kenkyū,' in N. Sakai, B. de Bary, and Iyotani T. (eds) *Deconstruction of Nationalism*, Tokyo, Kashiwa Shobō, 1996, p. 293.
32 Pollack, *Writing Against Culture*, footnote 22, p. 23. Original in Said, *Orientalism*, New York, Vintage, 1978, p. 225.
33 Huntington, S., *The Clash of Civilizations and the Remaking of World Order*, New York, Simon & Schuster, 1996, p. 20.
34 Ibid. Huntington divides the post-1989 world into nine civilizational groupings by means of a rather arbitrary and confusing mishmash of criteria: geographic (Latin American, African), religious (Islamic, Hindu, Buddhist, Russian-Orthodox), ethnic/linguistic (Sinic/Chinese), national (Japanese) and, the most arbitrary but seemingly self-explanatory category of them all, 'Western.'
35 Ibid., pp. 20–1.
36 Ibid., pp. 310–11.
37 Ibid., p. 20.

Bibliography

Abe, M., 'Introduction to Kitarō Nishida,' *An Inquiry into Good*, Masao Abe and Christopher Ives (eds). New Haven: Yale University Press, 1990.
Adorno, T., *Against Epistemology: A Metacritique – Studies in Husserl and the Phenomenological Antinomies*, W. Domingo trans. Oxford: Basil Blackwell, 1982.
Akase, M., 'Shōwa jūnen zengo,' in S. Wada (ed.), *Nihon no kindai Bungaku*. Tokyo: Dōkō Sha, 1982.
—— 'Tenkō Bungaku,' in S. Wada (ed.), *Nihon no kindai Bungaku*. Tokyo: Dōkō Sha, 1982.
Albritton, R., *A Japanese Reconstruction of Marxist Theory*. London: Macmillan, 1986.
—— *A Japanese Approach to Stages of Capitalist Development*. London: Macmillan, 1991.
—— *Dialectics and Deconstruction in Political Economy*. New York: Macmillan, 1999.
—— and Sekine, T., *A Japanese Approach to Political Economy: Unoist Variations*. London: Macmillan, 1995.
Anderson, B., *Imagined Communities: Reflections of the Origins and Spread of Nationalism* (rev. edn). London: Verso, 1991.
Anzai, I. and Yi, S. (eds), *Kurarute undō to Tane maku hito*. Tokyo: Ochanomizu Shobō, 2000.
Ara, M., 'Dai ni no seishun,' *Ara Masato chosaku shū*. Tokyo: San'ichi Shobō, 1983.
Asada, A., *Kōzō to chikara: kigōron o koete*. Tokyo: Keisō Shobō, 1983.
—— *Tōsō ron: sukizo kizzu no bōken*. Tokyo: Chikuma Shobō, 1984.
—— 'Infantile Capitalism and Japan's Postmodernism: A Fairy Tale,' in Masao Miyoshi and H. D. Harootunian (eds), *Postmodernism and Japan*. Durham: Duke University Press, 1989.
—— Sawa, T. and Shindō, M., 'Discussion: Posutomodan to Neomodan,' *Sekai*, April 1990.
Barshay, A., *State and Intellectual in Imperial Japan: The Public Man in Crisis*. Berkeley: University of California Press, 1988.
—— 'Postwar Social and Political Thoughts, 1945–90,' in B. Wakabayashi (ed.), *Modern Japanese Thought*. Cambridge: Cambridge University Press, 1998.
Baudrillard, J., *Simulacra and Simulation*, Shelia Faria Glaser (trans.). Ann Arbor: University of Michigan Press, 1994.
Benjamin, W., 'The Work of Art in the Age of Mechanical Reproduction,' in Harry Zorn (trans.), *Illuminations*. New York: Schocken, 1969.
Bourdieu, P., *Outline of a Theory of Practice*, R. Nice (trans.). Cambridge: Cambridge University Press, 1977.
Brennan, T., 'The National Longing for Form,' in Bill Ashcroft, Gareth Griffiths, and Helen Tiffin (eds), *The Post-Colonial Studies Reader*. London: Routledge, 1995.

Brenner, R., 'Uneven Development and the Long Downturn: The Advanced Capitalist Economies from Boom to Stagnation, 1950–1998,' *New Left Review* vol. 229, May/June 1998.

Bungei Shunjū (eds), *Sengo 50-nen: nihonjin no hatsugen*, vol. 1. Tokyo: Bungei Shunjū, 1995.

Chakrbarty, D., 'Afterword: Revisiting the Tradition/Modern Binary,' in Stephen Vlastos (ed.), *Mirror of Modernity: Invented Traditions of Modern Japan*. Berkeley: University of California Press, 1998.

Chiba, M., 'Seiji no haiboku, daga kibō wa sutenai,' *Sekai*, December 1996.

Chiba, S., 'Zen'ei geijutsu tono sōgū,' in Y. Miyoshi and T. Takemori (eds), *Kindai Bungaku*, vol. 5. Tokyo: Yūkaikaku, 1977.

Chikushi, T., *Zenkyōtō – sore wa nan datta no ka*. Tokyo: Gendai no Riron Sha, 1984.

Clammer, J., 'Consuming Bodies: Constructing and Representing the Female Body in Contemporary Japanese Print Media,' in Lise Skov and Brian Moeran (eds), *Women, Media, and Consumption in Japan*. Honolulu: University of Hawaii Press, 1995.

Clark, G., *Yunikuna nihonjin: G. Kuraku, kikite Takemura Ken'ichi*. Tokyo: Kōdan Sha, 1979.

Clarke, J. J., *Oriental Enlightenment: The Encounter Between Asian and Western Thought*. London: Routledge, 1997.

Combs-Schillings, M. E., *Sacred Performances: Islam, Sexuality, and Sacrifice*. New York: Columbia University Press, 1989.

Connolly, W. E., 'Identity and Difference in Global Politics,' in James Der Derian and Michael Shapiro (eds), *International/Intertextual Relations: Postmodern Readings of World Politics*. Lexington, MA: Lexington Books, 1989.

Cox, R., 'Social Forces, States and World Orders: Beyond International Relations Theory,' in R. Keohane (ed.), *Neorealism and Its Critics*. New York: Columbia University Press, 1986.

—— *Production, Power, and World Order: Social Forces in the Making of History*. New York: Columbia University Press, 1987.

—— 'Multilateralism and World Order,' *Review of International Studies*, 18, 1992.

—— 'Gramsci, Hegemony and International Relations,' in Stephen Gill (ed.), *Gramsci, Historical Materialism and International Relations*. Cambridge: Cambridge University Press, 1993.

—— 'Civilizations in World Political Economy,' *New Political Economy*, vol.1, no. 2, 1996.

—— 'Civilizations and the Twenty-first Century: Some Theoretical Considerations,' *International Relations of the Asia–Pacific*, vol. 1, 2001.

Cronin, R., *Japan, the United States, and Prospects for the Asia–Pacific Century: Three Scenarios for the Future*. New York: St. Martin's Press, 1992.

Cyamoto, S., 'Kusanone no han "fusen ketsugi"-ha,' *Sekai*, no. 608, May 1995.

de Bary, B., 'Nihon bassingu no jidai ni okeru Nihon kenkyū,' in N. Sakai, B. de Bary and T. Iyotani (eds), *Nashionaritii no datsukōchiku*. Tokyo: Kashiwa Shobō, 1996.

Derrida, J., *Of Grammatology* (Gayatri Spivak, trans.). Baltimore: Johns Hopkins University Press, 1976.

Doak, K., *Dreams of Difference: The Japan Romantic School and the Crisis of Modernity*. Berkeley: University of California Press, 1994.

—— 'Ethnic Nationalism and Romanticism in Early Twentieth-Century Japan,' *Journal of Japanese Studies*, vol. 22, no. 1, 1996.
Doi, M., Katayama, S., Horikoshi, T. and Yoshimura, T., *Sekaishi*. Tokyo: Sanseido, 1986.
Dower, J., *Empire and Aftermath: Yoshida Shigeru and the Japanese Experience, 1878–1954*. Cambridge: Harvard University Press, 1979.
—— *War Without Mercy: Race and Power in the Pacific War*. New York: Pantheon, 1986.
—— *Japan in War and Peace: Essays on History, Culture, and Race*. London: Harper Collins, 1995.
—— *Embracing Defeat: Japan in the Wake of World War II*. New York: Norton & Company, 2000.
Duus, P., *The Rise of Modern Japan*. Boston: Houghton Mifflin, 1976.
—— (ed.), *The Cambridge History of Japan*, vol. 6. New York: Cambridge University Press, 1988.
Eagleton, T., *The Ideology of the Aesthetic*. Oxford: Blackwell, 1990.
Etō, J., 'Kaisetsu,' *Ishihara Shintarō shū*, Shin Nihon Bungaku zenshū 5. Tokyo: Shūei sha, 1962.
—— 'Kaisetsu,' *Ishihara Shintarō shū*, Shinchō Nihon Bungaku 62. Tokyo: Shinchō Sha, 1969.
—— '"Chichi" no imeeji no kaifuku o,' *Bunmei taikoku o mezase*. Tokyo: Yomiuri Shinbun Sha, 1971.
—— *Seijuku to sōshitsu: 'ha ha' no hōkai*. Tokyo: Kawade Shobō Shinsha, 1975.
—— *Nichibei sensō wa owatte inai: shukumei no taiketsu – sono genzai, kakao, mirai*. Tokyo: Nesuko, 1987.
Field, N., 'Somehow: The Postmodern as Atmosphere,' *Postmodernism and Japan*, M. Miyoshi and H. D. Harootunian (eds). Durham: Duke University Press, 1989.
—— *In the Realm of a Dying Emperor*. New York: Vintage, 1993.
Fujiwara, A., *Nankin no Nihongun: Nankin daigyakusatsu to sono haikei*. Tokyo: Ōtsuki Shoten, 1997.
Fukuda, K., *Nippon no kakyō*. Tokyo: Shinchō sha, 1993.
Fukuda, T., 'Shinpo-shugi no jikogiman,' *Heiwa no rinen – Fukuda Tsuneari hyōron shū* 6. Tokyo: Sinchō Sha, 1966.
Fukui, H., 'Postwar Politics, 1945–1973,' in Peter Duus (ed.), *The Cambridge History of Japan, Vol. 6, The Twentieth Century*. New York: Cambridge University Press, 1988.
Furubayashi, T. and Satō, M., *Sengo no Bungaku*. Tokyo: Yūkaikaku, 1978.
Gerow, A., 'Consuming Asia, Consuming Japan: The New Neonationalist Revisionism in Japan,' *Bulletin of Concerned Asian Scholars*, vol. 30, no. 2, 1998.
Gluck, C., *Japan's Modern Myths: Ideology in the Late Meiji Period*. Princeton: Princeton University Press, 1985.
Gordon, A., *The Wages of Affluence: Labor and Management in Postwar Japan*. Cambridge: Harvard University Press, 1998.
—— (ed.), *Postwar Japan as History*. Berkeley: University of California Press, 1993.
Gotō, Ken'ichi, '"Daitōa sensō" kaihō-shikan no kyomō-sei,' *Sekai*, September 1994.
Gotō, M., 'Taishū shakai ronsō,' in *Sengo shisō no saikentō*, Tokyo Yuifutsuron Kenkyūkai (ed.). Tokyo: Shiraishi Shoten, 1986.
Gramsci, A., *Selections From the Prison Notebooks* (G. Hoare and G. Nowell-Smith eds. and trans.). New York: International Publishers, 1971.

Gupta, A., 'The Song of the Nonaligned World: Transnational Identities and the Reinscription of Space in Late Capitalism,' *Cultural Anthropology*, vol. 7, no. 1, February 1982.

Hagiwara, S., 'Nihon eno Kaiki,' *Hagiwara Sakutarō zenshū*, vol. 4. Tokyo: Shinchō Sha, 1960.

Hanasaki, K., 'Esunissitii toshite no nihonjin,' *Sekai*, September 1993.

Hanes, J., 'Urban Planning as National Progress.' Paper presented at the 'Competing Modernities in Twentieth-Century Japan, Series Part II: Empires, Cultures, Identities, 1930–1960,' University of California at San Diego, February 12th–16th, 1998.

Harootunian, H. D. 'Visible Discourse/Invisible Ideologies,' in M. Miyoshi and H. D. Harootunian (eds), *Postmodernism and Japan*. Durham: Duke University Press, 1989.

—— 'Disciplining Native Knowledge and Producing Place: Yanagita Kunio, Origuchi Shinobu, Tanaka Yasuma,' in T. Rimer (ed.), *Culture and Identity: Japanese Intellectuals During the Interwar Years*. Princeton: Princeton University Press, 1990.

—— 'America's Japan/Japan's Japan,' in M. Miyoshi and H. D. Harootunian (eds), *Japan in the World*. Durham: Duke University Press, 1993.

—— 'Jizoku suru kioku/Bōkyaku sareru rekishi,' *hihyō kūkan* II–24, 2000.

Harvey, D., *The Condition of Postmodernity: An Inquiry into the Origins of Cultural Change*. Oxford: Blackwell, 1990.

Hashikawa, B., 'Rekishi ishiki no mondai,' *Kindai-ka to Dentō*. Tokyo: Chikuma Shobō, 1959.

—— (ed.), *Chōkokka shugi*. Tokyo: Chikuma Shobō, 1964.

—— *Nihon Rōman-ha Hihan josetsu*. Tokyo: Mirai Sha, 1965.

—— 'Yōsetsu-sha no kinyoku,' *Nihon rōman-ha hihan josetsu*. Tokyo: Mirai Sha, 1965.

—— 'Han-kindai to kindai no chōkoku,' *Kindai Nihon seiji shisō no shosō*. Tokyo: Mirai Sha, 1968.

—— 'Nihon hoshu-shugi no taiken to shisō,' in B. Hashikawa (ed.), *Hoshu no shisō*. Tokyo: Chikuma Shobō, 1968.

—— 'Chūkan-sha no me,' *hihyō to kenkyū: Mishima Yukio*. Tokyo: Hōga Shoten, 1974.

—— 'Yasuda Yojūrō o dō toraeru ka,' a discussion with Kawamura Jirō, *Rekishi to seishin*. Tokyo: Keisō Shobō, 1978.

—— Kano, M. and Hiraoka, T. (eds), *Kindai Nihon shisō-shi no kiso chishiki*. Tokyo: Yūkaikaku, 1971.

—— and Takabatake, M., 'Nashonarizumu no gyakusetsu,' *Rekishi no seishin*. Tokyo: Keisō Shobō, 1978.

Hasumi, S., 'Taishō-teki Gensetsu to Hihyō,' in K. Karatani (ed.), *Kindai Nihon no hihyō, Meiji-Taishō-hen*. Tokyo: Fukutake Shoten, 1992

Havens, T. R. H., *Architecture of Affluence: The Tsutsumi Family and the Seibu-Saison Enterprises in Twentieth-Century Japan*. Cambridge: Harvard University Press, 1994.

Hayashi, F., *Daitōa sensō kōtei ron*. Tokyo: Kabushiki Gaisha Rōman, 1974

—— *Ikeda Hayato*. Tokyo: Sankei Shinbun Sha, 1968.

Hein, L. and Selden, M. 'Learning Citizenship from the Past: Textbook Nationalism, Global Context, and Social Change,' *Bulletin of Concerned Asian Scholars*, vol. 30, no. 2, 1998.

—— *Living With the Bomb: American and Japanese Cultural Conflicts in the Nuclear Age*. Armonk, NY: M. E. Sharpe, 1997.

Heisig, J. W. and Maraldo, J., *Rude Awakenings: Zen, The Kyoto School, and the Question of Nationalism*. Honolulu: University of Hawaii Press, 1994.

Hidaka, R. (ed.), *Kindai shugi*. Tokyo: Chikuma Shobō, 1964.
Himeoka, T., 'Onna no sengo 50-nen,' *Sengo 50-nen o doo miru ka*, vol. 2, Tokyo: Jinbun shoin, 1998.
Hirata, K., 'Kahei haaku to rekishi ninshiki,' *Shisō*, nos. 553, 554 and 556, 1970.
Hobsbawm, E. and Ranger, T. (eds), *The Invention of Tradition*. Cambridge: Cambridge University Press, 1983.
Honda, S., 'Kaisetsu,' *Ara Masahito Chosakushū*, vol. 1. Tokyo: San'ichi Shobō, 1983.
Honma, N., 'Taishū shakai ni okeru bunka no mondai,' *Shisō no kagaku*, 21, September 1960.
Hora, T., *Nankin daigyakusatsu no shōmei*. Tokyo: Asahi Shinbun Sha, 1986.
Hoston, G., *Marxism and the Crisis of Development in Prewar Japan*. Princeton: Princeton University Press, 1986.
—— 'Tenko: Marxism & the National Question in Prewar Japan,' *Polity* vol. 16, no. 1, 1983.
Huntington, S., *The Clash of Civilizations and the Remaking of World Order*. New York: Simon & Schuster, 1996.
Huyssen, A., *After the Great Divide: Modernism, Mass Culture, Postmodernism*. Bloomington and Indianapolis: Indiana University Press, 1986.
Ida, M., 'Nihon no sei, Part I & II,' *Bungeishunjū*, November 1995.
Iida, Y., 'Fleeing the West, Making Asia Home: Transpositions of Otherness in Japanese Pan-Asianism, 1905–1930,' *Alternatives*, 1997, July-Sept., vol. 22, no. 3,: 409–32.
—— 'Between the Technique of Living an Endless Routine and the Madness of Absolute Degree Zero: Japanese Identity and the Crisis of Modernity in the 1990s,' *Positions: East Asia Cultures Critique*, vol. 8: no. 2, 2000.
Ikeda, D., *Ikeda Kaichō zenshū*, vol. 1. Tokyo: Sōka Gakkai, 1967.
Ikeda, K. and Amano, K. (eds), *Kokusai-ka to iu fashizumu*. Tokyo: Shakai Hyōron Sha, 1988.
Inoue, S., 'Jyōhō to seikatusu-ishiki no henka,', in Masaichi Nomura (ed.), *Jyōhō to nihonjin*. Tokyo: Kyōbun Dō, 1992.
Irie, Y., 'The History of the Textbook Controversy,' *Japan Echo*, August 1997.
Ishihara, S., *Ishihara Shintarō*, Shin-Nihon Bungaku zenshū, vol. 5. Tokyo: Shūei Sha, 1962.
—— *Ishihara Shintarō Shū*, Shinchō Nihon Bungaku vol. 62. Tokyo: Shinchō Sha, 1969.
—— *Kaseki no mori; Taiyō no kisetsu*. Tokyo: Shinchō Sha, 1981 [1955].
—— and Morita, A., *'No' to Ieru Nihon*. Tokyo: Kōbunsha, 1989.
Ishikawa, M., *Sengo seijishi*. Tokyo: Iwanami Shoten, 1995.
Ishizaka, K., '"Fusen ketsugi" towa nani ka,' *Sekai*, September 1994.
Isoda, K., 'Kaisetsu,' *Nihon no Bungaku: Ishihara Shintarō, Kaikō Takeshi, Ōe Kenzaburō*. Tokyo, Chūō Kōron sha, 1968.
—— *Sengoshi no kukan*. Tokyo: Shinchō Sha, 1983.
Isoya, T., 'Yoshimoto Shigaku no meta-gengo ni tsuite,' *Yoshimoto Takaaki o yomu*. Tokyo: Gendai Kikakushitsu, 1980.
Itani, R., *Hisen no Shisō*. Tokyo: Kinokuniya Shoten, 1967.
Itō, M., *Ikeda Hayato: sono sei to shi*. Tokyo: Shiseidō, 1996.
—— Shirozuka, N., Hanzawa, H. and Yamada, M., *Sengo shisō no chōryu: sono kyozō to jitsuzō*. Tokyo: Shin Hyōron, 1978.

Ivy, M., 'Critical Texts, Mass Artifacts: The Consumption of Knowledge in Postmodern Japan,' in M. Miyoshi and H. D. Harootunian (eds), *Postmodernism and Japan*. Durham: Duke University Press, 1989.

Jameson, F., *The Political Unconscious: Narrative as a Socially Symbolic Act*. Ithaca, NY: Cornell University Press, 1981.

—— 'Cognitive Mapping,' in Cary Nelson and Lawrence Grossberg (eds), *Marxism and the Interpretation of Culture*. Chicago: University of Illinois Press, 1988.

—— *Late Marxism: Adorno, or, The Persistence of the Dialectic*. New York: Verso, 1990.

—— *Postmodernism, or, The Cultural Logic of Late Capital*. Durham: Duke University Press, 1991.

Jay, M., *Force Fields: Between Intellectual History and Cultural Critique*. London: Routledge, 1993.

—— *Cultural Semantics: Keywords of Our Time*. Amherst: University of Massachusetts Press, 1998.

Jōkyō Shuppan (ed.), *Maruyama Masao o Yomu*. Tokyo: Jōkyō Shuppan, 1998.

Kajiki, G., 'Kindai Bungaku – eikō to hisan,' in Dentō to Gendai Sha (ed.), *Sengo shisō no genzai*. Tokyo: Dentō to Gendai Sha, 1981.

Kamiya, T., 'Shin-kankaku-ha no hōhō,' in Y. Miyoshi and T. Takemori (eds), *Kindai Bungaku*, vol. 5. Tokyo: Yūkaikaku, 1977.

Kamiyama, M., *Yoshimoto Takaaki ronkō*. Tokyo: Shichō Sha, 1988.

Kan T., *Yoshimoto Takaaki ron*. Tokyo: Daisan Bunmei Sha, 1973.

—— *Han-Shōwa Shisō ron*. Tokyo: Renga Shobō Shinsha, 1985.

Kang, S., *Orientarizumu no kanata e*. Tokyo: Iwanami Shoten, 1996.

—— 'Guroobarizumu to posuto gendai,' *Jōkyō*, November 1998.

—— and Yoshimi, S., *Guroobaru-ka no enkinhō: Atarashii kūkan o motomete*. Tokyo: Iwanami Shoten, 2001.

Kaplan, D. and Marshall, A., *The Cult at the End of the World: The Incredible Story of Aum*. London: Hutchinson, 1996.

Karatani, K., 'Kodoku naru seiha,' *Yoshimoto Takaaki o yomu*. Tokyo: Gendai Kikakushitsu, 1980.

—— *Kotoba to higeki*. Tokyo: Daisan Bunmei Sha, 1989.

—— *Hihyō to posutomodan*. Tokyo: Fukutake Shoten, 1989.

—— 'One Spirit, Two Nineteenth Centuries,' in M. Miyoshi and H. D. Harootunian (eds), *Postmodernism and Japan*. Durham: Duke University Press, 1989.

—— 'Foucault to Nihon,' *Huumoa toshite no yuifutsu-ron*. Tokyo: Chikuma Shobō, 1993.

—— 'The Discursive Space of Modern Japan,' in M. Miyoshi and H. D. Harootunian (eds), *Japan in the World*. Durham: Duke University Press, 1993.

—— *Origins of Modern Japanese Literature* (Brett de Bary, trans.). Durham: Duke University Press, 1993.

—— 'Bijutsukan to shite no Nihon: Okakura Tenshin to Fenorosa,' *Hihyō kūkan* II-1, 1994.

—— *Architecture as Metaphor: Language, Number, Money* (Sabu Kohso, trans., Michael Speaks, ed.). Cambridge: MIT Press, 1995.

—— '1970-nen = shōwa 45-nen,' *Shūen o meggutte*. Tokyo: Kōdan Sha, 1995.

—— (ed.) *Kindai Nihon no hihyō, Shōwa-hen 1*. Tokyo: Fukutake Shoten, 1990.

—— (ed.) *Kindai Nihon no hihyō, Shōwa-hen 2*. Tokyo: Fukutake Shoten, 1991.

—— Murai, O., Kawamura, M. and Yamaguchi, M., 'Shokuminchi-shūgi to kindai Nihon,' *Hihyō kūkan*, I-7, 1992.

—— Asada, A., Hasumi, S. and Miura, M., *Kindai Nihon no hihyō, Meiji-Taishō-hen*. Tokyo: Fukutake Shoten, 1992.

—— Asada, A., Okazaki, K. and Isozaki, A., 'Geijutsu no rinen to "Nihon"', *Hihyō kūkan*, I-10, 1993.

—— Asada, A., Yamashiro, M., Fukuda, K., Nishatani, O., Suga, H. and Kobayashi, Y., '"Senzen" no shikō: 1930-nendai-teki jōkyō to genzai,' *Hihyō kūkan*, II-1, 1994.

Kasai, K., 'Fuyū suru mokushiroku-teki ishiki,' *Sekai*, June 1995.

—— 'Wangan sensō to mukonkyo na "heiwa"', *Gendai shisō*, vol. 19, May 1991.

Kasuya, K., *Sengo shichō: chishikijin-tachi no shōzo*. Tokyo: Nihon Keizai Shinbun, 1981.

Katō, K., 'Kamereon jidai no shisō-teki taikōjiku,' in K. Ikeda and K. Amano (eds), *Tenkō to yokusan no shisō-shi*. Tokyo: Shakai Hyōron Sha, 1989.

Katō, N., Kore wa hihyō dewa nai,' *Gunzō*, May 1991.

—— *Haisengo ron*. Tokyo: Kōdan Sha, 1997.

—— 'Coping with Japan's Postwar Schizophrenia,' *Asahi Evening News*, January 1st, 1998.

—— and Kang, S., 'Haisengo ron to aidentitii,' *Nashonarizumu o yomu*. Tokyo: Jōkyō Shuppan Sha, 1998.

Katō, S., 'Taishō Democracy as the Pre-Stage for Japanese Militarism,' in B. Silberman and H. D. Harootunian (eds) *Japan in Crisis: Essays on Taishō Democracy*. Princeton: Princeton University Press, 1974.

—— 'Tennō-sei o ronzu,' *Katō Shūichi chosaku shū*. Tokyo: Heibon Sha, 1978–79.

Katō, T., 'Sengo 50-nen to chishikijin,' *Sekai*, January 1995.

Katsura, K., *Nihon no jyoho-ka to jyaanarizumu*. Tokyo: Nihon Hyōron Sha, 1995.

Kawakami, T., et al., *Kindai no chōkoku*. Tokyo: Fuzanbō, 1979.

Kawamoto, J., *Dōjidai no Bungaku*. Tokyo: Tōju Sha, 1979.

Kawamura, M., *Sengo hihyō ron*. Tokyo: Kōdan Sha, 1998.

Kawashima, T., 'Nihon shakai no kazoku-teki kosei,' in R. Hidaka (ed.), *Kindai shugi*. Tokyo: Chikuma Shobō, 1964.

Kenney, M. and Florida, R., 'Japan's Role in A Post-Fordist Age,' *Futures*, April 1989.

Keyman, Emin Fuat, *Globalization, State, Identity/Difference: Towards a Critical Social Theory of International Relations*. Atlantic Highlands, New Jersey: Humanities Press, 1997.

Kinsella, S., 'Cuties in Japan,' in Lise Skov and Brian Moeran (eds), *Women, Media, and Consumption in Japan*. Honolulu: University of Hawaii Press, 1995.

—— 'Japanese Subculture in the 1990s: *Otaku* and the Amateur *Manga* Movement,' *Journal of Japanese Studies*, vol. 24, no. 2, 1998.

Kitagawa, T., 'Takeuchi Yoshimi to sengo Nashonarizumu,' *Sengo shisō no genzai*. Tokyo: Dentō to Gendai Sha, 1981.

Kobayashi, K., *Yoshimoto Takaaki ron*. Tokyo: Tabata Shoten, 1968.

Koestler, A., *Janus: A Summing Up*. London: Picador, 1978.

Kogawa, T., 'New trends in Japanese popular culture,' in G. McCormack and Y. Sugimoto (eds), *The Japanese Trajectory: Modernization and Beyond*. Cambridge: Cambridge University Press, 1988.

—— 'Nyū media jōkyō to tennō-sei,' *Mikuro porittikusu*. Tokyo: Heibon Sha, 1987.

Kōsaka, M., *Shiken kitai sareru ningen zō*. Tokyo: Chikuma Shobō, 1966.

Kōsaka, S., *Hizai no Umi: Mishima Yukio to sengoshakai no nihirizumu*. Tokyo: Kawade Shobō Shinsha, 1988.

Koschmann, V., 'Maruyama Masao and the Incomplete Project of Modernity,' in M. Miyoshi and H. D. Harootunian (eds), *Postmodernism and Japan*. Durham: Duke University Press, 1989.

—— 'Intellectuals and Politics,' in Andrew Gordon (ed.), *Postwar Japan as History*. Berkeley: University of California Press, 1993.

—— *Revolution and Subjectivity in Postwar Japan*. Chicago: University of Chicago Press, 1996.

—— 'National Subjectivity and the Uses of Atonement in the Age of Recession,' *South Atlantic Quarterly*, vol. 99 no. 4.

Kōzu, A., *Yoshimoto Takaaki shiron: sengo-shisō no chōkoku*. Tokyo: Ryūdō Shuppan, 1980.

Kuno, O. (ed.), *Gendai Nihon ron*, Sengo Nihon Shisō Taikei 15. Tokyo: Chikuma Shobō, 1974.

—— (ed.) 'Discussion: yuifutsuron to shutaisei,' *Gendai Nihon ron*, Sengo Nihon shisō taikei 15. Tokyo: Chikuma Shobō, 1974.

—— and Takabatake, M., 'Gendai Nihon-ron no keifu,' *Gendai Nihon ron*, Sengo Nihon Shisō Taikei 15. Tokyo: Chikuma Shobō, 1974.

—— Tsurumi, S. and Fujita, S. (eds), *Sengo Nihon no shisō*. Tokyo: Keisō Shobō, 1959.

Kurihara, A., *Kanri shakai to minshū risei*. Tokyo: Shinyō Sha, 1982.

—— '1930-nendai no shakai ishiki to Oomoto,' *Rekishi to Aidentitii*. Tokyo: Shinyō Sha, 1982.

—— 'Kuukyo na chūshin no jōen,' *Seiji no fookuroa*. Tokyo: Shinyō Sha, 1988.

—— 'Nihon minzoku shūkyō to minshū-teki misutiiku,' *Seiji no fookuroa*. Tokyo: Shinyō Sha, 1988.

—— Sugiyama, M. and Yoshimi, S. (eds), *Kiroku: tennō no shi*. Tokyo: Chikuma Shobō, 1992.

Lacoue-Labarthe, P. and Nancy, J.-L., *The Literary Absolute: The Theory of Literature in German Romanticism* (Philip Barnard and Cheryl Lester, trans.). Albany: SUNY Press, 1988.

Lakoff, G., *Women, Fire and Other Dangerous Things: What Categories Reveal About the Mind*. Chicago: University of Chicago Press, 1987.

Lapid, Y. and Kratochwil, F. (eds), *The Return of Culture and Identity in IR Theory*. Boulder: Lynne Rienner Publishers, 1996.

MacArthur, D., 'Message to the Japanese People on the First Anniversary of the Constitution,' in Supreme Commander for the Allied Powers, *The Political Reorientation of Japan, September 1945–September 1948, Report of the Governmental Section of SCAP*. Washington: US GPO, 1948.

Maruyama, K., *Bunka no fetishizumu*. Tokyo: Keisō Shobō, 1985.

Maruyama, M., 'Gendai ni okeru taido kettei,' *Sekai*, July 1960.

—— *Thought and Behavior in Modern Japanese Politics*. New York: Oxford University Press, 1963.

—— 'Chōkokka shugi no ronri to shinri,' in R. Hidaka (ed.), *Kindai shugi*. Tokyo: Chikuma Shobō, 1964.

—— 'Fukuzawa ni okeru chitsujo to ningen,' in R. Hidaka (ed.), *Kindai shugi*. Tokyo: Chikuma Shobō, 1964.

—— 'Fukuzawa Yukichi no tetsugaku,' in R. Hidaka (ed.), *Kindai shugi*. Tokyo: Chikuma Shobō, 1964.

—— *Gendai seiji no shisō to kōdō*. Tokyo: Mirai Sha, 1964.

—— 'Nihon ni okeru nashonarizumu,' in S. Ueyama (ed.), *Nihon no nashonarizumu*. Tokyo: Tokuma Shoten, 1966.

—— 'Rekishi ishiki no koso,' in M. Maruyama (ed.), *Nihon no shisō 6: rēkishi shisō shū*. Tokyo: Chikuma Shobō, 1972.

—— 'Aru jiyushugi-sha eno tegami,' *Maruyama Masao Shū*, vol.4. Tokyo: Iwanami Shoten, 1995.

—— 'Fukuzawa ni okeru jitsugaku no tenkai,' *Maruyama Masao Shū*, vol. 3. Tokyo: Iwanami Shoten, 1995.

—— *Maruyama Masao Zadan 2*. Tokyo: Iwanami Shoten, 1998.

—— Satō N. and Umemoto, K., *Sengo Nihon no kakushin shisō*. Tokyo: Gendai no Riron Sha, 1983.

Mashita, S., 'Shutaisei – Yuifutsuron no shutai-teki haaku to kanren shite,' *Mashita Shin'ichi chosaku shū*, vol. 1, *Gakumon to jinsei*. Tokyo: Aoki Shoten, 1979.

—— 'Yuifutsu benshōhō no tetsugaku-teki tachiba,' *Mashita Shin'ichi chosaku shu*, vol. 5, *Gakumon to jinsei*. Tokyo: Aoki Shoten,1980.

Matsumoto, K., 'Takeuchi Yoshimi ron,' *Takeuchi Yoshimi ron: kakumei to chinmoku*. Tokyo: Daisan Bunmei Sha, 1975.

—— 'Kaidai,' in Kawakami, T., and Takeuchi, Y., *Kindai no chōkoku*. Tokyo: Fuzanbō, 1979.

—— 'Maruyama Masao, Otsuka Hisao to kindai shugi,' in Dentō to Gendai Henshū-bu (ed.), *Sengo shisō no genzai*. Tokyo: Dentō to Gendai Sha, 1981.

—— 'Kindai no chōkoku Oboegaki,' *Rekishi no seishin*. Tokyo: Kashiwa Shobō, 1982.

—— 'Jizoku suru seishin,' in Takeuchi, Y., *Kindai no chōkoku*. Tokyo: Chikuma Shobō, 1983.

—— *Segno no seishin: sono sei to shi*. Tokyo: Sakuhinsha, 1985.

—— 'Sengo-waku no kanō to genkai,' *Shinpen Etō Jun Bungaku shūsei*, vol. 3. Tokyo: Kawade Shobō Shinsha, 1985.

—— *Mishima Yukio Bōmei Densetsu*. Tokyo: Kawade Shobō, 1987.

—— 'Posuto-modan kara Nishida Tetsugaku e,' *Shōwa saigo no hibi*. Tokyo: Ribu-repōto, 1989.

Matsushita, K., 'Taishū kokka no seiritsu to sono mondaisei,' *Shisō*, November 1956.

—— 'Taishū shakai ron no konnichi-teki kadai,' *Shisō*, October 1960.

—— *Sengo shisō no rekihi to shisō*. Tokyo: Chikuma Shobō, 1994.

McCormack, G., 'The Student Left in Japan,' *New Left Review*, vol. 65, 1971.

—— *The Emptiness of Japanese Affluence*. Armonk, NY: M. E. Sharpe, 1996.

—— 'From Number One to Number Nothing: Japan's *Fin de Siècle* Blues,' *Japanese Studies*, vol. 18, no. 1, April 1998.

—— 'New Tunes for an Old Song: War Memory, and Nationalism in Japan at the End of Century.' Unpublished paper presented at the Japan Policy Research Institute (JPRI) Conference, University of San Francisco, April 24th, 1998.

—— 'The Japanese Movement to 'Correct' History,' *Bulletin of Concerned Asian Scholars*, vol. 30, no. 2, 1998.

Mikami, O., 'Sengo nashonarizumu no taishū-teki kitei,' in Dentō to Gendai Henshū-bu (ed.), *Sengo shisō no genzai*. Tokyo: Dentō to Gendai Sha, 1981.

—— *Mishima, Kakuei, Etō Jun: Hoshu Shisō no kōzu*. Tokyo: Saryu Sha, 1984.

Miki, K., 'Fuan no shisō to sono chōkoku,' *Miki Kiyoshi zenshū*, vol.10. Tokyo: Iwanami Shoten, 1967.

Minamoto, R., 'The Symposium on "Overcoming Modernity",' in J. Heisig and J. Maraldo (eds), *Rude Awakenings: Zen, The Kyoto School, and the Question of Nationalism*. Honolulu: University of Hawaii Press, 1994.

Ministry of Education, *Kitai sareru ningen-zō*. Tokyo: Ministry of Education, 1966.
Mishima, Y., *Eirei no koe*. Tokyo: Kawade Shobō, 1976.
—— and Hayashi, F., *Taidan: Nihonjin ron*. Tokyo: Banchō Shobō, 1966.
—— and *Zenkyōtō, Tōron: Mishima Yukio vs. Zenkyōtō*. Tokyo: Shinchō Sha, 1969.
Mittelman, J., 'Coxian Historicism as an Alternative Perspective in International Studies,' *Alternatives*, vol. 23, 1998.
Miyadai, S., *Seikimatsu no sahō: owarinaki nichijō o ikiru chie*. Tokyo: Media Fakutorii, 1997.
—— Fujii, Y. and Nakamoro, A., *Shinseiki no riaru*. Tokyo: Asuka Shinsha, 1997.
—— and Suzuki, T., 'Shōhi sareru jiko,' in T. Suzuki (ed.), *Hayari no bunka chōkenkyu*. Kyoto: Seigen Sha, 1988.
Miyoshi, M., *As We Saw Them: The First Japanese Embassy to the United States*. Berkeley: University of California Press, 1979.
—— *Off Center: Power and Cultural Relations Between Japan and the United States*. Cambridge: Harvard University Press, 1991.
—— and Harootunian, H. D. (eds), *Postmodernism and Japan*. Durham: Duke University Press, 1989.
—— *Japan in the World*. Durham: Duke University Press, 1993.
Miyoshi, Y. (ed.) *Kindai nihon bungakushi*. Tokyo: Yūkaikaku, 1975.
—— 'Akutagawa Ryūnosuke no shi,' in Y. Miyoshi and T. Takemori (eds), *Kindai Bungaku*, vol. 5. Tokyo: Yūkaikaku, 1977.
—— *Kindai bungakushi hikkei*. Tokyo: Gakutō Sha, 1987.
Moore, J., 'Democracy and Capitalism in Postwar Japan, in Joe Moore (ed.), *The Other Japan: Conflict, Compromise, and Resistence Since 1945*. Armonk, NY: M. E. Sharpe, 1997.
Moriyama, K., 'Shisō-teki jiritsu to shin-teki ryōiki no teiritsu,' *Yoshimoto Takaaki o yomu*. Tokyo: Gendai Kikakushitsu, 1980.
Morris-Suzuki, T., *A History of Japanese Economic Thought*. London: Routledge, 1989.
—— 'The Invention and Reinvention of "Japanese Culture,"' *The Journal of Asian Studies* vol. 54, no. 3, August 1995.
—— 'Remembered Worlds: Rethinking Historical Space in a Global Age', *Geography Research Forum*, vol. 19, 1999.
—— *Re-Inventing Japan: Time, Space, Nation*. Armonk, NY: M. E. Sharpe, 1998.
—— *Shōwa: An Inside History of Hirohito's Japan*. London: Athlone, 1984.
—— 'Unquiet Graves: Katō Norihiro and the Politics of Mourning,' *Japanese Studies* vol. 18, no. 1, May 1998.
Muraishi, K., 'Takeuchi Yoshimi ni okeru kindai no chōkoku,' *Nihon kaiki: seiō kindai to Nihon no sōkoku*. Tokyo: Dentō to Kindai Sha, 1975.
Murakami, Y. (ed.), *21-seiki sisutemu no tenbō*. Tokyo: Ōkura-shō Insatsu-kyoku, 1987.
—— Kumon, S. and Satō, S., *Bunmei toshite no ie-shakai*. Tokyo: Chūō Kōron Sha, 1979.
Nagata, H., *Ōe Kenzaburo*, Gendai no Bungaku 28. Tokyo: Kōdan Sha, 1971.
Nagatomi, Y., *Kindai o koete: ko Ōhira Sōri no nokosareta mono*, vols 1 and 2. Tokyo: Ōkura Zaimu Kyōkai, 1983.
Najita, T. and Harootunian, H. D. 'Japanese Revolt against the West: Political and Cultural Criticism in the Twentieth Century', in Peter Duus (ed.), *The Cambridge History of Japan*, vol. 6. New York: Cambridge University Press, 1988.
Nakamasa, M., '"Doitsusei" no kigen o megutte,' *Jōkyō*, May 1998.

Nakamura, M., 'The History Textbook Controversy and Nationalism,' Kristine Dennehy (trans.), *Bulletin of Concerned Asian Scholars*, vol. 30: 2, 1998.
Nakamura, Y., *Nihon no shisō kai*. Tokyo: Keisō Shobō, 1967.
—— *Nishida Tetsugaku no datsu-kōchiku*. Tokyo: Iwanami Shoten, 1987.
Nakano, K., 'The Politics of Administrative Reform in Japan, 1993–1998,' *Asian Survey*, vol. XXXVIII, no. 3, 1998.
Nakata, M., 'Shin-kankaku-ha no tanjō,' *Yokomitsu Riichi: Bungaku to haiku*. Tokyo: Bensei Sha, 1997.
Narita, R., Komori, Y., Kan, S. and Satō, M., 'Taiwa no kairo o tozashita rekishikan o dō kokufuku suru ka,' *Sekai*, May 1995.
Nelson, C. and Grossberg, L. (eds), *Marxism and the Interpretation of Culture*. Chicago: University of Illinois Press, 1988.
Nikkei Sangyō Shinbun (ed.), *Kōdo jyōho shakai*. Tokyo: Nihon Keizai Shinbun Sha, 1984.
Nippon Hoso Kyokai (ed.), *Nihon no sengo*, vol. 1. Tokyo: Nippon Hoso Shuppan Kyokai, 1977.
Nishibe, S., 'Sekai wa mushiro boodaaafuru dearu,' *Kaien*, October 1995.
—— 'Why We Should Scrap the Constitution,' *Japan Echo*, August 1997.
Nishida, K., *Nishida Kitarō zenshū*. Tokyo: Iwanami Shoten, 1965.
Nishigaki, T., 'Sengen hitotsu no ichi,' in Y. Miyoshi and T. Takemori (eds), *Kindai Bungaku*, vol. 5. Tokyo: Yūkaikaku, 1977.
Nishikawa, N., *Nihon no sengo shōsetsu: haikyo no hikari*. Tokyo: Iwanami Shoten, 1988.
—— *Kokumin kokka ron no shatei*. Tokyo: Kashiwa Shobō, 1998.
Nishikawa, Y., 'Domestic Space as Literary History,' paper presented at the conference 'The Empire of Readers,' East Asia Program, Cornell University, November 6th–7th, 1998.
Nishio, K., 'Aum shinrikyō to gendai bunmei,' *Shinchō*, August 1995.
—— 'Rewriting Japanese and World History,' *Japan Echo*, August 1997.
Nishiyama, A., 'Kaeru basho go nai,' *Sekai*, March 1997.
Norman, E. H., *Origins of the Modern Japanese State: Selected Writings of E. H. Norman*. (John Dower, ed. and introduction). New York: Pantheon, 1975.
Oda, M., *Beheiren*. Tokyo: San'ichi Shobō, 1969.
—— and Tsurumi, S., *Hansen to henkaku*. Tokyo: Gakugei Shobō, 1968.
Odagiri, H., *Gendai Bungaku shi*, vol. 2. Tokyo: Shūei Sha, 1975.
Ōe, K., *Shuppatsuten*. Tokyo: Iwanami Shoten, 1980.
—— 'Sebuntiin,' *Ōe Kenzaburo Zensakuhin* 3. Tokyo: Shinchō Sha, 1966.
Ōgoshi, A., 'Mōhitotsu no 'katarikuchi no mondai': dono yō ni rekishi jijitsu to deau ka?,' *Sōbun*, April 1997.
Ōhashi, R., 'Shisō toshite no nihonbunka-ron,' *Chūō kōron* 103, 1988.
Ōkubo, N., 'Shōwa jūnen zengo,' in S. Wada (ed.), *Nihon no kindai Bungaku*. Tokyo: Dōkō Sha, 1982.
Okuda, Y., 'Purikura no tonari ni uttsute iru no wa dare ka?,' *Hayari no bunka chōkenkyu*. Kyoto: Seigen Sha, 1998.
Okumura, H., 'Hōjin-shugi no tasogare,' *Sekai*, March 1994.
Okuno, T., 'Kaisetsu,' in Dazai O., *Shayō/Ningen shikkaku*. Tokyo: Shinchō Sha, 1979.
Olson, L., *Ambivalent Moderns: Portraits of Japanese Cultural Identity*. Savage, Maryland: Rowman & Littlefield, 1992.
Ōmae, Ken'ichi, *Kinyukiki kara no saisei*. Tokyo: Presidento Sha, 1995.
Orwell, G., *Nineteen Eighty-four*. Harmondsworth: Penguin, 1990.

Ōsawa, M., 'Bamoidooki-shin no kao,' *Gunzō*, October 1997.

Ōtsuka, H., 'Kindai-teki Ningen Ruikei no soshutsu,' *Kindai-ka no ningen-teki kiso*. Tokyo: Chikuma Shobō, 1968.

Peretz, C., 'Microelectronics, Long Waves, and World Structural Change,' *World Development*, March 1985, vol. 13.

Pincus, L., *Authenticating Culture in Imperial Japan: Kuki Shuzo and the Rise of National Aesthetics*. Berkeley: University of California Press, 1996.

Polanyi, K., *The Great Transformation: The Political and Economic Origins of Our Time*. Boston: Beacon Press, 1944.

Pollack, D., *Writing Against Culture: Ideology and Narrative in the Japanese Novel*. Ithaca: Cornell University Press, 1992.

Porter, D., '*Orientalism* and its Problems,' in Patrick Williams and Laura Chrisman (eds), *Colonial Discourse and Post-Colonial Theory*. New York: Columbia University Press, 1994.

Pyle, K., 'Japan, the World, and the Twenty-first Century,' in Kumon Shumpei and Henry Rosovsky (eds), *The Political Economy of Japan, vol. 3: Culture and Social Dynamics*. Stanford: Stanford University Press, 1992.

—— *The Japanese Question: Power and Purpose in a New Era*. Washington D.C.: American Enterprise Institute Press, 1992.

Reischauer, E. O., *The Japanese*. Cambridge: Harvard University Press, 1977.

Ricoeur, P., *Time and Narrative*. Chicago: University of Chicago Press, 1983.

Rimer, T. (ed.), *Culture and Identity: Japanese Intellectuals During the Interwar Years*. Princeton: Princeton University Press, 1990.

Saeki, K., *Gendai Nihon no ideorogii: groobarizumu to kokka ishiki*. Tokyo: Kōdan Sha, 1998.

Said, E., *Orientalism*. New York: Vintage, 1978.

Sakai, N., 'Modernity and Its Critique: The Problem of Universalism and Particularism,' in M. Miyoshi and H. D. Harootunian (eds), *Postmodernism and Japan*. Durham: Duke University Press, 1989.

—— *Voices of the Past: The Status of Language in Eighteenth-Century Japanese Discouse*. Ithaca: Cornell University Press, 1991.

—— 'Return to the West/Return to the East: Watsuji Tetsuro's Anthropology and Discussions of Authenticity,' in M. Miyoshi and H. D. Harootunian (eds), *Japan in the World*. Durham: Duke University Press, 1993.

—— 'Maruyama Masao to sengo nihon,' *Sekai*, November 1995.

—— *Shisansareru nihongo, nihonjin: 'Nihon' no rekishi*. Tokyo: Shinyō Sha, 1996.

—— *Translation and Subjectivity: On 'Japan' and Cultural Nationalism*. Minneapolis: University of Minnesota Press, 1997.

—— de Bary, B. and Iyotani, T. (eds), *Nashionaritii no datsukochiku*. Tokyo: Kashiwa Shobō, 1996.

Sakurai, T., *Shisō toshite no 60-nendai*. Tokyo: Kōdan Sha, 1988.

Sasaki, M., *Kyōiku Chokugo*. Tokyo: Mizuho Shobō, 1986.

Satō, M., Kan, S., Komori, Y. and Narita, R., 'Taiwa no karo o tozashita rekishi-kan o do kokufuku suruka,' *Sekai*, May 1997.

—— *Sengo Bungaku*, Sinposiumu Nihon Bungaku, vol. 19. Tokyo: Gakusei Sha, 1977.

Sawa, T., 'Nihon-teki posuto modanizumu no ogori,' *Sekai*, April 1989.

—— *Heisei fukyō no seiji keizai gaku: seijukuka shakai eno jyōken*. Tokyo: Chūō Kōron Sha, 1994.

—— Shindō, M. and Sugiyama, M., *80-nendai ron*. Tokyo: Shinyō Sha, 1987.

Sayle, M., 'Nerve Gas and the Four Noble Truths,' *New Yorker*, April 1st, 1996.
Schaller, M., *The American Occupation of Japan: The Origins of the Cold War in Asia*. New York: Oxford University Press, 1985.
Schodt, F., *Dreamland Japan: Writing on Modern Manga*. Berkeley: Stone Bridge Press, 1996.
Sekine, T., *An Outline of the Dialectic of Capital*, 2 vols. London: Macmillan, 1997.
Shapiro, M. and Hayward Alker (eds), *Challenging Boundaries: Global Flows, Territorial Identities*. Minneapolis: University of Minnesota Press, 1996.
Shima, N., 'Shayō Nippon, yattsu no kūdo-ka,' *Bungeishunjū*, March 1995.
Shimao, T., *Shimao Toshio sakuhin shū*. Tokyo: Shōbun Sha, 1966.
Shimizu, I., *Ningen o kangaeru*. Tokyo: Bungei Shunjū, 1970.
—— *Sengo o utagau*. Tokyo: Kōdan Sha, 1980.
Shimomura, T., *Nishida Kitarō: hito to shisō*. Tokyo: Tokai daigaku shuppankai, 1977.
Shiroyama, S. and Nakamura, T., 'Heisei kyōko wa kuru ka,' *Bungeishunjū*, May 1995.
Skov, L. and Moeran, B. (eds), *Women, Media, and Consumption in Japan*. Honolulu: University of Hawaii Press, 1995.
Smith, S., Booth, K. and Marysia Zalewski (eds), *International Theory: Positivism & Beyond*. Cambridge: Cambridge University Press, 1996.
Sugiyama, M., 'Shin-kokkashugi to sengo shisō: gendai ideologii hihan,' *Sekai*, January 1986.
—— Sawa, T. and Shindo, M., *Hachijyū-nendai ron*. Tokyo: Shinyō Sha, 1987.
Sun, G. and Komori, Y., 'Kindai tennōsei tabuu no koozu,' *Sekai*, October 2000.
Supreme Commander for the Allied Powers (ed.), *The Political Reorientation of Japan, September 1945–September 1948, Report of the Governmental Section of SCAP*, 2 vols. Washington: US GPO, 1948.
Tachibana, T., 'Seijō to ijō no aida,' *Bungeishunjū*, March 1998.
Takabatake, M., *Nichijō no shisō*. Tokyo: Chikuma Shobō, 1970.
—— *Seiji no hakken*. Tokyo: San'ichi Shobō, 1983.
—— *Tōron: Sengo Nihon no seiji shisō*. Tokyo: San'ichi Shobō, 1977.
Takagi, M., *Zengakuren to zenkyōtō*. Tokyo: Kōdan Sha, 1985.
Takeda, S., 'Tennō toiu Kin'i,' *Gendai hihyō no enkinhō*. Tokyo: Kōdan Sha, 1998.
—— 'Yoshimoto Takaaki no genzai,' in S. Kōsaka, S. Takeda and H. Yamamoto (eds), *Gendai shisō nyūmon II*. Tokyo: JICC, 1990
Takeuchi, S., *Sengo shisō eno shikaku: shutai to gengo*. Tokyo: Chikuma Shobō, 1972.
Takeuchi, Y., 'Chūgoku no kindai to Nihon no kindai,' in S. Ueyama (ed.), *Nihon no nashonarizumu*. Tokyo: Tokuma Shoten, 1966.
—— *Nihon ideorogii*. Tokyo: Chikuma Shobō, 1971.
—— *Nihon to Ajia*. Tokyo: Chikuma Shobō, 1971.
—— 'Futatsu no ajia shikan,' *Takeuchi Yoshimi zenshū*, vol. 5. Tokyo: Chikuma Shobō, 1981.
—— 'Kindai no chōkoku,' *Kindai no chōkoku*. Tokyo: Chikuma Shobō, 1983.
—— 'Kindai-shugi to minzoku no mondai,' *Kindai no chōkoku*. Tokyo: Chikuma Shobō, 1983.
—— 'Kindai towa nani ka,' *Kindai no chōkoku*. Tokyo: Chikuma Shobō, 1983.
Tamamoto, M., 'Japan's Search for a World Role,' *World Policy Journal*, Spring 1994.
Tamura, Y., 'Unit 731,' in Haruko Taya Cook and Theodore F. Cook (eds), *Japan at War: An Oral History*. New York: The New Press, 1992
Tanaka, M., *Nankin jiken no sōkatsu: gyakusatsu hitei jyūgo no ronkyo*. Tokyo: Kenkō Sha, 1987.

Tanaka, S., *Japan's Orient: Rending Pasts into History*. Berkeley: University of California Press, 1993.
Tanaka, Y., *Nantonaku, kurisutaru*. Tokyo: Kawade Shobō Shin-sha, 1981.
Taniguchi, T., *Yoshimoto Takaaki no hō e*. Tokyo: Seikyūsha, 1987.
Tansman, A., 'Images of Loss and Longing in 1930s Japan.' Paper presented at the 'Competing Modernities in Twentieth-Century Japan, Series Part II: Empires, Cultures, Identities, 1930–1960,' University of California at San Diego, February 12th–16th, 1998.
Taylor, M. C., 'Introduction: System . . . Structure . . . Difference . . . Other,' in M. C. Taylor (ed.), *Deconstruction in Context: Literature and Philosophy*. Chicago: University of Chicago Press, 1986.
Tosaka, J., 'Nihon rinri-gaku to ningen-gaku,' in Y. Yuasa (ed.), *Watsuji Tetsuro*. Tokyo: San'ichi Shobō, 1973.
Treat, J., 'Yoshimoto Banana Writes Home: The *Shojo* in Japanese Popular Culture,' *Contemporary Japan and Popular Culture*. Richmond: Curzon Press, 1996.
Tsuda, S., 'Rekishi no gaku ni okeru hito no kaifuku,' *Tsuda Sōkichi zenshū*, vol. 20. Tokyo: Iwanami Shoten, 1965.
—— *Tsuda Sōkichi zenshū*, vol. 20. Tokyo: Iwanami Shoten, 1965.
Tsukimura, T., *Etō Jun ron: kanjusei no meiun*. Tokyo: Jiritsu Shobō, 1977.
Tsunoda, R., et al., *Sources of Japanese Tradition*, R. Tsunoda, W. T. de Bary and D. Keene (eds). New York: Columbia University Press, 1958.
Tsuzuki, T., *Sengo nihon no chishiki-jin: Maruyama Masao to sono jidai*. Tokyo: Seori Shobō, 1995.
Tucker, R. (ed.), *The Marx–Engels Reader*. New York: W. W. Norton & Company, 1978.
Uchida, R., *Shōhi shakai to kenryoku*. Tokyo: Iwanami Shoten, 1987.
Ueno, C., *Hatsujō sōchi: erosu no shinario*. Tokyo: Chikuma Shobō, 1998.
—— *Kindai kazoku no seiritsu to shūen*. Tokyo: Iwanami Shoten, 1994.
Ueyama, S., 'Dai tōa senso no shisōshi-teki imi,' in Yoshimoto, T. (ed.), *Kokka no shisō*, Sengo Nihon shisō taikei 5. Tokyo: Chikuma Shobō, 1969.
—— *Juyō to sōzō no kiseki*. Tokyo: Kadokawa Shoten, 1991.
—— *Nihon no shisō: dochaku to ohka no keifu*. Tokyo: Saimaru Shuppan, 1971.
—— 'Nishida Kitarō no tetsugaku shisō,' *Nihon no shisō: dochaku to ohka no keifu*. Tokyo: Saimaru Shuppan, 1971.
—— 'Rekishi-kan no mosaku,' *Shisō no kagaku* 1, 1959.
—— *Taiwa: Nihon no kokka o kangaeru*. Tokyo: Tokuma Shoten, 1985.
—— (ed.), *Nihon no nashonarizumu*. Tokyo: Tokuma Shoten, 1966.
—— and Hashikawa, B., 'Discussion seiji no ronri to shōchō no shōdō,' in B. Hashikawa (ed.), *Jidai to yoken*. Tokyo: Dentō to Gendai Sha, 1975.
Umehara, T., *Bi to shūkyō no hakken*. Tokyo: Chikuma Shobō, 1967.
—— *Bukkyō o kangaeru*. Tokyo: Shūeisha, 1984.
—— *Gendai Nihon o kangaeru*. Tokyo: Shūeisha, 1984.
—— 'Shinto and Buddhism in Japanese Culture,' *The Japan Foundation Newsletter*, July 1987.
Umemoto, K., 'Yuifutsuron to ningen,' *Umemoto Katsumi chosakushū*, vol. 1. Tokyo: San'ichi Shobō, 1977.
Uozumi, Y., 'Kadai,' in T. Umehara, *Tetsugaku no fukkoh*. Tokyo: Shueisha, 1984.
van Wolferen, K., *The Enigma of Japanese Power: People and Politics in a Stateless Nation*. London: Macmillan, 1989.

Vlastos, S., 'Tradition: Past/Present Culture and Modern Japanese Tradition,' in Stephen Vlastos (ed.), *Mirror of Modernity: Invented Traditions of Modern Japan*. Berkeley: University of California Press, 1998.

Vogel, E. F., *Japan As Number One: Lessons for America*. Tokyo: Charles E. Tuttle, 1979.

Wada, S. and Funato, Y. (ed.), *Nihon no kindai Bungaku*. Tokyo: Dōhō Sha, 1982.

Wakabayashi, Bob T. (ed.), *Modern Japanese Thought*. Cambridge: Cambridge University Press, 1998.

Wakamiya, Y., 'Sengo seiji ni okeru "Ajia ishiki",' *Chūō kōron*, February 1995.

Wallerstein, I., 'Culture as the Ideological Battleground of the Modern World-System,' in Mike Featherstone (ed.), *Global Culture: Nationalism, Globalization and Modernity*. London: Sage Publications, 1990.

—— 'The inter-state structure of the modern world system,' in Steve Smith, Ken Booth and Marysia Zalewski (eds), *International Theory: Positivism & Beyond*. Cambridge: Cambridge University Press, 1996.

Walker, R. B. J., 'Realism, Change, and International Political Theory,' *International Studies Quarterly*, 31, 1987.

—— 'The Concept of Culture in International Relations,' in Jongsuk Chay (ed.), *Culture and International Relations*. New York: Praeger, 1990.

—— 'Security, Sovereignty, and the Challenge of World Politics,' *Alternatives*, 15, 1990.

—— *Inside/Outside: International Relations as Political Theory*. Cambridge: Cambridge University Press, 1993.

Washida, K., *Zoho Yoshimoto Takaaki ron*. Tokyo: San'ichi Shobō, 1992.

—— *Gendai shisō ron*. Tokyo: San'ichi Shobō, 1988.

Waswo, A., 'The transformation of rural society, 1900–1950,' in Peter Duus (ed.), *The Cambridge History of Japan*, vol. 6. New York: Cambridge University Press, 1988.

Watsuji, T., *Ningen no gaku toshite no rinri-gaku*. Tokyo, Iwanami Shoten, 1934.

—— *Climate and Culture: A Philosophical Study* (Geoffrey Bownas trans.). New York: Greenwood Press, 1961.

—— *Kokumin tōgō no shōchō* (original publication, 1948), Watsuji Tetsurō zenshū, vol. 14. Tokyo: Iwanami Shoten, 1962.

—— *Watsuji Tetsurō zenshū*, vol. 14. Tokyo: Iwanami Shoten, 1962.

—— *Fūdo: ningengaku-teki kōsatsu*. Tokyo: Iwanami Shoten, 1979.

Wei-Hsun Fu, C. and Heine, S. (eds), *Japan in Traditional and Postmodern Perspectives*. New York: SUNY Press, 1995.

Whitworth, S., *Feminism and International Relations: Towards a Political Economy of Gender in Interstate and Non-Governmental Institutions*. New York: Macmillan Press, 1994.

Williams, R., *Keywords: A Vocabulary of Culture and Society*. London: Fontana, 1988.

Wolfe, A., 'Suicide and the Japanese Postmodern: A Postnarrative Paradigm, in Masao Miyoshi and H. D. Harootunian (eds), *Postmodernism and Japan*. Durham: Duke University Press, 1989.

—— *Suicidal Narrative in Modern Japan: The Case of Dazai Osamu*. Princeton: Princeton University Press, 1990.

Yamada, K., *Sengo shisō shi*. Tokyo: Aoki Shoten, 1989.

Yamamoto, H., *Gendai Nihon no yuifutsu ron*. Tokyo: Shinsen Sha, 1981.

—— '70-nendai no shisō no henbō to shakai jōkyō,' in S. Kōsaka, S. Takeda and H. Yamamoto (eds), *Gendai shisō nyumon II*. Tokyo: JICC, 1990.

—— *Gendai nihon no yuifutsu ron*. Tokyo: Yūkaikaku, 1978.

Yamamoto, Y., *Chisei no hanran*. Tokyo: Zen'eisha, 1969.

Yamamura, K., 'The Japanese Political Economy after the "bubble": *Plus Ca Change?*,' *Journal of Japanese Studies*, vol. 23, no. 2, 1997.
Yamazaki, M., *Ishihara, Shintaro*, Nihon Bungaku zenshū, vol. 49. Tokyo: Kawade Shobō, 1968.
Yasuda, Y., 'Ajia no haikyo,' *Yasuda Yojūrō senshū*, vol. 1. Tokyo: Kōdan Sha, 1971.
—— 'Bunmei kaika no ronri no shien ni tsuite,' *Yasuda Yojūrō senshū*, vol. 1. Tokyo: Kōdan Sha, 1971.
Yonahara, K., 'Mirareru shutai to sei,' *Hayari no bunka chōkenkyū*. Kyoto: Seigen Sha, 1998.
Yoshida, H., *Gensō seisei ron: Yoshimoto Takaaki sanbu-saku kaidoku no kokoromi*. Tokyo: Yamato Shobō, 1988.
Yoshida, K., *Zoku Yoshimoto Takaaki ron*. Tokyo: Parōru Sha, 1991.
Yoshida, M., *Sengo Shisōron*. Tokyo: Aoki Shoten, 1984.
Yoshida, Y., *Nihonjin no sensō-kan: sengo-shi no naka no henyō*. Tokyo: Iwanami Shoten, 1995.
—— 'Rekishi ishiki wa henka shita ka,' *Sekai*, September 1994.
Yoshimi, S., 'Wareware jishin no naka no Aum,' *Sekai*, July 1995.
Yoshimoto, T., 'Maruyama Masao ron,' in Etō Jun and Yoshimoto Takaaki (eds), *Warera no Bungaku*. Tokyo: Kōdan Sha, 1962.
—— *Masu imeeji ron*. Tokyo: Fukutake Shoten, 1984.
—— *Geijutsu-teki teikō to zasetsu*. Tokyo: Mirai Sha, 1963.
—— *Mosha to kagami*. Tokyo: Shunjū Sha, 1964.
—— 'Nihon no nashonarizumu,' in Yoshimoto Takaaki (ed.), *Nashonarizumu*. Tokyo: Chikuma Shobō, 1964.
—— *Yoshimoto Takaaki zen chosaku shū*, vol. 13. Tokyo: Keisō Shobō, 1969.
—— 'Machiu-sho shiron,' *Yoshimoto Takaaki zen chosaku shū*, vol. 4. Tokyo: Keisō Shobō, 1969.
—— *Kyōdō genso ron*, *Yoshimoto Takaaki zen chosaku shū*, vol. 11. Tokyo: Keisō Shobō, 1972.
—— *Shin-teki gensho-ron josetsu*, *Yoshimoto Takaaki zen chosaku shū*, vol. 10. Tokyo: Keisō Shobō, 1973.
—— *Hankaku iron*. Tokyo: Shinya Sōsho Sha, 1982.
—— (ed.) *Kokka no shisō*. Tokyo: Chikuma Shobō, 1969.
Yoshimura, K., *Ikeda seiken 1575 Days*. Tokyo: Gyōsei Mondai Kenkyū Jo, 1985.
Youngs, G. and Kofman, E. (eds), *Globalization: Theory and Practice*. New York: Pinter, 1996.
Yuasa, Y. (ed.), *Watsuji Tetsurō*. Tokyo: San'ichi Shobō, 1973.
Žižek, S., *The Sublime Object of Ideology*. New York: Verso, 1989.
—— 'Grimaces of the Real, or When the Phallus Appears,' *October*, vol. 58, 1991.

Index

Adorno, T. W. 9, 266
aestheticism 26, 57, 60, 259–60, 267–8; art 1, 2–3, 14; cultural renaissance 63, 65, 66; Fukuda 257; identity 61; *iki* 203; knowledge 10; romanticism 23, 44–8, 52–3, 55, 63–4, 66, 115, 161; Yasuda 205
age of culture 165, 166–8
Akutagawa Ryūnosuke 33–4
Albritton, Robert 265–6
Althusser, L. 10
Anpo movement 69, 92–5, 104, 111, 114–15, 121
Aono Suekichi 31
Ara Masato 67, 74, 75–6
Arendt, Hannah 250
Arishima Takeo 30–1
art 1, 13–14, 30
Asada Akira 61, 181, 183–4
Asahara Shoko 239
Asanuma Inejiro 93, 131
Asia 4, 15–16, 51, 56, 59–60, 106; Asianism 23; balance of power 275; counter-hegemonic discourse 110–11; economic recession 214–15, 217; English language 216; historical revisionism 197–8, 245, 246, 249; Japanese foreign investment 195, 217; Japanese war responsibility 72, 220, 224, 225, 249; Takeuchi 140–1; troubled relations with Japan 223–5
Aum Shinrikyō 8, 208, 210, 237–44, 254, 269
avant-garde literature 26, 30, 32–3

Barshay, Andrew 72
Barthes, Roland 201
Baudrillard, Jean 175
beauty 10, 44–5, 52, 65, 145, 148
Beheiren 121–3, 124, 126
Bell, D. 151
Benjamin, W. 254

body 128, 181–2, 232–3, 254, 255, 269
Brennan, Timothy 264
Brenner, Robert 214–15, 218
Buddhism 145, 146, 191, 203, 239

capitalism 4–5, 7, 106–7, 115, 253–4, 265–9; advertising 183; crisis of 253; historical revisionism 245; image creation 173; 'infantile' 181; 'information' 177; Matsushita 151, 152, 153, 154; nation-state 264; national identity 201, 260; postwar growth 155–6, 158, 161, 162; speculation 216, 253, *see also* economic growth
Chakrabarty, Dipesh 263–4
China 46, 90, 105, 111, 197–8, 204, 273, 275
Clammer, John 181–2
Clark, Gregory 187
class 103, 152, 153–4, 172–4
closed historical consciousness 271
Cold War 68, 72, 88, 89, 90–1, 111, 138, 208
colonialism 11–12, 23, 225
Communism 31–2, 34–5, 36, 73, 84, 88–91, *see also* Japan Communist Party
Confucianism 137, 203
conservatism 5, 158, 160–1, 201, 214, 262; critique of 216; economic growth 115–21, 133, 150–1, 168; Japan–Asia relations 224; postwar 84, 86, 89, 94, 104; progressive 218; realists 91; revisionism 247; US–Japan Security Treaty 93, *see also* neo-conservatism
Constitution of Japan 138, 139–40, 221, 223, 248–9
consumerism 7–8, 95, 114, 172–7, 178–82, 185–6, 200
corporate culture 230
corporations 118, 169–70, 172, 177, 187, 211, 216

Cox, R. 261
cultural identity 13, 14, 26, 58, 66, 189, 269
cultural particularism 14, 15, 61, 65, 104, 138; *nihonjinron* 199, 208; old liberals 84, 88
cultural renaissance 26, 35–48, 50, 58, 63, 65–6, 204
culturalism 188, 189, 199, 205
culture 5–6, 7, 13, 114, 152–3, 264; aesthetic formalism 204; 'age of' 165, 166–8; 'cute' 180–1, 227; deconstruction of 262–3; emperor system 149; homogeneity 173–4; hyperreality 175–6; *ie-society* 188, 189; material snobbism 177–9, 207; modern popular 226–32; *nihonjinron* 164, 165, 187–8; postmodern 185–6; Umehara 145–6, 189–91; urban space 174–5
'cute' culture 180–1, 227

Date Kyōko 228–9
Dazai Osamu 76–7
de Bary, Brett 272
democracy 5, 12, 27, 121, 151, 267; Anpo movement 92, 93, 94–5; critique of 69; decline of Enlightenment Project 95–8; Maruyama 78–83, 105; mass society 153–4; 'old liberals' 85–6, 88; postwar climate 67–8, 69–70, 71–2, 74, 77, 111–12; reverse course 88–92, 111; social transformation 151; Takeuchi 98; Yoshimoto 98, 99, 103, 104
Derrida, Jacques 180
Doak, Kevin 58
Doi Takako 224
Doi Takeo 188
Drucker, P. 151

Eagleton, Terry 1, 2, 6
economic growth 2, 7, 8, 11, 27, 269; conservatism 168; consumerism 95, 114; corporations 170, 171; fall in 161–2, 186; lack of subjectivity 202; new conservatism 115–21, 133, 150–1; postmodernity 164, 166, 187; romanticism 143; US resentment 196, *see also* capitalism
economics: global economy 275–6; recession 209, 213–19, 252–3
emperor system 5–6, 18, 148–50, 193, 207–8, 210–13, 259, *see also* Imperial Court
enlightenment 9, 10–11, 70–1, 266, 268; challenges to 99, 101, 104–5, 107–8, 112, 245; critique of 20, 21, 23; decline of project 95–8; postwar modernism 68, 78–83; rejection by old liberals 84, 85, 87–8; revisionism 245
ethics 38–9, 81, 144
ethnic conflict 270
ethnic nationalism 108, 109
ethnicity 108, 109, 191
Etō Jun 5, 134–7, 148, 157–8, 161, 163; Ishihara 128, 129–30; postmodernity 191–3, 199; revisionism 246–7; World War II 196
Eurocentrism 39, 49, 65, 142; anti-modernism 98, 105, 106; philosophy 144, 146; subjectivity 60; universalism 16
expansionism 15, 56–7, 65, 72

family 21, 119, 133–7, 210, 228, 229
fascism 23, 35, 101, 106, 269
fragmentation 7, 10, 11, 209, 254, 269, 270
fūdo 37, 38, 142
Fujii Yoshiki 233
Fujio Masayuki 198
Fujioka Nobukatsu 8, 245–8, 250–1, 252, 255, 257
Fukuda Kazuya 256–7
Fukuda Tsuneari 84–5
Fukuzawa Yukichi 12, 15–16, 50, 78, 80–2, 83

Galbraith, J. 151
Gellner, Ernest 261
gender 134, 135–6, 143, 229–32, 247
Gerow, Aaron 251
globalization 172, 270, 274
Gluck, Carol 19
Great Hanshin earthquake 237–8, 241
Great Kanto Earthquake 31
Gulf War 209, 219–23, 245, 246

Hagiwara Sakutarō 43, 44
Haniya Yutaka 74, 75
Harootunian, H. D. 59, 255
Hashikawa Bunzō 25, 46, 47, 62
Hasumi Shigehiko 28–30
Hata Ikuhiko 245
Hayashi Fusao 37, 43, 52–5, 63, 142–3, 148, 246–7, 252
Hegel, G. W. F. 266
hegemony 6, 11, 17, 98, 112, 205, 221; Asia 16; instability 269; late modernity 261, 263–5, 270–1, 275; modernization 57; power 272; social 115, 154, 226, 252, 253; transformation of national 7, 18–24; US 117, 127, 132, 138, 224; Western 13, 14–15, 49, 65, 105, 273
Heidegger, Martin 37, 40, 203
Hirano Ken 74, 76

Hirata Kiyoaki 155–6
Hirohito, Emperor 69, 208, 209, 210–11
history 87, 88, 96–7, 100, 107; relativism 138, 142; revisionism 8, 197–9, 208, 210, 220, 244–52, 255–7, 270; Romantic School 43–4, 46; Watsuji 37, 38, 60; *Zenkyōtō* 159–60
Hobsbawm, Eric 261, 262–3
Honda Shūgo 72, 74, 77
Horkheimer, M. 9
Hosokawa Morihiro 218, 224, 225
Huntington, Samuel 273–4
hyperreality 175–6, 177, 207

ie-society 188, 189
Ikeda Daisaku 146–7, 159
Ikeda Hayato 115, 116, 117–19, 120
iki 203
Imperial Court 41, 86, *see also* emperor system
imperialism 15, 16, 106, 140, 143
information society 165, 167–8, 172, 200, 209
International Research Centre for Japanese Studies (*Nichibunken*) 191, 195, 199
internationalism 209, 219, 245, 250–1, 274, 275
intolerance 274
irony 44, 45–7, 50, 55–6, 58–9, 62–3, 64
Ishihara Shintarō 114, 127–30, 131, 133, 157, 193, 196, 224
Ishikawa Takuboku 27–8
Islam 273
Isoda Kōichi 132
Isozaki Arata 183
Itō Jinsai 203
Itō Noe 31
Itō Seikou 220–2
Itō Toshiharu 183
Ivy, Marilyn 183

Jameson, Fredric 10, 252, 253
Japan Communist Party (JCP) 22, 31–2, 34–5, 36, 73, 89–91, 95
Japan Romantic School *see* Romantic School
Japan Socialist Party (JSP) 93, 95, 120–1, 224
Jay, Martin 64
JCP *see* Japan Communist Party
Jinbo Kōtarō 43
JSP *see* Japan Socialist Party

Kamei Katsuichirō 25, 36, 43, 53, 54–5, 63
Kang Sang-jung 247, 249
Kant, Immanuel 267

Karatani Kōjin 13, 28, 63, 157, 165, 202–4, 206, 221
Kasai Kiyoshi 221–3
Katō Norihiro 8, 245, 248–51, 252, 255–6, 257
Katsumata Seiichi 120
Kawabata Yasunari 33
Kawakami Tetsutarō 48–9, 50
Kawamura Minato 221
keiretsu 170–1, 177, 186, 216
Kinsella, Sharon 180–1, 227
Kishi Nobusuke 93, 116
knowledge 9–10, 11, 21, 40; postmodernism 165, 172, 183–4, 185, 200; Romantic School 45
Kobayashi Hideo 52, 55, 99
Kobayashi Takiji 34, 35
Kobe murders 234–7, 247, 254
Kogawa Testuo 176–7
kogyaru 226, 231–2
Koizumi Shinzō 91
Kojève, Alexandre 201
Kojima Nobuo 133, 134–5
Kokoro 85–8, 91, 93, 99, 103, 104, 141–2
kokugaku 25, 44, 47
kokutai 5, 9, 19, 20–1, 36, 59, 65, 86; essentialism 55; ethics 39; Nishida 41, 42; Pan-Asianism 111; Romantic School 56, 64, 66; Takeuchi 106, 108, 110; ultranationalism 101, 102; war ideology 62, 63
Komaki Oumi 30
Komori Yoichi 259, 269
Korea 15, 16, 143, 197, 198, 275
Korean War 90, 91, 138, 140
Kosaka Shuhei 162
Koschmann, Victor 70, 82, 255
Koyama Ken'ichi 155
Kuki Shuzo 203
Kumon Shunpei 169, 188
Kunikida Doppo 28
Kuno Osamu 78, 92, 93, 96
Kurahara Korehito 34–5, 73–4, 75
Kurihara Akira 173–4, 207
Kuwahara Takeo 195
Kyoto school 23, 40, 42, 50–2, 55–6, 60, 63; foundationalism 205; *Nichibunken* 195

Lacoue-Labarthe, Philippe 63–4
language 26, 28, 33, 206, 215, 216, 256–7
LDP *see* Liberal Democratic Party
Leftist groups 5, 23, 30–1, 35, 50, 58; criticisms of Matsushita 154–5; decline of 114, 120–1, 126; Ikeda policy 119; new Left 121–6; postwar 73–4, 78, 91, 95, 96; romantic 115, 161

Liberal Democratic Party (LDP) 115–16, 117–18, 120, 121, 133, 161; Anpo movement 93; capitalism 155; corporations 170; corruption 169; developmental guidelines 165, 168; Ikeda critique 146, 147; recession 213, 218–19; war revisionism 198; *Zenkyōtō* struggle 124
liberalism 70, 78, 84–8, 245, 249, 274, *see also* neo-liberalism; old liberals
literary movements 23, 25–6, 27–37, 44, 57, 72–7, 108
Literary World 50, 52, 53, 55

MacArthur, General 70–1, 89, 90
magazines 181–2
manga 226–7, 228
Mannheim, K. 153
market economy 155–6, 266–7
Maruyama Masao 7, 68, 91, 92, 111, 160; Anpo movement 93–4; critique of 100–1, 104; discursive space 202; Enlightenment Project 78–83, 96–7, 105, 112–13; militarism 144; political ethos 156; Yoshimoto comparison 99
Marx, Karl 266
Marxism 22, 23, 57–8, 63, 78, 104; critiques of 38, 46, 85, 91, 99; market society 156; Matsushita 151, 152–5; proletarian literature 31–2, 34; Romantic School 44, 47; suppression by US 88–9, 90; *tenkō* 35–7; universalism 142; Yoshimoto 185, 186
masculinity 130–3, 136, 143, 230
Mashita Shin'ichi 78, 99
mass media 71, 174–7, 182, 184, 200, 211, 231
mass society 114, 123, 126, 152–5, 156, 157, 185
Matsumoto Ken'ichi 96
Matsushita Keiichi 151–5, 156
Meiji restoration 12, 21, 53, 204
metaphysics 40–1, 87–8
militarism 19, 35, 144, 260, 275
Mishima Yukio 1–2, 5–7, 147–50, 158–60, 162, 163
Miyadai Shinji 232–4, 237, 254
Miyazaki, Tsutomu 227–8
modernism 68–9, 78, 141, 171, 185; critiques of 84–8, 141, 148; Maruyama 96, 100, 101, 105; rejection of 98, 99, 101–3, 107–8, 112, 144, *see also* progressivism
modernity 9, 10, 22–6, 260, 264, 268; hegemony 11, 270–1; overcoming 4, 48, 50–6, 64–6, 105, 205–6; postwar Japan 67–8; Romantic School 43–4, 47; Takeuchi 110; Tsuda critique 88
modernization 2–4, 9, 18–24, 25, 110, 166, 205; alienation 13; critiques of 144; Etō 191–2; family 134, 136; Hayashi 143; hegemony 57; identity 61; language 26; loss of religiosity 51, 53; Maruyama 81, 83; Meiji restoration 12; Overcoming modernity symposium 50–6; political 97; resistance 107; Romantic School 43; structural dualism 17; traditional culture 190
morality 80, 203–4, 231
Morita Akio 196
Morris-Suzuki, Tessa 249
Motoori Norinaga 44, 203–4
Murakami Yasusuke 169, 188, 189, 199

Nabeyama Sadachika 35–6
Nakagami Kenji 221
Nakamori Akio 233
Nakamura Mitsuo 53–4, 55
Nakamura Yūjiro 183
Nakane Chie 188
Nakano Shigeharu 35, 76
Nakano Yoshio 92
Nakasone Yasuhiro 194–5, 199
Nancy, Jean-Luc 63–4
nationalism 2–3, 4–6, 21–2, 60, 205, 209, 275; critiques of 259–60, 261–5; 'death of' 7; economic arguments 196; emperor system 211; Etō 192, 193; expansionism 56, 65; extra-rational aspects 10; Maruyama 78, 79, 83; 'new' 8–9, 210, 250–2, 257–8; new conservatism 118; *nihonjinron* 165, 196, 199; resurgence of 213; revisionism 197, 246, 248–9, 250–2; Shimizu 194; Takeuchi 106, 108, 109; World War II 56, 57; Yoshimoto 101–2, *see also* ultra-nationalism
Natsume Sōseki 17–18
naturalism (*shizen-shugi*) 23, 27–30, 57
neo-conservatism 165, 169, 171–2, 199, 219
neo-liberalism 116, 216, 219
neo-sensualism (*shin-kankaku-ha*) 30–1, 32–3
new academism 183, 184–5
'new world order' 209, 219
Nichibunken (International Research Centre for Japanese Studies) 191, 195, 199
nihilism 2, 3, 7, 8, 163, 193, 203; *Aum Shinrikyō* cult 243; identity 258; Mishima 148, 150; Miyadai 254; optimistic 200, 208

nihonjinron 3, 8, 164–5, 186–91, 195–6, 254; history 255; Katō 249, 250; postmodernism 206; revisionism 197, 208; significance of 198–201
Nishida Kitarō 23, 26, 36, 39–43, 58, 60, 65, 204–5
Nishio Kanji 243, 244, 245, 247
Nishitani Keiji 51–2

Oda Makoto 121–3
Odagiri Hideo 74, 91
Ōe Kenzaburō 127–8, 130–3, 137, 157, 183
Ogoshi Aiko 255–6
Ogyū Sorai 203
Ōhira Masayoshi 166, 169, 188, 199
Oi Kentaro 15
Okakura Tenshin 16, 202
Okuno Seisuke 198, 224–5
Okuno Takeo 76–7, 157
old liberals 84–8
Ōmae Ken'ichi 200, 215–16, 217
Orientalism 201–2, 271–2
Ōsawa Masachi 236
Ōsugi Sakae 31
otaku 226, 227–8, 243
Other 204, 205, 206–7, 252, 271

Pan-Asianism 16, 42, 56, 59–60, 111, 224–5
particularism 14, 15, 61, 65, 104, 138; *nihonjinron* 199, 208; old liberals 84, 88
peace movement 92
philosophy 144–6, 203–4
politics 7, 22, 149, 164, 233, 274; aestheticization 26, 66, 104–5, 112; age of culture 168; Anpo movement 92–5, 111; anti-Communist 88–92; anti-Japanese 196; anti-Western 193–4; art involvement in 30; conservative resurgence 114–15, 116–21, 158; corruption 169; East Asia 275; economic recession 213–14, 218–19; Etō 192; Gulf War 219–23; ideological control 19; Ikeda 146–7; Japan–Asia relations 224–5; *keiretsu* 171, 177; legitimacy crisis 168–9; Matsushita 152–5; Mishima 149, 150, 158–9, 160; multicivilizational 273; neo-conservatism 169; new Left 121–6; 'new world order' 209, 219; *nihonjinron* 201; Ōe 130–1; 'old liberals' 84–8; oppression 27, 31, 34–5, 90, 93; postwar intellectuals 75, 76, 77, 79; postwar occupation 67–72; realist 91, 93, 138, 140, 142, 194; representation 253, 268; structural transformation 151; *Zenkyōtō* movement 104, 123–6, 158–60, *see also* Communism; conservatism; democracy; Leftist groups; liberalism
Pollack, David 272–3
pornography 226–8
Porter, Dennis 271–2, 273
post-Fordism 170–1
post-industrial society 151, 181, 209
postmodernism 7–8, 165, 183–6, 200–3, 206–7, 220–3, 269
poststructuralism 160, 183–4, 249, 261, 272
power 17, 98, 272, *see also* hegemony
powerlessness 127, 128–9, 130
pragmatism 81–2
production 152, 154, 170–1, 197, 214, 215, 268
progressivism 84, 91, 96, 99, 104–5, 109, 111; Anpo movement 93; Kyoto School 52; Mishima 148; neo-conservatism 169; Shimizu 193; *Zenkyōtō* 124, 125, 160, *see also* modernism
proletarian literature 26, 30–2, 34–5, 36–7, 73, 74, 108
proletarianization 152, 154
Pyle, Kenneth 196

Ranger, Terence 261, 262
rationalism 3, 10, 24, 36, 50–1, 60, 166; Adorno 266; alienation 267; anti-modernist challenges 98, 100, 104; *Aum Shinrikyō* cult 241, 244; critiques of nationalism 260, 264; ideologies 20; Literary World 53; modernity 54, 88; postwar romanticism 144; *shizen-shugi* 29; Takeuchi critique 107–8, 109
realism: literary 27, 28, 73, 74, 156–7; political 91, 93, 138, 140, 142, 194; representation 64, 268; Romantic School 45, 47
Reischauer, Edwin 117
relativism 87, 97, 138–42, 274
religion 145, 146, 151, 189–90, 191; *Aum Shinrikyō* cult 239, 241; incorporation into politics 147; loss of religiosity 51, 53
representation 10, 50, 58–9, 64, 205
representational crisis 252–3, 268
reverse course 68, 88–92, 111
revisionism 8, 197–9, 208, 210, 220, 244–52, 255–7, 270
Romantic School 23, 50, 53, 58–9, 61–4, 66; anti-modernism 23, 43–8, 54–6, 144; Mishima 148; postwar condemnation 84; revisionism 256
romanticism 14, 115, 126–50, 158, 161, 204; Miyadai 233–4, 237; modernity 10–11, 22–3, 52–3, 64; *nihonjinron* 8, 199

Rostow, W. W. 117
Russian Revolution 30
Russo–Japanese war (1904–5) 4, 16, 22, 27

Saeki Keishi 247
Said, Edward 271–3
Saitō Minako 247
Sakai Naoki 15
Sakaiya Taichi 200
Sano Manabu 35–6
Sasaki Kiichi 74, 75, 156–7
Sasaki Soichi 86
Sato Eisaku 118
Satō Manabu 269–70
Satō Seizaburō 169, 188
SCAP *see* Supreme Commander for Allied Forces
Schodt, Frederik 226, 227, 228
science 159, 241
Sekine, Thomas 265–6
self 59–60, 61, 232–4, 243–4, 253, 269; literature 75–6; romantic irony 63; Western 271, 272–3
self-determination 92, 100, 112, 140; Etō 192; Takeuchi 55, 105, 106, 107, 109, 110–11
sexuality 127–33, 137, 227, 228, 229, 231, 251
shame 2, 4, 76–7
Shibata Shingo 154–5
Shiga Naoya 85
Shimada Masahiko 221
Shimao Toshio 134, 156
Shimizu Ikutarō 5, 78, 92, 93, 94, 193–4, 199
shin-kankaku-ha (neo-sensualism) 30–1, 32–3
Shintoism 146, 191, 204
shizen-shugi (naturalism) 23, 27–30, 57
Shōno Junzō 133
signs 179–80, 182, 185, 201, 206–7, 255, 268–9
simulacra 175
Sino–Japanese war (1894–5) 4, 16
Skov, Lise 179
snobbism 164, 177–9, 200, 203, 207
social changes 114–15
social imaginary 3, 8, 10–11, 156, 158, 253, 260
socialism 31, 74
Soviet Union 90, 91, 209, 219
state 16–17, 19, 20, 21, 85, 153; democracy 27; hegemonic power 264–5; political oppression 93; society relationship 82–3; sovereign reification 79–80
student movements 123–6

sub-cultures 177–81, 226–32
subjectivity 7, 65, 112–13, 255, 257, 260; absence of 201, 202; *Aum Shinrikyō* cult 243, 244; commercialization of 209; consumer culture 179, 200; destruction of 3, 47, 54; Eurocentric 60; fragmented 254, 269, 270; history 256; ironic subject 62; Maruyama 81; modernity 23, 25–6, 28, 39, 57, 59; 'old liberals' 85–7; postmodernity 165, 207–8; postwar literary circles 75; reconstitution of national 251; Takeuchi 109, 110; Yoshimoto 99; *Zenkyōtō* movement 125, 126
suicide 1, 34, 61, 150, 160, 230
Sun Ge 259–60
Supreme Commander for Allied Forces (SCAP) 68, 69–72, 82, 88–90, 98, 111, 171

Takahashi Kazumi 136
Takamura Kōtarō 85
Takeda Seiji 212, 257
Takemura Kenichi 187
Takeuchi Yoshimi 7, 49, 55–6, 202, 224, 259; Anpo movement 93, 94; challenge to enlightenment 67, 69, 98, 105–11, 112–13; relativism 140–1, 142
Takeyama Michio 141–2
Tanaka Giichi 34
Tanaka Kakuei 161–2, 169
Tanaka Masaaki 197
Tanaka, Stefan 59
Tanaka Yasuo 178, 221
Tanizaki Junichirō 85
technology 152, 154–5, 167, 176, 275
tenkō 35–7
Tocqueville, A. de 153
Tokunaga Sunao 34
trade 12, 17, 119, 187, 195–6, 214–15
truth 138–43
Tsuda Sōkichi 85, 87–8, 92
Tsuji Jun 34
Tsuru Shigeto 92

Ueyama Shumpei 138–41, 142, 143, 195, 246, 252
ultranationalism 78, 79, 83, 101, 105–6, 144, 206
Umehara Takeshi 144–6, 158, 159, 161, 189–90, 195, 199
Umemoto Katsumi 78, 99
Umesao Tadao 141–2, 195
United Nations (UN) 219, 220
United States (US) 3, 140, 144, 165, 187, 273; anti-American feeling 192, 194, 195–7, 199, 225, 247–8;

anti-Communist policy 88, 89, 90, 91; commercial treaty 11–12; economics 213, 214–15, 216, 217; family 134–5, 136, 137; Gulf War 209, 219–23, 246; hegemony 117, 127, 132, 138, 224; *keiretsu* 170, 171; Nixon shock 161; nuclear bombing of Japan 246; occupation 11, 68, 69–72, 88–91, 94, 98, 111, 245–6; US–Japan Security Treaty 68–9, 90, 92–5, 98, 111–12, 117, 122
universalism 18, 24, 64, 68, 106, 205, 268; critiques of 107, 110, 139–40, 141, 143, 271; global capital 260; Nishida 40; rejection of 195; Western 13, 14–15, 16, 273, 274
Uno Kozo 265

values 166, 167, 192, 201, 205, 250; 'foreign' 97; universal 273, 274
van Wolferen, Karel 196
Vietnam War 121, 122, 123
violence 17, 18, 128, 129–30, *see also* war
virtual media 228–9, 232
Vlastos, Stephen 262–3, 264
Vogel, Ezra 187, 188

war 26, 46–7, 54–5, 67, 92, 221
war criminals 84, 89–90
Watanabe Shōichi 193, 196
Watsuji Tetsurō 23, 26, 36–9, 42–3, 58–60, 65; human relations 85–6, 167; peace movement 92; Umesao comparison 142
welfare 117–18
Westernization 13, 149, 166, 205

White, Theodore 196
women 134–6, 137, 181–2, 227, 229, 230–2
World War I 30
World War II 2, 4, 8, 131, 142–3, 205; end of 67, 69, 72; Japan–Asia relations 224–5; Maruyama analysis 80; Nishida 41–2; old liberals 84; overcoming modernity 24, 41–2, 48–9, 51, 55–6, 59; reinterpretations 138–9, 194, 195, 196; revisionism 197–8, 199, 220, 245–6, 249; Shimizu 194; US interpretation 140; war responsibility 72, 220, 224, 225, 249

Yamaguchi Masao 183
Yamamoto Hiraku 172, 173, 175
Yamamoto Yoshitaka 125, 159
Yamamuro Shizuka 74
Yanagi Sōetsu 85
Yanagida Kunio 85
Yasuda Yojūrō 23, 25–6, 43–8, 55, 58, 60, 66; condemnation of 84; Fukuda 256; postmodernity 204, 205
Yasuoka Shōtarō 133, 134–5
Yokomitsu Riichi 32–3
Yomoda Inuhiko 183
Yoshida Shigeru 89, 118, 171
Yoshimoto Mitsuhiro 179
Yoshimoto Takaaki 7, 67, 69, 98–106, 112–13, 144, 185–6
Yoshino Gensaburō 92
Yoshino Sakuzō 27

Zenkyōtō 104, 123–6, 158–60

Printed in Japan
落丁、乱丁本のお問い合わせは
Amazon.co.jp カスタマーサービスへ